Google® Cloud Certified

Professional Cloud Database Engineer

Study Guide

Google® Cloud Certified

Professional Cloud Database Engineer

Study Guide

JAKE HOLMQUIST

To Annie, and our children, Johnny, Henry, and Nora, whose support made this possible.

And to anyone striving for certification, may this guide be a milestone in your ongoing journey of learning and growth.

Acknowledgments

While my name is on the cover, this study guide is the result of the collaboration, expertise, and support of many incredible people. The journey of writing a book is never a solo endeavor, and I am deeply grateful to everyone who contributed to its creation.

My journey in creating this guide began with Rob Morse, who first introduced me to the Database Engineer beta certification—thank you for sparking the initial idea. For their deep technical insights, I am indebted to several individuals. Thank you to Brice Nguoghia, who served as a fantastic technical resource for all things data management, and to Anu Ganesan, for her invaluable education on Cloud Spanner (and for her inspiring work toward solving global hunger). A special thanks also goes to Mona Mona for generously sharing her experiences and lessons learned from authoring the ML Engineer study guide, which provided a much-needed roadmap.

I must also extend my gratitude to the vibrant Google Champion Innovator and Google Developer Expert (GDE) communities. The opportunity to engage with so many brilliant subject matter experts has been invaluable. Your collective expertise, inspiration, and support were instrumental throughout this process. To all of my colleagues—past, present, and future—thank you for the daily collaboration. I continue to learn from each of you every day.

Finally, this book would not have crossed the finish line without the dedicated team who guided the authoring process. My sincere thanks to Kenyon Brown, Pete Gaughan, Caroline Define, Elizabeth Welch, Ashirvad Moses, and countless others for your unwavering guidance, support, and for keeping me on track. I am also incredibly grateful to Hitesh Hinduja for his meticulous technical review and insightful feedback, which has greatly improved the quality and accuracy of this guide.

—Jake Holmquist

About the Author

Jake Holmquist is a Google Cloud Field CTO at a large systems integrator, where he serves as a trusted adviser to business and technology leaders, helping them leverage the power of Google Cloud. As a Google Champion Innovator for Data Management and a recognized leader in the retail vertical, he specializes in bridging the gap between complex technology and strategic business objectives, with a focus on generative AI and deep expertise in solutions like Vertex AI Search for Commerce.

As a member of the first cohort to participate in the beta program for the Google Professional Cloud Database Engineer certification, Jake helped shape the exam by providing expert feedback on its content. This experience provided a deep, early understanding of the subject, grounded in years of practical expertise architecting and implementing cloud-native data solutions. Before his current role, Jake served as a chief information officer (CIO), where he led a major digital transformation by migrating complex, large-scale production systems to Google Cloud and establishing an enterprise-wide data and analytics program.

Jake is passionate about sharing his knowledge and mentoring others within the tech community. He is a frequent contributor to the Google Cloud publication on Medium under the handle `@cloud-jake` and has created numerous technical demos showcasing the power of Google Cloud. This commitment to helping others grow is also demonstrated through his work designing and delivering successful enablement programs that have helped numerous engineers achieve professional certifications. Jake is 8x Google Cloud certified and holds many technical expert badges and certifications from others such as Databricks and AWS. He is dedicated to empowering other professionals with the knowledge to succeed in their cloud journey. He can be reached at `jake.holmquist@gmail.com`.

Contents at a Glance

Introduction			*xxi*
Assessment Test			*xxxiv*
Answers to Assessment Test			*xxxix*
Chapter	**1**	Data Storage Technologies	1
Chapter	**2**	Database Storage Models and Data Types	35
Chapter	**3**	Databases in Google Cloud	61
Chapter	**4**	Database Capacity and Usage Planning	117
Chapter	**5**	Designing for High Availability and Disaster Recovery	137
Chapter	**6**	Designing Secure Database Connectivity and Access	159
Chapter	**7**	Monitoring, Troubleshooting, and Optimizing Performance	177
Chapter	**8**	Managing and Automating Database Operations	207
Chapter	**9**	Implementing Backup and Recovery Strategies	225
Chapter	**10**	Planning and Executing Database Migrations	245
Chapter	**11**	Deploying and Validating Database Solutions	269
Appendix		Answers to the Review Questions	295
Index			*337*

Contents

Introduction   *xxi*

Assessment Test   *xxxiv*

Answers to Assessment Test   *xxxix*

Chapter 1   Data Storage Technologies   1

Data Storage Design Considerations   3
Workload Characteristics   3
Performance and Scalability   4
Cost Optimization   4
Data Protection and Recovery   5
Security and Compliance   5
Storage Technologies   6
Block Storage   6
Persistent Disk   6
Hyperdisk   9
Local SSD   11
Comparing Block Storage Options in Google Cloud   12
Object Storage   12
Google Cloud Storage   13
File Storage   19
Google Cloud Filestore   20
Google Cloud NetApp Volumes   23
Storage Options Decision Tree   27
Summary   28
Exam Essentials   29
Review Questions   30

Chapter 2   Database Storage Models and Data Types   35

Database Storage Technologies   36
Types of Data   36
Structured Data   37
Unstructured Data   38
Semi-Structured Data   40
Vector Data   41
Types of Databases   43
In-Memory Databases   44
Relational Databases   44
NoSQL Databases   45
Vector Databases   45
In-Memory   45

Relational Databases	47
Transactional: OLTP Databases	47
Analytical: OLAP Databases	48
NoSQL Databases	50
Key-Value Databases	50
Document Databases	51
Vector	52
Summary	54
Exam Essentials	54
Review Questions	56

Chapter 3 Databases in Google Cloud — 61

Google Cloud Database Offerings	62
Unmanaged Databases	64
Key Characteristics	64
Examples	65
Advantages	65
Challenges	65
Common Use Cases	66
Google-Managed Databases	66
Key Characteristics	66
Examples	67
Advantages	67
Challenges	67
Common Use Cases	68
Partner-Managed Databases	68
Key Characteristics	68
Examples	69
Advantages	69
Challenges	70
Common Use Cases	70
Google-Managed Databases in Google Cloud	71
Memorystore	71
Key Characteristics	71
Key Features	71
Deployment Options	72
When to Choose	72
Cloud SQL	74
Key Characteristics	74
Key Features	74
Deployment Options	74
When to Choose	75

AlloyDB   76
    Key Characteristics   77
    Key Features   77
    Deployment Options   78
    When to Choose   79
  Cloud Spanner   80
    Key Characteristics   80
    Key Features   80
    Deployment Options   81
    When to Choose   82
    Other Considerations   82
  Cloud Bigtable   83
    Key Characteristics   83
    Key Features   83
    Deployment Options   84
    When to Choose   84
    Other Considerations   84
  Cloud Firestore   86
    Key Characteristics   86
    Key Features   86
    Deployment Options   87
    When to Choose   88
  BigQuery   89
    Key Characteristics   89
    Key Features   90
    Deployment Options   90
    When to Choose   91
Partner Databases in Google Cloud   93
  MongoDB   93
    Key Characteristics   94
    Key Features   94
    Deployment Options   94
    When to Choose   94
  Oracle   95
    Key Characteristics   96
    Key Features   96
    Deployment Options   96
    When to Choose   97
    Other Considerations   99
Self-Managed Database Options in Google Cloud   100
  Databases on Google Bare Metal Solution (BMS)   100
    Key Characteristics   101

Key Features	101
Deployment Options	101
When to Choose	101
Databases on Compute Engine	102
Key Characteristics	102
Key Features	102
Deployment Options	103
When to Choose	103
Databases on Google Kubernetes Engine (GKE)	104
Key Characteristics	104
Key Features	104
Deployment Options	104
When to Choose	105
Integrating Multiple Database Technologies	106
Federated Queries	106
Data Integration and Movement	106
Hybrid and Multicloud Deployments	106
Databases for Generative AI and LLMs	107
The Role of Vector Search in RAG	107
Google Cloud Database Solutions for AI/LLM	107
Meeting Regulatory and Compliance Requirements	108
Regulatory and Compliance Support	108
Aligning with Organizational Policies	109
Summary	109
Exam Essentials	110
Review Questions	111
Chapter 4 Database Capacity and Usage Planning	**117**
The Google Cloud Implementation Methodology	118
Assess Phase: Understanding the Current State	118
Inventory Applications	119
Map Dependencies	119
Build an Application Catalog	120
Assess Data	121
Understand Business Requirements	122
Gathering Current Environment Workload Metrics	122
Projecting Future Requirements	122
Plan Phase: Designing the Future State	123
Sizing Database Compute and Storage	123
Analyzing Costs of Google Cloud Database Solutions	125
Develop a Rollback Plan	126
Prepare a Communication Plan	127

Deploy Phase: Executing the Plan   127
  Set Up Google Cloud Resources   127
  Automate Deployments   128
  Migrate Data   128
  Configure Security   128
  Test the New Environment   129
Optimize Phase: Continuous Improvement   129
  Monitor Performance and Costs   129
  Fine-Tune Configurations   129
  Implement Automation   130
  Leverage Cloud-Native Features   130
Summary   131
Exam Essentials   131
Review Questions   132

Chapter 5   Designing for High Availability and Disaster Recovery   137

Evaluating Database High Availability and Disaster
    Recovery Options   138
Evaluating Trade-offs Between Multiregional, Regional,
and Zonal Deployment Strategies   140
  Zonal Deployment   140
  Regional Deployment   140
  Multiregional Deployment   141
Defining Maintenance Windows and Notifications Based on
Application Availability   143
  Maintenance Windows   144
  Notifications   144
Planning Database Upgrades for Google Cloud–Managed
Databases   145
  Minor Version Upgrades   145
  Major Version Upgrades   145
Designing Database Backup and Recovery Solutions   148
  Designing for RTO, RPO, and PITR   148
    Recovery Time Objective (RTO)   148
    Recovery Point Objective (RPO)   148
    Point-in-Time Recovery (PITR)   148
  Google Cloud Backup and Recovery Solutions   149
  Designing Your Backup and Recovery Strategy   149
Summary   151
Exam Essentials   151
Review Questions   153

Chapter 6   Designing Secure Database Connectivity and Access   159

Designing Secure Database Connection Patterns   160
   Designing for Scalability, High Availability, and Security   160
      Scalability   161
      High Availability   161
      Security   162
      Client-Side Resiliency: Exponential Backoff   162
   Configuring Networking and Security   163
      Cloud SQL Connection Methods   163
      The Cloud SQL Auth Proxy: A Layer of Identity-Aware Security   164
      Customer-Managed Encryption Keys (CMEK)   166
      SSL/TLS Certificates   166
   Justifying the Use of Session Pooler Services   167
   Assessing Auditing Policies for Managed Services   167
Determining Database Connectivity and Access Management Considerations   168
   Determining IAM Policies for Database Connectivity   168
   Managing Database Users, Including Authentication and Access Control   168
      Authentication   169
      Access Control   170
Summary   170
Exam Essentials   171
Review Questions   172

Chapter 7   Monitoring, Troubleshooting, and Optimizing Performance   177

Configuring Database Monitoring and Troubleshooting Options   178
Assessing Slow-Running Queries, Database Locking, and Identifying Missing Indexes   178
   Slow-Running Queries   178
   Troubleshooting Self-Managed Databases on Compute Engine   180
   Database Locking   182
   Identifying Missing Indexes   182
   Monitoring and Investigating Database Vitals: RAM, CPU, Storage, I/O, and Cloud Logging   183
      Cloud Monitoring   185
      Cloud Logging   186
   Monitoring and Updating Quotas   186

Investigating Database Resource Contention 187
Setting Up Alerts for Errors and Performance Metrics 188
Optimizing Database Cost and Performance in Google Cloud 189
Assessing Options for Scaling Up and Scaling Out 189
Scaling Database Instances Based on Current and
Upcoming Workload 190
Defining Replication Strategies 191
Optimize Queries for Cost and Performance 192
General Best Practices 192
Service-Specific Optimization Strategies 193
Summary 199
Exam Essentials 199
Review Questions 201

Chapter 8   Managing and Automating Database Operations   207

Automating Common Database Tasks 208
Performing Database Maintenance 208
Assessing and Managing Fragmentation 210
Scheduling Database Exports 212
Export Mechanisms and Automation 212
Managing Upgrades for Google Cloud–Managed Databases 213
Monitoring Database SLA/SLOs 214
Optimizing Database Cost and Performance in Google Cloud 215
Continuously Assessing and Optimizing Cost 216
Assessing Costs 216
Cost Optimization Strategies 216
Summary 217
Exam Essentials 218
Review Questions 219

Chapter 9   Implementing Backup and Recovery Strategies   225

Recommending Backup and Recovery Options 226
Options by Database Service 227
Cloud SQL 228
AlloyDB for PostgreSQL 229
Cloud Spanner 229
Bigtable, Firestore, and BigQuery 230
Configuring Automatic Scheduled Backups 231
Cloud SQL 232
Cloud Spanner, Bigtable, and Firestore 233
Configuring Export and Import of Data for Databases 234
Key Use Cases for Export/Import 234
Export/Import Procedures in Google Cloud 235

		Managing Data Retention	236
		Retention Mechanisms in Google Cloud	237
		Summary	238
		Exam Essentials	238
		Review Questions	240
Chapter	**10**	**Planning and Executing Database Migrations**	**245**
		Designing and Implementing Data Migration and Replication	246
		Developing and Executing Migration Strategies	247
		Extended Outage (Offline Migration)	247
		Near-Zero Downtime Migration	248
		Zero-Downtime Migration	250
		Creating Migration Plans, Including Fallback and Schema Conversion	251
		The Migration Plan	251
		DDL/DML Conversion (Schema Conversion)	252
		Fallback and Rollback Plan	253
		Configuring Reverse Replication from Google Cloud Back to the Source	254
		Pre-Migration Requirements for DMS	255
		Determining the Correct Database Migration Tools for a Given Scenario	256
		Common Migration Paths to Google Cloud Databases	259
		Summary	261
		Exam Essentials	262
		Review Questions	263
Chapter	**11**	**Deploying and Validating Database Solutions**	**269**
		Applying Concepts to Implement Highly Scalable and Available Databases	270
		Provisioning High Availability Database Solutions in Google Cloud	271
		Cloud SQL	271
		AlloyDB for PostgreSQL	272
		Cloud Spanner	273
		Bigtable	273
		Automating Database Instance Provisioning	275
		Terraform	276
		gcloud Command-Line Interface (CLI)	277
		Deploying and Scaling Read Replicas	278
		Connecting Applications to Replicas for Global Scale	279
		Application-Side Routing Strategies	279

Setting Up Multiregional Replication for Disaster Recovery 281
Creating a Cross-Region Replica 281
Testing High Availability and Disaster Recovery Strategies
Periodically 283
Testing High Availability (HA) 283
Testing Disaster Recovery 284
Executing and Verifying Failover and Promotion 285
Troubleshooting a Failed Failover 286
Configuring Monitoring for Highly Available Databases 286
Setting Up Alerts 287
Summary 288
Exam Essentials 289
Review Questions 290

Appendix   Answers to the Review Questions   295

Index   337

Introduction

Why should you become a Google Cloud Database Engineer? Because data is the foundation of modern business and artificial intelligence. In today's digital world, the amount of data being generated is staggering—in fact, the amount of data created each day is measured in hundreds of exabytes, and this rate of growth is accelerating exponentially. This explosion of information needs to be stored, managed, secured, and made accessible. By mastering Google Cloud's database services, you position yourself as a crucial expert in a rapidly expanding field. Regardless of the specific cloud or on-premises solutions you work with, understanding Google Cloud's powerful and integrated data platform will broaden your expertise and give you a significant professional edge. This expertise allows you to make informed decisions on how to design scalable, reliable, and cost-effective data solutions that power everything from simple web applications to complex analytics and groundbreaking AI models.

The Google Cloud Certified Professional Cloud Database Engineer certification is a credential that validates your expertise in designing, creating, managing, and troubleshooting Google Cloud database solutions. This exam certifies that you have the necessary skills to select the right database for the job—whether it's a relational database like Cloud SQL or Spanner, a NoSQL solution like Bigtable or Firestore, or an in-memory store like Memorystore. It proves you can not only deploy these systems but also handle migrations, manage day-to-day operations, and implement robust security and disaster recovery plans. Achieving this certification demonstrates to employers that you are a top-tier professional capable of handling their most critical data assets.

The purpose of this book is to provide you with everything you need to pass the Professional Cloud Database Engineer exam. Because the exam covers the full life cycle of cloud database management, those are the topics emphasized in this guide. You'll learn how to design database solutions for performance and scalability, migrate data from other systems, manage and monitor cloud databases effectively, and implement security and compliance best practices. We will dive deep into Google Cloud's suite of data tools, showing you how to unlock insights using powerful analytics services like BigQuery. Even after you've earned your certification, this book will remain an invaluable on-the-job reference for your day-to-day work.

Don't just study the questions and answers! The questions on the actual exam will be different from the practice questions included in this book. The exam is designed to test your knowledge of a concept or objective, so use this book to learn the objectives behind the questions.

The Google Cloud Certified Professional Cloud Database Engineer Exam

Google Cloud offers a robust and diverse portfolio of managed database services designed to meet the needs of any application, from small-scale projects to massive, globally distributed systems. The platform provides solutions for traditional relational workloads, highly scalable NoSQL use cases, globally consistent transactional systems, and powerful data warehouses for analytics. As a Cloud Database Engineer, your expertise in choosing, deploying, managing, and migrating to these services is critical for building modern, data-driven applications.

Why Become a Google Cloud Certified Professional Cloud Database Engineer?

In a competitive IT landscape, holding a certification is a key differentiator that validates your skills and dedication. Here are several powerful reasons to pursue your Google Cloud Database Engineer certification:

Accelerate Your Career Advancement   Certification serves as tangible proof of your professional achievement and expertise. It signals to your current and future employers that you have a deep understanding of Google Cloud's database solutions. According to Google, 8 in 10 Google Cloud learners say that having a certification contributes to faster promotion. By earning this credential, you position yourself as a leader and a go-to expert within your organization, opening doors for new responsibilities and career growth.

Increase Your Marketability to Employers   In today's job market, certified professionals stand out. Hiring managers are actively seeking candidates who have verified skills. Google reports that 8 in 10 leaders from organizations using Google Cloud say they prefer to recruit and hire professionals who hold cloud certifications. This certification makes you a more attractive candidate, can lead to a higher starting salary, and reduces the training burden for new employers.

Gain In-Demand, Job-Ready Skills   The process of studying for this certification isn't just about passing an exam; it's about acquiring practical, real-world skills. The curriculum is designed to equip you with the knowledge to design, manage, and troubleshoot complex database solutions on Google Cloud. As a result, 85 percent of Google Cloud learners say that cloud certifications give them the skills to fill in-demand roles. You will gain the confidence and competence to tackle challenging database projects from day one.

Build Credibility and Trust   The Professional Cloud Database Engineer certification is a respected credential that formally validates your technical abilities. This validation raises your credibility with peers, stakeholders, and clients, establishing you as a trusted database professional capable of managing an organization's most critical data assets.

Boost Customer and Stakeholder Confidence   Whether you work as a consultant or as part of an in-house team, your certification builds confidence. Clients and internal stakeholders are more likely to trust the recommendations and architectural decisions of a certified professional. This trust is essential when you are responsible for an organization's most critical asset: its data.

How to Become a Google Cloud Certified Professional Cloud Database Engineer

Earning your certification is a straightforward process. The primary requirement is to pass the Professional Cloud Database Engineer certification exam. This exam assesses your ability to design, implement, manage, and troubleshoot Google Cloud database solutions.

The exam is administered by Google and can be taken at a designated testing center or as a remotely proctored exam. To register, you will need to create an account on Webassessor (`https://webassessor.com/googlecloud`), Google's test delivery partner. From there, you can locate a nearby testing center or schedule a remote session that fits your schedule.

For the most up-to-date information on exam registration, fees, and testing locations, please visit the official Google Cloud certification website at `https://cloud.google.com/learn/certification`. Upon passing the exam, you will receive a digital certificate and a badge that you can add to your resume and professional networking profiles to showcase your achievement.

Exam policies can change from time to time. We highly recommend that you check both the Google Cloud and Webassessor sites for the most up-to-date information when you begin your preparing, when you register, and again a few days before your scheduled exam date.

What Does This Book Cover?

This book covers topics outlined in the Google Cloud Professional Cloud Database Engineer exam here:

```
https://cloud.google.com/learn/certification/
cloud-database-engineer
```

Chapter 1: Data Storage Technologies   This chapter introduces the fundamental concepts of data storage technologies on Google Cloud. It explores the differences between block, object, and file storage and examines specific Google Cloud options like Persistent Disk, Hyperdisk, Local SSD, and Google Cloud Storage, detailing their features and use cases.

Chapter 2: Database Storage Models and Data Types   This chapter categorizes data into structured, unstructured, semi-structured, and vector types, detailing the characteristics and use cases for each. It also provides an overview of the different database types available on Google Cloud, including in-memory, relational, NoSQL, and vector databases, explaining how to select the best option for specific needs.

Chapter 3: Databases in Google Cloud   This chapter offers a comprehensive overview of the specific database solutions on Google Cloud. It covers the differences between managed, unmanaged, and partner database offerings, how to select solutions that meet compliance requirements, and how to leverage these technologies for modern use cases like generative AI.

Chapter 4: Database Capacity and Usage Planning   Using the Google Cloud Implementation Methodology as a framework, this chapter focuses on database capacity and usage planning. It covers how to assess current workloads, project future requirements, size database compute and storage based on performance, and perform a comparative cost analysis to select the right solution.

Chapter 5: Designing for High Availability and Disaster Recovery   This chapter details how to design resilient database solutions on Google Cloud to meet uptime requirements. It evaluates the trade-offs between multiregional, regional, and zonal deployment strategies and covers the design of backup and recovery solutions based on RTO and RPO requirements, including point-in-time recovery (PITR).

Chapter 6: Designing Secure Database Connectivity and Access   This chapter covers how to secure database access using a defense-in-depth strategy. Topics include configuring networking, key management, and encryption, justifying the use of session poolers, assessing auditing policies, and determining Identity and Access Management (IAM) policies for database users.

Chapter 7: Monitoring, Troubleshooting, and Optimizing Performance   This chapter details the tools and techniques for monitoring, troubleshooting, and optimizing database performance and cost. It covers how to assess slow-running queries and database locking, monitor database vitals like RAM and CPU, set up alerts, and evaluate options for scaling up and scaling out.

Chapter 8: Managing and Automating Database Operations   This chapter focuses on automating common database tasks to improve operational efficiency. It covers performing database maintenance like rebuilding indexes, scheduling data exports, managing upgrades for managed databases, monitoring SLAs/SLOs, and continuously optimizing costs.

Chapter 9: Implementing Backup and Recovery Strategies   This chapter covers the implementation of backup and recovery strategies based on business requirements for RTO and RPO. It details how to recommend and configure backup options, such as automatic scheduled backups; configure data exports and imports; and manage data retention policies to meet compliance and cost objectives.

Chapter 10: Planning and Executing Database Migrations   This chapter provides a guide to planning and executing database migrations to Google Cloud. It covers developing migration strategies for different downtime requirements, including fallback plans and schema conversion. The chapter also details how to configure reverse replication and determine the correct migration tools for a given scenario.

Chapter 11: Deploying and Validating Database Solutions   This chapter focuses on implementing and validating scalable and highly available database solutions. It includes provisioning HA databases, automating provisioning with Infrastructure as Code, deploying and scaling read replicas, setting up multiregional replication, and periodically testing HA and DR strategies.

Who Should Buy This Book

This book is intended to help database administrators, data engineers, solutions architects, IT professionals, and developers gain expertise in the database services on the Google Cloud Platform and take the Professional Cloud Database Engineer exam. This book intends to take readers through the database management process starting from data modeling and moving on through database design, migration, and operations on Google Cloud. It also walks readers through best practices for when to pick custom database solutions versus managed services. Google Cloud's database technologies are presented through real-world scenarios to illustrate how IT professionals can design, build, and operate secure, scalable, and reliable cloud database environments to modernize and automate applications.

Anybody who wants to pass the Professional Cloud Database Engineer exam may benefit from this book. If you're new to Google Cloud, this book covers the updated database engineer exam course material, including Google Cloud SQL, AlloyDB, Spanner, Bigtable, Firestore, Memorystore, and BigQuery.

Since it's a professional-level study guide, this book is written with the assumption that you know the basics of the Google Cloud Platform, such as compute, storage, networking, and Identity and Access Management (IAM), or have taken the Google Cloud Associate-level certification exam. Moreover, this book assumes you understand the basics of database management in general. In case you do not understand a term or concept, we have included a glossary for your reference.

Study Guide Features

This study guide uses several common elements to help you prepare. These include the following:

Exam Objectives   Each chapter begins with a list of exam objectives that are covered in the chapter. You will find that the book doesn't cover the objectives in order. Instead, the content is organized thematically to create a more logical flow for learning.

SkillsBoost   Google Cloud SkillsBoost is an online platform that offers on-demand training and skill development in Google Cloud technologies. It's designed to help individuals and organizations build expertise in Google Cloud and develop practical experience through interactive labs, allowing learners to apply their knowledge directly.

Codelabs   A Google Codelab is a guided, interactive tutorial that walks learners through building real-world applications or adding features to an existing one. Codelabs are designed to provide hands-on experience with Google Cloud Platform (GCP) and other Google technologies.

Quickstarts   Google Cloud Jump Start Solutions (often referred to as quickstart solutions) are pre-built sample applications and infrastructure best-practices that you can deploy within a few clicks in your own Google Cloud account. They are designed to accelerate development by providing a fully functional, multi-service architecture—such as a dynamic web app, a load-balanced VM cluster, or a generative AI application—so you don't have to build the foundation from scratch. Each solution includes the underlying open-source Terraform code, interactive tutorials, and comprehensive documentation, allowing you to gain hands-on experience, explore how different cloud services work together, and customize the deployment for your specific use case.

Summaries   The summary section of each chapter briefly explains the chapter, allowing you to easily understand what it covers.

Exam Essentials   The exam essentials focus on major exam topics and critical knowledge that you should take into the test. The exam essentials focus on the exam objectives provided by Google Cloud.

Chapter Review Questions   A set of questions at the end of each chapter will help you assess your knowledge and whether you are ready to take the exam based on your knowledge of that chapter's topics.

The review questions, assessment test, and other testing elements included in this book are *not* derived from the actual exam questions, so don't memorize the answers to these questions and assume that doing so will enable you to pass the exam. You should learn the underlying topic, as described in the text of the book. This will let you answer the questions provided with this book *and* pass the exam. Learning the underlying topic is also the approach that will serve you best in the workplace—the ultimate goal of a certification.

Interactive Online Learning Environment and TestBank

Studying the material in the *Google Certified Professional Cloud Database Engineer Study Guide* is an important part of preparing for the Professional Cloud Database Engineer certification exam, but we provide additional tools to help you prepare. The online TestBank will help you understand the types of questions that will appear on the certification exam.

- The Practice Tests in the TestBank include all the questions in each chapter as well as the questions from the Assessment test. *In addition*, there are two practice exams with 60 questions each. You can use these tests to evaluate your understanding and identify areas that may require additional study.

- The Flashcards in the TestBank will push the limits of what you should know for the certification exam. There are two sets of flashcards with 100 questions each that are provided in digital format. Each flashcard has one question and one correct answer.

- The online Glossary is a searchable list of over 100 key terms introduced in this exam guide that you should know for the Professional Cloud Database Engineer certification exam.

To start using these to study for the Google Certified Professional Cloud Database Engineer exam, go to `www.wiley.com/go/sybextestprep` and register your book to receive your unique PIN. Once you have the PIN, return to `www.wiley.com/go/sybextestprep`, find your book, and click Register or Login and follow the link to register a new account or add this book to an existing account.

> Like all exams, the Professional Cloud Database Engineer certification from Google Cloud is updated periodically and may eventually be retired or replaced. At some point after Google Cloud is no longer offering this exam, the old editions of our books and online tools will be retired. If you have purchased this book after the exam was retired, or are attempting to register in the Sybex online learning environment after the exam was retired, please know that we make no guarantees that this exam's online Sybex tools will be available once the exam is no longer available.

How to Contact the Author

We appreciate your input and questions about this book! Email me at `jake.holmquist@gmail.com`, or follow me on Medium at `@cloud-jake`.

Conventions Used in This Book

This book uses certain typographic styles in order to help you quickly identify important information and to avoid confusion over the meaning of words such as on-screen prompts. In particular, look for the following styles:

- *Italicized text* indicates key terms that are described at length for the first time in a chapter. (Italics are also used for emphasis.)

- A `monospaced font` indicates the contents of configuration files, messages displayed at a text-mode shell prompt, filenames, text-mode command names, and Internet URLs.

- *Italicized monospaced text* indicates a variable—information that differs from one system or command run to another, such as the name of a client computer or a process ID number.

- **Bold monospaced text** is information that you're to type into the console, for example at a shell prompt. This text can also be italicized to indicate that you should substitute an appropriate value for your system.

In addition to these text conventions, which can apply to individual words or entire paragraphs, a few conventions highlight segments of text:

A note indicates information that's useful or interesting but that's somewhat peripheral to the main text. A note might be relevant to a specific database engine or a niche use case, for instance, or it may refer to a legacy feature or a new preview feature.

Real-World Scenario

A real-world scenario is a type of sidebar that describes a task or example that's particularly grounded in the real world. This may be a situation a database engineer has encountered, or it may be advice on how to architect solutions or work around problems that are common in real-world Google Cloud database deployments.

EXERCISES

An exercise provides a hands-on procedure to help you apply the concepts from the chapter. These labs reference official content from Google Cloud SkillsBoost or Google Codelabs. Don't stop at just the steps in the exercises, though! Experimenting with other configurations and features is the best way to gain a deep understanding of Google Cloud's database services.

Google Cloud Professional Database Engineer Objective Map

This study guide has been written to cover every Professional Cloud Database Engineer exam objective at a level appropriate to its exam weighting. The following table provides a breakdown of this book's exam coverage, showing you the weight of each section and the chapter where each objective or subobjective is covered:

Subject Area	% of Exam
Design innovative, scalable, and highly available cloud database solutions	32
Manage a solution that can span multiple database technologies	25
Migrate data solutions	23
Deploy scalable and highly available databases in Google Cloud	20
Total	100

OBJECTIVE	CHAPTER(S)
Section 1: Design innovative, scalable, and highly available cloud database solutions	
1.1 Analyze relevant variables to perform database capacity and usage planning.	1, 4
• Perform solution sizing based on current environment workload metrics and future requirements.	4
• Evaluate performance and cost tradeoffs of different database configurations (e.g., machine types, storage types).	1, 4
• Size database compute and storage based on performance requirements.	4
1.2 Evaluate database high availability and disaster recovery options given the requirements.	5
• Evaluate tradeoffs between multi-regional, regional, and zonal database deployment strategies.	5
• Define maintenance windows and notifications based on application availability requirements.	5

(Continued)

(Continued)

OBJECTIVE	CHAPTER(S)

1.3 Determine how applications will connect to the database.   6

- Configure networking, key management, encryption, and security.   6

- Justify the use of session pooler services.   6

- Assess auditing policies for managed services.   6

1.4 Evaluate appropriate database solutions on Google Cloud.   1, 2, 3, 4, 6

- Differentiate between managed and unmanaged database services.   2, 3

- Distinguish between SQL and NoSQL business requirements (e.g., structured, semi-structured, unstructured, vector).   2

- Analyze the cost of running database solutions in Google Cloud (comparative analysis).   4

- Assess application and database dependencies.   2, 4

- Identify solutions to support regulatory and compliance requirements.   1, 3, 6

- Understand implications of organizational policies on database strategy.   3

- Consider solutions that span multiple database technologies (e.g., federation, exports, hybrid deployments).   3

- Leverage database technologies to support generative AI and LLM use cases.   2, 3

Section 2: Manage a solution that can span multiple database technologies

2.1 Determine database connectivity and access management considerations.   6

- Determine Identity and Access Management (IAM) and policies for database connectivity and access control.   6

OBJECTIVE	CHAPTER(S)
• Manage database users including authentication and access.	6
2.2 Configure database monitoring and troubleshooting options.	7
• Assess slow running queries, database locking—identify missing indexes.	7
• Monitor and investigate database vitals—AM, CPU storage, I/O, and audit logging.	7
• Monitor and update quotas.	7
• Investigate database resource contention.	7
• Set up alerts for errors and performance metrics.	7
2.3 Design database backup and recovery solutions.	5, 9
• Given requirements, recommend backup and recovery options (automatic scheduled backups).	9
• Configure export and import data for databases.	9
• Design for RTO, RPO, and PITR.	5, 9
• Manage data retention.	9
2.4 Optimize database cost and performance in Google Cloud.	7, 8
• Assess scaling up and scaling out options.	7
• Scale database instances based on current and upcoming workload.	7
• Define replication strategies.	7
• Continuously assess and optimize the cost of running a database solution.	8
• Optimize queries for cost and performance.	7

(*Continued*)

(Continued)

OBJECTIVE	CHAPTER(S)
2.5 Automate common database tasks.	5, 8, 9
• Perform database maintenance (e.g., rebuilding indexes, data exports).	8
• Schedule database exports.	8, 9
• Manage upgrades for Google Cloud–managed databases.	5, 8
• Monitor database SLA/SLOs.	8
Section 3: Migrate data solutions	
3.1 Design and implement data migration and replication.	10
• Develop and execute migration strategies and plans, including zero/near-zero downtime, extended outage, and fallback.	10
• Reverse replication from Google Cloud to source.	10
• Plan and perform database migration, including fallback plans and DDL/DML conversion.	10
• Determine the correct database migration tools for a given scenario.	10
Section 4: Deploy scalable and highly available databases in Google Cloud	
4.1 Apply concepts to implement scalable and highly available databases in Google Cloud.	11
• Provision highly available database solutions in Google Cloud.	11
• Test high availability and disaster recovery strategies.	11
• Set up multi-regional replication for databases.	11

OBJECTIVE	CHAPTER(S)
• Deploy and scale read replicas.	11
• Automate database instance provisioning.	11
• Configure monitoring for highly available databases.	11

Assessment Test

1. Which storage type is most cost-effective for storing data that is accessed infrequently, such as backups or archival data?

    A. Block storage

    B. File storage

    C. Object storage

    D. In-memory storage

2. You are designing a data lake on Google Cloud to store a massive amount of unstructured data, including images, videos, and log files. This data will be accessed infrequently for batch analytics. Which storage class should you choose to minimize storage costs?

    A. Standard

    B. Nearline

    C. Coldline

    D. Archive

3. What is the key difference between OLTP (online transaction processing) and OLAP (online analytical processing) databases?

    A. OLTP databases handle high-volume reads; OLAP handles high-volume writes.

    B. OLTP databases prioritize data consistency; OLAP prioritizes data speed.

    C. OLTP databases focus on short, frequent transactions; OLAP focuses on complex queries over large datasets.

    D. OLTP databases are used for analytics; OLAP databases are used for transactions.

4. Which of the following are advantages of using a managed database service on Google Cloud? (Choose three.)

    A. Simplified management

    B. Automatic backups and updates

    C. Greater control over configuration and customization

    D. Reduced operational overhead

5. A company is migrating a large, complex Oracle database to Google Cloud. They require high performance, low latency, and the ability to leverage existing Oracle licenses. Which deployment option would best meet their needs?

    A. Cloud Spanner

    B. Oracle on Google Compute Engine

    C. Oracle on Bare Metal Solution (BMS)

    D. Cloud SQL

6. Which of the following Google Cloud database services is a fully managed in-memory data store that offers both Redis and Memcached options?

   A. Cloud SQL

   B. Cloud Spanner

   C. Cloud Bigtable

   D. Cloud Firestore

   E. Big Query

   F. Memorystore

7. Which phase of the Google Cloud Implementation Methodology involves continuously monitoring the performance and cost of your Google Cloud infrastructure?

   A. Assess

   B. Plan

   C. Deploy

   D. Optimize

8. What security best practice should be followed when configuring access to Google Cloud resources?

   A. Granting excessive permissions

   B. Using only Google-managed encryption keys

   C. Following the principle of least privilege

   D. Ignoring IAM roles and policies

9. Your development team is setting up a nonproduction test environment for a new application feature. They are considering deploying their Cloud SQL database in a single zone to minimize costs. What is the primary risk associated with this zonal deployment for even a nonproduction environment?

   A. Increased network latency for applications in different zones

   B. Higher operational costs due to single instance management

   C. Complete unavailability of the database if that specific zone experiences an outage

   D. Reduced performance during peak usage

10. A professional Cloud Database engineer is responsible for a critical Cloud SQL instance that serves a global application. To minimize user impact, they need to schedule maintenance for patches and updates. What is a key consideration when defining the weekly maintenance window for this instance?

   A. Setting the window during the application's highest traffic period to utilize cloud bursting capabilities

   B. Selecting a time when the database is fully quiesced for consistent backups

   C. Choosing a period of lowest expected application traffic across all relevant time zones

   D. Disabling maintenance windows entirely to ensure continuous availability

11. What is the primary reason why it is crucial to use SSL/TLS encryption for all data in transit between your application and a database, even when connecting over a private network?

    A. To reduce network latency

    B. To prevent eavesdropping and on-path attacks

    C. To increase database query performance

    D. To enable database engine upgrades

12. When designing a highly available database solution, which strategy ensures that your database can withstand infrastructure failures, such as a zonal outage or a hardware failure on the primary instance, with minimal disruption?

    A. Deploying the database in a single zone to centralize resources

    B. Implementing multizone or multiregional database deployments with failover mechanisms

    C. Relying on manual database restarts in case of failure

    D. Using public IP addresses to allow global accessibility

13. A database engineer wants to establish a baseline for the performance of a production Cloud SQL instance and identify potential resource bottlenecks. Which is the most appropriate Google Cloud service to collect and visualize metrics like CPU utilization, memory usage, and I/O operations for this instance?

    A. Cloud Logging

    B. Cloud Audit Logs

    C. Cloud Monitoring

    D. Cloud Storage

14. A read-heavy analytics application using Cloud SQL is hitting performance limits on its single primary instance. The team needs to improve read throughput. To improve read throughput for a Cloud SQL instance, which scaling strategy is generally most effective and targeted for this specific workload?

    A. Scaling up the primary instance by increasing its CPU and RAM

    B. Scaling out by adding one or more read replicas

    C. Migrating the entire database to Cloud Bigtable

    D. Implementing a custom caching layer in front of the database

15. A database engineer needs to understand the current cost allocation for their Google Cloud databases, broken down by project and specific database service (e.g., Cloud SQL, Cloud Spanner). Which Google Cloud tool provides the most granular and customizable insights for this purpose?

    A. Cloud Monitoring dashboards

    B. Cloud Billing Reports with billing export to BigQuery

    C. Google Cloud Quotas page

    D. Google Cloud Recommender

16. Your organization has a predictable, steady-state production workload running on a Cloud SQL database. To optimize the ongoing compute costs for this database, which Google Cloud cost optimization strategy would provide the most significant percentage discount over a multiyear period?

   A. Scaling down the instance every night

   B. Leveraging CUDs for 1 or 3 years

   C. Using HDD storage instead of SSD storage

   D. Migrating to an open source database on a Compute Engine VM

17. When designing a backup and recovery solution, what is the fundamental difference between a recovery time objective (RTO) and a recovery point objective (RPO)?

   A. RTO is the maximum acceptable data loss, whereas RPO is the maximum acceptable downtime.

   B. RTO is the maximum acceptable downtime, whereas RPO is the maximum acceptable data loss.

   C. RTO is the cost of recovery, whereas RPO is the duration of the recovery process.

   D. RTO is for hardware failures, whereas RPO is for software failures.

18. Your company frequently uses `bq extract` to export data from BigQuery tables to Cloud Storage for downstream processing. How can you automate these `bq extract` commands to run on a regular, scheduled basis using native Google Cloud services?

   A. By configuring a Cloud SQL export schedule

   B. By using a Cloud Scheduler job to trigger a Cloud Function that executes the `bq extract` command

   C. By manually running the `bq extract` command from a local machine daily

   D. By setting up a continuous Dataflow streaming job

19. A large e-commerce platform needs to migrate its core transactional MySQL database from on-premises to Cloud SQL for MySQL. The application can tolerate no more than 10 minutes of downtime for the entire migration. Which migration strategy is most appropriate for this scenario?

   A. Extended outage (offline migration)

   B. Zero-downtime migration

   C. Near-zero downtime migration

   D. Manual export/import

20. A large enterprise needs to move its entire petabyte-scale data warehouse, currently residing as flat files on-premises, to Cloud Storage. Their Internet bandwidth is limited, and they cannot afford a long online transfer time. Which Google Cloud service is specifically designed for physically transferring massive datasets when online transfer is not feasible?

A. Database Migration Service (DMS)

B. Datastream

C. Storage Transfer Service

D. Transfer Appliance

21. A company needs to ensure its Cloud SQL for MySQL database remains available with minimal downtime in case of a single zone failure within a region. Which replication strategy should be implemented for this Cloud SQL instance to achieve high availability against a zonal outage?

A. Create multiple read replicas across different regions.

B. Configure the Cloud SQL instance with a high availability (HA) setup.

C. Implement a manual backup and restore process to Cloud Storage.

D. Use a single zonal instance with no replication for cost savings.

22. A Google Cloud database engineer is tasked with standardizing the deployment of their Cloud SQL instances across multiple environments (development, staging, production) and projects. They want to ensure consistency, repeatability, and version control for their database infrastructure. Which Google Cloud tool is best suited for automating this provisioning process using infrastructure as code (IaC)?

A. Google Cloud Console's UI for manual instance creation

B. `gcloud` command-line interface (CLI) for scripting

C. Cloud Monitoring for resource utilization alerts

D. Terraform

Answers to Assessment Test

1. **C.** Object storage typically offers tiered storage options, allowing you to choose a lower-cost tier for infrequently accessed data, making it the most cost-effective choice for this use case.

    Block, file, and in-memory storage are generally more expensive for infrequently accessed data.

2. **C.** Coldline storage is the most cost-effective option for storing infrequently accessed data, making it suitable for data lakes used for batch analytics.

    Standard, Nearline, and Archive storage are more expensive for infrequently accessed data.

3. **C.** OLTP systems excel at handling many short, fast transactions. OLAP systems are designed for analytical queries across large datasets.

    The other options misrepresent the core functions of OLTP and OLAP databases.

4. **A, B, D.** With a managed database, simplified management saves time and resources by handling database provisioning, patching, and scaling. Automatic backups and updates ensure data protection and optimal performance without manual intervention. Reduced operational overhead eliminates the need for dedicated database administrators and infrastructure management.

5. **C.** Bare Metal Solution allows for high performance and low latency while fully supporting the use of existing Oracle licenses and offering complete control.

    Cloud Spanner is a different database system; Cloud SQL doesn't directly support existing Oracle licenses, and Oracle on Compute Engine offers less control.

6. **F.** Memorystore is a fully managed, in-memory data store service on Google Cloud. It provides high performance and low latency for caching, session management, and real-time data processing. It offers both Redis and Memcached options.

    All other options are managed database options on Google Cloud.

7. **D.** The Optimize phase focuses on ongoing monitoring and improvement of the migrated environment.

    The other phases have different focuses: assessment, planning, and deployment.

8. **C.** Granting only necessary permissions minimizes the attack surface, improving security.

    Excessive permissions increase risk. Using only Google-managed keys is one aspect of a broader security strategy. Ignoring IAM is fundamentally insecure.

9. **C.** A purely zonal deployment means the database instance resides entirely within one Google Cloud zone. If that entire zone experiences a widespread outage (e.g., due to a major power failure or network disruption), the database would become completely unavailable, leading to significant downtime.

A is incorrect because if the application is also in the same zone, latency would be minimal; latency is a concern when the application is in a different zone or region. B is incorrect as a single instance is generally the lowest cost configuration, not higher. D is incorrect because performance is typically a function of instance size and configuration, not solely its zonal deployment; a zonal instance can perform well if sized correctly.

10. C. For a global application, identifying periods of lowest expected traffic across all user bases and time zones is crucial to minimize disruption during maintenance. This ensures that the essential updates occur when they have the least impact on the majority of users.

    A is incorrect because performing maintenance during high traffic periods would maximize disruption and negatively impact user experience. B is incorrect as quiescing for backups is a separate, although important, operational task, not the primary consideration for scheduling a maintenance window for Google-managed updates. D is incorrect because maintenance is essential for security, performance, and new features; disabling it would compromise the database's health and security posture.

11. B. SSL/TLS (Secure Sockets Layer/Transport Layer Security) encrypts data as it travels over the network, protecting it from eavesdropping (unauthorized viewing) and on-path attacks, where an attacker might intercept and potentially alter the communication. This ensures the confidentiality and integrity of your data.

    A is incorrect because SSL/TLS adds a small overhead, which can slightly increase latency, not reduce it. C is incorrect because SSL/TLS is for security, not direct database query performance. D is incorrect as SSL/TLS has no direct relation to enabling database engine upgrades.

12. B. Implementing multizone or multiregional database deployments (e.g., Cloud SQL HA, Cloud Spanner) with automatic failover mechanisms is a fundamental strategy for high availability. This distributes the database across different failure domains, allowing it to withstand outages in one location with minimal downtime and disruption.

    A is incorrect because deploying in a single zone creates a single point of failure and does not provide high availability against zonal outages. C is incorrect because relying on manual restarts would lead to significant downtime and higher RTO, which is contrary to the goal of high availability. D is incorrect as using public IP addresses makes the database globally accessible but does not inherently improve its resilience against underlying infrastructure failures.

13. C. Cloud Monitoring is the central service for collecting, visualizing, and alerting on operational metrics and telemetry data from all Google Cloud services, including your database instances. It provides comprehensive insights into resource usage like CPU, memory, and I/O.

    A is incorrect because Cloud Logging collects log data, not performance metrics. B is incorrect because Cloud Audit Logs record administrative activities and data access events for compliance, not real-time performance metrics. D is incorrect because Cloud Storage is an object storage service and not used for real-time performance monitoring.

14. B. For a read-heavy workload on Cloud SQL, scaling out by adding read replicas is highly effective. Read replicas offload read queries from the primary instance, distributing the read load and significantly improving read throughput without impacting write performance on the primary.

A is incorrect because scaling up the primary instance might help overall but is less targeted and potentially more expensive for a read-heavy workload than dedicated read replicas. C is incorrect because migrating to Cloud Bigtable is a major architectural change to a NoSQL database, not a direct scaling strategy for an existing Cloud SQL relational database. D is incorrect because although caching can help, it's an application-level optimization and not a direct database scaling strategy for improving throughput on the database itself.

15. B. Cloud Billing Reports provide an overview, but exporting billing data to BigQuery enables highly granular and customizable analysis. You can write complex SQL queries to break down costs by project, service, SKU, and labels, and track trends over time for precise cost assessment.

A is incorrect because Cloud Monitoring focuses on performance metrics, not detailed cost breakdown. C is incorrect because the Quotas page shows service limits and usage, not cost analysis. D is incorrect because the Recommender provides optimization suggestions, not detailed historical cost breakdowns.

16. B. For predictable, steady-state workloads, purchasing CUDs for Cloud SQL (or other services like Spanner) offers the most significant percentage discount (up to 52 percent for 3 years) on compute (vCPU and memory) compared to on-demand pricing.

A is incorrect because scaling down daily is for intermittent workloads, and CUDs are for continuous use. C is incorrect because HDD vs. SSD affects storage cost and performance, not directly the compute cost. D is incorrect because although an open source database might initially seem cheaper, it incurs significant operational overhead and management costs that often outweigh perceived savings.

17. B. RTO defines the maximum acceptable duration of downtime after an incident. RPO defines the maximum acceptable amount of data loss, measured in time. They are the two crucial metrics for guiding the design of any recovery solution.

A is incorrect because it reverses the definitions. C is incorrect because RTO/RPO are objectives related to time and data loss, not direct costs or process duration, though they influence these. D is incorrect because RTO/RPO apply to recovery from all types of failures, not just specific ones.

18. B. To automate BigQuery exports, a common pattern is to use Cloud Scheduler to define the recurring schedule. This scheduler job then triggers a Cloud Function (or Cloud Run service) that contains the logic to execute the `bq extract` command using the BigQuery client libraries.

A is incorrect because Cloud SQL export schedules are for Cloud SQL, not BigQuery. C is incorrect because manual execution is not automation. D is incorrect because a Dataflow streaming job is for continuous, real-time data processing, not for scheduling batch `bq extract` operations.

19. C. A near-zero downtime migration uses continuous data replication to keep the source and target databases in sync, minimizing the final service interruption to a brief cutover window (typically a few minutes), which aligns with the 10-minute tolerance.

A is incorrect because an extended outage requires significant downtime, far exceeding the 10-minute tolerance. B is incorrect because a zero-downtime migration is much more complex and expensive than necessary for a 10-minute tolerance and typically involves significant application re-architecture. D is incorrect because manual export/import is an offline method with potentially long downtime.

20. D. Transfer Appliance is a physical hardware appliance that you load with your data on-premises and then ship to Google. Google then ingests the data into Cloud Storage. This is ideal for petabyte-scale migrations with limited network bandwidth where online transfer is impractical or too slow.

A is incorrect because DMS is for migrating transactional databases, not flat files. B is incorrect because Datastream is for real-time change data capture (CDC), not large-scale bulk offline transfer of flat files. C is incorrect because although Storage Transfer Service can transfer large datasets over a network, it does not involve a physical appliance for cases of severely limited bandwidth.

21. B. Configuring Cloud SQL with a high availability (HA) setup ensures that a synchronized standby instance is maintained in a different zone within the same region. In case of a zonal failure, Cloud SQL automatically fails over to the standby, providing high availability with minimal downtime.

A is incorrect because read replicas across regions are primarily for disaster recovery against regional failures or for read scaling, not for automatic HA within a single region. C is incorrect because manual backup and restore leads to significant downtime and data loss, failing HA requirements. D is incorrect because a single zonal instance is a single point of failure and provides no HA against zonal outages.

22. D. Terraform is a widely used open source infrastructure as code (IaC) tool that allows you to define and provision cloud infrastructure declaratively using configuration files. It ensures consistency, repeatability, and version control for database instance provisioning, making it ideal for standardizing deployments across multiple environments.

A is incorrect because manual UI creation is prone to human error and lacks version control. B is incorrect because although `gcloud` CLI can be used for scripting, Terraform's declarative nature and state management capabilities are superior for managing complex, version-controlled infrastructure. C is incorrect because Cloud Monitoring is for monitoring and alerting, not for provisioning infrastructure.

Chapter

1

Data Storage Technologies

GOOGLE CLOUD CERTIFIED PROFESSIONAL CLOUD DATABASE ENGINEER EXAM OBJECTIVES COVERED IN THIS CHAPTER:

✔ **1.1 Analyze relevant variables to perform database capacity and usage planning.**

- Evaluate performance and cost tradeoffs of different database configurations (machine types, HDD versus SSD, etc.).

✔ **1.4 Evaluate appropriate database solutions on Google Cloud.**

- Identify solutions to support regulatory and compliance requirements.

The amount of data created globally is exploding. Estimates suggest daily data creation will top 500 exabytes by 2025 (that's 500 million petabytes!), which means that the amount of data being generated is doubling every few years. Figure 1.1 shows the exponential rise in data generated year over year since 2010. As the amount of data generated grows, finding efficient and cost-effective ways to store and access this data is becoming increasingly important.

Traditionally, most data was structured, fitting neatly into tables with defined formats (like customer names and addresses). However, the rise of social media, sensor data, and multimedia content has led to a surge in unstructured data, which doesn't fit easily into predefined formats (like emails, videos, and social media posts).

FIGURE 1.1   Global data generated annually.

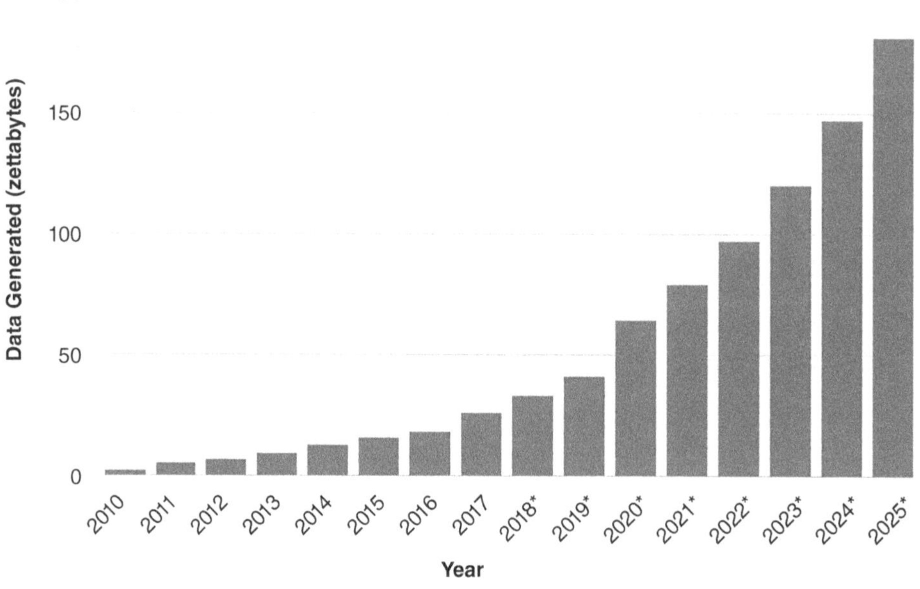

Organizations require ways to store this data that are not only secure and reliable, but also adaptable and efficient. Traditional on-premises storage and database solutions, while familiar, can struggle to keep pace with ever-growing data volumes and evolving business needs.

Turning to the cloud presents a compelling solution. Cloud storage and databases options offer inherent scalability, allowing you to effortlessly adjust resources up or down based on demand. This eliminates the need for costly hardware provisioning and management, freeing up IT resources for more strategic tasks. Additionally, cloud providers handle infrastructure maintenance and security, ensuring your databases are constantly protected and up-to-date.

For a Google Cloud Professional Database Engineer, understanding different storage solutions and where to apply them is crucial. In this chapter, we'll explore block, object, and file storage, then delve into structured, unstructured, transactional, and relational databases, highlighting their uses and how a database engineer leverages them as part of an overall architecture.

Data Storage Design Considerations

As a Google Cloud database engineer, designing optimal storage solutions requires careful consideration of various factors. This section explores some key aspects you should define before diving into the design process.

Workload Characteristics

Understanding your workload's characteristics is crucial for effective storage design. Consider factors such as data volume, growth rate, access patterns, durability requirements, retention policies, and any compliance or regulatory obligations. This information will help determine the appropriate storage solution and capacity needs.

For example, imagine that you are an online retail platform handling product catalogs, customer orders, and inventory management. You might identify for the following workload characteristics to inform your planning:

Data Volume: Several terabytes of product information, customer data, and order history

Growth Rate: Rapidly increasing product catalog and customer base, requiring frequent data additions

Access Patterns: High read volume for product catalogs and order lookup; frequent writes for new orders and inventory updates

Durability Requirements: High durability needed to prevent data loss as orders and customer information are critical

Retention Policies: Order data retained for 7 years for tax and compliance purposes; product catalog data updated frequently

Compliance: Adherence to Payment Card Industry Data Security Standards (PCI DSS) for handling payment information

Performance and Scalability

Define the performance requirements for your workload, including necessary IOPS and throughput. Assess the potential for future growth and the ability to scale storage resources to accommodate increasing demands. Establishing performance SLAs will help ensure that your storage solution meets your application's needs.

Imagine that your client is a high-frequency trading platform. What are some performance and scalability requirements?

Performance Requirements: Extremely low latency, high input/output operations per second (IOPS) for rapid order execution and market data ingestion. Throughput needs to handle thousands of transactions per second.

Scalability: Ability to quickly scale storage resources to handle increased trading volume during peak market hours.

Performance SLAs: Strict latency requirements, such as 99.999 percent of read operations completing within 1 millisecond.

Cost Optimization

To maximize cost efficiency, evaluate different storage options and their pricing models. Implement data life-cycle management strategies to move cold or infrequently accessed data to lower-cost storage tiers. Careful consideration of storage costs will help optimize your overall cloud expenditure.

For example, take a large-scale data warehousing application storing historical sales data. How could you identify cost optimization opportunities?

Storage Tiers: Evaluate different storage options like Nearline, Coldline, and Archive storage tiers offered by Google Cloud Storage.

Life-Cycle Management: Implement life-cycle policies to automatically move older sales data (e.g., data older than 3 years) to lower-cost storage tiers like Coldline or Archive.

Monitor Storage Usage: Analyze storage usage patterns to identify opportunities for optimization and cost savings.

Data Protection and Recovery

Develop comprehensive backup and recovery plans to safeguard your data. Determine the frequency of backups, retention periods, and recovery procedures. Additionally, consider disaster recovery strategies to protect against data loss in case of unforeseen events. Data encryption should also be implemented to protect sensitive information.

For example, some industries will have different tolerances for recovery time objective (RTO), or how quickly you must recover based on the cost of downtime. RTO is about how quickly systems must be restored (speed of recovery), whereas RPO is about how much data loss is acceptable (data currency). We will cover more about RTO and RPO in Chapter 5, "Designing for High Availability and Disaster Recovery."

What are some ways to design for these data protection and recovery requirements in Google Cloud?

Automated Backups: Leverage native automated backup tools such as Backup for GKE or Cloud SQL Backup.

Persistent Disk Snapshots: Create point-in-time copies of persistent disks for rapid recovery.

Data Encryption: By default, all data stored in Google Cloud is encrypted in transit and at rest.

Security and Compliance

Prioritize data security by implementing robust access controls to prevent unauthorized access. Ensure compliance with data residency regulations and other relevant industry standards. Establish auditing and logging procedures to monitor storage activities and maintain a strong security posture.

Imagine that you represent a large healthcare provider that needs to store sensitive patient data, including medical records, financial information, and personal details. They must comply with stringent regulations like HIPAA, GDPR, and CCPA while ensuring data privacy and accessibility for authorized personnel. What are some ways to address data security and compliance requirements?

Robust Access Controls: Implement IAM policies that limit data access based on user roles and grant users only the necessary permissions.

Data Residency: Store data in specific geographic locations to comply with laws. Replicate data across regions for disaster recovery while adhering to regulations.

While this is not an exhaustive list, documenting some of these requirements will help you start to determine the best storage solutions on Google Cloud.

Storage Technologies

Google Cloud provides a comprehensive suite of storage solutions to cater to diverse data management needs. These solutions are primarily categorized into three fundamental types: block, file, and object storage. Before delving into the specifics of each storage format, it's essential to understand their core characteristics:

Block Storage: Presents data as raw blocks, providing low-level access for applications requiring high performance and flexibility.

File Storage: Organizes data into hierarchical filesystems, offering a familiar structure for applications that need to manage and share files.

Object Storage: Stores data as objects with metadata, optimized for large amounts of unstructured data that requires high durability and availability.

In the subsequent sections, we will explore these formats in detail, highlighting their key features, use cases, and how they are delivered in Google Cloud.

Block Storage

Block storage is a type of digital storage that divides data into small, independently addressable chunks called *blocks*. This structure allows for rapid data access and modification, making it ideal for applications demanding high performance, such as databases and transaction processing systems. Similar to traditional storage systems used in data centers, block storage offers high IOPS and is often used in virtual machine (VM) environments. Google Cloud provides various block storage options as part of its Compute Engine service, catering to different performance and cost requirements. These block storage options are available in three different formats:

Persistent Disk: Dedicated hard-disk drives (HDD) and solid-state drives (SSD) for enterprise and database applications, offering durability and flexibility.

Hyperdisk: High-performance block storage decoupling performance from VM type with volumes that can be dynamically resized, providing scalability and efficiency.

Local SSD: High-performance, low-latency block storage directly attached to the virtual machine, ideal for I/O-intensive workloads.

Let's explore each type of block storage in detail, including key features, configuration options, and use cases.

Persistent Disk

Google Cloud Persistent Disks are block storage volumes that function as virtual hard disk drives (HDDs), solid-state disks (SSDs), or an option that balances price/performance for VMs on Google Compute Engine (GCE) and Kubernetes Engine (GKE).

Key Features

Key features include the following:

Durability: Data persists independently of the VM life cycle, ensuring information remains secure even after VM shutdown or termination.

Flexibility: Users can dynamically resize persistent disks on the fly to accommodate growing storage needs without impacting VM uptime.

Scalability: Multiple disks can be attached to a single VM for increased storage capacity.

Performance Options: Users can choose between high-performance SSDs for demanding applications or cost-effective HDDs for large datasets with less frequent access.

Configuration Options

When you configure a persistent disk, you can select one of the following disk types:

- **Standard Persistent Disks (pd-Standard):** HDD-based, cost-effective for workloads with moderate performance needs.
  - Suitable for large data processing workloads that primarily use sequential I/Os
  - Most cost-effective option
  - Backed by standard HDDs
- **Performance (SSD) Persistent Disks (pd-ssd):** SSD-based, provides higher performance and lower latency compared to standard persistent disk.
  - Suitable for enterprise applications and high-performance databases that require lower latency and more IOPS than standard persistent disks provide
  - Designed for single-digit millisecond latencies; the observed latency is application specific
  - Backed by SSDs
- **Balanced Persistent Disks (pd-Balanced):** SSD-based, offers a balance of price and performance.
  - An alternative to performance (pd-ssd) persistent disks
  - Balance of performance and cost. For most VM shapes, except very large ones, these disks have the same maximum IOPS as SSD persistent disks and lower IOPS per GiB. This disk type offers performance levels suitable for most general-purpose applications at a price point between that of standard and performance (pd-ssd) persistent disks
  - Backed by SSDs
- **Extreme Persistent Disks (pd-Extreme):** SSD-based; delivers the highest performance for demanding workloads.
  - Offer consistently high performance for both random access workloads and bulk throughput

- Designed for high-end database workloads
- Allow you to provision the target IOPS
- Backed by SSDs
- Available with a limited number of machine types

Feature Summary

Table 1.1 summarizes the differences between the various Persistent Disk types. The column definitions are as follows:

Backed By: Type of physical hard drive: HDD or SSD?

Performance: How much IOPS and throughput do you need?

Scalability: Do you need to be able to scale your storage up or down easily?

Cost: How much are you willing to spend on storage?

Use Cases

Use cases include the following:

Databases: High-performance databases like MySQL, PostgreSQL, and Oracle can benefit from the low latency and high throughput of Persistent Disks.

Virtual Machines: As the primary storage for Compute Engine instances, Persistent Disks are essential for running virtual machines with various workloads.

Big Data Analytics: Persistent Disks can be used for storing intermediate data for big data processing frameworks like Apache Spark and Hadoop.

Gaming and Media: Applications demanding high IOPS and low latency, such as online gaming and video editing, can leverage Persistent Disks.

TABLE 1.1   Comparison of persistent disk types

Persistent disk type	Backed by	Performance	Cost
Standard persistent disks	HDD	Moderate	Low
Performance (SSD) persistent disks	SSD	High	Moderate
Balanced persistent disks	SSD	Balanced	Low-moderate
Extreme persistent disks	SSD	Very High	High

Hyperdisk

Hyperdisk is Google Cloud's next-generation block storage solution designed to deliver exceptional performance, scalability, and flexibility for demanding workloads. It represents a significant leap forward in block storage technology compared to traditional Persistent Disks.

Key Features

Key features include the following:

High Performance: Hyperdisk offers substantially higher IOPS and throughput compared to Persistent Disk, making it ideal for performance-critical applications. With Hyperdisk, you get dedicated IOPS and throughput with each volume, as compared to Persistent Disk, where performance is shared between volumes of the same type.

Scalability: Hyperdisk lets you scale performance and capacity dynamically. For some Hyperdisk types, you can independently scale performance (IOPS and throughput) and capacity, providing granular control over resource allocation.

Integration: Seamlessly integrates with Compute Engine and Google Kubernetes Engine (GKE).

Configuration Options

The following Hyperdisk options are available depending on your workload:

- **Hyperdisk Balanced:** (customizable throughput, IOPS, shareable between VMs, bootable)
  - Optimized for most workloads, including databases, web servers, and enterprise applications
  - Offers a balanced combination of IOPS and throughput for general-purpose use cases
  - Provides a cost-effective option for workloads with moderate performance demands
- **Hyperdisk Balanced High Availability:** (customizable throughput, IOPS, shareable between VMs, bootable, synchronous replication for HA)
  - Optimized for most workloads, including databases, web servers, and enterprise applications
  - Offers a balanced combination of IOPS and throughput for general-purpose use cases
  - Protects your applications from a zonal outage by synchronously replicating the disk data across two zones in the same region

- **Hyperdisk Extreme:** (high IOPS/throughput, not shareable, not bootable)
  - Optimized for high-performance workloads, such as high-end databases (Oracle, SQL Server, SAP HANA), in-memory databases, and real-time analytics
  - Delivers the highest IOPS and throughput for demanding applications
  - Comes with a premium price due to its exceptional performance capabilities
- **Hyperdisk ML:** (customizable throughput, not IOPS, shareable between VMs in read-only mode, not bootable)
  - Optimized for machine learning workloads that require the highest throughput
  - Hyperdisk ML has the highest throughput available and the fastest data load times as a result
  - Faster data load times mean shorter accelerator idle times and lower compute costs
  - For large inference and training workloads, you can attach a single Hyperdisk ML volume to multiple VMs in read-only mode
- **Hyperdisk Throughput:** (customizable throughput, no IOPS, not shareable, not bootable)
  - Optimized for scale-out analytics workloads, cold storage, and cost-sensitive applications
  - Prioritizes throughput over IOPS, making it suitable for data-intensive workloads
  - Offers a more cost-efficient option compared to Balanced and Extreme for throughput-oriented applications

Feature Summary

Table 1.2 summarizes the differences between the various Hyperdisk types.

Use Cases

Use cases include the following:

High-Performance Databases: Databases like Oracle, SQL Server, and SAP HANA can benefit from Hyperdisk's exceptional performance and scalability.

In-Memory Databases: Applications requiring low-latency access to large datasets can leverage Hyperdisk.

Big Data Analytics: Hyperdisk can accelerate data processing and analytics workloads.

Gaming and Media: Applications demanding high IOPS and low latency, such as online gaming and video editing, can benefit from Hyperdisk.

TABLE 1.2   Comparison of Hyperdisk types

Hyperdisk type	Customizable throughput	Customizable IOPS	Shareable between VMs	Boot disk support
Hyperdisk Balanced	Yes	Yes	Yes	Yes
Hyperdisk Balanced High Availability	Yes	Yes	Yes	Yes
Hyperdisk Extreme	No	Yes	No	No
Hyperdisk ML	Yes	No	Yes	No
Hyperdisk Throughput	Yes	No	No	No

Local SSD

Google Cloud Local SSDs are a high-performance, low-latency storage option specifically designed for temporary data within Compute Engine virtual machines. Ideal for workloads demanding rapid data access, such as caching, scratch processing for data analytics or high-performance computing, and temporary data storage like SQL Server's tempdb, Local SSDs offer significantly superior IOPS and latency compared to Persistent Disk and Hyperdisk. This performance boost is attributed to their direct attachment to the host server.

However, it's crucial to remember that Local SSDs are not suitable for long-term data storage. Data on these disks can be lost if the VM stops or terminates. To ensure data durability, consider using Persistent Disk or Cloud Storage for non-temporary data. While Local SSDs provide exceptional performance, their use is limited to scenarios where data persistence is not a primary concern.

Key Features

Key features include the following:

High Performance: Local SSDs offer exceptional IOPS and low latency due to their physical attachment to the host VM.

Ephemeral Storage: Data stored on Local SSDs is not persistent and will be lost upon VM termination or instance reboot.

Cost-Effective: Compared to Persistent Disk, Local SSDs are generally more cost-effective for performance-sensitive workloads.

Scalability: You can attach multiple Local SSD partitions to a single VM for increased storage capacity.

Additional Considerations

Some additional considerations are as follows:

Data Durability: Since Local SSDs are ephemeral, data loss is a risk. Implement backup strategies for critical data.

Workload Characteristics: Carefully analyze your workload to determine if Local SSDs are the right fit. Consider factors like IOPS, latency, and data durability requirements.

Cost Optimization: Balance performance needs with cost considerations. Evaluate the trade-offs between Local SSDs and Persistent Disk for your specific use case.

Use Cases

Use cases include the following:

Caching: Storing frequently accessed data for faster retrieval.

Scratch Space: Temporary storage for intermediate data processing results.

Log Storage: Storing application logs for short-term analysis.

In-Memory Databases: Using Local SSDs as a temporary storage medium for in-memory databases.

High-Performance Computing (HPC): Storing intermediate data for HPC workloads.

Media Processing: Storing input and output files for video editing and rendering.

Comparing Block Storage Options in Google Cloud

Block storage options in Google Cloud are compared in Table 1.3.

Object Storage

Object storage is a type of data storage architecture designed to handle massive amounts of unstructured data.

Unlike traditional filesystems, which organize data in a hierarchical structure of folders and files, object storage treats data as individual units called *objects*. Each object consists of the data itself, metadata describing the data (such as size, creation date, and content type), and a unique identifier. Because these unique keys are in the form of URLs, this means that object storage interacts well with web technologies.

This flat structure makes object storage highly scalable and efficient for storing and managing large volumes of data. It is ideal for handling diverse data types like images, videos, audio files, and log data. Google Cloud Storage is a service that delivers object storage services in Google Cloud, providing features like high durability, availability, and accessibility from anywhere in the world.

TABLE 1.3 Comparing block storage options in Google Cloud

Feature	Persistent disk	Hyperdisk	Local SSD
Performance	High performance, suitable for most workloads	Highest performance, scalable, decoupled from VM	Very high performance, but ephemeral
Latency	Low latency	Lower latency	Extremely low latency
Throughput	High throughput	Highest throughput	Very high throughput
IOPS	High IOPS	Highest IOPS	Very high IOPS
Durability	Highly durable, with replication	Highly durable, with replication	Not durable, data lost on instance termination
Cost	Lower cost	Higher cost, but often cost-effective due to performance	Lowest cost for high IOPS and low latency workloads
Use Cases	General purpose workloads, databases, web servers	High-performance databases, big data analytics, machine learning	Temporary storage, burst workloads
Flexibility	Flexible, can be attached/detached from VMs	Highly flexible, with storage pools and dynamic scaling	Limited flexibility, tied to instance life cycle
Ephemeral	No	No	Yes
Managed vs. Unmanaged	Managed	Managed	Unmanaged

In the last section, you learned about block storage. Let's now take a look at how object storage differs from block storage. Table 1.4 compares some key differences between object and block storage.

Google Cloud Storage

Google Cloud Storage (GCS) is a highly scalable object storage service provided by Google Cloud. It allows you to store and retrieve any amount of data from anywhere in the world. Google Cloud Storage is used as an underlying storage solution for a number of services across Google Cloud. Cloud Storage's primary use is whenever binary large-object storage

TABLE 1.4 High-level comparison of object storage vs. block storage

Feature	Object storage	Block storage
Data organization	Objects with metadata	Blocks of data
Access	Through API	Through block device interface
Performance	Lower latency, higher throughput	Lower latency, higher IOPS
Cost	Typically lower	Typically higher
Scalability	Highly scalable	Less scalable
Use cases	Unstructured data, backups, archives	Structured data, databases, VMs

(also known as a "BLOB") is needed for online content such as videos and photos, for backup and archived data, and for storage of intermediate results in processing workflows.

Google Cloud Storage organizes data into buckets located in specific geographic regions for optimal performance. Google Cloud Storage does not have actual folders. Instead, it uses a hierarchical naming convention for objects within a bucket. This means you can use slashes (/) in object names to create a folder-like structure, but these are simply part of the object's name and not actual directories.

While there are no physical folders, many tools and interfaces, including the Google Cloud Console, simulate a folder structure for easier organization and navigation. Essentially, it's a virtual filesystem built on top of a flat object storage system.

Data objects in Google Cloud Storage are immutable, meaning new versions are created upon changes. Bucket versioning can be enabled to track object history, providing data recovery options. When you upload a file to GCS, it becomes an object. If you want to change the object, you create a new object with the updated content. With versioning enabled, GCS keeps track of all object versions, allowing you to revert to previous states if needed.

While objects themselves are immutable, metadata associated with an object (like object name, storage class, ACLs) can be modified without creating a new object. This immutability characteristic makes GCS a reliable choice for storing data that requires high integrity and durability, such as backups, archives, and large datasets.

Key Features

Key features include the following:

Scalability: Handle massive amounts of data effortlessly.

Durability: Data is replicated across multiple locations for high availability and durability.

Performance: Offers fast data access and transfer speeds.

Cost-Effective: Provides various storage classes to optimize costs based on data access patterns.

Security: Robust security features to protect your data.

Configuration Options

When setting up a Google Cloud Storage bucket, you can define several key parameters to manage cost, access, and data retention.

Storage Classes

A storage class sets costs for storage, retrieval, and operations, with minimal differences in uptime. When you create a GCS bucket, you'll choose if you want objects to be managed automatically or specify a default storage class based on how long you plan to store your data and your workload or use case.

The following Google Cloud storage classes are available depending on your workload:

- Standard
  - Highest performance and availability
  - Ideal for frequently accessed data
  - Best suited for active datasets
- Nearline
  - Optimized for infrequent access
  - Lower cost than Standard
  - Suitable for data accessed a few times per month
  - Incur a small retrieval fee
- Coldline
  - Designed for data accessed a few times per year
  - Lower cost than Nearline
  - Significant retrieval fee applies
  - Suitable for long-term data archiving
- Archive
  - Lowest-cost storage option
  - For data that is accessed very infrequently
  - Highest retrieval fee
  - Ideal for long-term data retention with minimal access needs

Table 1.5 summarizes the differences between the various Google Cloud Storage classes.

TABLE 1.5 Comparison of Google Cloud storage options

Storage class	Name for APIs and CLIs	Minimum storage duration	Retrieval fees	Typical monthly availability	Cost (approximate)
Standard	STANDARD	None	None	99.99%	Highest
Nearline	NEARLINE	30 days	Yes	99.95%	Medium
Coldline	COLDLINE	90 days	Yes	99.95%	Low
Archive	ARCHIVE	365 days	Yes	99.95%	Lowest

Autoclass

When Autoclass is selected, Google Cloud Storage will automatically transition each object to Standard or Nearline class based on object-level activity, to optimize for cost and latency. Autoclass is recommended if usage frequency may be unpredictable and can be changed to a default class at any time.

Location Types

Each storage class is available in one of the following location configurations:

- Region:
  - Lowest latency within a single region
  - Use when data primarily accessed from within a single region
  - Suitable for applications with lower availability requirements
  - Lowest-cost storage option
- Dual-region:
  - High availability and low latency across two regions
  - Data redundancy across two regions
  - Use when compliance requirements mandate data residency in specific regions
  - Ideal for applications requiring high availability and disaster recovery
  - Suitable for applications with moderate latency requirements
  - Typically the most expensive option
- Multiregion:
  - Highest availability across largest area
  - Use when you have global applications with users distributed across multiple regions
  - Ideal for applications that access data with stringent availability requirements
  - Suitable for applications that can tolerate slightly higher latency

- Higher storage price than regions, but lower than dual-regions
- Outbound data transfer charges always apply when reading data

Table 1.6 summarizes the difference between the various Google Cloud Storage location options.

Additional Storage Location Considerations

Additional factors to take into account are as follows:

Colocate Data and Compute for Optimal Performance and Cost-Efficiency: Store data in the same region as your applications.

Choose Storage Location Based on Data Access Patterns and Life Cycle: Frequent access data should be in the same region as compute resources, whereas long-term archival data can be stored in lower-cost storage classes.

Consider Data Durability, Availability, and Regulatory Requirements: Multiregion storage provides higher durability but may incur additional costs. Ensure compliance with data residency laws.

Implement Life-Cycle Management and Cost Optimization Strategies: Regularly review storage classes and retention policies to reduce costs.

Factor in Disaster Recovery and Business Continuity: Use multiregion storage for redundancy and develop data backup and recovery plans.

TABLE 1.6 Comparison of Google Cloud storage location options

Feature	Region	Dual-region	Multiregion
Availability	Cross-zone redundancy	Cross-region redundancy	Cross-region redundancy
Performance	Best performance within a single region (up to 200 Gbps per region)	Good performance across two regions (up to 200 Gbps per region)	Moderate performance across multiple regions (up to 50 Gbps per region)
Latency	Lowest latency within a single region	Lower latency across two regions	Higher latency across multiple regions
Costs	Lower cost than dual-region and multiregion	Higher storage cost than region. Adds redundancy cost	Higher storage cost than region; cost-effective for high availability needs
Typical Use Cases	Analytics, backup and archive	Analytics, backup and archive, disaster recovery	Content serving

Use Cases

Google Cloud Storage acts as a flexible and scalable data repository that seamlessly integrates with other Google Cloud services, enabling efficient data pipelines, machine learning workflows, analytics, and application development. Here are just some of the use cases that can leverage Google Cloud Storage and when to select each storage class:

- Standard Storage
  - **High-Performance Applications:** Serving web and mobile applications with frequent data access patterns.
  - **Real-Time Analytics:** Storing and processing data for immediate insights and decision-making.
  - **Content Delivery Networks (CDNs):** Distributing static content globally for fast delivery.
  - **Data Lakes:** Storing large volumes of raw data for exploratory analysis and machine learning.
  - **Machine Learning:** Store training data and models.
  - **Big Data Processing:** Stage data for processing with tools like Dataflow.
- Nearline Storage
  - **Long-Term Data Archiving:** Storing data for infrequent access, such as backup data or compliance requirements.
  - **Data Warehousing:** Storing large datasets for offline analytics and reporting.
  - **Disaster Recovery:** Storing backups of critical data for recovery in case of system failures.
  - **Media Archives:** Storing video, audio, and image files for long-term preservation.
  - **Internet of Things (IoT) Data:** Storing large volumes of sensor data for analysis and insights.
- Coldline Storage
  - **Deep Archives:** Storing data for very infrequent access, such as historical data or legal records.
  - **Disaster Recovery Cold Storage:** Storing long-term backups for disaster recovery purposes.
  - **Compliance and Regulatory Data:** Storing data for long-term retention to meet compliance requirements.
  - **Media Libraries:** Storing large media archives for occasional access.
  - **Research Data:** Storing large datasets for long-term preservation and analysis.

- Archive Storage

  - **Regulatory Compliance:** Storing data for long-term retention to meet regulatory requirements.

  - **Disaster Recovery Cold Storage:** Storing very long-term backups for disaster recovery.

  - **Historical Data:** Storing historical data for research or analysis purposes.

  - **Digital Preservation:** Storing digital assets for long-term preservation.

File Storage

File storage uses a hierarchical structure to organize data. This means data is arranged in a tree-like fashion with folders (or directories) acting as branches and files as leaves. File storage stores data in files, organized in hierarchical directories. Access is via file paths. File storage is similar to how your operating system stores and organizes your files. The following is a visual representation of a file storage hierarchy (Figure 1.2):

File storage is ideal for sharing data among multiple users and applications, especially when protocols such as NFS and SMB are preferred. While not as fast as block storage, file storage offers better organization and compatibility.

The following are some considerations for when to choose file storage:

Shared Access Is Required: Multiple users or applications need to access and modify the same data simultaneously.

Hierarchical Organization Is Essential: Data is naturally structured in folders and subfolders, making it easier to manage and find specific files.

Random Access Patterns Are Common: Frequent reads and writes to different parts of the filesystem are necessary.

FIGURE 1.2   Visual representation of a file storage hierarchy.

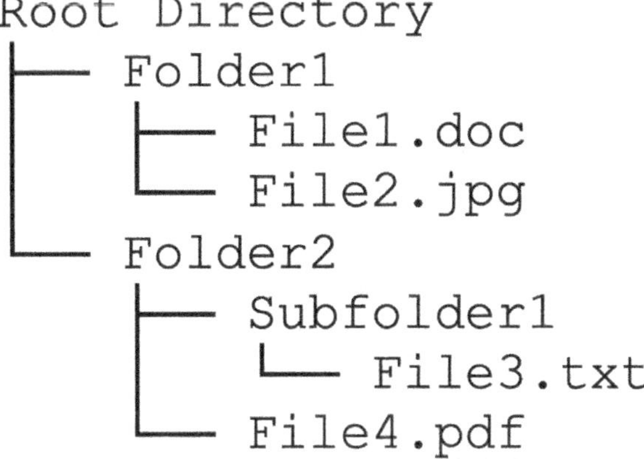

Compatibility Is a Priority: Existing applications and workflows rely on standard filesystem protocols (like NFS or SMB).

Performance Needs Are Moderate: While not as fast as block storage, file storage provides sufficient performance for many applications.

The two main services in Google Cloud that provide file storage services are Google Cloud Filestore and Google Cloud NetApp Volumes.

Google Cloud Filestore

Google Cloud Filestore is a fully managed network file storage service offered by Google Cloud Platform. It provides a scalable, high-performance, and reliable platform for storing and accessing data. Filestore is designed to simplify the management of file-based workloads by handling infrastructure and maintenance, allowing users to focus on their applications. It offers compatibility with standard NFS clients, making it easy to integrate with existing systems. With its ability to scale resources up or down based on demand, Filestore is suitable for a wide range of use cases, including media rendering, data analytics, and content management systems.

Google Cloud Filestore organizes data in a hierarchical structure, similar to traditional filesystems. This means data is stored in files and folders, allowing for easy navigation and management. It's designed to mimic the familiar filesystem structure used on local computers, making it intuitive for users and applications. This hierarchical organization enables efficient data access, sharing, and management within the cloud environment.

Key Features

Key features include the following:

Performance Tiers: Filestore offers different performance tiers to match varying workload requirements, ensuring optimal performance for different applications.

Scalability: You can easily scale Filestore instances up or down to accommodate changes in data volume or performance needs.

High Availability: Filestore is designed for high availability, providing redundancy and fault tolerance to minimize downtime.

Data Protection: Filestore incorporates data protection features such as encryption and snapshots to safeguard your data.

Deeply Integrated with the NFS Protocol: Filestore offers robust support for both NFSv3 and NFSv4.1 versions. This ensures broad compatibility with a wide range of operating systems and applications that rely on the NFS protocol for file sharing.

Integration with Other Google Cloud Services: Filestore seamlessly integrates with other Google Cloud services, such as Compute Engine, Kubernetes, and Cloud Storage, to create comprehensive cloud solutions.

Configuration Options

Google Cloud Filestore offers several service tiers to cater to different performance, capacity, and availability needs. The Basic tiers are cost-effective for development and testing, while the Zonal and Regional tiers provide higher performance and availability for production workloads.

Basic HDD:

- Cost-effective
- Lower performance
- Suitable for file sharing, software development, and use with GKE workloads
- Have a performance increase when the provisioned capacity exceeds 10 TiB

Basic SSD:

- Improved performance over HDD
- Suitable for workloads requiring moderate performance
- Higher cost than Basic HDD
- Performance of basic SSD instances is fixed regardless of the provisioned capacity

Zonal:

- Higher performance than Basic tiers
- Single zone availability
- Ideal for workloads requiring consistent performance within a zone
- Suitable for high-performance computing application requirements such as genome sequencing, and financial-services trading analysis
- When compared with basic SSD instances, zonal may provide a better option for users that require higher availability and lower capacity.
- When compared with regional instances, zonal may provide a more cost-effective option.

Regional:

- Highest availability among the listed tiers
- Replicated across multiple zones providing resiliency to zonal outages
- Suitable for mission-critical applications requiring high uptime
- Optimized for enterprise-grade network attached storage (NAS)

- Suitable for high availability for mission-critical, high-performance computing workloads running within a large namespace
- Supports linear performance that scales with capacity, within the parameters of the specified capacity range

Legacy service tiers

- Filestore's legacy service tiers include the following:
  - Standard
  - Premium
  - High scale SSD
  - Enterprise

  When creating new instances, users are strongly encouraged to use these replacements.
- Basic HDD replaces the standard service tier.
- Basic SSD replaces the premium service tier.
- Zonal replaces the high-scale SSD service tier.
- Regional replaces the enterprise service tier.

Use Cases

Here are some use cases:

- Basic HDD
  - **Development and Testing Environments:** Cost-effective storage for early-stage projects.
  - **File Sharing for Small Teams:** Basic collaboration needs within a limited user base.
  - **Web Hosting:** For static content serving with lower-performance requirements.
- Basic SSD
  - **Development and Testing Environments:** Faster performance for iterative development.
  - **Small-Scale Data Analytics:** Handling moderate data processing workloads.
  - **Media Streaming:** For lower-quality or less demanding video streaming applications.
- Zonal
  - **High-Performance Computing (HPC):** For applications requiring high throughput and low latency.
  - **Media Rendering and Transcoding:** Handling large media files and processing intensive tasks.
  - **In-Memory Databases:** As a high-performance storage backend for in-memory databases.

- Regional
  - **Mission-Critical Applications:** For workloads demanding high availability and low downtime.
  - **Database Backups:** Storing critical database backups for disaster recovery.
  - **Content Management Systems:** Managing large volumes of digital assets with high availability requirements.

Table 1.7 summarizes the four main Filestore configurations options and compares the key features of each.

Google Cloud NetApp Volumes

Google Cloud NetApp Volumes is a fully managed, high-performance file storage service offered by Google Cloud Platform in partnership with NetApp. It provides a scalable, reliable, and enterprise-grade platform for storing and accessing data. Designed to simplify the management of file-based workloads, NetApp Volumes handles infrastructure and maintenance, allowing

TABLE 1.7 Comparison of Google Cloud Filestore options

Feature	Basic HDD	Basic SSD	Zonal	Regional
Performance Tier	Entry	Standard	High	High
Maximum Throughput	Low	Medium	High	Highest
Workload Suitability	Low-to-medium IOPS, sequential workloads	Medium IOPS, mixed workloads	High IOPS, mixed workloads	Highest IOPS, mixed workloads
Price	Lowest	Low	Medium	Highest
Typical Use Cases	Development/test environments, low-performance file shares	General purpose file sharing, medium performance applications	Production environments requiring high availability and performance	High-performance, mission-critical applications requiring low latency and high throughput
Recommended for	Cost-conscious users with low performance requirements	Users needing balanced performance and cost	Users requiring high availability and performance	Users demanding the highest performance and availability

users to focus on their applications. It offers broad protocol support, including NFS and SMB, ensuring compatibility with a wide range of systems and applications. By providing features like instant capacity adjustments, performance tiers, and advanced data protection capabilities, NetApp Volumes is tailored to meet the demands of complex and performance-intensive enterprise workloads. It offers a hierarchical data organization similar to traditional filesystems, making it intuitive for users and applications to manage and access data efficiently.

Key Features

Key features include the following:

Fully Managed Service: Eliminates the need for infrastructure management and maintenance, allowing users to focus on applications.

Rapid Provisioning: Enables quick creation and deployment of storage volumes to accelerate application development and deployment.

Performance Tiers: Delivers consistent performance for demanding workloads, with options for different performance tiers to match specific needs.

Scalability: Offers flexible capacity provisioning and the ability to adjust resources on-demand to accommodate changing workloads.

Multiprotocol Support: Supports both NFS and SMB protocols and Active Directory (AD) integration, ensuring compatibility with a wide range of systems and applications.

Advanced Data Protection: Provides features like snapshots, backups, and replication to protect data from loss and ensure business continuity.

Hierarchical Data Organization: Offers familiar filesystem structure for easy data management and access.

Integration with Google Cloud: Seamlessly integrates with other Google Cloud services for comprehensive cloud solutions.

Configuration Options

Google Cloud NetApp Volumes offers multiple service tiers to cater to different performance needs:

- Flex
  - Highly available, general-purpose storage with up to 16 KiBps per GiB of pool capacity (shared across all volumes in the pool), up to a maximum of 1 GiBps per pool.
  - Ideal for common enterprise workloads like NFS/SMB file shares, SAP shared files, containerized workloads, and Google Cloud VMware Engine.
- Standard
  - Highly available, general-purpose storage with up to 16 KiBps per GiB of volume capacity. Maximum of 1 GiBps per volume.

- Suitable for common enterprise workloads like NFS/SMB file shares, SAP shared files, and Google Cloud VMware Engine.
- Premium
  - Highly available, high-performance storage with up to 64 KiBps per GiB dedicated to the volume. Maximum of 4.5 GiBps per volume.
  - Best for performance-critical workloads requiring low latency, like Windows/enterprise NFS, self-managed databases, file shares, VDI, and VMware Engine.
- Extreme
  - Highly available, high-throughput storage with up to 128 KiBps per GiB dedicated to the volume. Maximum of 4.5 GiBps per volume.
  - Optimized for performance-critical workloads needing high throughput and low latency, such as Windows/enterprise NFS, self-managed databases, file shares, VDI, and VMware Engine.

Additional Considerations

Additional factors to consider includes these:

Auto-Tiering: Available for Premium and Extreme tiers, allowing for cost optimization by moving infrequently accessed data to a lower-cost storage tier.

Large Volumes: Premium and Extreme tiers support larger volumes (up to 1 PiB) for specific use cases.

Performance Considerations: Workload characteristics (read/write ratio, block size, I/O concurrency) significantly impact performance.

Use Cases

Here are some use cases:

- Flex
  - **General-Purpose File Shares:** Suitable for shared filesystems used by multiple users or applications with moderate performance requirements.
  - **Development and Test Environments:** Provides a cost-effective option for nonproduction workloads.
  - **Backup and Archive Storage:** Can be used for storing less frequently accessed data.
  - **Home Directories:** Suitable for storing user home directories with moderate file sizes.
  - **Media Streaming:** Can be used for storing and serving media content with moderate performance needs.

- Standard
  - **Virtual Desktops:** Provides sufficient performance for basic user workloads in VDI environments.
  - **DevOps Environments:** Supports build and test environments with moderate performance demands.
  - **SAP Shared Files:** Handles SAP workloads with standard performance requirements.
  - **Database Backups:** Suitable for storing database backups with regular access patterns.
  - **Content Management Systems:** Can be used for storing and managing digital assets.
- Premium
  - **High-Performance Computing (HPC):** Offers the performance required for data-intensive workloads.
  - **Online Transaction Processing (OLTP) Databases:** Supports databases with high transaction rates and low latency requirements.
  - **Virtual Desktop Infrastructure (VDI):** Provides a better user experience for demanding VDI workloads.
  - **Media and Entertainment Workloads:** Handles high-resolution video and audio editing and rendering.
  - **Enterprise File Shares:** Supports demanding file sharing environments with large file sizes and high concurrency.
- Extreme
  - **Real-Time Analytics:** Provides the performance needed for processing large datasets with low latency.
  - **In-Memory Databases:** Supports high-performance in-memory databases with demanding workloads.
  - **Financial Trading Applications:** Handles high-frequency trading with ultra-low latency requirements.
  - **3D Rendering and Animation:** Supports complex 3D workloads with large datasets.
  - **High-Performance Data Analysis:** Ideal for data scientists and analysts requiring maximum performance.

TABLE 1.8   Comparison of Google Cloud NetApp Volumes options

Feature	Flex	Standard	Premium	Extreme
Performance Tier	Entry level	General purpose	High performance	Ultra-high performance
Maximum Throughput	16 MiBps per TiB pool capacity	16 MiBps per TiB volume capacity	64 MiBps per TiB volume capacity	128 MiBps per TiB volume capacity
Workload Suitability	Development, testing, small file shares	File shares, VMs, databases	File shares, VMs, databases, high-performance computing	OLTP databases, low-latency applications
Price	Most economical	Balanced	Higher performance, higher cost	Highest performance, highest cost
Typical Use Cases	Noncritical workloads, cost-sensitive environments	General-purpose workloads, medium-sized file shares	Performance-sensitive workloads, large file shares	Mission-critical workloads, demanding applications
Recommended for	Smaller datasets, lower IOPS requirements	Medium-sized datasets, moderate IOPS requirements	Large datasets, high IOPS requirements	Very large datasets, extremely high IOPS requirements

Table 1.8 summarizes the four main NetApp Volumes confirmation options and compares the key features of each.

Storage Options Decision Tree

The decision tree in Figure 1.3 guides you through the Google Cloud storage recommendations.

FIGURE 1.3 Google storage options decision tree.

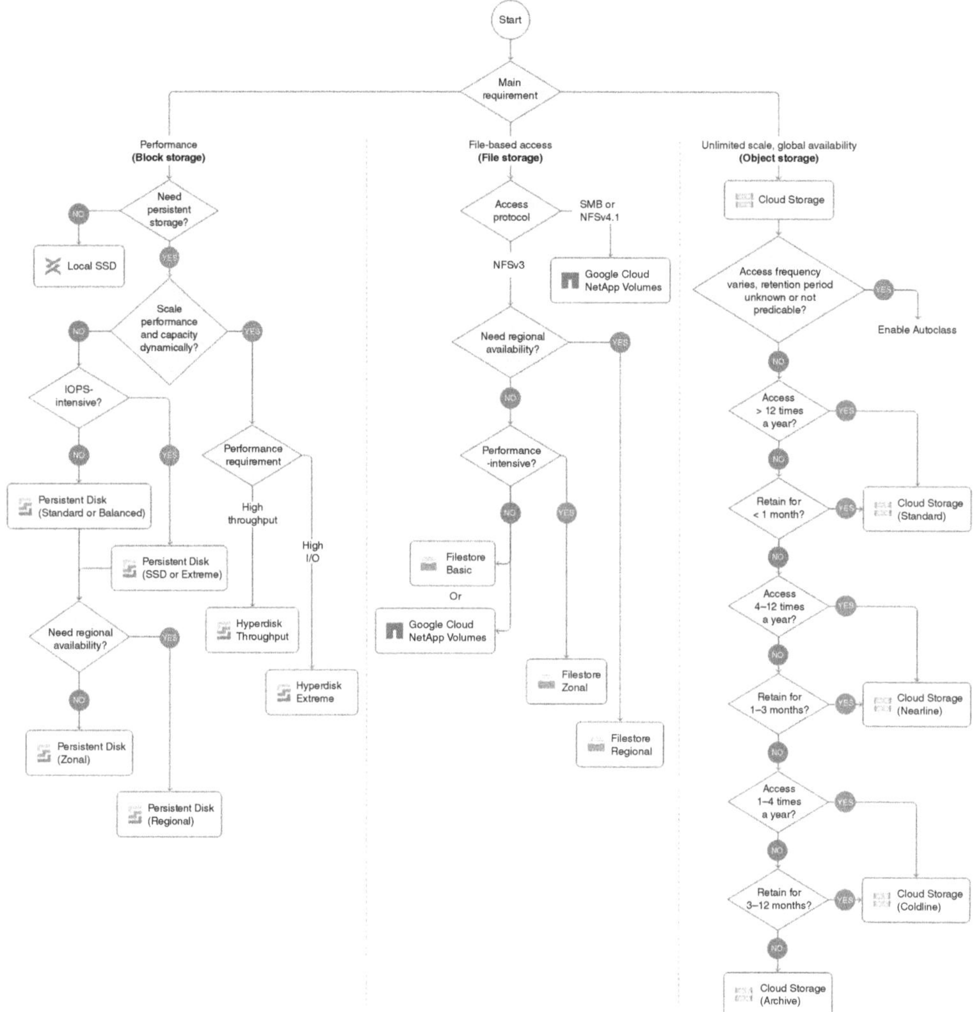

Summary

This chapter explored the fundamental concepts of data storage technologies within Google Cloud. It delved into the key differences between block, object, and file storage, highlighting their respective strengths and weaknesses. The chapter then examined the various storage options available within Google Cloud, including Persistent Disk, Hyperdisk, Local SSD, and Google Cloud Storage, providing a detailed analysis of their features, configuration options, and use cases.

Exam Essentials

Understand the evolving landscape of data.   Recognize the trends driving the growth of unstructured data and its impact on storage needs. Explain the challenges of managing exploding data volumes and the advantages of cloud storage solutions.

Master Google Cloud storage options.   Differentiate between block, object, and file storage formats in terms of their core characteristics, use cases, and access methods.

Describe the key features, configuration options, and use cases of Google Cloud's block storage options: Persistent Disk, Hyperdisk, and Local SSD.

Understand the different types of Persistent Disk (standard, performance, balanced, extreme) and their appropriate use cases.

Explain the advantages of Hyperdisk compared to Persistent Disk and identify the key benefits of each Hyperdisk type (balanced, high availability, extreme, ML, throughput).

Understand the strengths and limitations of Local SSDs and identify scenarios where they are most suitable.

Explore Google Cloud Storage (GCS).   Understand the fundamentals of object storage and its advantages compared to block storage.

Describe the key features, configuration options, and use cases of Google Cloud Storage (GCS).

Analyze the different storage classes (Standard, Nearline, Coldline, Archive) and their appropriate use cases.

Explain the concept of data immutability in GCS and its implications for data integrity.

Differentiate between the different GCS location types (region, dual-region, multi-region) and their impact on availability, latency, and cost.

Apply a systematic approach to storage solution selection.   Analyze workload characteristics such as data volume, growth rate, access patterns, durability requirements, retention policies, and compliance needs to inform your decision.

Consider factors like performance, scalability, cost optimization, data protection, and security to make informed storage design choices.

Review Questions

1. You are working on a project that involves storing large volumes of unstructured data, such as images, videos, and audio files. Which Google Cloud storage solution would be most appropriate for this scenario?

   A. Persistent Disk

   B. Google Cloud Storage

   C. Cloud Filestore

   D. Hyperdisk

2. You are tasked with designing a storage solution for a high-frequency trading platform. What is the most important consideration for this scenario?

   A. Cost optimization

   B. Data durability

   C. Performance and scalability

   D. Security and compliance

3. Which Google Cloud storage solution is directly attached to a virtual machine and is ideal for I/O-intensive workloads?

   A. Persistent Disk

   B. Hyperdisk

   C. Local SSD

   D. Google Cloud Storage

4. You are working on a project that requires high performance and low latency for data access. Which Google Cloud storage solution would you recommend?

   A. Standard Persistent Disk

   B. Balanced Persistent Disk

   C. Extreme Persistent Disk

   D. Hyperdisk

5. You are designing a storage solution for a large-scale data warehousing application. Which Google Cloud storage class would you recommend for older sales data that is accessed infrequently?

   A. Standard

   B. Nearline

   C. Coldline

   D. Archive

6. A social media company needs to store a massive amount of user-generated content, including images, videos, and text posts. The data is expected to grow rapidly. Which storage type is most suitable for this scenario?

   A. Block storage

   B. File storage

   C. Object storage

   D. In-memory storage

7. A database architect needs a storage solution for a virtual machine running a high-performance database that requires low latency and high throughput. The data stored on this volume must persist even if the virtual machine is terminated. Which storage option is most appropriate?

   A. Object storage

   B. Persistent Disk

   C. Local SSD

   D. Cloud storage

8. Which Google Cloud storage option offers the best performance but does not guarantee data durability?

   A. Persistent Disk

   B. Hyperdisk

   C. Local SSD

   D. Object storage

9. What is a key difference between Google Cloud Filestore and Google Cloud NetApp Volumes?

   A. Filestore is a Google-managed service, while NetApp Volumes is a partner-managed service.

   B. Filestore supports NFS, while NetApp Volumes supports SMB.

   C. Filestore is suitable for small-scale workloads, while NetApp Volumes is suitable for enterprise-grade workloads.

   D. Filestore offers lower performance, while NetApp Volumes offers higher performance.

10. A genomics research company needs to store and analyze massive datasets containing DNA sequences. The data is expected to grow rapidly over time. Which storage type is most suitable for this scenario?

   A. Block storage

   B. Object storage

   C. File storage

   D. In-memory database

11. Which Google Cloud storage solution is a fully managed network file storage service that is compatible with standard NFS clients?

A. Cloud storage

B. Cloud Filestore

C. Hyperdisk

D. NetApp Volumes

12. A company is migrating an on-premises application to Google Cloud. The application requires a filesystem that can be accessed concurrently by multiple virtual machines. Which storage service best meets this requirement?

A. Cloud Filestore

B. Cloud storage

C. Persistent Disk

D. Local SSD

13. Your company is migrating an on-premises Oracle database to Google Cloud. The database requires high IOPS and throughput for optimal performance. Which Google Cloud storage option is most suitable for this scenario?

A. Cloud storage

B. Persistent Disk (pd-standard)

C. Persistent Disk (pd-extreme)

D. Local SSD

14. A startup is building a video editing application on Google Cloud and requires high-performance storage to handle large video files and processing tasks. The application also needs low latency access to temporary files during the editing process. Which storage options would you recommend for this use case?

A. Persistent Disk (pd-standard) for video files and Local SSD for temporary files

B. Hyperdisk Extreme for video files and Persistent Disk (pd-balanced) for temporary files

C. Cloud Filestore for video files and Local SSD for temporary files

D. Cloud Storage Nearline for video files and Persistent Disk (pd-ssd) for temporary files

15. You are designing a disaster recovery strategy for a mission-critical application running on Google Cloud. You need to ensure that data is replicated across multiple geographic regions to protect against regional outages. Which Google Cloud Storage location type should you choose?

A. Region

B. Dual-region

C. Multiregion

D. None of the above

16. Your team is developing a new application that requires a shared filesystem accessible from multiple compute engine instances. You need a storage solution that offers high performance and low latency, and that supports the NFS protocol. Which Google Cloud storage option would you recommend?

    A. Cloud storage

    B. Cloud Filestore

    C. Persistent Disk

    D. Local SSD

17. You are working on a machine learning project that involves training a model on a massive dataset stored in Google Cloud Storage. The training process requires high throughput to read the data efficiently. Which storage class should you choose to optimize performance and minimize costs?

    A. Standard

    B. Nearline

    C. Coldline

    D. Archive

18. You need to store a large volume of data that is infrequently accessed but requires high durability and low cost. This data will be used for disaster recovery purposes and long-term archival. Which Google Cloud storage class best fits these requirements?

    A. Standard

    B. Nearline

    C. Coldline

    D. Archive

19. Your organization is subject to data residency regulations that require certain data to be stored within specific geographic regions. You need to choose a Google Cloud Storage location type that allows you to control data placement and ensure compliance. Which option should you select?

    A. Region

    B. Dual-region

    C. Multiregion

    D. Global

20. You have a requirement to store frequently accessed data for a web application. This data needs to be highly available and deliver low latency to users across the globe. Which Google Cloud Storage location type is most suitable for this scenario?

    A. Region

    B. Dual-region

    C. Multiregion

    D. None of the Above

Chapter

2

Database Storage Models and Data Types

GOOGLE CLOUD CERTIFIED PROFESSIONAL CLOUD DATABASE ENGINEER EXAM OBJECTIVES COVERED IN THIS CHAPTER:

✔ **1.4 Evaluate appropriate database solutions on Google Cloud.**

- Differentiate between managed and unmanaged database services.

- Distinguish between SQL and NoSQL business requirements (structured, semi-structured, unstructured, vector).

- Assess application and database dependencies.

- Leverage database technologies to support generative AI and LLM use cases.

In this chapter, we will explore the different storage technologies available on Google Cloud, detailing the advantages and limitations of each. You will learn how to identify and classify data as structured, unstructured, semi-structured, or vector, and the importance of matching the right data storage technology to the type of data. We will delve into the characteristics, use cases, and advantages and limitations of each data type. Furthermore, you will gain an understanding of the various database types offered on Google Cloud, including in-memory, relational, NoSQL, and vector databases, and learn how to choose the best option for your specific needs. This chapter will provide you with the essential knowledge of database storage technologies and data types necessary to successfully design and deploy robust and efficient database solutions on Google Cloud.

Database Storage Technologies

The storage layer is the engine that dictates how data is physically stored, managed, and retrieved. This architectural choice is critical—it directly impacts your application's performance, scalability, and resilience. Since different applications have vastly different needs, we use a variety of storage technologies, each purpose-built for specific workloads, data models, and access patterns.

Types of Data

Accurately identifying the type of data that you will be working with is crucial for selecting the appropriate storage technology. Mismatching storage and data type can lead to inefficiencies, performance issues, and increased costs. For the purpose of this book, we'll define the four most commonly recognized data categories:

Structured data

Unstructured data

Semi-structured data

Vector data

Structured Data

Structured data is information that adheres to a predefined data model. It's organized into a structured format, making it easily searchable, accessible, and understandable by both humans and computers. Think of it as data that resides in a well-defined container, with clear labels and compartments.

Key Characteristics

The key characteristics are as follows:

Defined Schema: A rigid structure dictates the data types and relationships.

Rows and Columns: Data is typically organized in tables with rows (records) and columns (fields).

Predictable Format: Consistent structure allows for efficient processing.

Quantitative Nature: Often numerical or categorical data, suitable for statistical analysis.

Examples of Structured Data

Examples of structured data include these:

Relational Databases: SQL-based databases like Google Cloud SQL, Cloud Spanner, and BigQuery.

Spreadsheets: Excel, Google Sheets.

CSV Files: Comma-separated values.

XML and JSON: While semi-structured, they can be transformed into structured formats.

Advantages of Structured Data

Advantages of structured data are as follows:

Efficient Querying: SQL and other structured query languages enable rapid data retrieval.

Data Integrity: Enforced schema ensures data consistency and accuracy.

Scalability: Structured databases can handle large datasets efficiently.

Performance: Optimized for fast read and write operations.

Data Analysis: Well suited for statistical analysis and reporting.

Challenges with Structured Data

Here are some challenges with structured data:

Schema Rigidity: Modifying the structure can be complex and time-consuming.

Data Redundancy: Potential for duplicate data across tables.

Data Normalization: Balancing performance and data integrity can be challenging.

Limited Flexibility: Not ideal for unstructured or semi-structured data.

Common Use Cases

Use cases include the following:

Customer Relationship Management (CRM): Storing customer information, sales data, and interactions.

Financial Systems: Managing transactions, accounts, and financial reports.

Inventory Management: Tracking product information, stock levels, and orders.

Human Resources: Storing employee data, payroll, and performance metrics.

Data Warehousing: Consolidating data for analysis and reporting.

Structured Data in Google Cloud

Google Cloud offers a variety of tools and services for handling structured data:

Cloud SQL: Fully managed relational database service.

Cloud Spanner: Globally distributed, strongly consistent relational database.

BigQuery: Serverless, highly scalable data warehouse.

Dataflow: For large-scale data processing pipelines.

Unstructured Data

Unlike structured data, which conforms to a predefined schema, unstructured data lacks a rigid format. This makes it challenging to store, manage, and analyze but also incredibly rich in potential insights.

Unstructured data is information that doesn't fit neatly into rows and columns. It's often text-heavy, but it can also include images, videos, audio, and other formats.

Key Characteristics

The key characteristics are as follows:

No Predefined Schema: Data is free-form and variable.

High Volume and Variety: Comes in diverse formats and sizes.

Complex Processing: Requires specialized tools and techniques.

Rich in Insights: Can reveal patterns and trends not apparent in structured data.

Examples of Unstructured Data

Examples of unstructured data include these:

Text Documents: Word documents, PDFs, emails.

Social Media: Posts, comments, likes, shares.

Images and Videos: Photos, videos, GIFs.

Audio: Voice recordings, music files.

Log Files: System and application logs; however, some logs may be semi-structured.

Advantages of Unstructured Data

Benefits of unstructured data include the following:

Richness: Contains valuable insights and context.

Real-Time Analysis: Can be processed for immediate insights.

Competitive Advantage: Unlocking hidden patterns can lead to innovation.

Challenges of Unstructured Data

Some challenges of unstructured data are as follows:

Storage: Requires large storage capacities due to volume.

Processing: Demands powerful computing resources.

Analysis: Complex to extract meaningful information.

Integration: Difficult to combine with structured data for comprehensive analysis.

Common Use Cases

Common use cases include these:

Customer Sentiment Analysis: Understanding customer opinions from social media.

Fraud Detection: Identifying patterns in unstructured data to detect anomalies.

Risk Assessment: Analyzing documents for potential risks.

Market Research: Gaining insights from customer reviews and surveys.

Image and Video Analysis: Object recognition, facial recognition, video content analysis.

Unstructured Data in Google Cloud

Google Cloud offers a range of services to handle unstructured data:

Cloud Storage: For storing and managing unstructured data.

Cloud Firestore: Store textual data like descriptions, comments, or articles

Cloud Dataflow: For processing large volumes of unstructured data.

Natural Language API: For understanding and extracting information from text.

Vision API: For analyzing images and videos.

Speech-to-Text API: For converting audio to text.

Semi-Structured Data

Semi-structured data occupies a middle ground between structured and unstructured data. It possesses some organizational properties, making it more manageable than unstructured data, but lacks the rigid schema of structured data.

Semi-structured data has a hierarchical structure, often with tags or markers to separate semantic elements. While it doesn't conform to a strict relational database model, it's more organized than unstructured data.

Key Characteristics

The key characteristics are as follows:

Hierarchical Structure: Data is organized in a tree-like or nested format.

Self-Describing: Contains metadata to define its structure.

Flexible Schema: Can accommodate changes in data structure.

Human and Machine-Readable: Both humans and computers can interpret the data.

Examples of Semi-Structured Data

Examples include:

XML: Extensible Markup Language.

JSON: JavaScript Object Notation.

CSV and TSV: Comma-separated values and tab-separated values files are fundamentally structured due to their inherent organization. However, depending on the specific data within them and the level of adherence to a consistent format, they can exhibit some characteristics of semi-structured data.

NoSQL Databases: Many NoSQL databases store data in semi-structured formats.

Advantages of Semi-Structured Data

Benefits of semi-structured data are as follows:

Flexibility: Adaptable to changing data structures.

Scalability: Can handle large volumes of data.

Queryability: Can be queried using specialized languages or tools.

Efficiency: Often more efficient to process than unstructured data.

Challenges of Semi-Structured Data

Challenges of semi-structured data are as follows:

Complexity: More complex to manage than structured data.

Schema Evolution: Changes in data structure can impact processing.

Data Integrity: Ensuring data consistency can be challenging.

Common Use Cases

Common use cases of semi-structured data include the following:

Web Applications: Storing user data, configurations, and preferences.

Data Exchange: Transferring data between systems in a standardized format.

Log Analysis: Parsing and analyzing log files.

NoSQL Databases: Storing large amounts of data with flexible schemas.

Semi-Structured Data in Google Cloud

Google Cloud offers several services to handle semi-structured data:

Cloud Storage: Storing and managing semi-structured data in various formats.

Cloud Firestore: Firestore's native format is similar to JSON, making it ideal for semi-structured data.

BigQuery: Handling semi-structured data, including JSON and nested data.

Cloud Dataflow: Processing large volumes of semi-structured data.

Cloud Pub/Sub: For real-time data ingestion and distribution.

Vector Data

Vector data, also known as vector embeddings, represents a fundamental shift in how we handle complex data for machine learning and AI-driven applications. Instead of storing raw data, vector data consists of high-dimensional numerical arrays (vectors) that capture the semantic meaning or features of an object, such as text, images, or audio. These vectors are generated by machine learning models and enable powerful similarity searches.

Key Characteristics

The key characteristics are as follows:

High-Dimensional: Vectors often have hundreds or thousands of dimensions, representing complex features.

Numerical Representation: All data, regardless of its original format (text, image), is converted into a numerical vector.

Semantic Similarity: The distance between two vectors in the vector space indicates their semantic similarity. For example, vectors for "cat" and "kitten" would be closer than vectors for "cat" and "car."

Examples of Vector Data

Examples include these:

Text Embeddings: Vectors representing the meaning of words, sentences, or entire documents.

Image Embeddings: Vectors capturing the visual features of images for object recognition or similarity matching.

Audio Embeddings: Vectors representing characteristics of sound for tasks like music recommendation or voice identification.

Advantages of Vector Data

Benefits of vector data are as follows:

Semantic Search: Enables searching based on meaning and context rather than just keywords.

Recommendation Engines: Powers sophisticated recommendation systems by finding items similar to what a user has liked.

Flexibility: Can represent virtually any type of data once an appropriate embedding model is used.

Challenges with Vector Data

Challenges of vector data are as follows:

High-Dimensionality: Searching in high-dimensional spaces is computationally expensive and requires specialized algorithms (e.g., approximate nearest neighbor [ANN]).

Embedding Model Dependency: The quality of the vectors is entirely dependent on the machine learning model used to create them.

Storage and Indexing: Requires specialized databases or indexes designed for efficient high-dimensional vector search.

Common Use Cases

Common use cases include these:

Semantic Search: Finding documents or images based on conceptual similarity.

Recommendation Systems: Suggesting products, movies, or music based on user preferences and item similarity.

Image Recognition and Search: Identifying similar images or objects within images.

Anomaly Detection: Identifying outliers in data by finding data points that are distant from all others in the vector space.

Vector Data in Google Cloud

Google Cloud provides powerful, integrated services for managing and searching vector data:

Vertex AI Vector Search: A fully managed, high-scale, and low-latency vector database service built for efficient similarity searches. It is the premier solution for dedicated vector workloads.

AlloyDB AI: This PostgreSQL-compatible database offers integrated vector support, allowing you to perform both transactional operations and vector similarity searches on your data within the same system.

BigQuery: Supports vector search functions, enabling you to perform similarity searches at scale on vector embeddings stored alongside your analytical data.

Cloud SQL for PostgreSQL: Can be used with the pgvector open source extension to store and query vector embeddings directly within a managed PostgreSQL database.

Memorystore for Redis: Google Cloud's fully managed service for the Redis in-memory database. When paired with modules that support vector search (like RediSearch), it enables real-time, extremely low-latency similarity searches, making it a powerful choice for caching layers and interactive applications.

Table 2.1 lists the types of data.

Types of Databases

Google Cloud offers a number managed, unmanaged, Google-native, and partner database options for all kinds of workloads. The database engineer should be familiar with the following types of databases available on Google Cloud.

TABLE 2.1 Types of data

Data type	Key characteristics	Common use cases	Google Cloud Services
Structured	Predefined schema, organized in rows and columns, predictable format	CRM systems, financial transactions, inventory management	Cloud SQL, Spanner, BigQuery, AlloyDB
Unstructured	No predefined schema, high volume and variety, often text-heavy or binary	Social media posts, images, videos, audio files, log files	Cloud Storage, Vision AI, Natural Language AI
Semi-structured	Flexible schema, self-describing, often hierarchical (e.g., nested)	Web application data (JSON), data exchange (XML), log analysis	Firestore, BigQuery, Cloud Pub/Sub
Vector	High-dimensional numerical arrays, represents semantic meaning, searched by similarity	Semantic search, recommendation engines, image recognition, generative AI	Vertex AI Vector Search, AlloyDB AI, BigQuery

In-Memory Databases

In-memory databases excel at handling extremely low-latency workloads by storing data entirely in RAM. Memorystore provides a managed environment for Redis and Memcached, offering high performance and scalability for caching, session management, and real-time applications.

Relational Databases

Relational databases structure data in tables with rows and columns, enforcing data integrity and consistency. Cloud SQL offers managed MySQL, PostgreSQL, and SQL Server instances for traditional applications. Spanner is a globally distributed relational database ensuring strong consistency and high availability for mission-critical workloads. AlloyDB is a PostgreSQL-compatible database optimized for demanding enterprise workloads, balancing transactional (OLTP) and analytical (OLAP) capabilities. BigQuery, while primarily an analytical database, supports some transactional operations through its DML capabilities.

Google Cloud also provides managed and unmanaged partner relational database offerings such as Oracle Database OCI (Oracle Cloud Infrastructure) or Bare Metal. Customers can also choose to run their own databases on Google Compute Engine (GCE).

NoSQL Databases

NoSQL databases offer flexible data models to handle unstructured and semi-structured data. BigTable is a key-value and wide-column store designed for massive datasets and low-latency lookups, ideal for analytical workloads. Firestore is a document database that provides real-time synchronization and offline capabilities, suitable for mobile and web applications. Google Cloud also offers managed partner NoSQL database offerings such as MongoDB Atlas.

Vector Databases

Vector databases are purpose-built to store, manage, and query high-dimensional vector embeddings. These embeddings are numerical representations of unstructured data—like text, images, and audio—generated by machine learning models. Instead of filtering on exact matches, these databases find data points that are semantically or contextually "similar" by calculating the distance between their vectors in a multidimensional space. This capability is foundational for building sophisticated AI features.

On Google Cloud, Vertex AI Vector Search (formerly Matching Engine) is the premier managed service for this workload. It provides a high-performance, scalable platform for finding the most similar items (nearest neighbors) from billions of vectors with extremely low latency. Additionally, vector search capabilities are being integrated into other services, such as AlloyDB for PostgreSQL and Cloud SQL for PostgreSQL (via the pgvector extension), allowing users to combine similarity searches with traditional relational queries.

In-Memory

In-memory databases represent a critical component of modern cloud architectures, offering unprecedented speed and performance by storing data entirely within a server's RAM. Google Cloud provides a robust in-memory database service called Memorystore, designed to simplify the deployment and management of these high-performance datastores.

Memorystore supports two primary open source in-memory data structures: Redis and Memcached. Redis, a versatile data structure store, offers a rich set of features beyond basic key-value storage. It supports data types such as strings, hashes, lists, sets, sorted sets, and bitmaps, enabling complex data modeling and operations. Redis also provides built-in data replication, persistence, and clustering capabilities, making it a suitable choice for applications requiring high availability, durability, and scalability.

Memcached, on the other hand, is a simpler key-value store optimized for performance and efficiency. It excels at caching frequently accessed data, reducing load on backend systems and improving application response times. Memcached is often used in conjunction with other datastores to offload read-heavy workloads and enhance overall system performance. Although Memcached lacks the advanced data structures and features of Redis, its simplicity and speed make it an excellent choice for specific use cases.

Google Cloud Memorystore provides a fully managed environment for both Redis and Memcached, abstracting away the complexities of infrastructure management and allowing developers to focus on application logic. It offers automatic scaling, high availability, and robust security features, ensuring optimal performance and reliability. By leveraging Memorystore, organizations can accelerate their application development and deliver exceptional user experiences.

Use Cases

In-memory datastores like Memorystore are ideal for applications that demand extremely low latency and high throughput. Here are some common use cases:

- Caching
  - **Web Applications:** Accelerate page load times by caching frequently accessed data like product catalogs, user profiles, or search results.
  - **API Responses:** Improve API performance by caching computed results or frequently requested data.
- Session Management
  - **User Sessions:** Store session data in-memory for fast access and reduced latency, enhancing user experience.
  - **Shopping Carts:** Maintain shopping cart contents efficiently for online stores.
- Real-Time Analytics
  - **Fraud Detection:** Process financial transactions in real time to identify suspicious activity.
  - **Recommendation Engines:** Provide personalized recommendations based on user behavior and preferences.
  - **Gaming Leaderboards:** Update and retrieve player scores with minimal latency.
- Pub/Sub and Messaging
  - **Real-Time Communication:** Handle high-volume messaging and event streams for applications like chat, social media, and IoT.
- Gaming
  - **Game State Management:** Store game objects and player data in-memory for rapid access and updates.
  - **Leaderboards:** Maintain real-time leaderboards for competitive gaming.

Key Considerations

Consider these factors when choosing an in-memory datastore:

Data Volatility: In-memory datastores typically don't offer the same durability as traditional databases, so consider data persistence requirements.

Cost: In-memory storage is generally more expensive than disk-based storage, so evaluate cost–benefit trade-offs.

Data Size: In-memory datastores are best suited for relatively small datasets that can fit entirely in memory.

Relational Databases

Relational databases structure data into tables with rows and columns, enforcing data integrity and relationships. These databases are foundational for many applications and are widely deployed. Online transaction processing (OLTP) systems excel at handling frequent, short-lived transactions like online purchases or bank transfers. They prioritize speed and concurrency. On the other hand, online analytical processing (OLAP) systems focus on complex queries over large datasets for tasks like business intelligence and data warehousing. They prioritize read performance and data aggregation.

Transactional: OLTP Databases

OLTP databases are optimized for handling frequent, short-lived transactions that require high speed and concurrency. Google Cloud offers a variety of OLTP database options to cater to different application needs.

Cloud SQL is a fully managed relational database service that provides support for popular SQL databases like MySQL, PostgreSQL, and SQL Server. It offers a familiar environment for developers and enterprises already invested in these database technologies. Cloud SQL handles database provisioning, patching, backups, and failover, allowing users to focus on application development. While primarily designed for regional deployments, Cloud SQL also supports multiregion configurations for increased availability.

Spanner, a globally distributed relational database, stands out for its strong consistency guarantees and horizontal scalability. It ensures that data is always consistent across multiple regions, making it ideal for mission-critical applications that require low latency and high availability. Spanner's unique architecture enables it to handle massive scale and complex transaction workloads while maintaining strong consistency, a feature not commonly found in other relational databases.

AlloyDB is a PostgreSQL-compatible relational database service designed for demanding enterprise workloads. It combines the flexibility and power of PostgreSQL with the scalability and performance optimizations required for large-scale applications. AlloyDB offers a high level of compatibility with existing PostgreSQL applications while providing enhanced performance and cost-effectiveness. It is well suited for OLTP workloads that require high transaction rates and low latency, such as online retail, financial services, and gaming while balancing the ability to simultaneously handle demanding OLAP workloads.

Oracle Database on Google Cloud represents a strategic partnership between Google Cloud and Oracle. This collaboration offers customers the flexibility to run Oracle databases on Google Cloud infrastructure. Oracle Database@Google Cloud is a fully integrated experience that brings together Oracle Cloud Infrastructure (OCI) and Google Cloud to help you simplify deployment and management, supercharging your journey to the cloud. OCI and Google Cross-Cloud Interconnect allows customers to deploy workloads across both OCI and Google Cloud regions with no cross-cloud data transfer charges and Oracle on

Google Compute Engine (GCE) enables customers to easily migrate and run Oracle database and applications on high-performance, reliable Google Cloud infrastructure.

Use Cases

Relational OLTP databases are the workhorses of many applications, excelling at handling a high volume of short, concurrent transactions. Here are some key scenarios where they shine:

- **E-commerce:** Managing online stores requires processing numerous transactions for product purchases, order fulfillment, and customer accounts. OLTP databases ensure fast and reliable handling of these critical operations.

- **Financial Services:** Banking applications, trading platforms, and payment gateways rely on OLTP databases for high-speed, accurate transaction processing. Data integrity and ACID properties (Atomicity, Consistency, Isolation, Durability) are crucial to maintain financial records and prevent errors.

- **Inventory Management:** Tracking stock levels, updating inventory in real time, and processing orders all benefit from the efficient transaction handling capabilities of OLTP databases.

- **CRM Systems:** Customer relationship management (CRM) applications often involve frequent updates to customer data, order history, and communication logs. OLTP databases ensure accurate and consistent data for managing customer interactions.

- **Social Media Platforms:** Handling user activity, posts, comments, and real-time updates requires a database that can manage a high volume of concurrent transactions. OLTP databases can efficiently handle this load and ensure data consistency.

Key Considerations

Consider these factors when choosing a relational OLTP database:

- **Transaction Volume and Complexity:** How many transactions does your application need to handle per second? Do these transactions involve complex joins or updates?

- **Scalability:** Will your application require horizontal scaling to handle increasing workload?

- **Data Consistency:** How critical is it to maintain strong data consistency across all transactions?

- **Cost:** Different OLTP database options on Google Cloud offer varying pricing structures. Evaluate your cost requirements and choose the best fit.

Analytical: OLAP Databases

OLAP databases are designed for complex queries over large datasets, enabling organizations to extract valuable insights and make data-driven decisions. Google Cloud offers powerful OLAP solutions to meet diverse analytical needs.

BigQuery is a fully managed, serverless data warehouse that excels at handling petabyte-scale datasets and complex SQL queries. Its columnar storage format, coupled with advanced query optimization, delivers lightning-fast query performance. BigQuery's ability to handle both batch and streaming data makes it suitable for a wide range of analytical workloads, from business intelligence and data warehousing to machine learning and data science.

AlloyDB, while primarily an OLTP database, also offers robust analytical capabilities. Its hybrid transactional and analytical processing (HTAP) architecture allows users to run both complex OLTP workloads and ad hoc analytical queries on the same dataset. This unified approach simplifies data management and reduces latency for analytical operations. While not as specialized as BigQuery for large-scale analytics, AlloyDB provides a convenient option for organizations that require both transactional and analytical capabilities within a single database.

Use Cases

Relational OLAP databases excel at handling complex queries over large datasets, providing valuable insights for businesses. Here are some key use cases:

Business Intelligence and Reporting: OLAP databases power interactive dashboards and reports that help organizations understand their performance, identify trends, and make data-driven decisions.

Data Warehousing: By consolidating data from various sources into a single repository, OLAP databases enable comprehensive analysis and reporting across the entire organization.

Customer Analytics: Analyzing customer behavior, preferences, and purchasing patterns helps businesses tailor marketing campaigns, improve customer satisfaction, and increase sales.

Financial Analysis: OLAP databases support complex financial modeling, forecasting, and risk assessment.

Market Analysis: Understanding market trends, competitor activities, and customer segmentation is crucial for business strategy. OLAP databases provide the tools to analyze market data effectively.

Key Considerations

Consider these factors when choosing a relational OLAP database:

Data Volume and Complexity: OLAP databases handle large datasets and complex queries, so evaluate the scale of your data and the complexity of your analysis.

Query Performance: OLAP databases are optimized for query performance, but the specific requirements of your workloads will influence your choice.

Scalability: Consider how your data and query needs will grow over time and select a database that can scale accordingly.

Integration: Ensure the OLAP database can integrate seamlessly with your existing data sources and reporting tools.

NoSQL Databases

NoSQL databases excel at handling unstructured and semi-structured data, offering flexibility and scalability.

Key-value stores, like BigTable, are optimized for simple data structures with rapid access, making them ideal for large-scale analytics and time-series data. On the other hand, document databases, such as Firestore, store data in flexible JSON-like documents, accommodating complex data models and enabling rapid application development. Partner offerings, such as MongoDB Atlas on Google Cloud, also incorporate key-value and document datastores.

Key-Value Databases

Key-value stores are adept at efficiently storing and retrieving large datasets using simple key-value pairs. BigTable, while built upon a key-value mechanism internally, is a wide-column NoSQL database optimized for handling massive datasets and achieving low-latency lookups. This makes it ideal for applications demanding rapid access to substantial data volumes, such as internet-scale analytics, recommendation systems, and time-series data processing. BigTable excels in scalability and performance, making it a powerful solution for these demanding workloads.

Use Cases

NoSQL key-value and wide-column databases, like BigTable, are ideal for applications that prioritize scalability, performance, and handling massive datasets with simple or semi-structured data. Here are some key use cases:

Large-Scale Analytics: BigTable excels at storing and analyzing massive datasets efficiently. This makes it a perfect fit for applications like log analysis, clickstream processing, and user behavior analytics.

Real-Time Applications: The low latency and high throughput of BigTable enables building real-time applications that require fast data access and updates. This can be crucial for applications like social media feeds, fraud detection systems, and IoT data processing.

Time-Series Data: BigTable's flexible schema is well suited for storing and analyzing time-series data, such as sensor readings, financial transactions, and network activity logs. This allows for efficient historical analysis and real-time monitoring.

Ad hoc Queries: While not primarily designed for complex queries, BigTable allows querying data based on row keys and column families when integrated with tools like BigQuery and Dataflow. This enables ad hoc analysis on large datasets without sacrificing performance.

Key Considerations

Here are some factors to consider when choosing a NoSQL key-value/wide-column database:

Data Size and Growth: If you anticipate massive datasets that will grow significantly over time, BigTable's horizontal scalability can be a major advantage.

Data Model Simplicity: Key-value stores like BigTable work best with simple data models or where data structure flexibility is less critical.

Query Complexity: BigTable excels at basic lookups and scans, but complex joins or aggregations might be better suited for other database types.

Document Databases

Document databases store data in flexible, JSON-like documents, making them well suited for applications with complex and evolving data structures. Firestore, a fully managed document database, provides real-time synchronization, offline capabilities, and automatic scaling. It is well suited for mobile and web applications that require flexible data modeling and rapid development. Firestore's strong consistency and low latency make it a popular choice for building modern, responsive applications. While Firestore's real-time sync scales well for moderate workloads, it may face challenges in applications with extremely high write throughput or globally distributed user bases. For such scenarios, integrating with services like Pub/Sub or BigQuery streaming may be necessary to handle the increased scale and complexity.

Use Cases

NoSQL document databases, like Firestore, offer a compelling choice for applications that require flexibility, scalability, and real-time data synchronization. Here are some key use cases where Firestore shines:

Mobile and Web App Development: Firestore's flexible document model and offline capabilities make it ideal for building dynamic mobile and web applications. It allows developers to store and manage complex data structures efficiently while enabling offline functionality for a smooth user experience.

Real-Time Applications: Firestore's real-time synchronization capabilities ensure immediate updates across all connected devices, fostering a seamless experience for users. This is crucial for applications like collaborative editing, chat, and live dashboards.

Rapid Development: Firestore's ease of use and flexible data model allow developers to iterate quickly and focus on building functionality rather than complex data management solutions. This is a major benefit for agile development cycles.

Scalability: Firestore automatically scales to accommodate growing data volumes, eliminating the need for manual database sharding or infrastructure management. This simplifies development and ensures your application can handle increasing user bases.

Offline Functionality: Firestore allows storing data locally on devices, enabling users to interact with the application even without an internet connection. This enhances user experience and is essential for applications in unreliable network environments.

Key Considerations

Here are some factors to consider when choosing a NoSQL document database:

Data Model Complexity: Firestore excels at handling complex and evolving data structures, making it suitable for applications with diverse data requirements.

Real-Time Needs: If your application requires real-time data updates and synchronization across devices, Firestore's capabilities can significantly enhance user experience.

Scalability Requirements: For applications that anticipate significant data growth, Firestore's automatic scaling ensures smooth operation without performance bottlenecks.

Offline Functionality: If your application needs to function offline, Firestore's local data storage capabilities can be a major advantage.

Vector

Vector databases are a new category of database designed specifically to store, manage, and search high-dimensional vector embeddings. They use specialized indexing algorithms, such as Approximate Nearest Neighbor (ANN), to perform similarity searches incredibly fast, even on billions of vectors. While traditional databases search for exact matches on structured data, vector databases search for items that are "most similar" in meaning or features.

Google Cloud offers a leading, managed solution for these workloads, Vertex AI Vector Search. It provides a high-performance, scalable service for finding the most similar vectors to a given query vector. Additionally, vector search capabilities are being integrated into existing Google Cloud databases to support multi-modal applications. For instance, AlloyDB AI integrates vector processing directly into the PostgreSQL-compatible database, and BigQuery now includes vector search functions.

Use Cases

Vector databases are the engine behind many modern AI applications:

AI-Powered Search: Building search engines that understand the intent and context of a query, not just the keywords.

Generative AI: Used in retrieval-augmented generation (RAG) to find relevant information to provide as context to a large language model (LLM), improving the accuracy and relevance of its responses.

Product Recommendations: Finding and recommending products that are visually or semantically similar to those a user has viewed.

Security and Fraud Detection: Identifying unusual patterns or behaviors by comparing new events against a database of known activities.

Key Considerations

Here are some key factors to take into consideration:

Performance vs. Accuracy: Vector searches often use ANN algorithms, which trade perfect accuracy for immense speed. This trade-off is configurable and is a key design consideration.

Scalability: As the number of vectors grows into the billions, the performance and scalability of the vector database are critical.

Integration: Consider how the vector database will integrate with your existing datastores and application architecture. Solutions like AlloyDB AI simplify this by combining transactional and vector data in one place.

Table 2.2 lists the types of databases.

TABLE 2.2   Types of databases

Database type	Primary use case	Key characteristics	Google Cloud examples
In-Memory	Caching, session management, real-time leaderboards, low-latency workloads	Stores data in RAM, extremely fast read/write operations	Memorystore (for Redis and Memcached)
Relational (SQL)	Transactional systems (OLTP), data warehousing (OLAP), applications requiring strong consistency (ACID)	Data in tables with rows/columns, enforces schema and data integrity	Cloud SQL, Spanner, AlloyDB, BigQuery
NoSQL	Handling large-scale, unstructured or semi-structured data, applications requiring high flexibility and scalability	Flexible data models (document, key-value, wide-column), horizontal scalability	Firestore, Bigtable, MongoDB Atlas
Vector	AI/ML applications, semantic search, recommendation systems, anomaly detection	Stores and indexes high-dimensional vectors, uses Approximate Nearest Neighbor (ANN) search	Vertex AI Vector Search, AlloyDB AI

Summary

This chapter introduced various database storage technologies on Google Cloud, emphasizing the importance of matching the right technology to data types, differentiating between managed and unmanaged database services, and comparing SQL and NoSQL solutions. It began by categorizing data into structured, unstructured, semi-structured, and vector types, detailing their characteristics, use cases, and Google Cloud services for handling each type. Structured data, like that in relational databases such as Cloud SQL, Spanner, and AlloyDB, has a defined schema and is suited for efficient querying and analysis, whereas unstructured data, like text, images, and audio, requires specialized tools such as Cloud Storage and Vision API. Semi-structured data, such as JSON and XML, provides a middle ground with a hierarchical structure and is well suited for web apps and can utilize services like Cloud Firestore and BigQuery. Vector data, consisting of high-dimensional numerical embeddings, is crucial for AI/ML applications like semantic search and is managed using services like Vertex AI Vector Search and AlloyDB AI.

The chapter further explained different types of databases, including in-memory, relational, NoSQL, and vector options. In-memory databases like Memorystore (Redis and Memcached) excel in low-latency scenarios, while relational databases, like Cloud SQL, Spanner, and AlloyDB, are categorized into transactional (OLTP) and analytical (OLAP) uses, handling various workloads and consistency requirements. Additionally, the chapter explored NoSQL databases like BigTable and Firestore, which offer flexibility and scalability for unstructured and semi-structured data, with BigTable as a key-value store and Firestore as a document database. We also covered the emergence of vector databases, like Vertex AI Vector Search, designed for efficient similarity search on vector embeddings.

Finally, we delved into the specific use cases and considerations for each database type, equipping readers with the knowledge to design and deploy efficient database solutions on Google Cloud.

Exam Essentials

Understand data types.   Identify and classify data as structured, unstructured, semi-structured, or vector.

Describe the key characteristics of each data type.

Understand the advantages and disadvantages of each data type.

Identify common use cases for each data type.

Differentiate between database types.   Differentiate between managed and unmanaged database services (self-managed, bare metal, Google-managed databases, and partner database offerings).

Understand the use cases and characteristics of the following database types:

In-memory databases (Memorystore)

Relational databases (Cloud SQL, Spanner, AlloyDB

NoSQL databases (BigTable, Firestore)

Vector databases (Vertex AI Vector Search)

Evaluate database solutions for different use cases. Identify the appropriate database solution based on data type, workload requirements, and business needs.

Consider factors such as scalability, performance, cost, and data consistency when selecting a database solution.

Understand the trade-offs between different database types and their suitability for specific use cases.

Assess application and database dependencies. Understand how application requirements and dependencies influence database selection.

Evaluate the impact of database choice on application performance and scalability.

Review Questions

1. Which of the following is *not* a characteristic of structured data?

   A. Defined schema

   B. Rows and columns

   C. Variable format

   D. Quantitative nature

2. What is the main advantage of using an in-memory database?

   A. High cost-efficiency

   B. High durability

   C. High performance and low latency

   D. High data security

3. Which type of database is optimized for handling complex queries over large datasets?

   A. In-memory database

   B. NoSQL database

   C. Relational OLAP database

   D. Relational OLTP database

4. Which type of NoSQL database stores data in flexible, JSON-like documents?

   A. Key-value store

   B. Document database

   C. Graph database

   D. Columnar database

5. Which type of database is most suitable for storing and analyzing large volumes of sensor data with a time-series component, such as temperature readings from IoT devices?

   A. Relational database

   B. In-memory database

   C. Key-value store

   D. Document database

6. A mobile gaming company needs a database solution to store player profiles, game progress, and real-time leaderboards. The database must be able to handle frequent updates and provide low latency access. What type of database would be most suitable?

   A. Relational database

   B. In-memory database

   C. Key-value store

   D. Document database

7. What is a key difference between structured and unstructured data?

  A. Structured data has a predefined schema, whereas unstructured data does not.

  B. Structured data is stored in tables, whereas unstructured data is stored in files.

  C. Structured data is quantitative, whereas unstructured data is qualitative.

  D. Structured data is easy to analyze, whereas unstructured data is difficult to analyze.

8. You need to design a storage solution for a financial application that requires frequent read and write operations with the highest level of data integrity and consistency. The application must be able to handle a large volume of transactions while ensuring that all data changes are ACID compliant. Which database type best meets these requirements?

  A. NoSQL database

  B. Key-value store

  C. Relational database (OLTP)

  D. Document database

9. A company wants to build a new search feature for its e-commerce site that allows customers to find products based on conceptual descriptions (e.g., "summer-style dresses") rather than exact keywords. Which data type is specifically designed to capture this kind of semantic meaning for advanced similarity searches?

  A. Structured data

  B. Semi-structured data

  C. Unstructured data

  D. Vector data

10. A company needs to store sensitive customer data, including names, addresses, and financial information. Which data type best describes this information, and what is a crucial consideration for its storage?

  A. Structured data; data security and compliance

  B. Unstructured data; scalability

  C. Semi-structured data; flexibility

  D. In-memory data; performance

11. Which type of database is designed for handling frequent, short-lived transactions and prioritizes speed and concurrency? (Choose three.)

  A. Key-value store

  B. In-memory database

  C. Document database

  D. Relational database

12. You are designing a data storage solution for a mobile gaming application. The application requires low-latency data access for storing user profiles, game state, and leaderboards. Which storage type would best meet these requirements? (Choose two.)

A. In-memory database

B. Relational database

C. Object storage

D. Document database

E. Key-value store

F. File storage

13. What distinguishes a managed database service like Cloud SQL from an unmanaged database service on Google Cloud?

A. Managed services handle tasks such as provisioning, backups, and patching, whereas unmanaged services require user configuration and administration.

B. Managed services offer higher performance and scalability than unmanaged services.

C. Managed services are only suitable for NoSQL databases, whereas unmanaged services are best for relational databases.

D. Managed services are more cost-effective for all types of workloads compared to unmanaged services.

14. Your application needs to store and query large amounts of data with a flexible schema, including user profiles, product catalogs, and social interactions. Which database type is the *most* suitable for this use case?

A. In-memory database

B. Document database

C. Key-value database

D. Relational database

15. You are designing a system to handle real-time analytics for a mobile gaming application. This system needs to process a high volume of events, such as player actions and game state updates, with very low latency. Which database type would be the *most* appropriate for this scenario?

A. Relational database

B. Key-value database

C. In-memory database

D. Document database

16. Vector databases often use Approximate Nearest Neighbor (ANN) algorithms for searching. What is the primary trade-off associated with using ANN?

    A. It increases storage costs in exchange for lower latency.

    B. It sacrifices some query accuracy for a massive increase in search speed.

    C. It requires a rigid schema, reducing data model flexibility.

    D. It provides stronger data consistency (ACID) at the expense of performance.

17. Your team is developing a generative AI application that uses a retrieval-augmented generation (RAG) model. To ensure the model provides the most accurate and relevant responses, you need a dedicated, high-performance database to perform low-latency similarity searches over billions of text embeddings. Which Google Cloud service is the premier, fully managed solution for this dedicated vector search workload?

    A. AlloyDB AI

    B. Vertex AI Vector Search

    C. BigQuery with vector search functions

    D. Cloud SQL for PostgreSQL with the pgvector extension

18. Which type of database stores data in a table format with rows and columns and is typically used for transactional workloads?

    A. In-memory database

    B. NoSQL database

    C. Relational database

    D. Key-value store

19. Which of the following is an advantage of using an unmanaged database service on Google Cloud?

    A. Simplified management

    B. Automatic backups and updates

    C. Greater control over configuration and customization

    D. Reduced operational overhead

20. Which of the following best describes semi-structured data?

    A. Data that conforms to a rigid schema with predefined data types and relationships

    B. Data that has a self-describing structure, often hierarchical or graph-like, but lacks a fixed schema

    C. Data that lacks a predefined schema and is typically text-heavy, such as emails, social media posts, or sensor data

    D. Data that is stored entirely in a server's RAM for ultra-fast access

Chapter

3

Databases in Google Cloud

✔ **1.4 Evaluate appropriate database solutions on Google Cloud. Activities include:**

- Differentiate between managed and unmanaged database services (e.g., self-managed, bare metal, Google-managed, Google Cloud native and partner database offerings).

- Identify solutions to support regulatory and compliance requirements.

- Understand implications of organizational policies on database strategy.

- Consider solutions that span multiple database technologies (e.g., federation, exports, hybrid deployments).

- Leverage database technologies to support generative AI and LLM use cases.

This chapter provides a comprehensive overview of the specific database solutions available on Google Cloud, including how they support modern use cases like generative AI and meet compliance needs. It covers the distinctions between managed and unmanaged database services, including self-managed, bare metal, Google-managed databases, and partner database offerings.

We will delve into how to select databases that meet stringent regulatory and compliance requirements and how internal organizational policies can shape your database strategy. We will also consider solutions that bridge multiple database technologies, such as data federation and hybrid deployments. Finally, this chapter will explore how to leverage Google Cloud's database technologies to power innovative generative AI and large language model (LLM) applications.

By the end of this chapter, you will be able to confidently assess the strengths and limitations of each database service and make informed decisions regarding the most appropriate database solution for your project, fully aligned with the latest Google Cloud certification standards.

Google Cloud Database Offerings

Before diving into the database offerings on Google Cloud, it's important to clarify the distinction between the different managed and unmanaged database options. Depending on your application and database requirements, one or more of the options may be better for you:

Managed Database Services   Google Cloud handles the underlying infrastructure, provisioning, patching, backups, and high availability. You focus on data modeling and application development. Within this category, we'll also explore Google-managed and partner-managed database offerings.

Unmanaged Database Services   You have much more control over the database environment, including hardware, software, and configuration. This requires significant expertise in database administration. Within this category we'll explore self-managed databases deployed on Google Compute Engine (GCE), Google Kubernetes Engine (GKE), and Google's Bare Metal Solution (BMS).

Table 3.1 compares the key features of managed and unmanaged database options.

TABLE 3.1   Comparison of managed vs. unmanaged database options

Feature	Managed database	Unmanaged database
Infrastructure Management	Google Cloud handles.	You manage.
Database Engine Management	Google Cloud handles.	You manage.
Patching and Updates	Google Cloud handles.	You manage.
Backups and Recovery	Google Cloud handles.	You manage.
High Availability and Disaster Recovery	Features like automatic failover or replication are generally built into managed databases.	You configure and manage.
Security	Shared responsibility (Google Cloud provides foundational security; you manage application-level security).	Full responsibility.
Cost	Cloud costs generally higher due to managed services but lower operational expenses.	Lower upfront costs but higher operational expenses.
Expertise Required	Minimal database administration skills.	Extensive database administration and infrastructure skills.
Time to Market	Faster deployment.	Longer deployment time.
Scalability	Typically easier to scale.	Requires manual intervention for scaling.
Control	Less control over database configuration.	More control over database configuration.
Examples on Google Cloud	Cloud SQL, Cloud Spanner, Cloud Bigtable.	SQL Server on Compute Engine, PostgreSQL on GKE, Oracle on BMS.

Unmanaged Databases

Unmanaged, also known as self-managed, databases on Google Cloud are database instances that you, as the administrator, have full control over. Unlike managed database services, where Google Cloud handles infrastructure, updates, and maintenance, with unmanaged databases, you are responsible for every aspect of the database environment. While the additional overhead of self-managed database options may seem daunting, organizations with extensive database administration experience can leverage their knowledge to fine-tune performance, implement advanced features, and potentially reduce costs.

Managed services often come with premium pricing, but building and managing your own database infrastructure can actually be more cost-effective, especially for workloads with predictable resource consumption. Additionally, for organizations with existing on-premises databases, migrating to an unmanaged database on Google Cloud can provide a more familiar environment and potentially reduce migration efforts.

Another compelling reason to choose an unmanaged database is control. With full control over the database environment, organizations have the flexibility to customize hardware, software, and configuration to meet specific performance or compliance requirements. This level of control is particularly valuable for applications with stringent performance demands or those handling highly sensitive data where granular security measures are essential.

It's important to note that the decision to use an unmanaged database involves significant operational overhead and requires specialized skills. Therefore, a careful evaluation of the trade-offs between cost, control, and operational complexity is crucial before making a decision.

Key Characteristics

Unmanaged, or self-managed, databases on Google Cloud offer maximum flexibility and control over the database environment; however, this means you are responsible for all aspects of the database, from provisioning infrastructure to managing the database software itself.

Full Control: You have complete authority over the database instance, including hardware, software, configuration, and security.

Infrastructure Management: You provision and manage the underlying compute resources (e.g., Compute Engine instances) and storage (e.g., Persistent Disk).

Database Software Management: You install, configure, patch, and upgrade the database software (e.g., MySQL, PostgreSQL, MongoDB).

Operational Overhead: You handle tasks such as backups, monitoring, security, and performance tuning.

Cost Efficiency: Potentially lower costs compared to managed services, especially for long-term, predictable workloads.

Examples

Common examples of unmanaged databases on Google Cloud include the following:

MySQL on Google Compute Engine (GCE): Deploying a MySQL database instance on a Compute Engine virtual machine

PostgreSQL on Google Kubernetes Engine (GKE): Deploying a PostgreSQL database instance on GKE

Oracle Database on Google Bare Metal Solution (BMS): Deploying an Oracle database instance on Bare Metal

Custom Database Solutions: Building custom database solutions using Compute Engine, GKE, or other Google Cloud services

Advantages

Unmanaged databases offer several advantages, including these:

Cost Optimization: Potential for lower costs compared to managed services, especially for long-term, predictable workloads

Flexibility and Control: Complete control over the database environment, allowing for customization to specific needs

Performance Optimization: Ability to fine-tune database performance through hardware and software configurations

Compatibility: Suitable for legacy applications or those requiring specific database versions or features

Challenges

Managing an unmanaged database comes with significant challenges:

Operational Overhead: Requires significant administrative effort for tasks like patching, backups, and security

Expertise: Demands in-depth database administration skills and knowledge

Risk: Higher risk of errors, downtime, and security breaches due to increased responsibilities

Scalability: More complex to scale compared to managed services, requiring manual intervention

Common Use Cases

Unmanaged databases are often used in the following scenarios:

Cost-Sensitive Workloads: When cost is a primary factor and the organization has the necessary expertise

Legacy Applications: For existing applications that require specific database versions or configurations

High-Performance Computing: When maximum control over hardware and software is needed for performance optimization

Custom Database Solutions: For building specialized database applications with unique requirements

Remember that while unmanaged databases offer flexibility and potential cost savings, they also require significant expertise and operational effort. Carefully evaluate the trade-offs before choosing this option.

Google-Managed Databases

Google Cloud offers a suite of managed database services designed to simplify database management and administration. Unlike unmanaged databases where you handle all aspects of the database environment, Google Cloud assumes responsibility for infrastructure, updates, backups, and maintenance. This allows database engineers to focus on application development and optimization rather than operational tasks.

Managed databases provide several advantages, including increased developer productivity, enhanced performance through Google's infrastructure and optimization expertise, and improved scalability to handle the most demanding workloads. Additionally, they often offer cost-efficiency through pay-as-you-go pricing models and the ability to scale resources based on demand. By abstracting away the underlying infrastructure, managed databases reduce management overhead and allow organizations to benefit from Google's security best practices.

Key Characteristics

Google Cloud offers a variety of managed database services, each with distinct characteristics tailored to specific workloads. These services handle database provisioning, scaling, backups, and maintenance, allowing engineers to focus on application development.

Fully Managed: Google Cloud assumes responsibility for database infrastructure, updates, and maintenance.

Scalability: Many services offer horizontal scaling to handle increasing workloads without downtime.

High Availability: Built-in redundancy and failover mechanisms ensure data durability and accessibility.

Security: Robust security features, including encryption, access controls, and vulnerability management.

Cost-Effective: Pay-as-you-go pricing models with options for optimizing costs based on usage patterns.

Examples

Google Cloud provides a comprehensive suite of managed database services to cater to diverse application requirements:

Relational Databases: Cloud SQL, Cloud Spanner, AlloyDB

NoSQL Databases: Cloud Firestore (Document), Firebase Realtime Database (Document), Cloud Bigtable (Key value)

Warehouse and Analytics: BigQuery

In-Memory: Memorystore

Advantages

Leveraging Google-managed database services offers several benefits:

Increased Developer Productivity: Focus on application logic rather than database administration.

Improved Performance: Benefit from Google's infrastructure and optimization expertise.

Enhanced Scalability: Easily adapt to changing workloads without manual intervention.

Cost Efficiency: Pay only for the resources consumed.

Reduced Management Overhead: Google handles database patching, backups, and monitoring.

Challenges

While Google-managed databases offer many advantages, there are potential challenges to consider:

Vendor Lock-In: Reliance on Google Cloud infrastructure might limit flexibility.

Cost Management: Careful monitoring and optimization are essential to avoid unexpected expenses.

Data Migration: Modernizing existing databases to Google Cloud can be complex and time-consuming.

Common Use Cases

Google-managed databases are suitable for a wide range of applications and workloads:

Cloud SQL: Suitable for web applications, online stores, and small to medium-sized databases.

Cloud Spanner: Ideal for globally distributed applications requiring strong consistency and low latency.

AlloyDB: Fully Postgres-compatible database well suited for transactional and analytical workloads.

Cloud Bigtable: Well suited for large-scale, high-performance analytics and operational workloads.

Cloud Firestore: Excellent choice for mobile and web applications requiring flexible data modeling and real-time tracking of inventory for ecommerce applications.

BigQuery: Optimized for large-scale data analytics and business intelligence.

Memorystore: Improve application performance by storing frequently accessed data in-memory.

While managed database services may initially be more expensive and have limitations in customization compared to unmanaged databases, for many organizations, the advantages of managed databases outweigh these considerations, making them an attractive option for various workloads.

Partner-Managed Databases

Partner-managed databases on Google Cloud offer a specialized database service where a third-party partner assumes primary responsibility for the database engine, management, and support, while leveraging Google Cloud's infrastructure. This collaborative approach combines the deep database expertise of the partner with the scalability and reliability of Google Cloud. Unlike fully managed services provided by Google Cloud, partner-managed databases offer tailored solutions for specific database engines and use cases.

Partner-managed databases provide several advantages, including in-depth database expertise, flexible customization options, and the ability to leverage the partner's existing ecosystem. Additionally, they benefit from Google Cloud's robust infrastructure, global network, and security measures.

Key Characteristics

Partner-managed databases on Google Cloud offer a managed database service where a third-party partner provides the database engine, infrastructure, and management while leveraging Google Cloud's underlying infrastructure. This approach combines the expertise of both Google Cloud and the database partner to deliver a robust and scalable database solution.

Shared Responsibility Model: Google Cloud manages the underlying infrastructure (compute, storage, networking), while the database partner manages the database engine, updates, backups, and support.

Database Engine Focus: These solutions specialize in specific database engines, offering deep expertise and optimization.

Customization: Partners often provide customization options to tailor the database to specific application requirements.

Integration: Deep integration with Google Cloud services for enhanced capabilities and seamless management such as Cloud Functions and Pub/Sub for event-driven processing.

Examples

Examples include the following:

MongoDB Atlas on Google Cloud: A fully managed MongoDB database service that leverages Google Cloud's infrastructure for high performance and scalability.

Oracle Databases@Google Cloud: A managed database service that allows customers to run Oracle workloads on Oracle Cloud Infrastructure (OCI) hosted within Google Cloud data centers, with simplified management.

Advantages

Partner-managed databases offer several advantages:

Deep Database Expertise: Partners have in-depth knowledge of their specific database engine, leading to optimized performance and troubleshooting.

Managed Service: Handles database administration tasks, freeing up your team to focus on application development.

Scalability: Leveraging Google Cloud's infrastructure, these solutions can scale to meet varying workloads.

Compliance: Many partners offer compliance certifications to meet industry regulations.

Cost-Efficiency: Optimized resource utilization and potential cost savings compared to self-managed databases.

Hybrid and Multicloud Flexibility: Some partners support hybrid and multicloud environments.

Challenges

While partner-managed databases offer many benefits, there are also potential challenges:

Vendor Lock-in: Reliance on a specific partner and database engine might limit flexibility.

Cost: Pricing models can be complex, and costs might vary depending on usage and features.

Performance Limitations: Performance can be impacted by factors beyond the partner's control, such as network latency or underlying infrastructure issues.

Common Use Cases

Partner-managed databases are suitable for various use cases:

Applications with Specialized Database Requirements: When demanding performance, scalability, or specific database features are needed. A hedge fund requiring a high-performance, low-latency database for real-time risk analysis and trading decisions may choose MongoDB or Redis Enterprise, which can provide the necessary performance and scalability for their demanding workloads. An online retailer that needs a database that can handle massive spikes in traffic during peak shopping seasons might choose Elastic Search on Google Cloud.

Organizations Lacking Database Expertise: For companies without in-house database administration skills. For example, hospitals and clinics can benefit from SAP HANA Enterprise Cloud on Google Cloud, which offers managed services for HANA database administration and maintenance, freeing up IT staff to focus on patient care.

Hybrid and Multicloud Environments: To extend existing database infrastructure to Google Cloud. Large retailers can extend their on-premises Oracle databases to Google Cloud, enabling seamless integration and leveraging the benefits of both on-premises and cloud environments.

Compliance-Driven Workloads: When industry regulations require specific database and security controls. Government agencies can utilize Microsoft SQL Server on Google Cloud, which offers robust security features, compliance certifications (e.g., SOC 2, ISO 27001), and encryption to meet stringent data security and privacy regulations.

While Google Cloud offers a number popular managed database services, a partner-managed database service can supplement these options where specialized applications require a partner solution.

Google-Managed Databases in Google Cloud

Google Cloud (`https://cloud.google.com/products/databases`) offers a comprehensive suite of managed database services, each tailored to specific use cases and requirements. These services provide high availability, scalability, and performance while simplifying database management and maintenance.

For database engineers, understanding the nuances of each service is crucial for choosing the right fit for different applications and workloads. This section provides an in-depth overview of key characteristics, features, and considerations for each service.

Memorystore

Memorystore (`https://cloud.google.com/memorystore`) is a fully managed in-memory data store service that offers both Redis and Memcached options. It provides high performance and low latency for caching, session management, and real-time data processing.

Key Characteristics

Key characteristics include these:

- **Type:** In-memory datastore
- **Database Engines:** Redis, Memcached
- **Cost Structure:**
    - **Memorystore for Memcached:** Free tier for up to 1 GB of memory, pay-per-use for larger instances
    - **Memorystore for Redis:** Pay-per-use, based on the amount of memory used and the duration of usage
- **Location:** Regional
- **SLA:** 99.99 percent availability for Redis Cluster, 99.9 percent availability for Redis and Memcached

Key Features

Some key features are as follows:

High Performance and Low Latency: Designed for high-throughput read and write operations, ideal for caching and real-time applications.

Scalability: Easily scale instances up or down to accommodate changing workloads.

Data Persistence: Memorystore for Redis offers optional data persistence, allowing data to be saved to disk for recovery.

Security: Built-in security features like TLS encryption, access control, and authentication.

AI/ML Use Cases: Can be used as a low-latency vector database for real-time similarity searches in RAG applications.

Integration with Other Google Cloud Services: Seamless integration with other Google Cloud services like Cloud Functions and Cloud Run.

Open Source Compatibility: Compatible with Redis and Memcached clients and tools.

Deployment Options

Deployment options include the following:

Memorystore for Memcached: Fully managed Memcached service for Google Cloud

Memorystore for Redis: Fully managed Redis service for Google Cloud

Memorystore for Redis Cluster: Fully managed Redis service that distributes (or "shards") your data across primary nodes and replicates your data across optional replica nodes to ensure high availability

See Table 3.2 for a comparison of deployment options.

When to Choose

Considerations when choosing include the following:

Caching: For storing frequently accessed data for faster retrieval.

Session Management: For managing user sessions in web applications.

Real-Time Data Processing: For applications requiring low latency and high throughput.

Data Durability: Memorystore for Memcached does not offer data persistence, so data is lost on instance restart.

Cost: Memorystore for Redis can be expensive for large instances, especially with data persistence enabled.

Memorystore for Redis Cluster: The horizontally scalable cluster architecture provides better performance over vertically scalable architecture because Redis performance is better on many smaller nodes instead of fewer larger nodes.

TABLE 3.2 Comparison of Memorystore deployment options

Feature	Memorystore for Memcached	Memorystore for Redis	Memorystore for Redis Cluster
Data Structure Support	Key-value pairs	Strings, hashes, lists, sets, sorted sets, bitmaps, HyperLogLogs, geospatial indexes, streams, Pub/Sub	Strings, hashes, lists, sets, sorted sets, bitmaps, HyperLogLogs, geospatial indexes, streams, Pub/Sub
qweer	No	Optional (Redis DataBase – RDB, Append Only File – AOF)	Optional (RDB, AOF)
High Availability	Yes (single zone)	Yes (multizone)	Yes (multizone, distributed)
Scalability	Horizontal scaling	Vertical and horizontal scaling	Horizontal scaling
Clustering	Not supported	Not supported	Built-in clustering
Use Cases	Caching, session management	Caching, session management, real-time analytics, pub/sub, queuing, rate limiting	Large-scale applications, high throughput, low latency
Typical Workloads	High read workloads, low write workloads	Mixed read and write workloads, complex data structures	High throughput, low latency, complex data structures

EXERCISE 3.1

Caching Data from a Spring Boot App with Memorystore

```
https://codelabs.developers.google.com/codelabs/
cloud-spring-cache-memorystore
```

In this exercise, you will configure Memorystore for Redis to serve as a high-performance cache for a Spring Boot application. Accessed via the URL provided, this walkthrough offers hands-on practice deploying what you learned earlier in the chapter. You will focus on integrating the fully managed service to boost application speed and scalability, ensuring you understand the practical steps required to leverage caching without the overhead of managing complex infrastructure.

Cloud SQL

Cloud SQL (`https://cloud.google.com/sql`) is a fully managed relational database service that offers PostgreSQL, MySQL, and SQL Server engines. It provides high availability, scalability, and security for traditional relational database workloads.

Key Characteristics

Characteristics include the following:

Type: Relational database

Database Engines: PostgreSQL, MySQL, SQL Server

Location: Regional

SLA: 99.95 percent availability for Enterprise, 99.99 percent for Enterprise Plus

Key Features

Key features are as follows:

High Availability: Automatic failover and replication ensure continuous availability.

Scalability: Easily scale instances up or down to accommodate changing workloads.

Security: Built-in security features like TLS encryption, access control, and authentication.

Data Backup and Recovery: Automated backups and point-in-time recovery options.

Integration with Other Google Cloud Services: Seamless integration with other Google Cloud services like Cloud Functions and Cloud Run and federated querying directly from BigQuery.

Database Management Service (DMS): Provides frictionless migration from MySQL, PostgreSQL, and SQL Server instances running on Compute Engine, on-premises, or in other clouds.

Vector Search: Cloud SQL for PostgreSQL supports the `pgvector` extension, enabling it to function as a vector database for AI/ML applications.

Deployment Options

Cloud SQL is available in two editions to support various business and application needs. Each edition (`https://cloud.google.com/sql/docs/editions-intro`) provides different performance and availability characteristics (see Table 3.3):

TABLE 3.3   Comparison of CloudSQL Enterprise editions

	Enterprise	**Enterprise Plus**
Pricing model	Enterprise pricing	Enterprise Plus pricing
Database Engine	MySQL PostgreSQL SQL Server	MySQL PostgreSQL SQL Server
Machine type	General-purpose machine family	Performance-optimized N family Memory-optimized family (for Cloud SQL for SQL Server)
Zonal Availability	Highly Available	Highly available
Availability SLA	99.95%	99.99%
Maintenance downtime	<60 seconds	<1 second
Data cache	No	Yes
Automatic Storage Increases	Enabled	Enabled
Point-in-time log retention	Up to 7 days	Up to 35 days Not available for SQL Server
Automated Backups	Enabled	Enabled
Storage Options	HDD, SSD	SSD

Cloud SQL Enterprise Edition: Provides all core capabilities of Cloud SQL and is suitable for applications requiring a balance of performance, availability, and cost.

Cloud SQL Enterprise Plus Edition: Provides the best performance and availability to run applications requiring the highest level of availability and performance in addition to the capabilities of the Cloud SQL Enterprise edition.

When to Choose

Considerations when making your choice include these:

Traditional Relational Database Workloads: For applications requiring ACID properties, data integrity, and structured data storage.

High Availability and Scalability: For applications requiring continuous availability and the ability to scale resources on demand.

Data Backup and Recovery: For applications requiring reliable data backup and recovery capabilities.

Cloud-Based Alternative: Cloud SQL provides a cloud-based alternative to local MySQL, PostgreSQL, and SQL Server databases. You should use Cloud SQL if you want to spend less time managing your database and more time using it.

Cost: Cloud SQL can be expensive for large instances and high-volume workloads. In these cases, AlloyDB could be a more cost-effective option for regional workloads and Cloud Spanner for multiregion workloads.

Performance: For very high-performance applications, consider other options like Cloud Spanner or AlloyDB.

SQL Server Compatibility: Because SQL Server for Cloud SQL is delivered as a Linux container, there are some features that are not supported, including Azure Active Directory authentication, row-level security, and SQL Server Analysis Services (SSAS). For a full list of unsupported features, go to `https://cloud.google.com/sql/docs/sqlserver/features`.

EXERCISE 3.2

Creating and Managing Cloud SQL for PostgreSQL Instances

`www.cloudskillsboost.google/course_templates/652`

In this exercise, you will migrate, configure, and manage Cloud SQL for PostgreSQL instances to support robust data operations. Accessed via the URL provided, this walkthrough offers hands-on practice deploying what you learned earlier in the chapter. You will focus on executing these critical administrative tasks, ensuring you understand the practical steps required to maintain a healthy and scalable database environment.

AlloyDB

AlloyDB (`https://cloud.google.com/alloydb`) is Google's fully managed, PostgreSQL-compatible relational database service designed for high-performance transactional workloads and analytical queries. AlloyDB pairs a Google-built database engine with a cloud-based, multinode architecture to deliver enterprise-grade performance, reliability, and availability.

Key Characteristics

Here's a list of key characteristics:

Type: Relational database.

Engine: PostgreSQL-compatible.

Regional: AlloyDB is available in multiple regions globally.

SLA: 99.99 percent availability.

Key Features

Here's a list of key features:

Index Advisor: An index adviser helps you find opportunities to optimize your database schema using new indexes based on your usage patterns.

Columnar Engine: A columnar engine can accelerate the performance of analytical queries by storing data in memory using a columnar format. This lets AlloyDB use advanced processing techniques to efficiently scan a large amount of table data when needed.

Autovacuum: An adaptive variation of the PostgreSQL stale-data autovacuum feature automatically adjusts vacuum-related parameters to best suit the shape of your workload.

Memory and Storage Management: Automatic memory and storage management systems take advantage of the Google-built, cloud-based environment that AlloyDB runs on, continuously allocating and releasing memory and storage as needed to keep your cluster running with optimal performance and resource efficiency.

High Performance: Delivers high transaction throughput and low query latency.

Scalability: Allows you to scale your database instances horizontally and vertically.

Intelligent Database Management: Manages crucial aspects of the database, including PostgreSQL vacuuming, storage allocation, memory usage, and data placement.

Performance Enhancements: Data tiering feature ensures optimal performance and cost-efficiency by strategically distributing data across different storage tiers. Index Advisor analyzes query patterns to recommend suitable indexes, provisioning up to 4× performance of standard Postgres.

Hybrid Transaction/Analytical Processing (HTAP): Provides capabilities for both transactional and analytical workloads.

Backup and Recovery: Provides automated backups and point-in-time recovery.

Nondisruptive Maintenance: AlloyDB maintenance operations are designed to minimize disruptions to your database. Primary and secondary instances have a downtime of less than a second, while read pools remain continuously available with no downtime.

Vector Search: Fully integrated support for the `pgvector` extension, offering high-performance vector search that is significantly faster than standard PostgreSQL.

Deployment Options

AlloyDB is available in two different deployment options (see Table 3.4):

AlloyDB: A fully managed, cloud-native relational database service that is PostgreSQL-compatible. It offers high performance, scalability, and reliability.

AlloyDB Omni: A downloadable database software package that allows you to deploy a streamlined edition of AlloyDB for PostgreSQL in your own computing environment. It provides flexibility and portability.

A managed AlloyDB deployment in a given region organizes its resources into a cluster. That cluster is deployed within a single Virtual Private Cloud (VPC) and leverages a Google cloud–based filesystem that is optimized for AlloyDB.

A cluster contains several nodes, which are VMs that are dedicated to running a PostgreSQL-compatible database engine that applications use to query your cluster's data.

TABLE 3.4   Comparison of AlloyDB deployment options

Feature	AlloyDB	AlloyDB Omni
Deployment Model	Google Cloud-Managed Database	Customer installed and managed on-premises, AWS, Azure, Google Cloud
Data Residency	Data stored in Google Cloud	Data stored in chosen environment
Management	Managed by Google Cloud	Requires on-premises or third-party management
Use Cases	Ideal for transactional workloads, data warehousing, and real-time analytics within Google Cloud; high-performance vector search for AI/ML	Suitable for applications requiring hybrid cloud deployment, data portability, multicloud access, and edge computing

AlloyDB organizes nodes into instances, each of which has a private, static IP address in your VPC.

AlloyDB has two kinds of instances:

Primary Instance: Handles read and write operations. Can be highly available (HA) with an active and standby node, or basic with a single node.

Read Pool Instance: Handles read-only operations and can be scaled independently.

Applications connect to instances, which then distribute queries to nodes. AlloyDB automatically balances load across read pool instances.

When to Choose

AlloyDB is a great option for applications that require both transactional and analytical workloads.

High-Performance Transactions: For applications requiring high transaction throughput and low latency.

High-Performance AI/ML Applications: Use AlloyDB as a high-performance vector database for demanding RAG and similarity search workloads.

Demanding PostgreSQL Workloads: When you need better performance, availability, and scalability than standard PostgreSQL.

Analytical Queries: For applications that need to perform complex queries on large datasets.

Hybrid Workloads: For applications that combine transactional and analytical workloads.

Hybrid Cloud Strategy: Use AlloyDB Omni to maintain a consistent database platform across on-premises and cloud environments.

AlloyDB: Best for applications requiring high performance, scalability, and Google Cloud integration. Ideal for organizations fully committed to Google Cloud and its managed services.

AlloyDB Omni: Best for applications needing hybrid cloud deployments, data portability, and multicloud access. Suitable for organizations with complex infrastructure and data residency requirements.

PostgreSQL Compatibility: AlloyDB is PostgreSQL-compatible but may have some differences in syntax and functionality, especially for extensions.

Creating and Managing AlloyDB Instances

`www.cloudskillsboost.google/course_templates/642`

In this exercise, you will create and manage AlloyDB instances to handle enterprise-grade database workloads. Accessed via the URL provided, this walkthrough offers hands-on practice deploying what you learned earlier in the chapter. You will focus on migrating data from PostgreSQL, administering the database, and accelerating analytical queries using the AlloyDB Columnar Engine, ensuring you possess the practical skills to optimize database performance.

Cloud Spanner

Google Cloud Spanner is a globally distributed, relational database service that offers a powerful combination of scalability, high availability, and strong consistency. Built on Google's own distributed database technology, Spanner provides a unique solution for handling mission-critical applications requiring the highest levels of performance and reliability.

Spanner separates data storage and processing. This allows for flexible scaling of computing power without affecting data management. By handling data distribution and replication automatically, Spanner simplifies database management and ensures optimal performance.

Key Characteristics

Key characteristics include the following:

Type: Relational database.

Database Engines: Cloud Spanner supports standard SQL and a PostgreSQL dialect.

Location: Globally distributed, with regional, dual-region, and multiregion instances.

SLA: 99.99 percent for regional, 99.999 percent availability for dual and multiregion.

Key Features

Essential features include the following:

Global Distribution and Strong Consistency: Spanner ensures data consistency across multiple regions, eliminating the need for complex sharding or data replication schemes. This provides a single, global view of data with strong consistency guarantees.

High Availability and Scalability: Spanner automatically replicates data across multiple zones, ensuring high availability and seamless failover in case of failures. It also scales horizontally to handle massive amounts of data and traffic.

Transaction ACID Properties: Spanner guarantees atomicity, consistency, isolation, and durability for all transactions, ensuring data integrity and reliability.

Built-in Backup and Recovery: Spanner has the ability to schedule full and incremental backups of your data, allowing for point-in-time recovery and disaster recovery scenarios.

SQL Compatibility: Spanner supports a standard SQL dialect, making it easy for developers to transition from traditional relational database systems.

Postgres Interface for Spanner: Applications can connect to a PostgreSQL interface-enabled Spanner database using native Spanner clients or PGAdapter, a lightweight proxy that implements the open PostgreSQL wire protocol.

Deployment Options

Cloud Spanner is available in regional and multiregion instances (see Table 3.5).

Regional Instance: A regional instance consists of three read-write replicas in three separate zones within the same region. A single read-only replica could additionally be deployed to another region.

TABLE 3.5 Comparison of Cloud Spanner deployment options

Feature	Regional	Multiregion
Location	Single region (e.g., Iowa)	Multiple regions (e.g., Iowa, Salt Lake City, Oklahoma)
Compute	Compute capacity is provisioned as processing units (PUs) or nodes (1 node = 1,000 processing units) PUs start at 100, increase by increments of 100 to 1,000, then by increments of 1,000.	Compute capacity is provisioned as processing units (PUs) or nodes (1 node = 1,000 processing units) PUs start at 100, increase by increments of 100 to 1,000, then by increments of 1,000.
Replicas	3 read-write replicas in 3 separate zones within the region	2 read-write replicas in primary region (Iowa), 2 read-write replicas in secondary region (Salt Lake City), 1 witness replica in private GCP region (Oklahoma)
Optional read-only replicas	Up to 1 in other regions	Up to 1 in other regions, including secondary region
Availability SLA	99.99%	99.999%

Multiregion Instance: A multiregion instance consists of two read-write replicas deployed in the primary region (default leader), two read-write replicas deployed in a secondary region, and one witness replica in a third region.

We'll explore failover in Cloud Spanner, including leader election, in Chapter 11, "Deploying and Validating Database Solutions."

When to Choose

Here are some factors to help you decide which to choose:

Mission-Critical Applications: Applications requiring high availability, low latency, and strong consistency.

Global Data Distribution: Applications needing to access data from multiple geographic locations with consistent data views.

Large-Scale Data Volumes: Applications handling massive amounts of data and requiring a scalable database solution.

Strict ACID Compliance: Applications demanding strict transaction integrity and data consistency.

Other Considerations

Latency: Regional deployments typically offer lower latency for applications within the same region. Multiregion deployments may introduce higher latency for read operations due to the potential need to access replicas in a different region.

Disaster Recovery: Multiregion deployments provide enhanced protection against regionwide failures.

Data Distribution: Multiregion deployments can improve read performance by distributing data across multiple regions.

Cost: Spanner is a premium service and can be more expensive than regional databases like Cloud SQL or AlloyDB.

EXERCISE 3.4

Creating and Managing Cloud Spanner Instances

`www.cloudskillsboost.google/course_templates/643`

In this exercise, you will apply the concepts covered earlier in this chapter by accessing the lab environment via the provided link. This activity provides hands-on practice deploying what you learned, allowing you to build proficiency in provisioning and managing Cloud Spanner resources. You will create instances, load data using various techniques, and perform critical operations such as database backups and schema definitions. Finally, you will connect a deployed web application to a live instance, solidifying your understanding of how to integrate this database into a modern architecture.

Cloud Bigtable

Google Cloud Bigtable (`https://cloud.google.com/bigtable`) is a fully managed, NoSQL key-value and wide-column store database service designed for large-scale, high-performance data workloads. It offers a scalable and reliable platform for storing and accessing massive datasets with low latency and high availability. Bigtable uses a flexible data model with row keys, column families, and qualifiers, enabling efficient handling of diverse data structures.

Bigtable is built on top of Google's own distributed storage technology, ensuring data integrity and resilience. Bigtable decouples compute resources from data storage, which makes it possible to transparently adjust processing resources. Each additional node can process reads and writes equally well, providing effortless horizontal scalability. Bigtable optimizes performance by automatically scaling resources to adapt to server traffic, handling the sharding, replication, and query processing.

Bigtable is ideal for applications requiring high-throughput, low-latency data access, global availability, and scalability, making it suitable for various use cases such as real-time analytics, social media platforms, and large-scale data storage.

Key Characteristics

Some important characteristics are as follows:

Type: NoSQL, wide-column store

Database Engines: Apache HBase, Cloud Bigtable

Location: Global, with regional data replication (eventual consistency)

SLA: 99.9 percent single cluster, 99.99 percent two clusters across two regions, 99.999 percent multicluster routing policy across three or more regions

Key Features

Here are some important features to consider:

High Scalability: Bigtable can handle massive datasets and high throughput requests, scaling horizontally to meet demanding workloads.

Low Latency: Designed for fast data access with low latency reads and writes, ideal for real-time applications.

Strong Consistency: Guarantees strong consistency across all replicas, ensuring data integrity.

Global Availability: Provides high availability with global replication across multiple regions.

Flexible Data Model: Supports a flexible data model with row keys, column families, and qualifiers, allowing for diverse data structures such as time-series data and user profiles

Built-in Data Integrity: Offers built-in data integrity features with automatic replication and recovery.

Storage and Compute Separation: Allows for independent scaling of compute nodes and storage, optimizing cost and performance.

Deployment Options

To use Bigtable, you create instances, which contain clusters that your applications can connect to. You can choose to deploy one or more clusters in different regions. Each cluster contains nodes, the compute units that manage your data and perform maintenance tasks. See Table 3.6 for Bigtable configuration options.

When to Choose

When making a choice, consider the following:

Large-Scale Analytics and Operational Workloads: Ideal for applications like IoT data ingestion, real-time analytics, and personalization engines

Time Series Data: Excellent for storing and analyzing large volumes of time-stamped data

Large Datasets: Suitable for handling massive amounts of data, especially when dealing with unstructured or semi-structured data

High Throughput and Low Latency: Ideal for applications requiring high read and write performance, especially for real-time scenarios

Global Availability: Needed for applications requiring global data access and high availability

Flexibility: Suitable for scenarios where a flexible data model is required

Other Considerations

Other considerations include the following:

Eventual Consistency: By default, replication for Bigtable is eventually consistent. This means that when you write a change to one cluster, you will eventually be able to read that change from the other clusters in the instance, but only after the change is replicated among the clusters.

TABLE 3.6 Cloud Bigtable configuration options

Configuration option	Description	Impact on performance/cost
Cluster Location	Geographic location of Bigtable clusters. Clusters are regional. You may choose to create one or more clusters in different regions.	Affects latency, data locality, and cost.
SLA	99.9% single cluster, 99.99% 2 clusters across 2 regions, 99.999% multicluster routing policy across 3 or more regions.	Affects latency, data locality, and cost.
Storage Tier	SSD or HDD storage for data.	SSD offers higher performance but is more expensive.
Replication	Data replication across multiple regions.	Improves high availability and disaster recovery but increases costs.
Column Family	Group of columns within a table.	Affects read/write performance and storage efficiency.
GC Rule	Garbage collection policy for data expiration.	Impacts storage costs and data retention.

Data Modeling: Requires careful consideration of data modeling, as Bigtable's wide-column store design differs from traditional relational databases.

Cluster Resizing Without Downtime: You can increase the size of a Bigtable cluster for a few hours to handle a large load, then reduce the size of the cluster again—all without any downtime. After you change a cluster's size, it typically takes just a few minutes under load for Bigtable to balance performance across all of the nodes in your cluster.

SLA: Bigtable instances with a multicluster routing policy across three or more regions are covered by a 99.999 percent monthly uptime percentage. Bigtable supports 99.99 percent monthly uptime percentage for all instances with a multicluster routing policy across less than three regions and 99.9 percent monthly uptime percentage for all instances with a single-cluster routing policy.

EXERCISE 3.5

Creating and Managing Bigtable Instances

`www.cloudskillsboost.google/course_templates/650`

In this exercise, you will create and manage Bigtable instances to support high-throughput, scalable applications. Accessed via the URL provided, this walkthrough offers hands-on practice deploying what you learned earlier in the chapter. You will focus on designing schemas, querying data, and executing administrative tasks—such as monitoring performance and configuring node autoscaling and replication—ensuring you understand the practical steps to maintain optimal database efficiency.

Cloud Firestore

Google Cloud Firestore (`https://cloud.google.com/firestore`) is a fully managed, flexible, and scalable NoSQL document database designed to store and sync app data at global scale. It's particularly well suited for building mobile and web applications. Cloud Firestore is essentially the evolution of Cloud Datastore. It builds upon the foundation of Datastore while introducing significant enhancements and new features.

Firestore's primary strength lies in its real-time capabilities, making it ideal for applications requiring instant data updates and synchronization across multiple users. It's a highly adaptable solution, readily integrating with various Google Cloud services and offering a powerful SDK for seamless development.

Key Characteristics

Key characteristics include these:

Type: NoSQL document database

Location: Global, with regional data replication for high availability and low latency

SLA: 99.99 percent for regional, 99.999 percent for multiregion

Key Features

Key features include these:

Scalability and High Availability: Firestore scales automatically to handle large amounts of data and traffic. Data is replicated across multiple regions to ensure high availability and low latency.

Document Model: Firestore uses a document model, which is well suited for storing structured and semi-structured data like user profiles, product catalogs, and more.

Offline Capabilities: Firestore supports offline capabilities, allowing users to interact with the database even when they are not connected to the Internet. Data changes are automatically synced when the device comes back online.

Real-Time Data Synchronization: Firestore provides real-time data synchronization, enabling applications to respond to changes in data immediately.

Query Optimization: Firestore features robust query capabilities with support for composite indexes, range queries, and more. These features allow for efficient retrieval of data based on various criteria.

Firebase Integration: Firestore is fully integrated with Firebase, a platform for building web and mobile applications. This provides a straightforward way to get started and leverage other Firebase services.

Firestore Cloud Bundle Extension: The Firestore Bundle Builder (`firestore-bundle-builder`) extension deploys an HTTP function that serves Cloud Firestore data bundles. You define the bundles in Firestore documents, and the extension serves static binary file data bundle via HTTP requests, along with various built-in caching mechanisms using Firebase Hosting CDN or Cloud Storage.

Deployment Options

Cloud Firestore offers two primary modes of operation (see Table 3.7):

Native Mode: Optimized for mobile and web applications. Cloud Firestore in Native Mode leverages real-time capabilities, offline support, and client-side SDKs for seamless user experiences, making it ideal for applications requiring rapid data synchronization and responsiveness.

TABLE 3.7 Comparison of Cloud Firestore modes

Feature	Native mode	Datastore mode
Target Audience	Mobile, web	Server-side, App Engine
SDKs	Client-side (iOS, Android, web)	Server-side
Real-time	Yes	No
Offline support	Yes	No
Scaling	Automatic	Automatic
Data Model	Flexible, document-oriented	Entity-oriented

Datastore Mode: Backward-compatible with Google Cloud Datastore. Cloud Firestore in Datastore Mode is designed for server-side applications and App Engine environments, providing automatic scaling, high performance, and access to established Datastore server architectures.

When to Choose

Factors to take into account when making a choice include the following:

Native Mode: Best for mobile and web apps that require real-time updates, offline functionality, and a flexible data model.

Datastore Mode: Ideal for server-side applications, existing Datastore users, and those needing to leverage established Datastore server architectures.

Mobile and Web Applications: Firestore is ideal for mobile and web applications that require a flexible data model, real-time updates, and offline capabilities.

Scalable Applications: Firestore's automatic scaling and high availability make it suitable for applications that experience variable traffic and data growth.

Social Media Applications: Firestore is often used for building social media applications that require real-time updates and efficient data management.

Gaming Applications: The real-time capabilities of Firestore are well suited for developing gaming applications that require low latency and fast data synchronization.

Cost: Both modes are generally priced similarly, but factors like data volume, read/write operations, and storage can influence costs. A free tier is available for a limited amount of data and operations.

Performance: Native mode often offers lower latency for client-side operations due to real-time capabilities. Datastore mode can handle high throughput for server-side workloads.

Data Model: Native mode provides a flexible document-oriented model, while Datastore mode uses an entity-oriented model with stricter schema requirements.

Data Model Flexibility: While Firestore's document model is flexible, it can be challenging to implement complex data relationships like those found in relational databases.

Firebase Realtime Database: While Firestore is generally preferred for new projects, Firebase Realtime Database might still be suitable for specific use cases where:

Data structure is simple and flat.
Real-time updates are the primary requirement.
You have existing code using Realtime Database.

Datastore: Firestore is the next generation of Datastore. Firestore can operate in Datastore mode, making it backward-compatible with legacy Cloud Datastore. With Firestore in Datastore mode, you can access Firestore's improved storage layer while keeping Datastore system behavior. Firestore in Datastore mode removes several legacy Cloud Datastore limitations.

EXERCISE 3.6

Cloud Firestore Web Codelab

`https://firebase.google.com/codelabs/firestore-web`

In this exercise, you will build a restaurant recommendation web application to demonstrate the capabilities of Cloud Firestore. Accessed via the URL provided, this walkthrough offers hands-on practice deploying what you learned earlier in the chapter. You will focus on writing complex queries, listening to real-time data changes, and implementing Firebase Authentication, ensuring you understand the practical steps required to secure and manage dynamic web data.

BigQuery

Google Cloud BigQuery (`https://cloud.google.com/bigquery`) is a fully managed, serverless data warehouse that allows you to analyze massive datasets with blazing speed. It offers a cost-effective and scalable solution for businesses of all sizes, making it a powerful tool for data analysis, business intelligence, and machine learning.

BigQuery can independently scale storage and compute based on demand, optimizing resource utilization and minimizing costs. This architecture allows for massive data storage at low cost while enabling high-performance query processing through the flexible allocation of compute resources, ultimately delivering significant cost savings and efficient data analysis capabilities.

Key Characteristics

Key characteristics include these:

Type: Relational Data warehouse, analytics database

Database Engines: SQL—Standard SQL, Legacy SQL (backward compatibility), Google SQL (Google Standard SQL)

Location: Global, with data stored in multiple regions

SLA: 99.9 percent Standard edition, 99.99 percent Enterprise and Enterprise Plus

Key Features

Some key features are as follows:

Serverless Architecture: No infrastructure to manage, allowing you to focus on data analysis.

High Performance: Optimized for petabyte-scale data analysis, leveraging Google's global infrastructure.

Scalability: Automatically scales to accommodate growing data volumes and query demands.

SQL Support: Provides a familiar and powerful SQL interface for querying and manipulating data.

Machine Learning: Integrates with BigQuery ML for building and deploying machine learning models, including LLMs, directly on your data using SQL.

Vector Search: Supports vector search capabilities for finding similar items within large datasets.

Federation: Can query data directly from Cloud SQL, Spanner, Bigtable, and Cloud Storage.

Data Exploration: Offers interactive tools like BigQuery Studio and Looker Studio for exploring and visualizing data.

Cost-Effective: Pay only for the resources you use, offering a cost-effective solution for data analysis.

Deployment Options

BigQuery is available as a pay-as-you-go (PAYG) pricing model as well as Editions pricing tier. BigQuery Editions (`https://cloud.google.com/bigquery/docs/editions-intro`) represent a tiered pricing model for the serverless data warehouse. Each edition offers different features, performance levels, and pricing structures to cater to various workloads:

Standard Edition: Provides a balance of cost and performance, suitable for general-purpose analytics. A mid-sized marketing agency may choose Standard Edition to analyze website traffic data from Google Analytics and run ad hoc queries, generate reports on campaign performance, and build basic dashboards.

Enterprise Edition: Delivers higher performance and additional features like advanced data protection and compliance options. A large financial institution that conducts real-time fraud detection analysis might choose Enterprise Edition to process high-velocity data streams, perform complex machine learning models, and ensure strict data security and compliance.

Enterprise Plus Edition: Offers the highest performance and broadest feature set, including disaster recovery and advanced analytics capabilities. Enterprise Plus would be a good fit for a global e-commerce company that needs to analyze massive datasets from various sources, including web logs, customer interactions, and IoT devices. They require the highest level of performance, advanced analytics capabilities, and robust disaster recovery.

When choosing an edition, you can also specify the number of slots to reserve (see Table 3.8). Slots are the unit of compute capacity in BigQuery. They determine how much computational power is allocated to process your queries.

On-Demand Slots: Automatically provisioned as needed, providing flexibility but can be more expensive

Reserved Slots: Pre-purchased slots offering cost savings but require upfront commitment

Slot Autoscaling: Dynamically adjusts the number of slots based on workload, optimizing cost and performance

When to Choose

Consider these factors when making your choice:

Large-Scale Data Analysis: When dealing with massive datasets exceeding terabytes or petabytes.

Real-Time Analytics: Analyzing data in near real time for immediate insights.

Business Intelligence: Creating interactive dashboards and reports for data visualization and reporting.

Machine Learning at Scale: Building and deploying machine learning models using BigQuery ML without moving data.

Centralized Data Warehouse: Acting as the single source of truth for an organization's analytical data.

Cost Optimization: Understanding BigQuery's pricing model and optimizing queries for cost efficiency is important. Inefficient queries can lead to higher-than-expected costs. BigQuery query costs are primarily determined by the amount of data processed. Optimized queries reduce costs by minimizing the amount of data scanned and processed, achieved through techniques like filtering data early, using appropriate join types, and leveraging partitioning and clustering for efficient data access.

Not for OLTP: BigQuery is an analytical database (OLAP) and is not designed for high-throughput, low-latency transactional (OLTP) workloads.

TABLE 3.8 Comparison of BigQuery editions

	Standard	Enterprise	Enterprise Plus	On-demand pricing
Pricing model	Slot-hours (1 minute minimum)	Slot-hours (1 minute minimum)	Slot-hours (1 minute minimum)	Pay per query with free tier
Compute model	Autoscaling	Autoscaling + Baseline	Autoscaling + Baseline	On-demand
Monthly Service Level Objective (SLO)	>=99.9%	>=99.99%	>=99.99%	>=99.99%
VPC Service Controls	No VPC Service Controls Support	VPC Service Controls Support	VPC Service Controls Support	VPC Service Controls Support
Storage encryption	Google-owned and Google-managed keys	Google-owned and Google-managed keys	Customer-managed encryption keys (CMEKs) Google-owned and Google-managed keys	Customer-managed encryption keys (CMEKs) Google-owned and Google-managed keys
Business Intelligence acceleration	No access to query acceleration through BI Engine	Query acceleration through BI Engine	Query acceleration through BI Engine	Query acceleration through BI Engine
Integrated machine learning	No access to BigQuery ML	BigQuery ML	BigQuery ML	BigQuery ML
Multi-cloud analytics	No access to BigQuery Omni support	BigQuery Omni support	BigQuery Omni support	BigQuery Omni support

Building a Data Warehouse with BigQuery

`www.cloudskillsboost.google/course_templates/624`

In this exercise, you will construct a data warehouse using BigQuery to perform advanced data operations, including joining datasets, troubleshooting common join errors, and appending data with unions. Accessed via the URL provided, this walkthrough offers hands-on practice deploying what you learned earlier in the chapter. You will focus on optimizing query performance and managing complex data structures by creating date-partitioned tables and working directly with JSON, arrays, and structs, ensuring you understand the practical steps required to handle large-scale analytics efficiently.

Partner Databases in Google Cloud

Google Cloud maintains a robust ecosystem of partner database services that allows you to leverage third-party engines with the benefits of cloud-native integration. These partnerships enable you to deploy, manage, and scale databases such as MongoDB and Oracle using familiar tools and workflows while utilizing high-performance Google Cloud infrastructure. By offering these managed services directly, Google Cloud ensures that you can utilize the specific capabilities of these engines—such as the document model of MongoDB or the enterprise features of Oracle—without the operational overhead of managing the underlying physical hardware.

MongoDB

MongoDB (`https://cloud.google.com/monqodb`) is a leading NoSQL document database known for its flexibility, scalability, and ease of use. Its document-oriented approach allows for storing data in JSON-like documents, providing a more flexible and dynamic data structure than traditional relational databases. This flexibility makes MongoDB ideal for modern applications requiring rapid development, complex data models, and high performance.

MongoDB on Google Cloud is offered through various deployment options, from the fully managed Cloud MongoDB Atlas to self-managed deployments on GKE or Compute Engine.

Key Characteristics

Some key characteristics are as follows:

Type: NoSQL, Document Database

Database Engines: MongoDB 4.0, 4.2, 4.4, 5.0, and 5.5

Location: Regional, with instances available in multiple regions worldwide

SLA: 99.95 percent availability for dedicated clusters, and 99.9 percent availability for shared clusters

Key Features

Some key features are as follows:

Document Model: Stores data in flexible JSON-like documents, providing high-level schema flexibility

High Scalability and Availability: Supports horizontal scaling through sharding and replication, achieving high performance and availability

Advanced Querying: Offers powerful query capabilities with full-text search and aggregation features, enabling complex data analysis

Rich Ecosystem: Extensive ecosystem of tools, drivers, and libraries for seamless integration with various applications and languages

Deployment Options

Here are your deployment options:

- **Cloud MongoDB Atlas:** A fully managed MongoDB service, providing easy setup, scaling, and administration with various pricing tiers.
- **Self-Managed**
  - **Google Kubernetes Engine (GKE):** Deploy MongoDB clusters within GKE for more control and customization, offering greater flexibility but requiring more management overhead.
  - **Compute Engine:** Deploying MongoDB on Compute Engine provides you with full control over the MongoDB deployment, allowing you to customize the database configuration and environment to meet specific application requirements.

When to Choose

When making your choice, take the following into account:

High Data Volume and Rapid Growth: MongoDB's horizontal scaling and document model handle large datasets efficiently.

Flexible Data Structures: The schema-less nature of documents enables storing data of various formats and evolving data structures without rigid schemas.

Complex Queries and Analysis: Powerful aggregation and full-text search capabilities facilitate complex data analysis and insights.

Real-Time Applications: MongoDB's strong performance and low latency make it suitable for applications requiring real-time data access.

Data Consistency: MongoDB offers tunable consistency, but its default settings prioritize availability over the strong consistency found in databases like Spanner.

Existing MongoDB Deployments: Customers already leveraging MongoDB could benefit from migrating their existing MongoDB databases and applications to Google Cloud.

EXERCISE 3.8

Getting Started with MongoDB Atlas on Google Cloud

`www.cloudskillsboost.google/course_templates/731`

In this exercise, you will set up MongoDB Atlas to operate as a fully managed database-as-a-service within Google's data cloud. Accessed via the URL provided, this walkthrough offers hands-on practice deploying what you learned earlier in the chapter. You will focus on harnessing the platform's speed, scale, and security to manage modern database systems efficiently, demonstrating how a DBaaS approach frees teams to prioritize high-value activities over infrastructure maintenance.

Oracle

Oracle Databases on Google Cloud (`https://cloud.google.com/solutions/oracle`) is a relatively new partnership between Google and Oracle. Previously, the only way to run Oracle on Google Cloud was to leverage Google's Bare Metal Solution (BMS), which allowed customers to install Oracle on bare metal hardware. Until recently, license and support restrictions did not allow for installing Oracle on Google Cloud Compute Engine or Containers.

Oracle on Google Cloud represents a partnership between Google and Oracle that allows customers to run and access Oracle Database services in Google Cloud through the following options:

- Oracle Database@Google Cloud (partner-managed)
- OCI and Google Cross-Cloud Interconnect

- Oracle on Google Compute Engine (self-managed)
- Bare Metal Solution (BMS) (self-managed)

Key Characteristics

Some key characteristics are as follows:

Type: Relational database

Database Engines: Oracle Database and Exadata

Location: Regional, offering high availability within a specific region.

SLA: Up to 99.95 percent availability for managed services

Key Features

And here are some key features:

Flexible Options to simplify and help accelerate migrating their Oracle databases to Google Cloud, including compatibility with proven migration tools such as Oracle Zero-Downtime Migration.

A Simplified Purchasing and Contracting Experience via Google Cloud Marketplace that enables customers to purchase Oracle database services using their existing Google Cloud commitments and leverage their existing Oracle license benefits, including Bring Your Own License (BYOL) and discount programs such as Oracle Support Rewards (OSRs).

Unified Customer Experience and support from Google Cloud and Oracle.

The simplicity, security, and latency of a **unified operating environment** (datacenter) within Google Cloud to deploy the entire portfolio of Oracle database services, including Oracle Exadata Database Service, Oracle Autonomous Database Service, MySQL Heatwave, Oracle Database Zero Data Loss Autonomous Recovery Service, Oracle GoldenGate, and Oracle Data Safe.

Access to Google AI Solutions—connecting their Oracle data with Google's industry-leading AI services including Vertex AI and Gemini foundation models to bring enterprise truth to AI applications and agents for customer service, employee services, creative studios, developer environments, and more.

Deployment Options

Here are your deployment options:

Oracle Database@Google Cloud (OCI): Oracle Database@Google Cloud (see Figure 3.1) offers a seamless experience for deploying and managing Oracle databases on Google Cloud's infrastructure powered by Oracle Cloud Infrastructure

(OCI) hardware. Users can leverage the advanced capabilities of Autonomous Database and migrate critical databases to the high-performance Exadata Database Cloud Service, all within the familiar Google Cloud environment.

OCI and Google Cross-Cloud Interconnect: Cross-Cloud Interconnect (see Figure 3.2) allows customers to deploy workloads across both Oracle Cloud Infrastructure (OCI) and Google Cloud regions with no cross-cloud data transfer charges. Cross-Cloud Interconnect provides a low-latency, high-throughput, private connection between Google Cloud and Oracle datacenters with seamless interoperability.

Oracle on Google Compute Engine: Migrate or install Oracle Database and applications on Google's managed Compute Engine service (see Figure 3.3). The option provides the most flexible configuration options but also requires that you manage the application and configuration. Bring your own Oracle license and playbooks.

Bare Metal Solution (BMS): BMS (see Figure 3.4) gives users the ability to run Oracle databases the same way they may currently do on-premises, on a fully managed end-to-end infrastructure, including compute, storage, and networking. Billing, support, and SLA are provided by Google Cloud.

When to Choose

When making your choice, consider the following:

Oracle Database@Google Cloud (OCI): This option is best suited for customers seeking to take advantage of Google Cloud for workloads that require Oracle databases.

FIGURE 3.1 Oracle Database@Google Cloud.

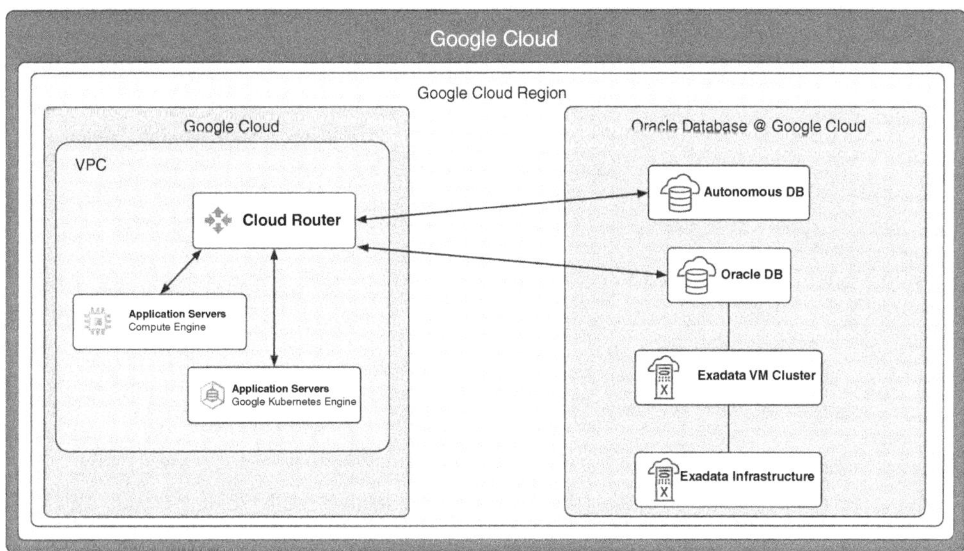

FIGURE 3.2   OCI and Google Cross-Cloud Interconnect.

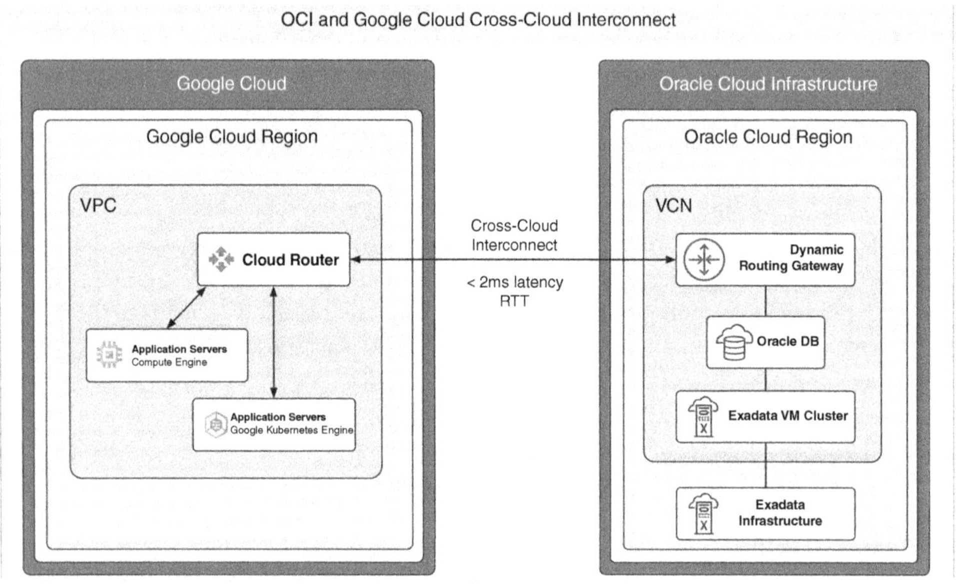

FIGURE 3.3   Oracle on Google Compute Engine.

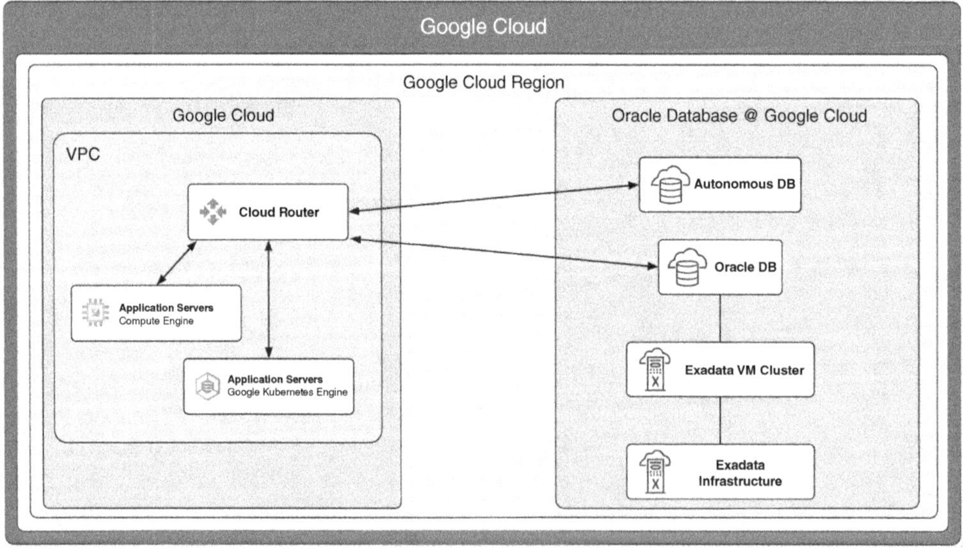

FIGURE 3.4 Oracle on bare metal solution (BMS).

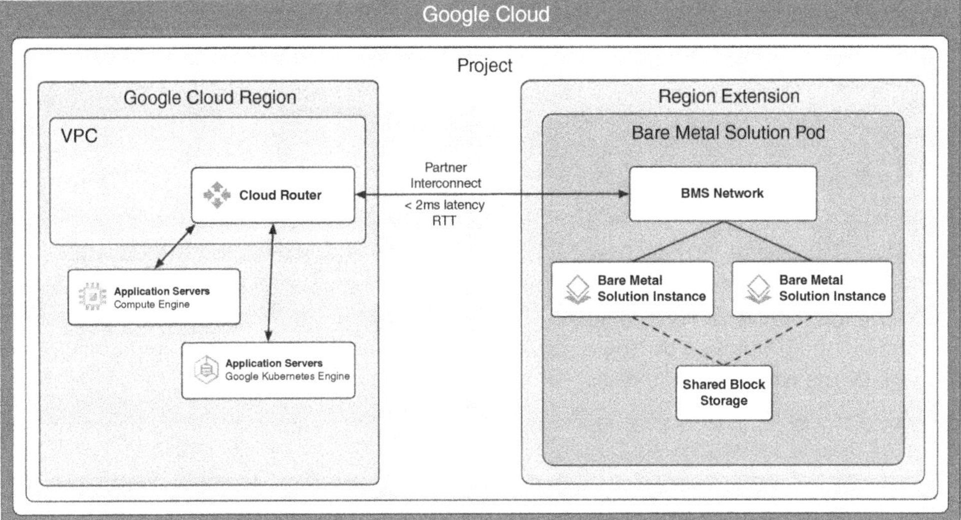

OCI and Google Cross-Cloud Interconnect: This option provides customers with existing workloads in OCI a seamless way to integrate their applications running on Google Cloud with existing databases in OCI.

Oracle on Google Compute Engine: Oracle on Compute Engine is a great option for quickly migrating lift-and-shift workloads with minimal changes to your application.

Bare Metal Solution (BMS): Customers who are looking to exit on-premises data centers and prefer to retain additional control over hardware configurations will find this to be the most effective path for migrating Oracle Workloads to the cloud with the least amount of changes to applications.

Other Considerations

Here are other factors to consider:

Bare Metal Solution (BMS): Oracle Databases@Google Cloud is a relatively new option. For many years, Oracle on Google Cloud Bare Metal Solution (BMS) had been the only option for hosting Oracle on Google Cloud. Therefore, BMS should be the primary option of deploying Oracle on Google Cloud until other solutions are more widely documented.

Database Migration Service (DMS) for Oracle to PostgreSQL on Cloud SQL: Google Cloud Database Migration Service (DMS) is a managed service designed to streamline the migration of databases to Cloud SQL. It specifically supports the migration of Oracle databases to PostgreSQL on Cloud SQL through data replication and translation of Oracle database schemas and data types into their PostgreSQL equivalents.

Migrating Oracle Workloads into Cloud SQL for PostgreSQL by Using Database Migration Service

```
https://cloud.google.com/database-migration/docs/
oracle-to-postgresql/quickstart
```

In this exercise, you will convert an Oracle database to PostgreSQL syntax and migrate the data to Cloud SQL using the Database Migration Service. Accessed via the URL provided, this walkthrough offers hands-on practice deploying what you learned earlier in the chapter. You will focus on the complete migration life cycle—from preparing the source and converting schemas to monitoring and promoting the job—ensuring you understand the practical steps required to modernize Oracle workloads efficiently.

Self-Managed Database Options in Google Cloud

While Google Cloud provides a comprehensive suite of managed database services, certain architectural patterns or business requirements necessitate direct control over the underlying infrastructure. Self-managed options allow you to replicate on-premises environments within the cloud, granting you the ability to fine-tune the operating system, install specific database versions, and manage distinct file system configurations. These solutions are particularly valuable when performing "lift-and-shift" migrations of legacy systems or when your application relies on a database engine that is not currently offered as a managed service.

Databases on Google Bare Metal Solution (BMS)

Google Cloud Bare Metal Solution (BMS) offers dedicated, physical servers within Google's data centers or a regional extension, providing a highly customized and powerful infrastructure solution (`https://cloud.google.com/bare-metal`). It's a unique offering in the cloud space, blending the control and performance of on-premises solutions with the scalability and flexibility of the cloud. BMS is most often associated with the migration of Oracle workloads from on-premises to the cloud.

Key Characteristics

Key characteristics are as follows:

Type: Physical servers

Database Engines: Installed by customer, but typically associated with databases such as Oracle that have hardware or license restrictions

Location: Regional, within Google Cloud data centers and regional extensions

SLA: 99.9 percent for BMS infrastructure

Key Features

Some key features are as follows:

Complete Control: Users have full control over the physical server, including the operating system, software, and configurations.

Customizability: Tailor server configurations to meet specific performance and security requirements.

Scalability: Provision additional servers as needed for growing workloads, leveraging Google Cloud's global network infrastructure.

Deployment Options

Unlike most Google Cloud services, Bare Metal Solution (BMS) requires a more extensive procurement process starting with a BMS Order Form. After you've executed a simplified, one-time Bare Metal Solution Order Form, you can order your Bare Metal Solution resources online by creating procurements through the Google Cloud console. Procurements let you order resources as you scale, without having to execute a new Bare Metal Solution Order Form every time.

When to Choose

Considerations when choosing include the following:

Full Control and Flexibility: For applications requiring full control over the underlying hardware and software stack.

Legacy Applications: Migrate on-premises applications to the cloud without requiring significant application changes.

Compliance Requirements: For industries with stringent security and compliance regulations where dedicated hardware is essential.

Cost: Bare metal servers can be more expensive than virtual machines, especially for smaller deployments.

Management: Users are responsible for managing and maintaining the server, including patching and security updates.

Scalability: While Google Cloud offers scalability, provisioning additional servers can be less immediate than scaling virtual machines.

Availability: Google Cloud offers a high level of availability for its infrastructure, but users should consider their own redundancy strategies for critical applications.

Databases on Compute Engine

Google Cloud Compute Engine (GCE) is a flexible IaaS platform that allows you to run your own databases on virtual machines (`https://cloud.google.com/compute`). It offers a wide range of customization options, allowing you to tailor the environment to your specific needs. However, it requires significant technical expertise to manage and maintain the infrastructure and database instances. GCE is a good option for organizations that need a highly customized database environment, have specific engine requirements, or want to optimize costs. However, it is important to consider the added responsibility and complexity associated with managing the underlying infrastructure.

Key Characteristics

Key characteristics are as follows:

Type: Infrastructure-as-a-service (IaaS)

Database Engines: Supports any database engine, including open source and proprietary options like MySQL, PostgreSQL, MongoDB, Oracle, and SQL Server

Location: Global, with availability in multiple regions and zones

SLA: Varies depending on the chosen VM instance type and region/zone

Key Features

Some key features are as follows:

Virtual Machine Instances: Offers a wide range of VM types with different CPU, memory, and storage configurations to suit your database needs

Persistent Disk Options: Provides reliable and durable storage for your databases, with options for different performance and cost characteristics

Networking: Supports various networking options, including private and public IP addresses, load balancing, and firewalls

Deployment Options

Multiple machine types and images are available, allowing customers to customize software and VM configuration and performance. The customer is responsible for installing and configuring database software as well as any license requirements.

The Google Cloud Marketplace offers partner images for popular database and software options.

When to Choose

Considerations when choosing include the following:

High Customization Requirements: GCE allows you to fully control the underlying infrastructure and configure the database environment according to your specific needs.

Specific Database Engine Needs: You can choose any database engine you prefer, including those not offered by managed database services.

Cost Optimization: You can tailor the resources and configuration to optimize for cost, especially for smaller or less demanding databases.

Legacy Migration: GCE can be a good option for migrating legacy databases to the cloud with minimal disruption to existing applications.

Maintenance: You are responsible for maintaining and patching the operating system and database software on GCE VMs.

Security: You need to implement security best practices and manage security updates to protect your database.

Cost: You need to manage costs for VM instances, storage, and other resources.

Complexity: Managing a database on GCE requires technical expertise and knowledge of the underlying infrastructure.

EXERCISE 3.10

Setting Up MySQL on Google Compute Engine

```
https://cloud.google.com/compute/docs/instances/sql-server/
setup-mysql
```

In this exercise, you will manually install and configure MySQL on a Google Compute Engine instance. Accessed via the URL provided, this tutorial offers hands-on practice deploying what you learned earlier in the chapter. You will focus on the end-to-end setup process and customization options, ensuring you possess the technical proficiency to manage a database environment when granular control is required.

Databases on Google Kubernetes Engine (GKE)

GKE (`https://cloud.google.com/kubernetes-engine`) is a managed Kubernetes service offering on Google Cloud Platform, providing a robust and scalable environment for deploying and managing containerized applications. While not a direct database service itself, GKE serves as a versatile platform for hosting and managing databases by leveraging the power of containers. Similar to running database workloads on Compute Engine, GKE requires significant technical expertise to manage and maintain the infrastructure and database instances. GKE may be a good voice for customers who can leverage existing knowledge in Kubernetes, but aren't ready or capable of leveraging a managed database service like Cloud SQL.

Key Characteristics

Key characteristics are as follows:

Type: Container Orchestration Platform

Database Engines: Supports any database engine that can be containerized, including popular options like MySQL, PostgreSQL, MongoDB, Redis, and Cassandra

Location: Global, with regional availability for individual clusters

SLA: 99.95 percent for GKE control plane, but individual database instances depend on their underlying infrastructure and configuration

Key Features

Some key features are as follows:

Automated Deployment and Scaling: GKE simplifies the deployment and scaling of databases by managing container orchestration, load balancing, and self-healing capabilities.

High Availability and Disaster Recovery: GKE offers various mechanisms for ensuring database availability through features like replica sets, stateful sets, and multi-cluster deployments.

Flexible Deployment Options: Allows deploying databases in different ways, including stateless containers, stateful sets, and deployments with persistent volumes.

Open Source Ecosystem: Leverages the vast open source Kubernetes ecosystem, providing access to a wide range of tools, libraries, and community support.

Deployment Options

Multiple machine types are available, allowing customers to customize performance. The customer is responsible for installing and configuring database software as well as any license requirements.

The Google Cloud Marketplace offers click-to-deploy containers for popular database and software options.

When to Choose

Considerations when choosing include the following:

Flexibility and Control: For databases that support containerization, GKE provides the highest level of control and flexibility for database deployment, enabling customization and tailoring to specific needs.

Complex Database Environments: Ideal for managing complex database deployments with specific requirements or for integrating with existing applications and services.

Cost Optimization: GKE allows for fine-grained resource management and optimization, reducing costs by scaling resources up or down based on demand.

Integration with Existing Kubernetes Infrastructure: If already using Kubernetes for other applications, GKE seamlessly integrates for consistent infrastructure and management.

Operational Complexity: Managing databases on GKE requires expertise in containerization, Kubernetes, and database administration.

Security and Compliance: GKE offers robust security features, but requires careful configuration and ongoing monitoring to maintain compliance with industry standards.

Backup and Recovery: Implementing a comprehensive backup and recovery strategy is crucial, as GKE itself doesn't provide automatic backup functionality for databases.

EXERCISE 3.11

Deploying a Stateful MySQL Cluster on GKE

```
https://cloud.google.com/kubernetes-engine/docs/tutorials/
stateful-workloads/mysql
```

In this exercise, you will deploy a highly available MySQL topology on Google Kubernetes Engine, utilizing InnoDB Clusters and ClusterSets for resilience and disaster recovery. Accessed via the URL provided, this tutorial offers hands-on practice deploying what you learned earlier in the chapter. You will focus on configuring stateful workloads, implementing router middleware, and performing failover simulations, ensuring you understand the critical steps for maintaining robust, stateful database operations in a containerized environment.

Integrating Multiple Database Technologies

Modern applications rarely rely on a single database. Instead, they often use a combination of technologies to meet diverse needs. Google Cloud provides several tools and strategies to manage and integrate these multi-database environments effectively.

Federated Queries

Federation allows you to query data across multiple sources without moving or copying it. This is incredibly powerful for real-time analysis and simplified data access.

BigQuery Federated Queries: BigQuery is the central hub for federation in Google Cloud. It can directly query data residing in:

Cloud SQL (MySQL & PostgreSQL): Run analytical queries on your live transactional data.

Cloud Spanner: Query operational data in a globally distributed database.

Cloud Storage: Query unstructured data in formats like CSV, JSON, Parquet, and Avro.

Cloud Bigtable: Analyze large NoSQL datasets.

Data Integration and Movement

When data needs to be moved, transformed, or synchronized between systems, Google Cloud offers robust pipeline and migration services.

Dataflow: A fully managed service for building batch and streaming ETL/ELT pipelines. It can read from and write to nearly any database, making it ideal for complex data transformations.

Database Migration Service (DMS): A serverless service for migrating databases to Google Cloud with minimal downtime. It supports homogeneous migrations (e.g., on-premises PostgreSQL to Cloud SQL for PostgreSQL) and heterogeneous migrations (e.g., Oracle to Cloud SQL for PostgreSQL).

Hybrid and Multicloud Deployments

Organizations often need to run databases across on-premises data centers and multiple cloud providers.

AlloyDB Omni: A downloadable edition of AlloyDB that can be run anywhere—on-premises, in other clouds (like AWS or Azure), or at the edge. This provides a consistent PostgreSQL-compatible database experience across all environments.

Oracle on Google Cloud: Google provides multiple paths for Oracle workloads, including the OCI and Google Cross-Cloud Interconnect, which creates a low-latency, private connection between Google Cloud and Oracle Cloud Infrastructure (OCI). This allows applications in Google Cloud to interact with Oracle databases in OCI as if they were in the same data center.

Google Distributed Cloud: Extends Google Cloud's infrastructure and services to the edge and your data centers, allowing you to run managed databases like Cloud SQL in your own environment.

Databases for Generative AI and LLMs

Generative AI and large language models (LLMs) have introduced new data management challenges. Databases are critical for storing the vast amounts of data needed for training, and more importantly, for implementing patterns like retrieval-augmented generation (RAG).

The Role of Vector Search in RAG

RAG enhances the quality and relevance of LLM responses by grounding them in external, up-to-date information. The process like this:

1. A user asks a question.

2. The application converts the question into a vector embedding.

3. The application uses this query vector to search a *vector database* for the most similar and relevant documents/data chunks.

4. The retrieved information is combined with the original prompt and sent to the LLM.

5. The LLM generates an answer based on both its internal knowledge and the provided context.

    This makes vector databases a cornerstone of modern GenAI applications.

Google Cloud Database Solutions for AI/LLM

Google Cloud integrates specialized features across its database portfolio to support the rapid development of artificial intelligence and large language model (LLM) applications. By embedding vector search, machine learning inference, and open source framework compatibility directly into the data layer, these solutions allow you to build generative AI workflows—such as retrieval augmented generation (RAG)—without complex data movement. The following list highlights the primary database solutions for AI and LLM workloads.

AlloyDB and Cloud SQL for PostgreSQL: Both services support the `pgvector` open source extension, turning them into powerful, fully managed vector databases. This allows you to store and query vector embeddings alongside your structured business data in the same database, simplifying your architecture.

BigQuery ML: Allows you to perform machine learning, including inference with LLMs, directly within your data warehouse using simple SQL commands. You can use BigQuery ML to generate vector embeddings from your data and call Vertex AI foundation models for tasks like text summarization or classification.

LangChain Integration: Google Cloud databases, particularly AlloyDB and Cloud SQL, offer robust integrations with popular application development frameworks like LangChain. These integrations provide pre-built components that make it easy to connect your database to LLMs and build RAG-based applications.

Meeting Regulatory and Compliance Requirements

Choosing a database is not just a technical decision; it's also driven by security, regulatory, and organizational policies. Google Cloud provides a robust framework to help organizations meet these requirements.

Regulatory and Compliance Support

Google Cloud's infrastructure and services undergo regular independent verification of security, privacy, and compliance controls, achieving certifications against global standards. This helps customers meet requirements for regulations such as these:

- GDPR (General Data Protection Regulation)
- HIPAA (Health Insurance Portability and Accountability Act)
- PCI DSS (Payment Card Industry Data Security Standard)
- ISO/IEC 27001/27017/27018

Key database features that support compliance include:

Data Residency: You can control where your data is stored by selecting specific regions for your database instances (e.g., Cloud SQL, Spanner, AlloyDB). This is crucial for meeting data sovereignty laws.

Encryption: Google Cloud encrypts all data at rest and in transit by default. For more control, you can use Customer-Managed Encryption Keys (CMEKs), where you manage the encryption keys in Cloud Key Management Service (KMS).

Audit Logging: Cloud Audit Logs provides detailed records of who did what, where, and when within your Google Cloud projects, which is essential for security analysis and compliance auditing.

Aligning with Organizational Policies

Internal company policies heavily influence database strategy.

Data Retention and Deletion: Organizational policies often dictate how long data must be kept and when it must be deleted. Database features like Time-to-Live (TTL) policies in Cloud Bigtable or scheduled deletion scripts can automate this.

Security Posture: A company's security standards will guide the configuration. VPC Service Controls can be used to create a service perimeter around your sensitive data, preventing data exfiltration. Identity and Access Management (IAM) policies ensure that users and applications have only the minimum necessary permissions (principle of least privilege).

Cost Management: Organizational budgets may lead to choosing serverless options like Firestore or BigQuery to avoid paying for idle resources, or using self-managed databases on Compute Engine to leverage existing licenses and expertise for cost savings.

Summary

In this chapter, we explored the various database solutions available on Google Cloud, equipping database engineers with the knowledge necessary to choose the optimal service for their needs. We explored the distinctions between managed and unmanaged database services, encompassing self-managed, bare metal, Google-managed, and partner-managed offerings. We covered strategies for integrating multiple databases through federation and hybrid deployments, and how specific services like AlloyDB and BigQuery are leveraged for modern generative AI use cases. Finally, we discussed how to select solutions that meet stringent regulatory, compliance, and organizational policy requirements.

Exam Essentials

Differentiate between managed and unmanaged database services.   Understand the trade-offs between managed (less operational overhead) and unmanaged (more control) services in terms of cost, expertise, scalability, and security.

Evaluate Google-managed database services.   Describe the key features and primary use cases for Memorystore, Cloud SQL, AlloyDB, Cloud Spanner, Cloud Bigtable, Cloud Firestore, and BigQuery.

Evaluate partner- and self-managed options.   Understand when to use partner solutions like MongoDB Atlas or the various Oracle on Google Cloud options. Know the use cases for self-managing on BMS, GCE, and GKE (e.g., licensing, legacy apps, customization).

Identify solutions for regulatory compliance.   Explain how features like data residency controls, CMEK, VPC Service Controls, and Cloud Audit Logs help meet compliance requirements like GDPR and HIPAA. Understand how internal organizational policies (e.g., cost, security) impact database choice.

Consider solutions spanning multiple technologies.   Explain how BigQuery Federated Queries allow you to query data in place across Cloud SQL, Spanner, and Cloud Storage.

Describe how services like AlloyDB Omni and Cross-Cloud Interconnect enable hybrid and multicloud database strategies.

Leverage databases for generative AI.   Explain the role of vector search in retrieval-augmented generation (RAG). Identify which Google Cloud databases (AlloyDB, Cloud SQL, BigQuery, Memorystore) support vector search and can be used to build AI-powered applications.

Review Questions

1. Which Google Cloud service is designed for storing and managing large amounts of unstructured data?

   A. Cloud SQL

   B. Cloud Spanner

   C. Cloud Storage

   D. Cloud Filestore

2. A company is developing an application that uses a large language model (LLM) and needs to implement retrieval-augmented generation (RAG) to improve the quality of the model's responses. They need a database that can store and efficiently search through a large collection of text documents to find relevant information to provide as context to the LLM. Which Google Cloud database feature is most relevant to this requirement?

   A. Cloud SQL's high availability features

   B. Cloud Firestore's real-time synchronization

   C. BigQuery's federated query capabilities

   D. AlloyDB's support for the `pgvector` extension

3. Which Google Cloud database service excels at handling petabyte-scale datasets and complex analytical queries?

   A. Cloud BigQuery

   B. Cloud SQL

   C. Cloud Spanner

   D. Cloud Datastore

4. A healthcare organization needs to store and analyze large volumes of patient data, including medical images and clinical notes. The data is subject to strict HIPAA regulations, requiring data residency in a specific region and robust security controls. Which Google Cloud features are most critical for meeting these requirements?

   A. VPC Service Controls and Dataflow

   B. Regional instance deployment and customer-managed encryption keys (CMEKs)

   C. Cloud Audit Logs and BigQuery Omni

   D. Firebase Realtime Database and Cloud Functions

5. A retail company wants to analyze customer purchasing patterns by querying data stored in both their on-premises Oracle database and their Google Cloud Storage buckets. They need a solution that allows them to run a single query across both data sources without moving or replicating the data. What Google Cloud feature would enable this?

    A. BigQuery Omni

    B. Database Migration Service

    C. Cloud Dataflow

    D. BigQuery Federated Queries

6. You are designing a mobile gaming app that requires real-time data synchronization, offline capabilities, and a flexible data model. Which Google Cloud database service is best suited for this scenario?

    A. Cloud SQL

    B. Cloud Spanner

    C. Cloud Firestore

    D. BigQuery

7. A company wants to migrate its on-premises Oracle database to Google Cloud while minimizing application changes. The company requires full control over the underlying hardware and software stack to meet specific security and compliance requirements. Which Google Cloud deployment option is the most suitable for this scenario?

    A. Cloud SQL

    B. Bare Metal Solution (BMS)

    C. Compute Engine

    D. Google Kubernetes Engine (GKE)

8. Your team needs to build a data warehouse to store and analyze vast amounts of sales data. They require a highly scalable and cost-effective solution that offers SQL support and seamless integration with Google's machine learning services. Which Google Cloud service is best suited for this scenario?

    A. Cloud Bigtable

    B. BigQuery

    C. Cloud Spanner

    D. AlloyDB

9. You are developing a social media application that requires storing user profiles, posts, and comments in a flexible and scalable manner. Which Google Cloud database service is the most appropriate choice for this scenario?

    A. Cloud SQL

    B. Cloud Spanner

    C. Cloud Firestore

    D. BigQuery

10. A company wants to move its existing MongoDB database to a managed service on Google Cloud. They are looking for a service that provides easy setup, automatic scaling, and a high level of availability. Which deployment option is the best fit for this scenario?

    A. Cloud SQL

    B. MongoDB Atlas on Google Cloud

    C. Bare Metal Solution (BMS)

    D. Compute Engine

11. You are building an e-commerce application that requires strong ACID properties, data integrity, and the ability to scale to handle peak traffic during shopping seasons. Which Google Cloud database service is the most suitable choice for this use case?

    A. Cloud Bigtable

    B. BigQuery

    C. Cloud Firestore

    D. Cloud SQL

12. An application development team is building a web app that requires low-latency data access for caching, session management, and real-time data processing. The team prefers a fully managed service with high performance and minimal operational overhead. Which Google Cloud service best fits these requirements?

    A. Memorystore

    B. Cloud SQL

    C. Cloud Spanner

    D. BigQuery

13. A company's database needs have outgrown its existing Cloud SQL deployment. They are seeking a Google-managed, PostgreSQL-compatible database service for both high-performance transactional workloads and analytical queries. Which service best addresses these requirements?

    A. AlloyDB

    B. Cloud Spanner

    C. Cloud Bigtable

    D. BigQuery

14. You need to build an application that requires a globally distributed database with strong consistency and low latency for users around the world. Which Google Cloud database service is the best fit for this use case?

    A. Cloud SQL

    B. Cloud Spanner

    C. Cloud Firestore

    D. BigQuery

15. A team is building a real-time analytics dashboard to track sensor data from IoT devices. They need a database that offers high throughput, low latency, and the ability to handle massive amounts of time-series data. Which Google Cloud database service is the best choice for this use case?

A. Cloud SQL

B. Cloud Bigtable

C. Cloud Spanner

D. BigQuery

16. A company is migrating a legacy application to Google Cloud and needs to choose a database solution. The application requires a specific version of MySQL that is not supported by Cloud SQL. Which Google Cloud deployment option offers the most flexibility in terms of database engine choices?

A. Bare Metal Solution (BMS)

B. Compute Engine

C. Google Kubernetes Engine (GKE)

D. Cloud SQL

17. A development team is building a microservices-based application on Google Kubernetes Engine (GKE) and needs a database solution that seamlessly integrates with their existing infrastructure. They are comfortable managing the database deployment lifecycle and require a high degree of customization. Which Google Cloud deployment option is most suitable for this scenario?

A. Cloud SQL

B. MongoDB Atlas on Google Cloud

C. Bare Metal Solution (BMS)

D. Google Kubernetes Engine (GKE)

18. A company is designing a new application and wants to choose between Cloud Firestore and Firebase Realtime Database. Their data structure is expected to be simple and flat, and real-time updates are a primary requirement. Which service is a more appropriate choice for this specific use case?

A. Cloud Firestore in Native Mode

B. Cloud Firestore in Datastore Mode

C. Firebase Realtime Database

D. Cloud Datastore

19. You are migrating an Oracle database to Google Cloud and want to simplify the process while leveraging your existing Google Cloud commitments. You also want access to unified support from both Google Cloud and Oracle. Which Google Cloud option best addresses these requirements?

   A. Oracle on Google Compute Engine

   B. Oracle on Bare Metal Solution (BMS)

   C. Oracle Databases@Google Cloud

   D. OCI and Google Cross-Cloud Interconnect

20. What distinguishes Google-managed databases from unmanaged databases on Google Cloud?

   A. Google-managed databases offer autoscaling and automated backups, while unmanaged databases provide complete control over server configuration.

   B. Google-managed databases are hosted on Google's infrastructure, while unmanaged databases utilize third-party data centers.

   C. Google-managed databases primarily use NoSQL engines, while unmanaged databases support only SQL engines.

   D. Google-managed databases are generally more expensive than unmanaged databases due to licensing fees.

Database Capacity and Usage Planning

GOOGLE CLOUD CERTIFIED PROFESSIONAL CLOUD DATABASE ENGINEER EXAM OBJECTIVES COVERED IN THIS CHAPTER:

✔ **1.1 Analyze relevant variables to perform database capacity and usage planning.**

- Perform solution sizing based on current environment workload metrics and future requirements.
- Size database compute and storage based on performance requirements.

✔ **1.4 Evaluate appropriate database solutions on Google Cloud.**

- Analyze the cost of running database solutions in Google Cloud (comparative analysis).
- Assess application and database dependencies.

For a Google Cloud Professional Database Engineer, the ability to accurately analyze workloads, forecast future needs, and translate those requirements into a right-sized and cost-effective Google Cloud solution is a fundamental skill. A database that is too small will fail under load, leading to outages and poor user experiences. A database that is too large will incur unnecessary costs, wasting valuable budget.

This chapter focuses on the methodologies for assessing current database workloads and planning for future requirements. To provide a structured approach, we will use the framework of the Google Cloud Implementation Methodology. We will explore how to perform solution sizing by analyzing key metrics during the Assess phase and how to design and cost the solution in the Plan phase. This will enable you to make informed decisions that balance performance, scalability, and budget.

The Google Cloud Implementation Methodology

The Google Cloud Implementation Methodology provides a structured, iterative framework to guide database migrations and deployments in Google Cloud. It prioritizes minimizing risks, reducing errors, and ensuring a smooth transition with minimal disruption to your business operations. It consists of four key phases: assess, plan, deploy, and optimize.

Assess Phase: Understanding the Current State

The assess phase is vital for a successful Google Cloud project. It involves thoroughly understanding your existing applications, their dependencies, and their performance requirements. This knowledge provides a clear picture of your current environment and serves as the foundation for planning and executing a successful migration.

Inventory Applications

To effectively scope a migration, you must first understand the complete inventory of your current environment. This includes applications, their underlying technologies, and their hardware configurations. Building this inventory can be a challenging task, but it is essential for identifying all the elements critical to a successful migration.

Acme Corp. Application Inventory

The Acme team creates an inventory to catalog their systems (Table 4.1). This gives them a high-level view of the applications that are reliant on the databases and provides a baseline for sizing cloud services.

TABLE 4.1   Application inventory

Name	Technologies	Dependencies	System resources requirements
E-commerce Platform	Custom-built, MySQL	MySQL database, payment gateway	8 CPU cores, 32 GB of RAM
Inventory Management	Proprietary app, Oracle	Oracle database, E-commerce platform	32 CPU cores, 128 GB of RAM
Customer Relationship Mgt.	Proprietary app, PostgreSQL	PostgreSQL database, marketing tools	16 CPU cores, 32 GB of RAM
Clickstream Analytics	Flat Files	None	4 CPU cores, 16 GB of RAM

Map Dependencies

A dependency map goes a level deeper, identifying the specific relationships between systems. This is critical for understanding the potential impact of a migration. Moving a central database without understanding its dependencies can cause a cascade of failures in other applications.

Acme Corp. Dependency Map

The team creates a detailed map to understand which systems would be affected by their migration plans (Table 4.2).

TABLE 4.2 Dependency map

Dependency type	Dependent component	Dependent on	Notes
Application-to-Database	E-commerce Platform	MySQL	Stores product catalogs, orders, payments.
Application-to-Database	Inventory Management	Oracle	Manages inventory data.
Application-to-Application	E-commerce Platform	Inventory Management	E-commerce platform retrieves inventory data for order fulfillment.
Database-to-Database	MySQL	Oracle	MySQL references Oracle data for inventory during order fulfillment.

Build an Application Catalog

With inventory and dependency data, you can categorize applications based on their importance, complexity, and dependencies. This helps prioritize the migration effort and identify potential challenges early on.

Acme Corp. Application Catalog

The team summarizes their findings into a catalog to prioritize migrations and flag potential difficulties (Table 4.3).

TABLE 4.3   Application catalog

	Has dependencies	Difficulty
Mission Critical		
E-commerce Platform	Yes	Hard
Inventory Management	Yes	Hard
Customer Relationship Mgt.	Yes	Medium
Non–Mission Critical		
Clickstream Analytics	No	Easy

Assess Data

The next crucial step involves a thorough assessment of the data itself. This analysis focuses on key characteristics like size, structure, quality, and sensitivity. Understanding data structure (structured, unstructured, semi-structured) is critical for choosing the right Google Cloud database solution. Assessing data quality is paramount to ensure that you are not migrating inconsistencies or inaccuracies into the new environment.

Acme Corp. Data Assessment

While assessing the Clickstream Analytics data, the Acme team discovers the data is stored in inconsistent flat file formats (some CSV, some JSON). They decide that a data cleansing and transformation step will be required during the migration to standardize the data before loading it into BigQuery for analysis. This prevents issues with querying the data in the target environment.

Understand Business Requirements

Finally, it is essential to understand the business goals and objectives that the migration is intended to achieve. This involves clarifying desired business outcomes with stakeholders, including performance targets (query response times), uptime expectations (SLAs), security needs, and any compliance requirements (like GDPR or HIPAA) that the new database environment must meet.

Acme Corp. Business Requirements

The Acme leadership team tells the database engineer that a key business goal is to reduce operational overhead by 25 percent. This requirement directly influences the choice of database solution. The engineer will prioritize fully managed services like AlloyDB or Cloud SQL over a self-managed database on a Compute Engine VM, as the managed options offload tasks like patching, backups, and scaling, thus contributing directly to the cost-reduction goal.

Gathering Current Environment Workload Metrics

To properly size a new database environment in Google Cloud, you must first benchmark your existing system. This involves collecting key performance and usage metrics over a representative period, ensuring you capture daily, weekly, and monthly cycles, as well as peak-load events.

Key metrics to collect include:

Compute Utilization: CPU and RAM usage (average and peak)

Storage Performance: IOPS (input/output operations per second), throughput (MB/s), and latency

Database-Specific Metrics: Queries per second (QPS), active connections, and total storage capacity

Projecting Future Requirements

Sizing for today's workload is not enough. You must also account for future growth by collaborating with business and application teams to understand their roadmap.

Consider the following factors for your forecast:

Business Growth: Projected increases in users or sales volume

Application Roadmap: New features that may change data volume or query patterns

Data Growth Trends: Historical data growth rates

Seasonality: Predictable peaks in traffic (e.g., retail holidays)

By combining current metrics with future projections, you can create a comprehensive profile of the workload your new database must support over its lifecycle.

Sizing Based on Future Requirements

The Acme Corp. business team informs the database engineer that they project a 50 percent increase in online sales over the next 18 months due to an international expansion. The engineer analyzes the current e-commerce database workload (500 GB, growing at 20 GB/month) and combines it with the business forecast.

Current 18-month growth: 20 GB/month × 18 months = 360 GB
Projected size without expansion: 500 GB + 360 GB = 860 GB
Additional growth from expansion (50%): 860 GB × 0.50 = 430 GB
Total projected size: 860 GB + 430 GB = 1290 GB

Based on this analysis, the engineer plans for at least 1.5 TB of storage to accommodate the projected growth and provide a safe buffer of 10–15 percent. They also note that the increased user traffic will require a more scalable compute solution, making a service like Cloud Spanner or AlloyDB a better long-term fit than a single Cloud SQL instance that would require manual resizing.

This calculation assumes linear growth. Real-world growth patterns may vary due to data compression, archiving policies, and usage changes.

Plan Phase: Designing the Future State

With a thorough understanding of your existing environment and goals, you can now develop a detailed plan. This phase involves designing the future state architecture, choosing migration approaches, sizing the solution, estimating costs, and addressing potential roadblocks.

Sizing Database Compute and Storage

With a clear understanding of your performance requirements from the Assess phase, you can now translate them into specific Google Cloud resources. This involves selecting the right machine types and storage options.

Sizing Compute Resources (vCPU and RAM)

In Google Cloud, compute resources for managed databases like Cloud SQL and AlloyDB are defined by the number of virtual CPUs (vCPUs) and the amount of RAM.

vCPUs: The number of vCPUs directly impacts the database's ability to handle concurrent queries and perform CPU-intensive operations.

RAM: Memory is critical for database performance, as it is used for caching frequently accessed data (the buffer pool), reducing the need for slower disk I/O.

When sizing compute, you cannot always do a direct 1:1 mapping from an on-premises environment. Google Cloud's modern infrastructure and managed database optimizations can often deliver better performance on smaller machine sizes.

Sizing Storage (Type and Capacity)

Choosing the right storage is a balance between performance (IOPS and throughput) and cost.

SSD Persistent Disk: The standard choice for most database workloads.

Balanced Persistent Disk: A lower-cost option for less intensive workloads.

Hyperdisk: Offers the highest levels of IOPS and throughput for the most demanding enterprise workloads.

To size storage:

Determine Performance Needs: Use the IOPS and throughput metrics you collected. For persistent disks, performance scales with the size of the disk.

Calculate Capacity: Start with your current storage footprint, add a buffer for overhead, and apply your data growth projections.

Sizing Based on Performance Requirements

Acme's on-premises Inventory Management System is an OLTP workload with a critical performance requirement: It must sustain 35,000 write IOPS during peak restocking events. The database engineer evaluates storage options for a Cloud SQL for PostgreSQL migration:

SSD Persistent Disk: Performance scales with size. To achieve 35,000 write IOPS, they would need to provision a disk of approximately 1,200 GB (since SSDs provide 30 write IOPS per GB).

The engineer concludes that a 1.2 TB SSD Persistent Disk is the correct choice. Even if the database itself only contains 400 GB of data, they must provision the larger disk size specifically to meet the IOPS performance requirement. This demonstrates a scenario where performance, not capacity, is the primary driver for storage sizing.

Analyzing Costs of Google Cloud Database Solutions

After sizing the technical resources, a key responsibility is to evaluate solutions on cost. The Google Cloud Pricing Calculator is an indispensable tool for this analysis.

When estimating costs, you must consider several factors:

Compute: Billed per vCPU-hour and GB-hour of RAM.

Storage: Billed per GB-month for the storage you provision.

High Availability (HA): Configuring a database for HA (with a standby instance) can significantly impact cost.

Networking: Data egress (traffic leaving Google Cloud) incurs costs.

Backups: You are charged for the storage consumed by your database backups.

Licensing: For services like Bare Metal Solution for Oracle, you must factor in license costs. License costs refer to the right to use the database software itself.

Comparative Cost Analysis

For Acme's CRM migration, the team performs a comparative analysis between two fully PostgreSQL-compatible managed services: Cloud SQL for PostgreSQL and AlloyDB for PostgreSQL (Table 4.4).

Scenario:
Workload: Acme's CRM database
Sizing: 8 vCPU, 64 GB RAM, 250 GB Storage
Requirement: High Availability (HA) configuration
Region: us-central1

TABLE 4.4   Comparative cost analysis

Cost component	Cloud SQL for PostgreSQL (HA)	AlloyDB for PostgreSQL (HA)	Notes
Primary Instance	~$1.15/hour (8 vCPU, 64 GB RAM)	~$1.15/hour (8 vCPU, 64 GB RAM)	Compute costs for the primary instance are often comparable.
HA Standby Instance	~$1.15/hour (8 vCPU, 64 GB RAM)	N/A (Included in primary cost)	Key difference: Cloud SQL HA provisions a separate standby instance. AlloyDB's architecture includes HA capabilities in its base pricing model, though specific configurations may vary.

(Continued)

TABLE 4.4   (Continued)

Cost component	Cloud SQL for PostgreSQL (HA)	AlloyDB for PostgreSQL (HA)	Notes
Storage	~$0.17/GB-month × 250 GB × 2 (for HA) = ~$85/month	~$0.25/GB-month × 250 GB = ~$62.50/month	AlloyDB's storage is priced differently and is inherently regional, so you don't pay double for HA storage.
Estimated Monthly	~$1,753 (Compute) + ~$85 (Storage) = ~$1,838	~$835 (Compute) + ~$62.50 (Storage) = ~$897.50	Estimates are illustrative. Use the official Pricing Calculator for exact figures.

In this HA scenario, AlloyDB is significantly more cost-effective primarily because its architecture does not require a full-priced standby instance for high availability. This type of comparative analysis is crucial for making a sound recommendation.

Develop a Rollback Plan

Even with meticulous planning, unforeseen issues can arise. A robust rollback plan provides a safety net, outlining a clear, tested strategy to revert to the previous state if necessary. This plan is not an afterthought; it is a critical component of risk management.

Acme Corp. Rollback Plan

For the migration of their PostgreSQL CRM database to AlloyDB using the Database Migration Service (DMS), the Acme team defines a clear rollback plan. Since DMS maintains continuous replication, the on-premises database remains nearly in sync with the AlloyDB instance until the final cutover. Their rollback plan is as follows:

Decision Point: If post-migration testing reveals critical errors within the first 60 minutes, initiate rollback.

Halt Traffic: Immediately stop the application services to prevent further data changes.

Reverse Direction: Point the application's database connection string back to the on-premises PostgreSQL server.

Restart Services: Restart the application services.

Because the on-premises database was kept "warm" via replication, the data is current, and downtime for the rollback is minimized to the time it takes to reconfigure and restart the application. The potential for data loss, though small, occurs with any new data written exclusively to AlloyDB after the final cutover but before the rollback is initiated.

Prepare a Communication Plan

Effective communication is key to managing expectations and ensuring a smooth migration process. A comprehensive communication plan outlines how, when, and what you will communicate to various stakeholders, from technical teams to business leaders.

Acme Corp. Communication Plan

For the CRM migration, the database engineer prepares a targeted communication plan:

- **To IT Leadership (Weekly Email):** High-level status updates, progress against milestones, and budget tracking.
- **To Application Development Teams (Daily Standup & Chat Channel):** Detailed technical timeline, code freeze reminders, and coordination for testing cycles.
- **To Business Stakeholders (Marketing & Sales Teams) (Pre- and Post-Migration Emails):** Announce the scheduled maintenance window (e.g., Saturday, 2–4 a.m.), explain the expected benefits (e.g., faster report generation), and provide contact information for post-migration support.

Deploy Phase: Executing the Plan

The Deploy phase is where the carefully crafted migration plan is put into action. This phase requires careful orchestration of several key activities to build the new environment, move the data, and validate the result.

Set Up Google Cloud Resources

This is the foundational step where you lay the groundwork for your new database environment. It involves creating Google Cloud projects, configuring network settings, and provisioning the chosen database service with the configurations determined during the Plan phase.

Acme Corp. Resource Setup

Following their plan, the Acme team creates a new Google Cloud project named acme-crm-prod. Within this project, they configure a VPC network with specific firewall rules to only allow traffic from their application servers. They then provision an AlloyDB for PostgreSQL instance, ensuring they select the us-central1 region and enable the High Availability option.

Automate Deployments

To ensure the deployment process is smooth and repeatable, you should automate it using infrastructure as code (IaC) tools like Terraform. Describing your infrastructure in code creates a reliable, version-controlled process that minimizes configuration drift.

Acme Corp. IaC

Instead of manually clicking through the Google Cloud console, the Acme team uses Terraform to define their AlloyDB instance, VPC network, and firewall rules. This code is stored in a Git repository. When they need to create a similar staging environment for testing, they can reuse the same Terraform code, ensuring consistency.

Migrate Data

This is the heart of the deployment phase. For near-zero downtime migrations of compatible databases, the Google Database Migration Service (DMS) is a powerful, fully managed tool that automates many complex tasks, including continuous replication and data validation.

Acme Corp. Data Migration

For the CRM migration, the Acme team configures a DMS migration job. They monitor the replication lag in the DMS console. Once it is near zero, they schedule a brief maintenance window to stop the source application, allow DMS to replicate the final transactions, and then point the application to the new AlloyDB instance.

Configure Security

Security must be integrated throughout the deployment. A key principle is least privilege, granting only the access absolutely necessary for each user and service account. Leverage features like customer-managed encryption keys (CMEK) and the Cloud SQL Auth Proxy for secure connections.

Acme Corp. Security Configuration

The Acme team creates a dedicated IAM service account for their CRM application and grants it only the "Cloud AlloyDB Client" role (`roles/alloydb.client`). For the AlloyDB instance, they configure a CMEK using a key they manage in Cloud KMS. All connections from the application to the database are routed through the Cloud SQL Auth Proxy, which handles authentication and encryption automatically.

Test the New Environment

Testing is a critical phase to validate that the migrated system meets all operational requirements. This is a comprehensive process covering functionality, performance, and data integrity.

Acme Corp. Testing

After the CRM data migration, the Acme QA team runs a suite of automated tests. They verify functionality, run scripts to compare row counts and checksums for data integrity, and use a load testing tool to simulate 500 concurrent users to validate performance against the targets defined in the Assess phase.

Optimize Phase: Continuous Improvement

The optimization phase begins after the initial deployment and continues as an iterative process of refining and enhancing the migrated environment to maximize performance, cost efficiency, and business value.

Monitor Performance and Costs

Monitoring the performance and costs of your migrated databases is critical for ensuring they run smoothly, efficiently, and affordably. Use Cloud Monitoring to track key metrics like CPU usage and query latency. Use Cloud Billing reports to analyze spending patterns and identify cost-saving opportunities.

Acme Corp. Performance Monitoring

Two weeks after migrating the CRM database to AlloyDB, the Acme team notices in Cloud Monitoring that the CPU utilization for the instance has never exceeded 30 percent, even during peak business hours. They also receive a rightsizing recommendation from the Google Cloud Recommender service suggesting a smaller instance size.

Fine-Tune Configurations

Fine-tuning is a crucial step toward maximizing performance and minimizing costs. This involves analyzing performance data from tools like Cloud Monitoring and Cloud Logging, understanding usage patterns, and making informed adjustments to database configurations and scaling options. This is an iterative process: monitor, analyze, adjust, and repeat.

Acme Corp. Fine-Tuning

Based on the monitoring data and the rightsizing recommendation, the Acme team schedules a maintenance window to change their AlloyDB instance from an 8-vCPU machine to a 4-vCPU machine. This change reduces their compute costs by nearly 50 percent with no impact on application performance, directly contributing to their business goal of reducing operational overhead.

Implement Automation

Automating routine tasks like backups, patching, and scaling is crucial for reducing operational overhead and ensuring the ongoing health of your database. Rely on the managed features for scheduled backups, point-in-time recovery (PITR), and the automated replication and failover mechanisms built into services like Cloud SQL and AlloyDB.

Acme Corp. Automation

The Acme team configures their AlloyDB instance to take automatic daily backups at 1 a.m., with a retention policy of 14 days. This automated approach ensures they can recover from data loss or corruption with minimal manual effort, freeing up the database team to focus on more strategic initiatives.

Leverage Cloud-Native Features

Explore and adopt cloud-native features to further enhance your database environment. Managed backups, robust disaster recovery solutions, and integrated machine learning capabilities can significantly improve efficiency and provide deeper insights.

Acme Corp. Leveraging Cloud-Native Features

The Acme marketing team wants to analyze customer purchasing patterns stored in the newly migrated CRM database. Instead of building a complex ETL pipeline, the database team uses the built-in integration between AlloyDB and Vertex AI. This allows them to run machine learning models directly on their transactional data to generate customer segments for targeted marketing campaigns, unlocking new business value from their existing data.

Summary

This chapter walked you through the essential aspects of database capacity and usage planning, framed by the Google Cloud Implementation Methodology. The Assess phase is foundational, requiring a thorough inventory of applications, dependencies, and business requirements, complemented by collecting workload metrics and projecting future growth. In the Plan phase, these findings are translated into a concrete design, where compute and storage are sized based on performance needs, and a comparative cost analysis guides the selection of the most appropriate Google Cloud services. The Deploy phase brings the plan to life through automated, secure, and well-tested processes. Finally, the Optimize phase establishes a continuous cycle of monitoring, fine-tuning, and leveraging cloud-native features to ensure the database solution remains performant and cost-effective over time. Mastering this structured approach is fundamental to designing and managing successful database solutions in Google Cloud.

Exam Essentials

Analyze relevant variables to perform database capacity and usage planning.   Know how to analyze workload metrics like CPU, RAM, IOPS, throughput, and storage consumption from an existing environment.

Understand how to forecast future requirements by considering business growth, application changes, and data trends.

Be able to evaluate the performance and cost trade-offs between different machine types and storage options.

Size database compute and storage based on performance requirements.   Know how to translate workload requirements into vCPU, RAM, and storage resources in Google Cloud.

Understand that managed services like AlloyDB often outperform self-managed databases due to various optimizations that enable smaller instance sizes to handle the same workload efficiently.

Be able to calculate required storage capacity based on current size, growth projections, and operational overhead.

Evaluate appropriate database solutions on Google Cloud.   Understand how to use the Google Cloud Pricing Calculator to analyze the costs of different database solutions.

Be able to perform a comparative cost analysis, considering all components like compute, storage, HA, and networking.

Recognize how architectural differences between services (e.g., Cloud SQL vs. AlloyDB for HA) can lead to significant cost variations.

Review Questions

1. Acme Corp. is migrating its e-commerce platform's transactional database from a single-region MySQL instance to the globally distributed Cloud Spanner. Their primary requirements are to minimize application downtime during the cutover and ensure transactional consistency. Which migration approach best meets these core requirements?

   A. Scheduled maintenance (offline migration)

   B. Continuous replication

   C. Split read/write

   D. Data access microservice (Strangler pattern)

2. During the Assess phase of the Google Cloud Implementation Methodology, what is a crucial first step for a successful database migration?

   A. Designing the target architecture

   B. Estimating migration costs

   C. Building an application catalog

   D. Inventorying applications and mapping dependencies

3. What Google Cloud tool helps estimate the total cost of ownership (TCO) for migrating to Google Cloud?

   A. Cloud Monitoring

   B. Cloud Billing

   C. Google Cloud Pricing Calculator

   D. Cloud Resource Manager

4. Which migration approach is best suited for applications with high downtime tolerance?

   A. Continuous replication

   B. Split read/write

   C. Scheduled maintenance

   D. Data access microservice

5. Acme Corp. wants to migrate its clickstream data (currently flat files) to Google Cloud. What service is best suited for storing and analyzing this data?

   A. Cloud SQL

   B. Cloud Spanner

   C. Cloud Storage and BigQuery

   D. Cloud Datastore

6. What is a crucial aspect of the Plan phase in the Google Cloud Implementation Methodology?

    A. Setting up Google Cloud resources

    B. Migrating data to Google Cloud

    C. Monitoring database performance

    D. Designing the target architecture and choosing a migration approach

7. What Google Cloud service simplifies database migrations to GCP and supports various database engines?

    A. Cloud Resource Manager

    B. Cloud SQL

    C. Cloud Spanner

    D. Google Cloud Database Migration Service (DMS)

8. During the Deploy phase, why is automating deployments crucial?

    A. To reduce the time it takes to migrate the data

    B. To reduce the risk of human error and ensure consistency

    C. To reduce the time it takes to monitor the database

    D. To reduce the amount of security controls required

9. What is a key benefit of using a data access microservice during a database migration?

    A. It simplifies the migration process and can enable seamless transition between database systems while keeping clients unaware of changes.

    B. It ensures that all data is migrated correctly.

    C. It speeds up the data migration process significantly.

    D. It automatically handles all security configurations.

10. The Optimize phase focuses on what key aspects of a database environment?

    A. Initial infrastructure setup

    B. Data migration and validation

    C. Monitoring performance and costs, fine-tuning configurations, and implementing automation

    D. Planning the migration approach

11. In the context of database migration, what does a proof-of-concept (PoC) help validate?

    A. The chosen architecture and migration approach

    B. The final cost of the migration

    C. The team's ability to use Google Cloud

    D. The application's scalability

12. Which Google Cloud service is particularly useful for analyzing large datasets like clickstream data?

A. Cloud Storage

B. Cloud SQL

C. Cloud Spanner

D. BigQuery

13. During the Optimize phase, what is a key strategy for reducing database load and improving read speeds?

A. Reducing the number of database instances

B. Implementing caching strategies

C. Increasing the size of database instances

D. Decreasing the amount of data stored

14. What does infrastructure as code (IaC) provide for database deployments?

A. Easier monitoring

B. More manual configuration options

C. Consistency and repeatability

D. Increased security vulnerabilities

15. What is a critical step to take after deploying a migrated database?

A. Immediately begin the optimization phase.

B. Stop monitoring the database environment.

C. Thoroughly test the new environment for functionality, performance, and data integrity.

D. Ignore the existing disaster recovery plan.

16. What is the best approach to identify potential migration challenges in the early stages of a cloud migration project?

A. Assume everything will go smoothly and just proceed with the migration.

B. Conduct a proof-of-concept (PoC).

C. Wait until the deployment phase to identify issues.

D. Migrate a small portion of the data and hope for the best.

17. Which Google Cloud service allows you to schedule tasks and workflows for automated database maintenance?

A. Cloud Monitoring

B. Cloud Logging

C. Cloud Scheduler

D. Cloud Composer

18. When evaluating database solutions on Google Cloud, what factors should be considered, besides cost?

   A. Only the type of database

   B. Only scalability

   C. Application and database dependencies, performance expectations, and compliance requirements

   D. Nothing else

19. What strategy helps ensure business continuity in case of a primary database instance failure?

   A. Regularly backing up the data

   B. Implementing automated replication and failover mechanisms

   C. Manually switching over to a standby instance

   D. Point-in-time recovery (PITR)

20. In the Assess phase, what is meant by "mapping dependencies"?

   A. Identifying which developers worked on which components of the system

   B. Documenting relationships between applications, databases, and other infrastructure components

   C. Identifying which operating system is used for each system

   D. Checking the database version number

Designing for High Availability and Disaster Recovery

GOOGLE CLOUD CERTIFIED PROFESSIONAL CLOUD DATABASE ENGINEER EXAM OBJECTIVES COVERED IN THIS CHAPTER:

✔ **1.2 Evaluate database high availability and disaster recovery options given the requirements.**

- Evaluate tradeoffs between multi-regional, regional, and zonal database deployment strategies.

- Define maintenance windows and notifications based on application availability requirements.

✔ **2.3 Design database backup and recovery solutions.**

- Design for RTO, RPO, and PITR.

For business-critical cloud applications, ensuring continuous data accessibility, consistency, and security is paramount, even in the face of unforeseen events. This chapter details how to architect resilient database solutions within Google Cloud, focusing on their ability to withstand failures and meet stringent uptime requirements. We will explore various strategies, principles, and practical considerations—from fundamental deployment choices like regional versus multiregional deployments and the use of managed services, to intricate backup and recovery methodologies, including point-in-time recovery and snapshotting, and advanced concepts like data replication and failover mechanisms. All these elements are designed to build a robust and resilient data foundation for your applications.

Building a Resilient E-Commerce Architecture on Google Cloud

Consider a large e-commerce platform processing millions of transactions daily. A sudden, unexpected outage in a single data center could cripple operations, leading to significant financial losses and reputational damage. However, by architecting a resilient database solution across multiple Google Cloud regions, implementing automated failover, and regularly practicing disaster recovery drills, this platform can ensure that even if one region experiences a complete failure, customer orders continue to flow seamlessly, data remains consistent, and sensitive information stays secure. This proactive approach transforms potential catastrophe into a minor blip, safeguarding both business continuity and customer trust.

Evaluating Database High Availability and Disaster Recovery Options

High availability (HA) and disaster recovery (DR) are two cornerstones of resilient system architecture, often discussed together due to their shared goal of ensuring business continuity. However, it is crucial to understand that while complementary, they address distinct types of failures and possess differing objectives.

High availability primarily focuses on minimizing downtime and ensuring continuous operational capability during localized disruptions. Such events might include common occurrences such as the failure of a single server, a software malfunction, or even a power outage affecting a specific rack or zone within a data center. The goal of HA is to keep the system running with minimal interruption, often through redundancy and automatic failover mechanisms.

In contrast, disaster recovery is concerned with the ability to recover from large-scale, catastrophic events that extend beyond localized failures and could impact an entire geographical region. Such disasters might encompass natural calamities like earthquakes, floods, or widespread service disruptions that render an entire Google Cloud region inaccessible. DR strategies are designed to bring systems back online in a different, unaffected location, often with a greater tolerance for initial downtime but with the ultimate aim of restoring full operational capability.

Table 5.1 outlines the primary characteristics of HA and DR.

Google Cloud, recognizing the critical importance of these concepts, offers a comprehensive suite of deployment strategies and built-in features across its managed database services. These offerings are meticulously engineered to help organizations achieve varying levels of HA and DR, allowing for a tailored approach based on specific application requirements for uptime, data consistency guarantees, and, crucially, cost-effectiveness. The selection among these options necessitates a thorough understanding of their inherent capabilities and the trade-offs involved.

TABLE 5.1   Comparing HA and DR

Feature	High availability (HA)	Disaster recovery (DR)
Primary Goal	Minimize downtime; ensure continuous operation	Recover from catastrophic, widespread failures
Scope of Failure	Localized (e.g., server, rack, zone outage)	Widespread (e.g., regional outage, natural disaster)
Recovery Time	Seconds to minutes (often automated failover) Example RTO: <1 minute	Minutes to hours (can involve manual intervention) Example RTO: <4 hours
Data Loss	Typically zero (synchronous replication)	Minimal to some (asynchronous replication, RPO defined)
Mechanisms	Redundancy, automatic failover, within-region replication	Cross-region replication, backups, separate recovery sites
Cost	Moderate to High	High to Very High

Evaluating Trade-offs Between Multiregional, Regional, and Zonal Deployment Strategies

When designing a highly available database solution on Google Cloud, a foundational understanding of zonal, regional, and multiregional deployments is essential. Each paradigm presents a unique combination of advantages and disadvantages for resilience, performance, and cost.

Zonal Deployment

Zonal deployment represents the most fundamental level of database instance placement within Google Cloud. In this configuration, your database instance is deployed entirely within a single Google Cloud zone, which is an isolated location within a region. This setup inherently provides a degree of protection against localized failures such as individual server hardware malfunctions, software crashes on a specific virtual machine, or even isolated power outages affecting a particular rack or segment within that zone's data center. However, the high availability offered by a purely zonal deployment is inherently limited. Should the entire zone experience a widespread outage—perhaps due to a significant network disruption or a large-scale power failure impacting the entire zone—your database would become entirely unavailable, leading to significant downtime.

While some managed services, notably Cloud SQL, allow for enhanced zonal resilience by enabling you to configure a failover replica in a *different* zone within the *same* region, thereby protecting against a single zonal failure, a stand-alone zonal deployment offers minimal inherent disaster recovery capabilities against such a comprehensive zonal outage. The primary advantages of opting for a zonal deployment are its comparatively lowest cost, as it requires fewer duplicated resources, and its lowest network latency for applications that are also deployed within the same zone. This co-location can be crucial for performance-sensitive workloads. Conversely, its most significant drawback is the existence of a single point of failure at the zonal level. This inherent vulnerability makes a purely zonal strategy generally unsuitable for mission-critical applications that demand continuous operation and that have stringent uptime requirements. Consequently, this strategy is typically best suited for development and testing environments, or for applications with less demanding recovery time objective (RTO) and recovery point objective (RPO) requirements that can genuinely tolerate significant periods of downtime.

Regional Deployment

Regional deployment elevates the level of resilience by distributing the database service across multiple distinct zones within a single Google Cloud region. This architectural pattern typically employs synchronous replication of data between these zones. This means that a transaction is considered committed only after it has been successfully written to the primary instance and at least one replica in another zone, ensuring that all data is consistent across these zones. In the highly critical event of a zonal failure, where an entire zone becomes unavailable, the system is designed to automatically detect this outage and seamlessly reroute application traffic to a healthy, operational zone where a replica can be promoted to become the new primary. This mechanism ensures continuous operation with minimal disruption. This configuration provides a high level of high availability, offering robust resilience against zonal outages, with the synchronous data replication guaranteeing strong consistency and, crucially, zero data loss upon failover.

However, it is important to acknowledge that while highly resilient against zonal failures, regional deployment offers limited disaster recovery capabilities against region-wide disasters. A complete outage affecting the entire Google Cloud region—perhaps due to a widespread natural disaster or a major regional network disruption—would still impact the database, as all components reside within that single geographical boundary.

The benefits of regional deployment are substantial: excellent high availability within a region, strong consistency guarantees, and automatic failover, often with lower latency compared to multiregion setups due to the closer proximity of zones within a region. The trade-offs include a higher cost than purely zonal deployments, given the need for duplicated resources and inter-zonal data transfer, and the inherent vulnerability to full regional outages. Despite this, regional deployments are widely considered ideal for the vast majority of production-grade applications that demand high availability and strong consistency within a defined geographical area.

Prominent examples of services offering regional high availability include Cloud SQL HA configurations, where a standby instance in another zone is kept in sync; Cloud Spanner regional instances, which distribute data across multiple zonal replicas; and Firestore in Native Mode, which also leverages multizonal replication for resilience.

Multiregional Deployment

Multiregional deployment represents the pinnacle of resilience for database services, involving the distribution of data and infrastructure across two or more geographically distinct Google Cloud regions. This advanced configuration frequently leverages asynchronous replication between regions, where data is copied from the primary region to secondary regions with a slight delay. This approach prioritizes performance and allows for greater geographical separation.

Certain mission-critical services, most notably Cloud Spanner, provide synchronous multiregion options, ensuring strong global consistency by requiring transactions to be committed across multiple regions before acknowledgment, albeit with higher latency. This multiregion strategy delivers exceptionally high availability, offering robust resilience against catastrophic regional outages. If one region becomes entirely unavailable due to a widespread disaster, the application can seamlessly fail over to a database instance in another, unaffected region, providing unparalleled disaster recovery capabilities designed to withstand the most severe disruptions.

However, multiregional deployments come with the highest cost of the three types, primarily due to the significant increase in infrastructure duplication, the complexity of managing distributed systems, and substantial data transfer costs between regions. It is worth noting that for Cloud Spanner, the cost of this inter-region replication is factored into the service's pricing, which can simplify cost management compared to other solutions. Multiregional deployments also inherently introduce higher data latency because of the geographical distances involved, a factor particularly pronounced with synchronous replication across continents. Synchronous multiregion setups like Cloud Spanner can see tens to hundreds of milliseconds added to write latency depending on region distance. Asynchronous replication, while offering improved performance, carries the potential for eventual consistency, meaning there might be a small window of potential data loss during a failover if the primary region fails before all transactions have been replicated to the secondary.

Designing applications for effective multiregion failover can add considerable complexity, requiring careful consideration of global load balancing, data consistency models, and application re-pointing mechanisms. Despite these complexities and costs, this strategy is typically reserved for the most mission-critical global applications with extremely stringent uptime requirements and minimal tolerance for data loss, such as global financial trading systems, large-scale e-commerce platforms, or critical government services.

Cloud Spanner multiregion instances, with their unique global consistency guarantees, are a prime example, as are custom solutions built with services like Cloud SQL read replicas deployed across different regions to serve as disaster recovery targets.

When evaluating these deployment strategies, you must understand the distinct paths to high availability and disaster recovery offered by different Google Cloud database services. For Cloud SQL, the journey toward resilience is a progression: a basic zonal instance, while offering protection against single server failures, provides no automatic failover in the event of a full zonal outage. To achieve high availability, a regional (HA) Cloud SQL instance is deployed, which provides automatic failover across zones within a single region. This ensures that if the primary zone becomes unavailable, the database seamlessly switches to a standby in another zone, minimizing downtime and achieving strong consistency.

For true disaster recovery against a regional failure, a cross-region replica is required. Promoting a cross-region replica is a manual process that involves a brief outage. Because the replication is asynchronous, a small amount of data loss is possible due to replication lag. When a failover is initiated, the replica is promoted to become a new, stand-alone primary instance, offering protection against widespread regional disasters.

In contrast, Cloud Spanner offers a fundamentally unified and integrated model for resilience. A regional Spanner instance is inherently highly available by design, distributing data synchronously across multiple zones within that region and automatically handling zonal failures without manual intervention or application-visible downtime. This built-in multizonal architecture means that a regional Spanner instance already provides the level of availability that Cloud SQL achieves with its HA configuration. To reach the highest tier of availability and built-in, automated disaster recovery capabilities, a multiregion Spanner instance is deployed. This configuration synchronously replicates data across multiple geographically distant regions, providing an industry-leading 99.999 percent availability SLA and automated failover in the event of a full regional outage, making it the go-to choice for global, mission-critical workloads with the most stringent uptime and data consistency requirements.

TABLE 5.2   Summary of deployment strategies

Strategy	Scope of protection	Data consistency on failover	Latency	Cost	Availability SLA (typical)	Google Cloud example services
Zonal	Instance	Strong	Lowest	Lowest	~99.95%	Basic Cloud SQL instance
Regional	Zonal	Strong	Medium	Medium	99.95%–99.99%	Cloud SQL with HA, AlloyDB, Regional Spanner
Multiregional	Regional	Strong (synchronous) / Eventual (asynchronous)	Highest	Highest	99.99%–99.999%	Multiregion Spanner, Bigtable with multicluster routing

Table 5.2 compares the zonal, regional, and multiregional deployment strategies discussed in this chapter.

When interpreting the table, it's important to note a few distinctions. The "Strong" consistency for zonal and regional strategies refers to transactional consistency within a single region, ensuring that failovers (like with Cloud SQL HA) do not result in data loss. For a multiregion synchronous service like Cloud Spanner, this is elevated to strong global consistency, guaranteeing transactional integrity across geographic regions. Similarly, while Bigtable offers a multiregion solution, it's crucial to remember that it provides eventual consistency for writes, making it unsuitable for workloads that require strict, immediate transactional consistency across regions.

Defining Maintenance Windows and Notifications Based on Application Availability

Google Cloud–managed databases, like all sophisticated software and hardware systems, undergo periodic maintenance. This essential process involves applying security patches, rolling out minor and major version updates, performing routine health checks, and optimizing underlying infrastructure.

While Google Cloud's operational teams strive to minimize the impact of these activities, some maintenance operations may, by their very nature, necessitate brief periods of downtime or result in temporary performance degradation. Consequently, defining appropriate maintenance windows and configuring robust notification mechanisms are absolutely critical for effective application availability management and ensuring that these necessary operational tasks align seamlessly with your business's operational requirements and acceptable service levels.

Maintenance Windows

Maintenance windows serve the crucial purpose of scheduling these essential maintenance activities during periods of lowest expected application traffic or minimal business impact. For many managed database services, such as Cloud SQL, you are typically afforded the flexibility to configure a preferred weekly maintenance window. For example, you might specify Tuesday from 2 a.m. to 4 a.m. as your preferred slot. Google Cloud will then endeavor to schedule the maintenance for your instance within this designated timeframe, respecting your operational preferences.

When defining these windows, it is paramount to deeply consider your application's tolerance for downtime. A clear understanding of whether your application can gracefully handle even a few minutes of connection disruption or if it requires near-zero downtime is key to making an informed decision. For global applications serving users across multiple time zones, it becomes vital to account for these different time zones and identify their respective low-traffic periods to minimize disruption across all user bases. This might involve setting different maintenance windows for instances serving different geographical regions.

Furthermore, a critical step in dependency mapping involves identifying all applications and upstream/downstream services that rely on the database. You must then ensure that their maintenance windows align, or, crucially, that these dependent systems are designed with sufficient resilience to gracefully handle temporary database unavailability without cascading failures. This proactive planning prevents unexpected service interruptions for your end users.

Notifications

Notifications are designed to keep administrators, development teams, and relevant business stakeholders promptly informed about upcoming maintenance events, their real-time status, and any potential issues that may arise during or after the maintenance period. To effectively configure these notifications, you should leverage Google Cloud's robust suite of monitoring and logging services, primarily Cloud Monitoring and Cloud Logging. Cloud Monitoring allows you to create custom alerts based on specific database metrics (e.g., CPU utilization, connection count drops) or by parsing logs that explicitly indicate maintenance activities. This provides proactive warnings that can be routed to various channels, such as email, SMS, PagerDuty, or Slack, enabling your team to prepare or react swiftly.

Cloud Logging, on the other hand, captures detailed operational logs. These logs can be configured to export relevant entries related to maintenance events to Pub/Sub topics or Cloud Storage buckets, enabling automated processing by Cloud Functions or other custom scripts for more sophisticated notification workflows. Beyond automated alerts, it is highly advisable to regularly check the Google Cloud Service Health Dashboard. This centralized resource provides real-time updates on the status of all Google Cloud services and announces broader service-wide incidents or planned maintenance that might affect your resources.

Critically, beyond technical configurations, establishing a clear and transparent communication plan for internal teams and, when necessary, external stakeholders (e.g., customers, partners) regarding maintenance schedules and any unexpected outages is paramount. This proactive communication fosters trust, manages expectations, and facilitates effective incident management during critical periods.

Planning Database Upgrades for Google Cloud–Managed Databases

Upgrading database versions (e.g., PostgreSQL 11–12, MySQL 5.7–8.0) is a crucial and continuous part of database life-cycle management. These upgrades are not merely administrative tasks; they are essential for leveraging new features, realizing performance improvements, ensuring compatibility with evolving application frameworks, and, critically, applying essential security patches that protect your data from emerging threats. All these factors contribute significantly to the long-term health, efficiency, and security posture of your database environment.

For Google Cloud–managed databases, the upgrade process can typically be categorized into two main approaches: in-place upgrades, which often require a brief period of downtime, or more involved migration processes that aim to minimize or eliminate service interruption. There are generally two distinct types of upgrades to consider.

Minor Version Upgrades

Minor version upgrades (e.g., from MySQL 5.7.X to 5.7.Y) are handled automatically by Google Cloud within your predefined maintenance window. These updates primarily focus on applying bug fixes, small performance enhancements, and security patches that do not introduce breaking changes.

While Google Cloud manages the complexity of these updates, they do require the instance to be restarted. This results in a short period of downtime, the duration of which depends on factors like the instance configuration and the nature of the patch. For instances configured with HA, this downtime is typically very brief, often lasting less than a minute. Google Cloud manages the complexities of these updates to ensure your database remains secure and performant with minimal operational overhead for you.

Major Version Upgrades

In contrast, Major version upgrades (e.g., PostgreSQL 11–12, MySQL 5.7–8.0) involve significant changes to the database engine, introducing new features, architectural improvements, and sometimes deprecating older functionalities. These upgrades often require more extensive planning and potentially some downtime due to the fundamental changes involved. For services like Cloud SQL, major version upgrades can be performed in-place, which entails a period of unavailability while the upgrade process completes. Alternatively, for applications with stricter uptime requirements, a migration process to a newly provisioned instance running the desired major version can be employed, allowing for a controlled cutover with significantly reduced, or even near-zero, downtime.

When evaluating planning considerations for major upgrades, thorough testing is paramount. You must rigorously test your application with the new database version in a dedicated nonproduction environment that closely mirrors your production setup. This step is critical for identifying any compatibility issues with your application code, detecting potential performance regressions, or uncovering breaking changes in SQL syntax, stored procedures, or driver behavior before they impact your live system.

A robust backup strategy must be in place immediately before initiating the upgrade. This ensures you have a reliable and consistent rollback point in case the upgrade encounters unforeseen issues or if the new version proves incompatible with your application. Evaluating your application's downtime tolerance is also a crucial decision point. For applications with very low downtime tolerance, the strategy of setting up a new database instance with the upgraded version and then migrating your data using specialized replication tools (like logical replication) or export/import utilities can facilitate a controlled cutover with minimal interruption, often measured in seconds or a few minutes. Conversely, for applications that can tolerate a more substantial, but still planned, downtime window, an in-place upgrade might present a simpler and less resource-intensive option.

Comprehensive monitoring should be implemented during and immediately after the upgrade process. This involves tracking key database metrics (e.g., CPU, memory, I/O, active connections, query latency) and application logs to quickly detect any performance degradation, increased error rates, or unexpected behavior. Furthermore, a clear and well-documented rollback plan is essential. This plan should detail the steps to revert to the previous database version, which might involve restoring from a pre-upgrade backup or switching back to a previously maintained replica.

Be prepared to make necessary application code changes to accommodate new features, deprecated functions, or changes in behavior introduced by the new database version; these changes should ideally be tested and deployed concurrently with the database upgrade.

Finally, clear, timely, and transparent communication of the upgrade plan, expected downtime, and potential impact to all internal stakeholders (development, operations, business teams) and, if applicable, external customers, is vital for managing expectations, minimizing disruption, and maintaining trust.

Designing for a Global SaaS Platform

GlobalConnect is a rapidly growing (fictional) software-as-a-service (SaaS) platform that provides real-time collaboration tools for distributed teams worldwide. GlobalConnect's primary database stores critical customer data, project files, and real-time communication logs. The business has ▪ defined strict requirements: a maximum of 5 minutes of downtime per year for any planned or unplanned event (translating to a very high availability target), and an absolute intolerance for data loss, especially for active project data. Furthermore, GlobalConnect serves customers across North America, Europe, and Asia, necessitating low latency for users in each region.

Initially, GlobalConnect deployed its primary database using a Cloud SQL PostgreSQL instance in a regional configuration (HA) in us-central1. This provided excellent high availability against zonal failures within us-central1, ensuring automatic failover to a standby instance in another zone with zero data loss. This met their initial regional HA needs and provided the required strong consistency. However, as GlobalConnect expanded globally, they recognized that a single-region deployment, while resilient to zonal outages, remained vulnerable to a full regional disaster in us-central1. To address this, they established cross-region read replicas in europe-west1 and asia-southeast1. While these replicas provided read-scaling benefits and a disaster recovery target, they operated with asynchronous replication, meaning a small RPO window existed in the event of a primary region failure, and failover would require manual intervention, impacting their RTO.

To meet their evolving global low-latency requirements and the stringent 99.999 percent availability target with zero data loss across regions, GlobalConnect decided to migrate their core transactional database to Cloud Spanner in a multiregion configuration. This allowed them to deploy a single logical database that automatically distributed and synchronously replicated data across us-central1, europe-west1, and asia-southeast1. This design inherently provided automated failover. Zonal failures were handled transparently within seconds. In the rare event of a full regional outage, the system could fail over to another continent in typically under a minute, achieving their aggressive RTO and RPO goals and ensuring strong global consistency. For their less critical, high-volume analytics data, they opted for Bigtable with multicluster routing across the same regions. This leveraged an eventual consistency model for high throughput. If a regional cluster became unavailable, traffic would automatically redirect to the nearest healthy cluster, usually within a few seconds, ensuring high availability for their analytical workloads.

For maintenance, GlobalConnect established distinct maintenance windows for their Cloud Spanner instances in each geographical region, aligning them with the lowest traffic periods for their respective customer bases (e.g., us-central1 maintenance at 2 a.m. EST, europe-west1 at 2 a.m. GMT, asia-southeast1 at 2 a.m. SGT). They configured Cloud Monitoring alerts to notify their SRE team via PagerDuty for any unexpected performance degradation or service health issues during these windows, and also subscribed to Cloud Logging exports to a Pub/Sub topic. This Pub/Sub topic triggered a Cloud Function that automatically posted detailed maintenance notifications to their internal Slack channels, ensuring all relevant development and operations teams were aware of upcoming and in-progress maintenance activities, allowing them to proactively manage application dependencies and communicate with customers if necessary.

Designing Database Backup and Recovery Solutions

A robust backup and recovery solution is the cornerstone of any effective disaster recovery strategy. Its design is inextricably driven by two critical metrics: the recovery time objective (RTO) and the recovery point objective (RPO). These metrics serve as the guiding principles that dictate both the speed with which data must be restored and the maximum acceptable amount of data loss the business can tolerate.

Designing for RTO, RPO, and PITR

Effective disaster recovery planning relies on three primary metrics to balance business requirements against infrastructure costs and technical complexity.

Recovery Time Objective (RTO)

The recovery time objective (RTO) defines the maximum acceptable downtime following an incident, essentially answering the question, "How quickly must we recover?" A low RTO, which indicates a need for rapid recovery, profoundly impacts the design of the solution. It necessitates approaches that enable swift restoration, such as leveraging services with built-in HA and automatic failover like Cloud SQL HA or Cloud Spanner, maintaining warm or hot standbys, and using automated recovery scripts. However, achieving a low RTO almost invariably comes with higher costs due to the required duplicated infrastructure and increased operational complexity.

Recovery Point Objective (RPO)

The recovery point objective (RPO) represents the maximum acceptable amount of data loss, measured in time, that a business can tolerate. It addresses the critical question, "How much data can we afford to lose?" A low RPO, indicating minimal tolerance for data loss, demands solutions designed to minimize this window. This can be achieved through various strategies, including synchronous replication, which provides an RPO of zero (as seen in Cloud SQL HA and Spanner), asynchronous replication, which introduces a small RPO window (common with Cloud SQL cross-region replicas), and frequent backups to reduce the time between recovery points. Similar to RTO, achieving a low RPO often incurs higher costs due to increased replication overhead, network bandwidth consumption, and storage for frequent backups.

Point-in-Time Recovery (PITR)

Point-in-time recovery (PITR) is a powerful capability for protecting against logical data corruption, such as user errors or application bugs. This feature works by combining a full backup with a continuous stream of transaction logs, allowing for the restoration of a database to a specific second within a defined retention period. The management of these logs depends heavily on the environment. In a managed database service like Google Cloud SQL, enabling PITR automatically turns on and configures the required transaction logs for you. In contrast, when enabling PITR in a self-managed instance, you must ensure the correct transaction logs are enabled for your specific database, whether for MySQL, PostgreSQL, or SQL Server. Regardless of the environment, while PITR provides a very low RPO, it is not suitable for all "zero data loss" requirements. For instance, in a catastrophic failure where the most recent logs are also destroyed, some data loss may occur, distinguishing it from true zero-data-loss solutions.

Google Cloud Backup and Recovery Solutions

Google Cloud provides a diverse and robust set of mechanisms to implement comprehensive backup and recovery strategies.

For services like Cloud SQL, managed backups offer a streamlined approach with automated daily backups and the flexibility for on-demand manual backups. This service is the foundation for PITR that allows you to restore a database to a specific second within a retention window, making it invaluable for recovering from user errors.

For databases deployed on Compute Engine, persistent disk snapshots are an efficient, block-level backup method. These snapshots are incremental, saving storage and time, but it is crucial that the database is quiesced before taking a snapshot to ensure data consistency.

Another method is export/import, or logical backups, which involves extracting data into a portable format like SQL or CSV. While excellent for data archival and migration, this method is generally too slow for low RTO/RPO scenarios.

Replication, through read replicas and cross-region replicas, plays a dual role in both high availability and disaster recovery, allowing a replica to be promoted to a primary in case of failure.

Finally, Cloud Spanner is engineered for resilience from the ground up, using synchronous replication across zones and regions to provide extremely low RTO and RPO by design, with automatic failover that is often transparent to the application.

Table 5.3 compares the common backup and recovery solutions on Google Cloud.

Designing Your Backup and Recovery Strategy

Designing an effective backup and recovery strategy requires a systematic, multifaceted approach.

The process begins with defining the RTO and RPO for each application in close collaboration with business stakeholders to understand the true cost of downtime and data loss.

TABLE 5.3   Google Cloud backup and recovery solutions

Solution	Description	Best for/use case	Key consideration
Managed Backups (Cloud SQL)	Automated daily and on-demand full backups of a database instance	General-purpose, reliable data protection for Cloud SQL; foundation for PITR	Retention period for full backups configurable up to 365 days.
Point-in-Time Recovery (PITR)	Restores a database to a specific second by combining a full backup with transaction logs	Recovering from logical errors (e.g., accidental DELETE) with near-zero RPO	In Google-managed databases, enabling PITR automatically manages the required transaction logs. For self-managed databases, logs (e.g., MySQL binary logs, PostgreSQL WAL) must be manually enabled and managed. PITR log retention is typically 7 days by default.
Persistent Disk Snapshots	Incremental, block-level snapshots of a VM's disk	Efficient backups for databases running on Compute Engine	Database must be quiesced (writes paused) and ideally application writes suspended to ensure full transactional consistency.
Export/Import (Logical Backup)	Extracts data into a portable format (e.g., SQL, CSV)	Data archival, migration between database types, and portability	Generally too slow for low RTO/RPO scenarios.
Replication (Read/ Cross-Region)	Creates a copy of the database that can be promoted to primary	Achieving low RTO for HA (read replica) or DR (cross-region replica)	Asynchronous replication introduces a small RPO (potential data loss).
Cloud Spanner	Inherently resilient via synchronous replication across zones/ regions	Mission-critical global applications needing extremely low RTO and RPO	Highest level of resilience, but also higher cost and complexity.

Next, it is essential to identify and classify critical data to determine which datasets demand the most stringent protection. Based on these objectives, you can then choose the appropriate tools from Google Cloud's portfolio that align with your targets.

A crucial element is to implement automation for all backup and recovery processes to reduce human error and accelerate recovery times. A backup is only truly effective if it can be successfully restored, which is why regular testing through disaster recovery drills is non-negotiable. This validates your plan and identifies any gaps.

Finally, this entire strategy must be supported by comprehensive monitoring and alerting to track key metrics and clear, up-to-date documentation to ensure recovery efforts are well coordinated and efficient during a crisis.

Summary

Designing for high availability and disaster recovery is an integral part of architecting robust database solutions on Google Cloud. By carefully evaluating the trade-offs between zonal, regional, and multiregional deployments, organizations can lay a solid foundation for their database infrastructure. Meticulous management of maintenance windows and strategic planning for upgrades ensure that your database environment remains secure and performant. Most critically, defining clear RTO and RPO metrics serves as the guiding principle for designing a comprehensive backup and recovery solution. Leveraging Google Cloud's rich portfolio of managed services, combined with a well-defined, automated, and regularly tested strategy, will empower your organization to build truly resilient database systems that protect your invaluable data.

Exam Essentials

Evaluate database high availability and disaster recovery options given the requirements.   Understand the fundamental differences between high availability (HA), which handles localized failures, and disaster recovery (DR), which handles catastrophic, widespread failures.

Know how to evaluate the trade-offs between zonal, regional, and multiregional deployments, considering their impact on resilience, performance, cost, and data consistency.

Know how to match specific Google Cloud database services, such as Cloud SQL with HA or a multiregion Cloud Spanner instance, to application requirements for uptime and data loss.

Understand how to define maintenance windows and configure notification systems to align with business operations and minimize disruption.

Design database backup and recovery solutions.   Understand how recovery time objective (RTO) dictates the maximum acceptable downtime and how recovery point objective (RPO) dictates the maximum acceptable data loss.

Know how to design a backup strategy using Google Cloud tools like managed backups, persistent disk snapshots, and replication to meet specific RTO and RPO targets.

Understand the function of point-in-time recovery (PITR) as a powerful defense against logical data corruption, allowing for granular recovery to a specific second.

Know how to create a comprehensive recovery plan that includes automation, regular testing through DR drills, monitoring, and clear documentation.

Review Questions

1. To ensure proactive management of database maintenance and potential issues, a company wants to set up robust notification systems for their Cloud SQL instances. Which Google Cloud services should they leverage to monitor for maintenance events and dispatch alerts to their operations team?

   A. Cloud DNS and Cloud CDN

   B. Cloud Monitoring and Cloud Logging

   C. Cloud Storage and Cloud Functions

   D. BigQuery and Dataflow

2. After implementing a comprehensive backup and recovery strategy for your production databases on Google Cloud, your manager asks about validating its effectiveness. What is the most important ongoing activity to ensure your recovery solutions will work as expected during an actual disaster?

   A. Daily review of backup logs

   B. Regular testing of recovery procedures through disaster recovery drills

   C. Increasing backup frequency to hourly

   D. Implementing additional monitoring tools

3. A small business uses a basic zonal Cloud SQL instance for their inventory management system. They recently experienced a brief outage when the specific zone became temporarily unavailable. To prevent future similar disruptions within the same region, they decide to upgrade their database. Which Cloud SQL configuration should they choose to achieve higher availability against zonal failures?

   A. Convert to a multiregional deployment.

   B. Configure a HA instance.

   C. Migrate to a custom PostgreSQL deployment on Compute Engine.

   D. Increase the storage size of the current zonal instance.

4. As a professional Cloud Database engineer, you are tasked with improving the reliability and speed of your company's disaster recovery procedures for their databases. Which principle is paramount to achieve faster and more consistent recovery outcomes?

   A. Manual intervention and approval for every recovery step

   B. Automation of backup schedules and recovery orchestration

   C. Reducing the frequency of backups to save storage costs

   D. Relying solely on a single type of backup mechanism

5. You are managing a custom PostgreSQL database deployed on a Compute Engine instance with a persistent disk. To ensure data integrity for backups, you plan to take regular disk snapshots. What crucial step must be performed on the database itself before taking a Persistent Disk snapshot to guarantee a consistent backup?

    A. Stop the Compute Engine instance to ensure all data is written to disk.

    B. Ensure the database is "quiesced" or placed into a consistent state to flush pending writes.

    C. Increase the persistent disk size to accommodate the snapshot.

    D. Disable all network connectivity to the database.

6. A financial services firm with a global presence needs to protect its Cloud SQL primary database against a complete regional outage. They are willing to accept a small amount of data loss in a disaster scenario if it means maintaining application resilience across regions. Which replication strategy would best support this cross-region disaster recovery objective?

    A. Cloud SQL HA within a single region

    B. Cloud SQL with a cross-region read replica

    C. Cloud Spanner with a multiregion configuration

    D. Managed backups to Cloud Storage

7. A company has implemented a Cloud SQL cross-region replica for disaster recovery. While this provides protection against regional outages, the primary database engineer warns that there is a potential for some data loss if the primary region fails. Why might this data loss occur with a Cloud SQL cross-region replica?

    A. Cross-region replicas automatically purge old data.

    B. Cross-region replication for Cloud SQL is typically asynchronous, leading to replication lag.

    C. Cloud SQL cross-region replicas are read-only and cannot be promoted.

    D. The replica only contains schema, not actual data.

8. When designing a comprehensive backup and recovery strategy, it's crucial to prioritize data protection efforts. What initial step helps determine which datasets require the most stringent RTO and RPO targets?

    A. Automating all backup schedules

    B. Performing a data classification exercise and business impact analysis (BIA)

    C. Migrating all databases to Cloud Spanner

    D. Purchasing the most expensive storage options

9. When implementing a multiregion database strategy for disaster recovery, the application itself needs to be designed to leverage this resilience. What is a key consideration for the application to effectively handle a failover to a different region?

    A. The application must only connect to the database via its IP address.

    B. The application should be able to re-point its database connection to the healthy region.

    C. The application must store local copies of all database data.

    D. The application should be designed to handle eventual consistency across all regions.

10. Your business demands extremely low RTO and RPO targets for its core transactional database. As the database engineer, you need to explain the financial implications of these stringent requirements to management. What is the main reason why achieving very low RTO and RPO typically incurs higher costs?

    A. It requires more frequent manual backups by engineers.

    B. It necessitates duplicated infrastructure, continuous replication, and complex management.

    C. It means using only open source database solutions.

    D. It reduces the need for specialized cloud services.

11. A global financial services application needs a database solution that can withstand a complete Google Cloud region outage with extremely low RPO and RTO, while maintaining strong global consistency. The application can tolerate higher latency due to geographical distribution. Which Google Cloud database service and deployment strategy would best meet these requirements?

    A. Cloud SQL with cross-region read replicas

    B. Cloud Spanner with a multiregion configuration

    C. Cloud Bigtable with multi-cluster routing

    D. Compute Engine instance running PostgreSQL with logical replication to another region

12. Your company plans to upgrade a Cloud SQL for MySQL 5.7 instance to MySQL 8.0. This is a major version upgrade for a critical production database. What is the most critical preparatory step you must undertake before initiating this upgrade?

    A. Automatically accept the upgrade as minor versions are non-disruptive.

    B. Perform a full backup of the database and rigorously test the upgrade in a nonproduction environment.

    C. Inform Google Cloud Support to manually perform the upgrade during business hours.

    D. Scale up the instance size to accommodate the upgrade process.

13. A database engineer notices that their Cloud SQL instance has been automatically updated to a newer patch version (e.g., PostgreSQL 14.1–14.2) without any manual intervention or significant downtime. Later, they plan to upgrade from PostgreSQL 14 to PostgreSQL 15, which they know will require more careful planning. What is the fundamental difference between these two types of upgrades in the context of Google Cloud–managed databases?

A. The former is a major version upgrade requiring significant downtime, whereas the latter is a minor version upgrade that is typically nondisruptive.

B. Minor version upgrades are generally nondisruptive and automated by Google Cloud, whereas major version upgrades often introduce breaking changes and require more planning and potential downtime.

C. Minor version upgrades are manual processes, whereas major version upgrades are automatically applied by Google Cloud.

D. Major version upgrades apply security patches, whereas minor version upgrades introduce new features.

14. A critical application experienced accidental data deletion due to a user error. The business requires the ability to recover the database to a state just seconds before the accidental deletion, without losing any subsequent legitimate transactions. Which Cloud SQL feature is essential to meet this low RPO requirement?

A. Automated daily backups

B. On-demand manual backups

C. Point-in-time recovery (PITR)

D. Read replicas for load balancing

15. A data archiving project requires moving historical transactional data from an active Cloud SQL database to Cloud Storage for long-term retention. While mysqldump (export/import) is being considered, the team has concerns about its suitability for certain DR scenarios. For which recovery objective is the Export/Import method generally *not* recommended?

A. Achieving very low RTO

B. Ensuring data portability across different database systems

C. Creating a complete logical backup for auditing purposes

D. Archiving old data to cost-effective storage

16. An application that handles real-time stock trading needs extremely rapid recovery in the event of a database failure, minimizing any interruption to trading activities. This requirement directly relates to which key disaster recovery metric?

A. Recovery point objective (RPO)

B. Recovery time objective (RTO)

C. Service level agreement (SLA)

D. Data consistency index (DCI)

17. A social media platform's analytics database collects vast amounts of user activity data. While continuous availability is important, the business can tolerate losing up to 15 minutes of recent data in a catastrophic failure. This tolerance defines which crucial disaster recovery metric?

A. Recovery time objective (RTO)

B. Recovery point objective (RPO)

C. Mean time to recovery (MTTR)

D. Uptime percentage

18. Cloud SQL's point-in-time recovery (PITR) is a powerful feature for minimizing RPO. How does Cloud SQL enable this granular recovery capability?

A. By creating a full database snapshot every second

B. By performing daily full backups and continuously archiving transaction logs

C. By synchronously replicating data to multiple regions

D. By allowing manual restoration from any previous full backup

19. Your organization is preparing for a major version upgrade of a mission-critical Cloud SQL database. The application it supports has a very low tolerance for downtime. What is the most appropriate strategy to minimize the service interruption during this upgrade?

A. Perform an in-place upgrade, as Cloud SQL handles all downtime automatically.

B. Provision a new instance with the upgraded version, replicate data, and then perform a controlled cutover.

C. Schedule the upgrade during peak business hours to get it done quickly.

D. Postpone the upgrade indefinitely to avoid any downtime.

20. Following a successful disaster recovery drill, the team identifies an area for improvement: ensuring that all future recovery operations are executed consistently and efficiently, especially under pressure. Which aspect of DR planning is most critical for achieving this?

A. Minimizing the RPO to reduce data loss

B. Comprehensive monitoring and alerting

C. Maintaining clear, concise, and up-to-date documentation and runbooks

D. Reducing the cost of recovery infrastructure

Designing Secure Database Connectivity and Access

GOOGLE CLOUD CERTIFIED PROFESSIONAL CLOUD DATABASE ENGINEER EXAM OBJECTIVES COVERED IN THIS CHAPTER:

✔ **1.3 Determine how applications will connect to the database.**

- Configure networking, key management, encryption, and security.
- Justify the use of session pooler services.
- Assess auditing policies for managed services.

✔ **2.1 Determine database connectivity and access management considerations.**

- Determine Identity and Access Management (IAM) and policies for database connectivity and access control.
- Manage database users including authentication and access.

Database security is a critical concern in any cloud environment. It's more than just protecting data at rest or in transit; it's a complete strategy for controlling who and what can connect to the database and what they can do. A connectivity breach can expose sensitive data, disrupt services, and cause significant financial and reputational damage. For a database engineer, designing a strong security posture for database connections is a top priority.

This chapter covers securing database access on Google Cloud using a defense-in-depth strategy. You will learn how to architect connection patterns for security, scalability, and high availability. The discussion moves from network-level controls like firewalls and private IP to specific tools like the Cloud SQL Auth Proxy. The chapter concludes with identity and access management, covering both Google Cloud IAM and internal database controls to ensure only authorized users and applications can access your data.

Designing Secure Database Connection Patterns

The way applications connect to a database is the foundation of its security. A weak connection architecture can create lasting vulnerabilities, whereas a strong one provides built-in security and simplifies management. A good design balances the demands of scalability, high availability, and security.

Designing for Scalability, High Availability, and Security

A modern cloud application is dynamic. It must handle fluctuating user loads, survive infrastructure failures, and defend against a constantly evolving threat landscape. Your database connection strategy must be equally dynamic.

Scalability

As an application's user base grows, the number of concurrent connections to its database will increase. Each database connection consumes resources, including memory and CPU cycles, on both the client and the server. Exceeding a database's connection limit leads to connection refusals, application errors, and poor performance. A scalable connection pattern anticipates this growth and manages resources efficiently. The two primary tools for achieving this are connection pooling and load balancing.

A *connection pooler* is a service or library that maintains a cache of active database connections. Establishing a new database connection is a resource-intensive process involving a network handshake, authentication, and session setup. Instead of creating a new connection for every request and then tearing it down, an application can "borrow" an existing, authenticated connection from the pool. When the application is finished, it returns the connection to the pool, making it available for another request. This reuse of connections dramatically reduces latency and the resource overhead on the database server, allowing it to handle a much higher throughput of short-lived requests.

A *load balancer* distributes incoming network traffic across a group of backend resources—in this case, multiple database instances. For read-heavy workloads, you can create several read replicas of your primary database. For example, with *Cloud SQL*, an internal load balancer can distribute read queries evenly across these replicas, preventing any single replica from becoming a bottleneck. This not only improves read performance but also enhances availability, because the load balancer can detect an unhealthy replica and stop sending traffic to it.

High Availability

Your database is often the most critical stateful component of your application stack. If the database is unavailable, the application is down. High availability (HA) design ensures that your database can withstand infrastructure failures—such as a zonal outage or a hardware failure on the primary instance—with minimal disruption.

A fundamental strategy for HA is deploying a multizone or multiregional database setup. For a service like Cloud SQL, a high availability configuration automatically provisions a primary instance and a standby instance in different zones within the same region. All data written to the primary is synchronously replicated to the standby. If the primary instance becomes unresponsive, Cloud SQL automatically initiates a failover to the standby instance. This process is seamless to the application; the connection endpoint remains the same, and traffic is simply redirected to the new primary.

For a global application requiring maximum availability and scalability, a multiregional Spanner configuration is the ideal choice, providing a recovery point objective of zero (RPO = 0) and a low recovery time objective (RTO).

Consider an application deployed in us-central1, which is also configured as the Spanner leader region. This region handles all write operations to achieve transactional consistency. If the us-central1 region experiences an outage, Spanner's internal systems automatically detect the failure and elect a new leader in a designated failover region, such as us-east1. This internal promotion process is fast, typically completing within 10–15 seconds.

However, a successful application failover depends on more than just Spanner's automatic leader election. Your architecture must be designed to handle the event. Traffic from your application, typically managed by a global load balancer, must be redirected away from the failed region to a healthy one. While no data is lost during this event, writes will fail during the brief leader election window. Afterward, writes originating from any region will be routed to the new leader in us-east1, which can increase write latency for clients not located near the new leader region.

Security

Security must be built into the fabric of your connection pattern, not added as an afterthought. A secure pattern uses multiple layers of defense.

First, always connect to your database over a *private network*. By assigning a private IP address to your database instance within your Virtual Private Cloud (VPC), you ensure it is not accessible from the public Internet. This immediately eliminates a vast range of external threats.

Second, *VPC firewall rules* act as a gatekeeper for traffic within your VPC. You should configure firewall rules based on the principle of least privilege, denying all ingress traffic to your database by default and then creating specific rules to allow connections only from your application servers, identified by network tags or service accounts.

Third, all data in transit between your application and the database must be encrypted using Secure Sockets Layer/Transport Layer Security (SSL/TLS). This prevents eavesdropping and on-path attacks, ensuring that if an attacker could intercept the network traffic, the data would be unreadable.

Finally, services like the *Cloud SQL Auth Proxy* provide another layer of security by integrating directly with Google Cloud's Identity and Access Management (IAM) for authentication and authorization.

Client-Side Resiliency: Exponential Backoff

In addition to server-side architecture, client applications need to be designed to handle connection problems effectively. *Exponential backoff* is a standard error handling strategy where a client retries a failed request with increasing wait times between attempts.

For example, if a connection to a database fails, the client might wait 1 second before retrying. If that fails, it waits 2 seconds, then 4 seconds, and so on, up to a maximum backoff time. Adding random jitter to these intervals prevents multiple clients from retrying simultaneously. This strategy is critical for resiliency. During a transient issue, such as a brief network partition or a database failover event that might take a few seconds to complete, exponential backoff prevents clients from overwhelming the database with a rapid-fire storm of retry attempts. This "backing off" gives the service time to recover. Many Google Cloud client libraries have exponential backoff built-in, but it is an important concept to understand and implement in any custom application code that interacts with a database.

Configuring Networking and Security

A database engineer needs to know how to implement these design patterns using Google Cloud tools. This section covers the specifics of configuring networking and security components, with a focus on the primary connection methods for Cloud SQL.

Cloud SQL Connection Methods

When connecting to Cloud SQL, you must choose between using a public IP address, which is accessible over the Internet, or a private IP address, which is only accessible from within your VPC network.

Public IP with Authorized Networks

This method assigns a public IPv4 address to your Cloud SQL instance, making it reachable from the Internet. To secure it, you must configure an *Authorized Networks* list. This list acts as a firewall, only allowing connections from the specific CIDR ranges you define.

Use Case: This approach is necessary when you need to connect from an external source that is not within your VPC, such as a corporate office, a data center, or a developer's workstation with a static IP address.

Security: While all connections should still be encrypted with SSL/TLS, this method is inherently less secure than using private IP because the database instance has a public presence. It requires diligent management of the IP allowlist to ensure that only trusted sources are included.

EXERCISE 6.1

Codelab: Connecting to Cloud SQL: Public IP and Authorized Networks

```
https://codelabs.developers.google.com/codelabs/cloud-sql-
connectivity-ips-public
```

In this exercise, you will create a Cloud SQL instance and configure it to allow connections from authorized public IP addresses. Accessed via the link provided, this codelab offers hands-on practice deploying what you learned earlier in the chapter. You will focus on the practical steps for enabling external connectivity for development and testing, ensuring you understand how to authorize networks using both the Google Cloud Console and command-line tools.

Private IP

Configuring your Cloud SQL instance with a private IP address is the recommended approach for most applications running within Google Cloud. This assigns an internal IP address to your instance from a VPC network, making it completely inaccessible from the public Internet. All traffic stays within Google's network.

Use Case: This is the standard for connecting from applications hosted on Compute Engine, GKE, Cloud Run, or other services within the same or a peered VPC network.

Security: This is the most secure option as it removes the public attack surface. You still use VPC firewall rules to control which resources *within* the VPC can access the database, providing an additional layer of internal security.

The Cloud SQL Auth Proxy: A Layer of Identity-Aware Security

Regardless of whether you use a public or private IP, the Cloud SQL Auth Proxy provides a critical layer of security. It is a utility that creates a secure, encrypted tunnel to your database, and its primary benefit is that it uses IAM for authorization, removing the need to manage connections via static IP addresses.

Here's a breakdown of its key benefits:

Secure Authorization: The proxy provides a powerful security layer by using IAM permissions to authorize who can connect. A service account or user must have the `roles/cloudsql.client` IAM role to establish a secure, encrypted tunnel to the database instance. While this centralizes connection authorization, your application must still authenticate with the database itself, typically using a username and password. To enable true password-less access, you can pair the proxy with the optional Cloud SQL IAM database authentication feature.

Automatic Encryption: All traffic between the proxy and the Cloud SQL instance is automatically encrypted with SSL/TLS, securing your data in transit without manual certificate management.

Simplified Network Configuration: Because connection authorization is handled by IAM, you don't need to manage IP allowlists (Authorized Networks). This is ideal for environments with dynamic or nonstatic IP addresses, such as Google Kubernetes Engine (GKE), Cloud Run, or App Engine.

Recommended Pattern: Private IP with the Cloud SQL Auth Proxy

The most secure and recommended pattern is to combine these two features. You configure your Cloud SQL instance with a private IP and have your applications connect to it via the Cloud SQL Auth Proxy. This provides multiple layers of security:

- The database has no public Internet presence.

- Traffic is confined to your private VPC network.

- Connections are authenticated using strong, short-lived IAM credentials, not static passwords or IP addresses.

- Traffic is always encrypted.

For a GKE workload, this is implemented by running the proxy as a *sidecar container* in the same pod as the application. The application connects to localhost, and the sidecar securely forwards the traffic to the Cloud SQL instance's private IP address.

Codelab: Connecting to Cloud SQL: Compute Engine, Private IP and Cloud SQL Proxy

```
https://codelabs.developers.google.com/codelabs/cloud-sql-
connectivity-gce-private
```

In this exercise, you will establish a secure connection between a Google Compute Engine virtual machine and a Cloud SQL instance using a private IP address and the Cloud SQL Proxy. Accessed via the link provided, this walkthrough offers hands-on practice deploying what you learned earlier in the chapter. You will focus on minimizing Internet exposure by restricting traffic to internal IPs and offloading SSL management to the proxy, ensuring you understand the practical steps required to securely migrate and run stateful applications in the cloud.

Table 6.1 compares the commonly used Cloud SLQ connection methods in Google Cloud. When running a legacy Oracle database on the Bare Metal Solution, network security is configured differently. You establish a secure Cloud Interconnect link between your VPC

TABLE 6.1   Comparison of Cloud SQL connection methods

Connection method	Security	Management overhead	Use case
Private IP + Auth Proxy	Highest	Low	Recommended for all applications within Google Cloud (GKE, GCE, Cloud Run, etc.).
Private IP Only	High	Medium	Good for internal services where IAM database authentication is not used. Requires firewall rules.
Public IP + Auth Proxy	Medium	Low	For connecting from outside Google Cloud without static IPs. Better than just an allowlist.
Public IP + Authorized Networks	Medium	High	For connecting from external sources with static IPs. Requires careful management of IP allowlists.

and the Bare Metal environment. You then use VPC firewall rules to strictly control which Compute Engine instances can communicate with the Oracle database servers over this private, low-latency connection.

Customer-Managed Encryption Keys (CMEK)

By default, all user data stored in Google Cloud's managed databases is encrypted at rest using Google-managed encryption keys. For organizations with specific compliance or regulatory requirements, customer-managed encryption keys (CMEKs) provide an additional layer of control.

CMEK allows you to use encryption keys that you manage within Cloud Key Management Service (Cloud KMS) to protect your database data. For example, to secure a Cloud SQL instance with CMEK, the process involves:

1. Creating a symmetric encryption key in a Cloud KMS keyring.

2. Granting the Cloud SQL service account the *cloudkms.cryptoKeyEncrypterDecrypter* IAM role on that specific key.

3. Selecting your key during the creation of the database instance or a backup.

Google Cloud uses a technique called *envelope encryption*. Your CMEK is used to encrypt a data encryption key (DEK), and the DEK is then used to encrypt your actual database data. This is highly efficient and secure. The primary benefit of CMEK is control. You control the key's rotation policy, and most importantly, you can disable or destroy the key at any time. If a key is disabled or destroyed, all data encrypted with it becomes permanently inaccessible, providing a "crypto-shred" capability.

SSL/TLS Certificates

While the Cloud SQL Auth Proxy handles encryption automatically, there are scenarios where you might need or want to connect directly to a database instance. For example, connecting to a Cloud SQL instance from a local client tool that cannot run the proxy requires manual SSL/TLS configuration to ensure data is encrypted in transit.

This involves a few steps:

1. On the Cloud SQL instance, specify that all connections must use SSL.

2. From the Google Cloud Console or gcloud CLI, create a client certificate and private key for your application.

3. Download the server's Certificate Authority (CA) certificate. This is used by your client to verify the identity of the database server it's connecting to.

4. Configure your application's database connection string to use the client key, client certificate, and server CA certificate.

This setup enables mutual TLS (mTLS), where both the client and the server authenticate each other's identity using certificates before establishing a secure connection. While more complex to manage than the proxy, it provides a very high level of security for direct connections.

Justifying the Use of Session Pooler Services

Connection pooling is essential for scalability, but its importance extends beyond performance. In cloud environments with autoscaling and serverless architectures, connection management is a significant challenge that poolers are well suited to address.

AlloyDB for PostgreSQL, for example, has a built-in connection pooler. For a serverless application on Cloud Run that needs to connect to AlloyDB, this is critical. Without the pooler, a sudden traffic spike causing Cloud Run to scale to 500 instances would try to create 500 database connections, overwhelming the primary instance. With the built-in pooler, these 500 application requests are efficiently managed through a much smaller, stable set of backend connections, ensuring high performance and stability. This effectively decouples the number of application instances from the number of database connections, allowing your application to scale massively without overwhelming the database.

For other databases like Cloud SQL, you might deploy an external pooler like PgBouncer on a dedicated Compute Engine VM. The key justification is that a session pooler is not just a performance optimization; it is an essential architectural component for building scalable and resilient cloud-native applications that rely on a relational database.

Assessing Auditing Policies for Managed Services

Auditing is the process of generating and retaining logs that record who did what, and when. For a database engineer, auditing is essential for security analysis, troubleshooting, and compliance. Google Cloud provides a robust, multilayered auditing framework.

Cloud Audit Logs is the centralized logging service for Google Cloud. It captures administrative changes and data access events for your cloud resources, including your databases. There are three types of audit logs:

Admin Activity Logs: These logs record administrative actions that modify the configuration or metadata of a resource. Examples include creating a new Cloud SQL instance, deleting a Spanner database, or changing an IAM policy. These logs are always enabled and are retained for 400 days at no cost.

Data Access Logs: These logs record API calls that read the configuration or metadata of resources, as well as user-driven API calls that create, modify, or read user-provided resource data. For a financial application running on Spanner that must comply with Sarbanes–Oxley (SOX), you would enable data access audit logs for the Spanner API. This captures every read and write operation. You can then create a log sink to export these audit logs to BigQuery, where you can run queries to prove to auditors that only specific, authorized service accounts have accessed sensitive financial tables.

System Event Logs: These logs record actions taken by Google Cloud systems rather than by users. For example, a log is generated when an automatic failover occurs on an AlloyDB cluster. These logs are always enabled.

While Cloud Audit Logs provide a platform-level view, they often don't capture the fine-grained activity *within* the database. For that, you need *database-native auditing*. For example, Cloud SQL for PostgreSQL supports the `pgaudit` extension, which can be configured to log specific events like all `SELECT` statements executed against a table containing sensitive data, or all failed login attempts. A comprehensive strategy combines both types of auditing.

Determining Database Connectivity and Access Management Considerations

Secure connectivity gets your application traffic to the database's doorstep. Access management determines who is allowed in and what they can do inside. This is managed through two complementary systems: Google Cloud IAM and the database's internal user management.

Determining IAM Policies for Database Connectivity

IAM is the primary tool for access control in Google Cloud. It governs access to all cloud resources, including the ability to manage and connect to databases. When designing your IAM policies for databases, you must adhere to the principle of least privilege: grant only the permissions necessary to perform a required task.

For databases, IAM roles can be broadly categorized into roles for managing the infrastructure and roles for connecting to the data. Table 6.2 highlights the key IAM roles for database access.

A critical best practice is separation of duties. For example, a data analytics team needs to query production data from a Spanner database but must not be able to modify it. You would grant the Google Group for this team the predefined IAM role `roles/spanner.databaseReader`. This role allows them to execute read queries against the data but denies them permissions to alter the data or schema, adhering to the principle of least privilege.

Managing Database Users, Including Authentication and Access Control

IAM controls access *to* the database service, but the database engine itself has its own internal security model with users, roles, and privileges.

TABLE 6.2   Key IAM roles for database access

Role	Purpose	Scope	Example service
`roles/ cloudsql.admin`	Full control over instances, including creation, deletion, and editing.	Administrative	Cloud SQL
`roles/ alloydb.admin`	Full control over AlloyDB clusters and instances.	Administrative	AlloyDB
`roles/spanner. databaseAdmin`	Can manage schema (`CREATE/ALTER/DROP`) and database-level IAM policies, but cannot delete the parent Spanner instance.	Administrative	Spanner
`roles/cloudsql. client`	Permission to connect to an instance, typically using the Auth Proxy.	Connectivity	Cloud SQL
`roles/alloydb. client`	Permission to connect to an AlloyDB cluster.	Connectivity	AlloyDB
`roles/spanner. databaseUser`	Can read, write, and execute DML statements (`SELECT, INSERT, UPDATE, DELETE`). Cannot alter schema (`DDL`).	Data Access	Spanner
`roles/spanner. databaseReader`	Read-only access to data and schema. Ideal for analytics, reporting, or auditing users.	Data Access	Spanner

Authentication

How do users prove their identity to the database? There are two primary methods:

Password-Based Authentication: This is the traditional method. You create a user within the database (e.g., `CREATE USER myapp WITH PASSWORD` '...') and configure your application with that username and password. When using Cloud SQL, the recommended practice is to store these credentials in a secure service like Secret Manager. Your application can then be granted an IAM role that allows it to fetch the database password from Secret Manager at startup, avoiding hardcoded secrets.

IAM Database Authentication: This is a more modern, cloud-native approach available for Cloud SQL (PostgreSQL and MySQL) and Spanner. It allows a user or service account to authenticate to the database using their Google Cloud identity, completely eliminating the need for passwords. When a user with an appropriate IAM role attempts to connect, the database service validates their identity with IAM and grants them a short-lived access token. This centralizes authentication within IAM and simplifies credential management.

Access Control

Once a user is authenticated, the database's internal access control model determines what they can do. Using standard SQL commands like `GRANT` and `REVOKE`, you can assign fine-grained permissions.

For example, to provide a new application service account with access to an **AlloyDB** instance, you would use IAM database authentication combined with internal roles. First, you create a role within the database: `CREATE ROLE app_writer;`. Then, you grant it specific permissions: `GRANT INSERT, UPDATE ON orders TO app_writer;`. Finally, you map the IAM service account to this database role: `CREATE USER "service-account-email@example.com" WITH LOGIN IN ROLE app_writer;`. This allows the service account to authenticate without a password and only perform the specific actions granted to the `app_writer` role.

Summary

This chapter covered the components for designing secure and reliable access to cloud databases. The discussion started with the foundational requirements for any connection strategy: scalability, high availability, and security. You learned how to implement these requirements using patterns like load balancing, multizone HA configurations, and a defense-in-depth security posture with private networking and firewalls. The chapter also introduced client-side resiliency through strategies like exponential backoff.

The chapter then covered specific Google Cloud tools. You learned how the Cloud SQL Auth Proxy simplifies secure connectivity and how CMEK provides a key layer of data control. We also reviewed the use of session poolers for dynamic environments and the creation of a complete auditing strategy using both Cloud Audit Logs and database-native features. Finally, you learned how to manage access control at two levels: using IAM for platform access and using internal database users and roles for fine-grained permissions, based on the principle of least privilege.

With a solid understanding of how to securely connect to and manage database access, you are ready for the next chapter. It builds on this foundation by focusing on database health and efficiency, covering monitoring, performance tuning, and troubleshooting.

Exam Essentials

Design scalable, highly available, and secure database connection patterns.   You must be able to design a connection architecture that effectively uses connection pooling for scalability, multizone/regional deployments for high availability, and layered controls like private IP, firewalls, and SSL/TLS for security.

Configure networking and security.   You need to know the specific use cases and configuration details for key security components, especially the Cloud SQL Auth Proxy, understanding its benefits for authentication and encryption. You should also understand when and why to use CMEK and manual SSL/TLS configurations.

Justify the use of session pooler services.   Be prepared to explain why connection pooling is not just a performance enhancement but a critical architectural requirement for scalable and serverless applications to avoid exhausting database connection limits.

Assess auditing policies for managed services.   You must be able to differentiate between Cloud Audit Logs (Admin Activity, Data Access) and database-native auditing, and explain how to use them together to meet security and compliance goals.

Determine identity and access management (IAM) policies for database connectivity.   You need to apply the principles of least privilege and separation of duties to assign appropriate IAM roles (e.g., `cloudsql.client` vs. `cloudsql.admin`) for both administrative and connectivity tasks.

Manage database users, including authentication and access control.   You must be able to compare and contrast password-based authentication (with Secret Manager) and IAM Database Authentication. You should also be able to describe how to use database-native roles and `GRANT/REVOKE` commands to implement fine-grained access control.

Review Questions

1. What is the fundamental difference between authentication and access control in the context of database security?

   A. Authentication determines what actions a user can perform, while access control verifies a user's identity.

   B. Authentication verifies a user's identity, while access control determines what actions they are permitted to perform.

   C. Authentication is managed by Google Cloud IAM, while access control is managed only within the database.

   D. Authentication applies to data at rest, while access control applies to data in transit.

2. Your application on Google Kubernetes Engine (GKE) needs to connect securely to a Cloud SQL for MySQL instance. The connection must use strong authentication, automatically encrypt traffic, and not require managing IP allowlists for dynamic GKE pod IPs. What is the recommended and most efficient way to achieve this connectivity?

   A. Configure a public IP on Cloud SQL and manually add GKE node IPs to authorized networks.

   B. Use direct SSL/TLS connections with client certificates and private keys.

   C. Deploy the Cloud SQL Auth Proxy as a sidecar container within the GKE application pod.

   D. Establish a VPN connection between the GKE cluster and the Cloud SQL instance.

3. A database engineer needs to implement an auditing solution for a Cloud Spanner database to track all changes to the database schema, such as `CREATE TABLE` or `ALTER INDEX` operations. Which type of Cloud Audit Log should be primarily enabled and monitored for this purpose?

   A. Data Access Logs

   B. Admin Activity Logs

   C. System Event Logs

   D. Operational Logs

4. A critical internal application, deployed on Compute Engine instances within a specific VPC, needs to connect to a new Cloud SQL database. To maximize security and minimize exposure, how should the Cloud SQL instance be configured to allow connections only from these Compute Engine instances without public Internet access?

   A. Configure the Cloud SQL instance with a public IP and enable Allow All External Connections.

   B. Assign a private IP to the Cloud SQL instance within the application's VPC and configure VPC firewall rules.

   C. Use the Cloud SQL Auth Proxy for all connections and disable all other network settings.

   D. Enable IAM database authentication and rely solely on client certificates for security.

5. A new serverless application on Cloud Run is experiencing connection issues with its Cloud SQL database under heavy load. The database logs show "too many connections" errors, even though the database instance has been scaled up. What is the most likely cause and what architectural pattern would help alleviate this problem?

   A. The database instance is undersized; scale up CPU and memory.

   B. Each Cloud Run instance is creating its own database connection, exhausting the limit; use a session pooler.

   C. The application is not using private IP, causing network latency.

   D. The Cloud SQL Auth Proxy is misconfigured, leading to connection drops.

6. For a critical Cloud SQL instance, the database engineer has enforced SSL/TLS for all connections directly on the instance. A legacy internal application, however, cannot use the Cloud SQL Auth Proxy. What is the manual configuration required on the application side to establish a secure, encrypted connection to this Cloud SQL instance?

   A. Only the database username and password

   B. The server's public IP address and port

   C. The client's private IP and the server's DNS name

   D. The server's Certificate Authority (CA) certificate, client certificate, and client private key

7. Your team needs to enable comprehensive security auditing for a Cloud SQL for MySQL instance. This requires logging all administrative changes to the instance (e.g., resizing, user creation) and also all data access events (e.g., `SELECT`, `INSERT` queries). Which combination of auditing capabilities is necessary?

   A. Enabling MySQL's slow query log and general query log

   B. Configuring Cloud Audit Logs (Admin Activity and Data Access) and enabling MySQL's native auditing features

   C. Using Cloud Monitoring for CPU and memory usage

   D. Only relying on connection logs from VPC Flow Logs

8. Your company needs to log all `SELECT` statements executed by a specific application user against a highly sensitive table in your Cloud SQL for PostgreSQL database for auditing purposes. Where would you configure this fine-grained logging?

   A. In Cloud Audit Logs by enabling Data Access logs for Cloud SQL

   B. By enabling the pgaudit extension within the Cloud SQL for PostgreSQL instance

   C. By setting up a custom metric in Cloud Monitoring to count `SELECT` queries

   D. By routing all network traffic through a Cloud Load Balancer with logging enabled

9. A highly sensitive financial application is deployed on Google Cloud, using Cloud SQL as its transactional database. Due to strict compliance requirements, the organization must ensure that the encryption keys used for data at rest are fully controlled by them, including the ability to disable or destroy the key at any time to render data inaccessible. Which security feature should they configure?

    A. SSL/TLS certificates for client-server encryption

    B. Cloud SQL Auth Proxy for strong authentication

    C. Customer-managed encryption keys (CMEKs)

    D. Private IP for network isolation

10. An application is designed with client-side resiliency features. When a transient database connection error occurs, the application attempts to reconnect with increasingly longer delays between retries. This strategy is known as exponential backoff. What is the primary benefit of using exponential backoff during transient failures?

    A. It speeds up the initial connection time.

    B. It prevents clients from overwhelming the database with rapid retry attempts during recovery.

    C. It eliminates the need for SSL/TLS encryption.

    D. It ensures strong data consistency across distributed systems.

11. A security analyst requires read-only access to all data in a Spanner database for auditing purposes. They must not be able to make any modifications to the data or schema. Which Google Cloud IAM role should be granted to the security analyst to adhere to the principle of least privilege?

    A. `roles/spanner.databaseAdmin`

    B. `roles/spanner.databaseUser`

    C. `roles/spanner.databaseReader`

    D. `roles/owner`

12. Your team is evaluating the use of IAM Database Authentication for Cloud SQL for PostgreSQL. What is the primary advantage of this authentication method over traditional password-based authentication for Cloud SQL instances?

    A. It allows direct SSH access to the database server.

    B. It integrates with Google Cloud IAM, eliminating the need to manage database passwords in application code.

    C. It provides faster query execution times.

    D. It enables multiregion failover automatically.

13. A professional Cloud Database engineer is setting up a new Cloud SQL instance and wants to use a traditional username and password for application connectivity. To avoid hardcoding sensitive credentials in application code and enhance security, where should the database password be securely stored?

    A. In a plaintext file on the Compute Engine instance

    B. As an environment variable on the application server

    C. In Google Cloud Secret Manager

    D. Directly in the Cloud SQL user configuration file

14. Your application connects to a legacy Oracle database running on Google Cloud's Bare Metal Solution. You need to ensure secure and low-latency connectivity from your Compute Engine VMs in your VPC to this Oracle database. How should this connectivity primarily be established and secured?

    A. Directly over the public Internet with a public IP for the Oracle server

    B. Using Cloud Interconnect to establish a private, dedicated connection, secured by VPC firewall rules

    C. Through the Cloud SQL Auth Proxy, as it supports all database types

    D. By deploying a bastion host in the public subnet and SSH tunneling

15. An organization needs to provide an application with administrative access to a Cloud SQL instance, allowing it to create new databases and manage users. Which specific IAM role is most appropriate for the service account associated with this application?

    A. `roles/cloudsql.client`

    B. `roles/cloudsql.viewer`

    C. `roles/cloudsql.admin`

    D. `roles/iam.serviceAccountUser`

16. An application running on multiple Compute Engine instances within a VPC needs to connect to a new Cloud SQL instance. To simplify connection management and enhance security, the database engineer decides to use the Cloud SQL Auth Proxy. When running the Auth Proxy, where should the application connect to the database (from its perspective)?

    A. To the Cloud SQL instance's private IP address directly

    B. To `localhost` on the same machine where the Auth Proxy is running

    C. To the Cloud SQL instance's public IP address

    D. To a global DNS endpoint managed by Google Cloud

17. You are configuring a Cloud SQL instance and want to allow a specific Google Group of developers to connect to it from their local machines using the Cloud SQL Auth Proxy. What is the minimum IAM role required for these developers to successfully connect via the Auth Proxy?

   A. `roles/cloudsql.admin`

   B. `roles/cloudsql.viewer`

   C. `roles/cloudsql.client`

   D. `roles/editor`

18. A company is migrating a legacy application that relies heavily on a large number of database connections to an AlloyDB for PostgreSQL cluster. The application's existing connection patterns are not easily changed to incorporate an external connection pooler. What feature of AlloyDB helps address this challenge and ensure connection efficiency?

   A. AlloyDB's automatic sharding feature

   B. AlloyDB's built-in connection pooler

   C. AlloyDB's read replicas automatically handle connection distribution

   D. AlloyDB's support for direct public IP connections

19. A database engineer needs to understand when Google Cloud performed an automatic failover of their Cloud SQL HA instance. Which type of Cloud Audit Log would provide this information?

   A. Admin Activity Logs

   B. Data Access Logs

   C. System Event Logs

   D. Export Logs

20. A database engineer is reviewing the trade-offs for different Cloud SQL connection methods. What is the main security implication of using a public IP with authorized networks for a Cloud SQL instance, compared to using the Cloud SQL Auth Proxy?

   A. Public IP with authorized networks provides stronger encryption.

   B. Public IP with authorized networks simplifies IAM integration.

   C. Public IP with authorized networks relies on IP allowlisting, potentially exposing the database to the Internet.

   D. Public IP with authorized networks is suitable for dynamic, autoscaling environments.

Monitoring, Troubleshooting, and Optimizing Performance

✔ **2.2 Configure database monitoring and troubleshooting options.**

- Assess slow running queries, database locking—identify missing indexes.

- Monitor and investigate database vitals—RAM, CPU storage, I/O, and audit logging.

- Monitor and update quotas.

- Investigate database resource contention.

- Set up alerts for errors and performance metrics.

✔ **2.4 Optimize database cost and performance in Google Cloud.**

- Assess scaling up and scaling out options.

- Scale database instances based on current and upcoming workload.

- Define replication strategies.

- Optimize queries for cost and performance.

This chapter covers the critical aspects of maintaining a healthy and efficient database environment in Google Cloud. It details the tools and techniques for monitoring databases, troubleshooting performance issues, and optimizing for both cost and performance.

A proficient Cloud Database engineer must be skilled not only in designing and implementing database solutions but also in ensuring their smooth day-to-day operation. This chapter provides the knowledge to proactively identify and resolve issues, ensuring databases are performant, reliable, and cost-effective.

Configuring Database Monitoring and Troubleshooting Options

Effective monitoring and troubleshooting are fundamental to a sound database management strategy. Identifying and addressing potential issues before they escalate are essential for maintaining high availability and performance. Google Cloud provides a suite of tools for monitoring databases, diagnosing problems, and taking corrective action. This section details how to configure and utilize these tools for effective database management.

Assessing Slow-Running Queries, Database Locking, and Identifying Missing Indexes

Slow-running queries, database locking, and missing indexes are common causes of poor database performance. Identifying and addressing these issues are critical skills for any database engineer. Google Cloud offers several tools and features to help pinpoint these problems.

Slow-Running Queries

Slow-running queries can degrade application performance. Identifying these queries is the first step toward optimization.

Cloud SQL Query Insights: For Cloud SQL, Query Insights is an effective tool for identifying resource-intensive queries. Its visual dashboard shows which queries consume the most CPU time, allowing engineers to examine the query plan for bottlenecks. Query Insights also provides performance improvement recommendations.

AlloyDB for PostgreSQL: As AlloyDB is fully PostgreSQL-compatible, it also integrates with Query Insights, providing the same capabilities for identifying and analyzing expensive queries. Standard PostgreSQL tools like the `pg_stat_statements` extension can also be used to track execution statistics for all SQL statements.

Cloud Spanner Query Statistics: Cloud Spanner provides detailed query statistics through the Google Cloud Console and the Cloud Monitoring API. These statistics include information on query latency, CPU utilization, and rows scanned, which helps in identifying poorly performing queries.

Bigtable: In Bigtable, performance issues typically manifest as high-latency read or write operations and are often related to schema design, specifically row keys. Client-side latency metrics should be tracked using Cloud Monitoring. The Key Visualizer is the primary tool for diagnosing hotspotting. It generates a visual heatmap of your table's row keys, allowing you to instantly see if reads or writes are concentrated on a narrow key range.

BigQuery Query Execution Details: For BigQuery, the query execution details provide extensive information about query execution, including the query plan, time spent in each stage, and bytes shuffled. This information is used to identify bottlenecks and optimize queries.

Diagnosing a Slow Query with Cloud SQL

An e-commerce site using Cloud SQL for its product catalog experiences slow page loads. A database engineer uses Query Insights and discovers that a query joining products, reviews, and inventory tables has high average latency and CPU consumption. The query plan reveals a full table scan on the reviews table. By adding an index on the `product_id` column of the reviews table, the database engineer reduces query execution time by 90 percent, and page load times return to normal.

Once a slow-running query or operation is identified, several optimization techniques can be applied:

Adding Indexes: For relational databases, indexes can improve query performance by allowing the database to locate data more quickly.

Optimizing Schema and Row Key Design: For NoSQL databases like Bigtable, an effective row key design that distributes reads and writes evenly across the table is critical for performance.

Rewriting the Query: A query can sometimes be rewritten more efficiently—for instance, by using a different join strategy or avoiding a subquery.

Analyzing the Query Plan: The query plan shows how the database executes a query. Analyzing the plan can reveal inefficiencies that can be addressed to improve performance.

EXERCISE 7.1

Codelab: Introduction to Query Insights for Cloud SQL

```
https://codelabs.developers.google.com/codelabs/cloud-sql-
insights-intro
```

In this exercise, you will configure a Cloud SQL for PostgreSQL instance to support a Node.js application and enable comprehensive performance monitoring. Accessed via the URL provided, this walk-through offers hands-on practice using what you learned earlier in the chapter. You will focus on using Query Insights to detect and diagnose query performance problems, ensuring you understand how to identify root causes and optimize database interactions using self-service diagnostic tools.

Troubleshooting Self-Managed Databases on Compute Engine

While Google Cloud-managed services offer integrated tools like Query Insights, you are responsible for configuring and managing monitoring for self-managed databases running on Compute Engine VMs. A common operational task is identifying slow queries on a self-managed MySQL instance.

Enabling Slow Query Logs for MySQL on Compute Engine

To troubleshoot slow queries on a self-managed MySQL instance, you must first enable the slow query log. This can be done in two ways:

Modify the MySQL Configuration File (`my.cnf`): This is the persistent method. Edit the `my.cnf` file (typically located at `/etc/mysql/my.cnf` or `/etc/my.cnf`) and add or modify the following lines under the `[mysqld]` section (ensure that the `mysql` os user has write permissions to this path):

```
slow_query_log = 1
long_query_time = 2
slow_query_log_file = /var/log/mysql/mysql-slow.log
```

`slow_query_log = 1`: Enables the slow query log.

`long_query_time = 2`: Defines the threshold in seconds. Queries taking longer than this will be logged.

`slow_query_log_file`: Specifies the path for the log file.

You must restart the MySQL service for these changes to take effect.

Use `SET GLOBAL` **Commands:** This method enables logging dynamically without a server restart, but the settings will be reset upon the next restart.

```
SET GLOBAL slow_query_log = 'ON';
SET GLOBAL long_query_time = 2;
```

Accessing Logs and Integrating with Cloud Logging

Once enabled, the slow query logs are written to the local filesystem of the Compute Engine VM (e.g., `/var/log/mysql/mysql-slow.log`). While you can SSH into the VM to view these files directly, the best practice for centralized analysis is to integrate them with Cloud Logging.

To do this, you install and configure the *Ops Agent* on the Compute Engine VM. The Ops Agent automatically collects system metrics and logs, including custom log files, and streams them to Cloud Logging.

Configuration for Ops Agent

You would define a configuration file for the agent (e.g., `/etc/google-cloud-ops-agent/config.yaml`) to specify the path to your MySQL slow query log:

```
logging:
  receivers:
    mysql_slow_queries:
      type: files
      include_paths:
        - /var/log/mysql/mysql-slow.log
  processors:
    mysql_slow_queries:
      type: parse_multiline
      # Add parsing rules for MySQL log format
  service:
    pipelines:
      default_pipeline:
        receivers: [mysql_slow_queries]
        processors: [mysql_slow_queries]
```

After you configure and start the Ops Agent, the slow query logs from your self-managed MySQL instance will appear in the Logs Explorer in the Google Cloud Console. From there, you can search, analyze, create log-based metrics, and set up alerts just as you would for a managed service.

Database Locking

Database locking is a mechanism that prevents concurrent modification of the same data. While necessary for data integrity in transactional databases, it can cause performance problems if not managed correctly.

Identifying Locking Issues: In Cloud SQL and AlloyDB, the `pg_locks` view (PostgreSQL) or the `information_schema.innodb_locks` table (MySQL) can be used to identify which transactions are holding or waiting for locks. For Cloud Spanner, the `SPANNER_SYS.LOCK_STATS` system table provides information about lock contention.

Locking in Bigtable: Bigtable does not use traditional database locks. It handles concurrent writes to the same row with a "last write wins" approach based on timestamps. Contention issues in Bigtable are typically due to hotspotting on a single row rather than locking.

Resolving Database Locking in AlloyDB

A financial application using AlloyDB experiences frequent timeouts during its end-of-day batch processing. The engineer queries the `pg_locks` view and discovers that a long-running reporting transaction holds an `EXCLUSIVE` lock on a key summary table, blocking numerous smaller update transactions. The issue is resolved by modifying the reporting job to query a read replica instance. This prevents it from locking the primary table and allows the update transactions to proceed without contention.

Resolving Locking Issues: Once a locking issue in a relational database is identified, several steps can be taken to resolve it:

Optimizing Transactions: Keep transactions as short as possible to minimize the duration that locks are held.

Using Optimistic Locking: This strategy assumes that conflicts are rare and checks for conflicts before committing a transaction, rather than locking data.

Choosing the Right Isolation Level: The transaction isolation level determines how a transaction is isolated from others. Selecting the appropriate isolation level can help reduce lock contention.

Identifying Missing Indexes

In relational databases, missing indexes are a common cause of slow query performance. An index allows the database to quickly find rows that match a query's WHERE clause, avoiding a full table scan.

Cloud SQL and AlloyDB Index Advisors: For Cloud SQL for PostgreSQL and AlloyDB, the Index Advisor analyzes the query workload and recommends new indexes to improve performance.

Cloud Spanner Key Visualizer: While not a direct index advisor, the Key Visualizer for Cloud Spanner helps analyze key usage patterns. This can identify hot spots and inform a more efficient schema design, which may include adding or modifying secondary indexes.

Bigtable Row Keys as Indexes: In Bigtable, the row key serves as the primary index. There are no secondary indexes in the same sense as a relational database. A poorly designed row key is analogous to a missing or incorrect primary key index. The Key Visualizer is the primary tool for diagnosing issues with row key design.

Using Key Visualizer to Improve Spanner Performance

A social media application using Cloud Spanner experiences high read latency when fetching a user's timeline. The engineer uses the Key Visualizer tool and finds a significant hotspot on the `Posts` table, concentrated on a narrow range of keys corresponding to recent timestamps. The application queries posts by `user_id` and `creation_timestamp`. To resolve this, a secondary index is created on `(user_id, creation_timestamp DESC)`, and the application is updated to use this index. This change distributes the read load, eliminating the hotspot and improving timeline-fetching latency.

Manual Analysis: Queries and schema can also be manually analyzed to identify missing indexes. Look for queries that perform full table scans or filter on unindexed columns.

Table 7.1 summarizes the tools available for assessing these common performance issues across different Google Cloud database services.

Monitoring and Investigating Database Vitals: RAM, CPU, Storage, I/O, and Cloud Logging

Monitoring the vital signs of a database is essential for maintaining its health and performance. This includes tracking resource utilization and analyzing logs, including audit logs for security and compliance. Google Cloud provides a comprehensive set of tools for this purpose.

TABLE 7.1 Identifying performance issues in Google Cloud databases

Issue	Cloud SQL	AlloyDB	Cloud Spanner	Bigtable	BigQuery
Slow-Running Queries	Query Insights	Query Insights, `pg_stat_statements`	Query Statistics	Key Visualizer, Cloud Monitoring Metrics	Query Execution Details
Database Locking	`pg_locks` (PostgreSQL), `information_schema.innodb_locks` (MySQL)	`pg_locks`	`SPANNER_SYS.LOCK_STATS`	N/A (Row Contention)	N/A (Concurrency Model)
Missing Indexes	Index Advisor (PostgreSQL)	Index Advisor	Key Visualizer	Key Visualizer (Row Key)	N/A (Columnar storage, no traditional indexes)

Cloud Monitoring

Cloud Monitoring is the central service for monitoring all Google Cloud services, including databases. It provides metrics to track the health and performance of database instances.

Key metrics to monitor include the following:

CPU Utilization: High CPU utilization can indicate an under-provisioned database or inefficient queries.

Memory Usage: High memory usage can lead to swapping and poor performance.

Storage Usage: Monitor storage usage to avoid running out of space.

I/O Operations: High I/O can indicate a bottleneck from excessive disk reads and writes.

Network Traffic: Monitor network traffic to identify unusual patterns or potential security issues.

Active Connections: A large number of active connections can strain a database.

Diagnosing Bigtable Hotspotting with Cloud Monitoring

An IoT platform using Bigtable to store time-series data from sensors starts experiencing high write latencies. An engineer checks the Bigtable dashboard in Cloud Monitoring and observes that the CPU Utilization - Hottest Node metric is consistently at 95–100 percent, while other nodes are at 30–40 percent. This indicates severe hotspotting. The investigation reveals the row key design (`sensor_id-timestamp`) is causing all new writes to target a single node. The row key is redesigned to use a salted prefix, which distributes writes evenly across the table and resolves the latency issue.

Custom dashboards can be created in Cloud Monitoring to visualize these metrics for a quick overview of database health. These dashboards provide a single pane of glass for observing the performance of one or more database instances, even across different Google Cloud services. A well-designed dashboard can correlate key performance indicators (KPIs) like CPU utilization, I/O operations, and query latency with relevant log entries, such as error logs. This allows engineers to quickly identify the root cause of an issue. For example, a dashboard could display a chart of Cloud SQL CPU usage next to a logs panel showing recent slow query logs, making it easy to see if a spike in CPU corresponds to a specific inefficient query.

Skillsboost: Monitoring and Managing Google Cloud Resources

`www.cloudskillsboost.google/course_templates/653`

In this exercise, you will manage IAM permissions, configure monitoring agents, and deploy an event-driven Cloud Run function. Accessed via the URL provided, this walk-through offers hands-on practice deploying what you learned earlier in the chapter. You will focus on mastering the operational controls needed to secure and observe database interactions, ensuring you can maintain robust performance and strict access governance for your data layer.

Cloud Logging

Cloud Logging is a managed service for storing, searching, analyzing, and alerting on log data from Google Cloud services. For databases, logs are a critical source of information for troubleshooting.

Types of logs to monitor include:

Error Logs: Contain information about database errors and are essential for troubleshooting.

Slow Query Logs: For supported databases like Cloud SQL and AlloyDB, these logs contain information about queries that execute slowly, which helps in optimization.

Audit Logs: Provide a record of all database activity, such as administrative changes and data access events, for security and compliance purposes.

You can use the Logs Explorer in the Google Cloud Console to search and analyze logs. You can also create log-based metrics and alerts to provide notifications for important events.

Monitoring and Updating Quotas

Quotas are limits that Google Cloud places on the use of its services to protect both customers and Google from unforeseen usage spikes. It is important to monitor quota usage and request increases as needed to avoid service disruptions.

Types of quotas include:

Rate Quotas: Limit the number of requests that can be made to a service in a given time period.

Resource Quotas: Limit the amount of resources that can be used, such as the number of database instances or the amount of storage.

Managing Cloud SQL API Quotas

An analytics pipeline that frequently queries a Cloud SQL instance starts failing with "quota exceeded" errors. The engineer checks the Quotas page in the IAM & Admin section of the console and finds that the Cloud SQL Admin API Queries Per Minute Per User Quota is at 100 percent utilization. A recent pipeline update that increased parallelism caused the spike. The engineer requests a quota increase and, in the interim, throttles the pipeline's API requests to stay within the current limit.

You can view quota usage in the Google Cloud Console. If a quota limit is being approached, you can request an increase through the console. It is advisable to request quota increases in advance, as approval can take time.

Investigating Database Resource Contention

Resource contention occurs when multiple processes or transactions compete for the same resources, such as CPU, memory, or I/O, which can lead to poor performance and deadlocks.

To identify resource contention, remember the following:

High CPU Utilization: Can be a sign of resource contention.

High I/O Wait: Can indicate that the database is waiting for disk I/O, a sign of contention for storage resources.

Lock Waits: Can be a sign of contention for data resources.

Resolving I/O Contention for Oracle on Bare Metal

A legacy CRM system running on Oracle on Bare Metal Solution becomes sluggish during peak business hours. The DBA uses Oracle's Automatic Workload Repository (AWR) reports and finds high DB File Sequential Read wait events, pointing to severe I/O contention. The underlying storage is struggling to keep up with demand. The team resolves this by provisioning higher-performance storage logical unit numbers (LUNs) for the Bare Metal instance and rebalancing the data files to alleviate the I/O bottleneck.

To resolve resource contention, keep the following in mind:

Scale Up or Scale Out: If a database consistently experiences resource contention, it may need to be scaled up to a larger instance or scaled out by adding more read replicas.

Optimize Queries: Inefficient queries can consume excessive resources and lead to contention.

Tune Your Database: Many database configuration parameters can be tuned to improve performance and reduce resource contention. For instance, increasing the size of the database's memory buffer cache (e.g., Oracle's SGA) allows more data to be served from RAM, directly reducing disk I/O contention. Similarly, tuning parameters that control query parallelism can ensure that large analytical queries use resources more efficiently without overwhelming the system.

Setting Up Alerts for Errors and Performance Metrics

Setting up alerts is a crucial part of a proactive monitoring strategy, providing notification of potential problems before they impact users. The workflow involves creating an alerting policy in Cloud Monitoring that watches a specific metric. When the metric crosses a defined threshold, the policy is triggered and sends a message to a configured notification channel.

Alerts can be created in Cloud Monitoring based on any of its collected metrics. For example, you could configure an alert to be sent if:

- CPU utilization exceeds 90 percent for more than 5 minutes.

- A database instance becomes unavailable.

- The number of errors in the log exceeds a certain threshold.

Alerts can be configured to send notifications to a variety of channels, including:

- Email

- SMS

- PagerDuty

- Slack

- Webhooks

For more complex, automated responses, the notification channel can be a Pub/Sub topic. A Cloud Function or Cloud Run service can then subscribe to this topic to take automated action, such as scaling a resource, logging a detailed ticket in a system like Jira, or triggering a workflow to gather more diagnostic information.

Creating a Latency Alert for Spanner

A global gaming application uses a multiregion Cloud Spanner instance. To ensure a good user experience, the team needs to be notified if latency increases for players in Europe. An engineer creates an alerting policy in Cloud Monitoring for the `spanner.googleapis.com/api/request_latencies` metric, filtered for the europe-west1 region. The condition is set to trigger if the 99th percentile latency exceeds 100 ms for 5 minutes. The alert is configured to notify the on-call team via PagerDuty and Slack for rapid response.

By setting up alerts for key metrics and errors, you can be notified of any potential problems with your databases, allowing for quick corrective action.

EXERCISE 7.3

Codelab: Alerts: Uptime Checks to Pub/Sub Topics

```
https://codelabs.developers.google.com/alert-uptime-check-pubsub
```

In this exercise, you will configure an uptime check for a deployed application and set up a Pub/Sub topic to serve as a notification channel for those alerts. Accessed via the URL provided, this walk-through offers hands-on practice deploying what you learned earlier in the chapter. You will focus on integrating Cloud Monitoring with Pub/Sub to create flexible alerting pipelines, ensuring you understand how to programmatically route availability notifications to other systems or third-party tools.

Optimizing Database Cost and Performance in Google Cloud

Optimizing databases for cost and performance is an ongoing process. As workloads change, the database configuration must be continually evaluated and adjusted to ensure the best possible performance at the lowest possible cost.

Assessing Options for Scaling Up and Scaling Out

When a database can no longer handle its workload, there are two primary scaling options. It is important to understand the different scaling models:

Scaling Up (Vertical Scaling): This involves adding more resources (e.g., CPU, RAM, storage) to a single database instance. This is the primary scaling method for traditional monolithic databases like Cloud SQL. While simple to implement, it often has a hard performance ceiling determined by the largest available machine type.

Scaling Out (Horizontal Scaling): This involves adding more nodes or instances to a database cluster. This is the native scaling method for distributed databases like Cloud Spanner, BigQuery, and Bigtable, which are designed to scale linearly. Linear scaling means that doubling the number of nodes will roughly double the performance capacity (throughput and storage). This is a key advantage for handling massive, growing workloads, as there is no theoretical performance ceiling.

Scaling a Cloud SQL Instance

An internal reporting tool running on a single Cloud SQL instance becomes slow as more employees run complex reports. The team evaluates two options: (1) scale up the machine type, which is simple but has a higher continuous cost, or (2) scale out by adding a read replica, which is more cost-effective and targets the read-heavy workload but requires application changes to direct traffic. Since the issue is primarily with read-heavy reports, they choose to scale out, providing a more targeted and cost-effective solution.

The best scaling strategy for a database depends on various factors, including the workload, budget, and operational capabilities. Table 7.2 compares the two scaling strategies.

Scaling Database Instances Based on Current and Upcoming Workload

To make informed scaling decisions, a good understanding of the current and upcoming workload is necessary.

Analyzing Historical Data: The metrics in Cloud Monitoring can be used to analyze historical workload patterns, which can help identify trends and predict future growth.

Capacity Planning: Based on the analysis of historical data and any known upcoming events (such as a marketing campaign or a new product launch), capacity planning can be performed to determine future resource needs.

TABLE 7.2 Scaling strategies in Google Cloud

Feature	Scaling up (Vertical)	Scaling out (Horizontal)
Complexity	Simpler	More complex
Cost	Can be more expensive	Can be more cost-effective
Performance	Can improve both read and write performance	Primarily improves read performance (replicas) or both (nodes)
Availability	Does not improve availability	Can improve availability
Example	Increasing the machine type of a Cloud SQL instance	Adding a read replica to a Cloud SQL instance or nodes to a Bigtable cluster

Automated Scaling: For some database services, such as Cloud Spanner and BigQuery, Google Cloud can automatically scale resources based on the workload. For other services, such as Cloud SQL, instances must be scaled manually.

Proactive Scaling for an AlloyDB Workload

A retail company using AlloyDB for its sales system is preparing for its annual Black Friday sale, which historically sees a 10x increase in traffic. By analyzing Cloud Monitoring metrics from last year's sale, the team identifies that CPU and active connections were saturated. Two weeks before the sale, they perform capacity planning and schedule a maintenance window to scale up the primary instance's vCPU and RAM and scale out the read pool. After the sale, they scale the resources back down to optimize costs.

Proactive scaling is crucial. Scaling should occur before a database struggles to handle its workload to avoid performance degradation or downtime.

Defining Replication Strategies

Replication is the process of copying data from one database instance to another for high availability, disaster recovery, and read scaling:

High Availability: Replicating data to a standby instance in a different zone ensures that the database remains available in the event of a zonal failure.

Disaster Recovery: Replicating data to a different region protects the data from a regional disaster.

Read Scaling: Replicating data to one or more read replicas can offload read traffic from the primary instance and improve read performance.

Google Cloud offers a variety of replication options for its database services. The best replication strategy for a database will depend on its specific requirements for availability, disaster recovery, and performance:

Cloud SQL: Supports both high availability (with a standby instance in a different zone) and read replicas.

AlloyDB for PostgreSQL: Offers a highly available architecture with a primary instance and a standby instance in a different zone. It also supports read pools for scaling read traffic.

Cloud Spanner: A globally distributed database that automatically replicates data across multiple regions, providing both high availability and disaster recovery.

Bigtable: Replication allows for increased availability and durability of data by storing a copy of it in a separate cluster.

Bigtable Replication for DR and Low Latency

A media company uses Bigtable to serve personalized content to users in North America and Europe. To ensure high availability and low latency, they configure a multicluster routing policy with one cluster in us-central1 and a replicated cluster in europe-west1. Application requests are automatically routed to the nearest cluster. If the U.S. cluster becomes unavailable, traffic fails over to the European cluster, ensuring continuous service.

When defining a replication strategy, the following factors should be considered:

Recovery Time Objective (RTO): How quickly the database needs to be recovered in the event of a failure.

Recovery Point Objective (RPO): How much data can be lost in the event of a failure.

Cost: Replication can add to the cost of the database environment.

By carefully considering these factors, a replication strategy that meets specific needs can be designed.

Optimize Queries for Cost and Performance

An inefficient query can be a major source of both poor performance and high cost, especially in cloud databases where payment is often based on resource consumption. Optimizing queries is a critical skill for any database engineer.

General Best Practices

To achieve consistent performance across any database engine, engineers should adhere to fundamental SQL optimization principles that minimize resource overhead.

Select Only Necessary Columns: Avoid using `SELECT *`. Explicitly list the columns needed to reduce the amount of data read from storage and transferred over the network.

Filter Early and Often: Use `WHERE` clauses to filter data as early as possible in the query. This reduces the size of the dataset that subsequent operations (like joins and aggregations) need to process.

Analyze Execution Plans: Use tools like `EXPLAIN` (in SQL databases) or the query execution details (in BigQuery and Spanner) to understand how the database is executing a query. This can reveal inefficiencies like full table scans or suboptimal join strategies.

Service-Specific Optimization Strategies

While general principles like filtering early and selecting only necessary columns apply broadly, each Google Cloud database service offers unique internal mechanisms that require specialized tuning strategies to balance performance and cost.

Optimizing Cloud SQL Performance

Cloud SQL provides a familiar relational environment, but because it often serves as the transactional backbone of an application, its performance is highly sensitive to query efficiency and resource provisioning. Unlike distributed services that scale horizontally by default, Cloud SQL primarily relies on vertical scaling for write operations.

Query Optimization and Indexing   Effective query performance in Cloud SQL is driven by minimizing resource-intensive operations like full table scans.

> **Cloud SQL Query Insights**   This visual dashboard allows engineers to identify which queries consume the most CPU time. It provides a drill-down into query plans to identify specific bottlenecks.

> **Index Advisor**   For PostgreSQL users, the Index Advisor analyzes the query workload and recommends specific new indexes that could significantly reduce execution time by avoiding full table scans.

Scaling and Availability Levers   Because Cloud SQL is often a monolithic instance, managing its growth requires a mix of vertical and horizontal strategies.

> **Vertical Scaling (Scale Up)**   Increasing the machine type (vCPU and RAM) is the primary method to improve write performance and handle complex batch jobs.

> **Read Replicas (Scale Out)**   To alleviate pressure on the primary instance, read-heavy workloads (such as reporting) should be offloaded to one or more read replicas.

> **High Availability (HA)**   Configuring a standby instance in a different zone ensures the database remains available during a zonal failure, though this is primarily for reliability rather than performance.

Optimizing AlloyDB Performance

AlloyDB is a fully PostgreSQL-compatible service designed for high-end transactional and analytical workloads, featuring a decoupled compute and storage architecture that allows for more flexible scaling than standard Cloud SQL.

Advanced Diagnostic Tools   AlloyDB integrates deeply with the PostgreSQL ecosystem while offering Google-native enhancements for visibility.

> **Enhanced Query Insights**   AlloyDB uses Query Insights to pinpoint expensive queries and provide performance recommendations tailored to its specialized storage layer.

> **Standard Extensions**   Engineers can utilize the pg_stat_statements extension to track execution statistics for all SQL statements over time, identifying "creeping" performance degradation.

Lock Management   To resolve resource contention, the pg_locks view is essential for identifying which transactions are holding EXCLUSIVE locks that block smaller update transactions.

Specialized Architecture and Scaling   AlloyDB's architecture provides unique levers for managing massive workloads that exceed the capabilities of standard PostgreSQL.

Read Pools   Instead of individual replicas, AlloyDB uses "read pools"—a collection of nodes that can scale horizontally to handle intense reporting or analytical traffic.

Dynamic Scaling   The primary instance can be scaled up (vCPU/RAM) during anticipated peaks, such as seasonal sales, to handle increased concurrent connections and transaction volume.

Contention Resolution   For long-running reporting jobs that cause database locking, the best practice is to route that traffic specifically to a read pool node, preventing it from blocking the primary writer.

Manual Execution Analysis   For MySQL and SQL Server, engineers should manually analyze query plans using EXPLAIN to identify inefficient join strategies or unindexed column filters.

Optimizing Cloud Spanner Performance

Cloud Spanner provides a unique combination of relational semantics and horizontal scalability. However, because it is a distributed system, achieving peak performance requires more than just standard SQL tuning; it requires an understanding of how data and execution plans are managed across nodes and regions.

Managing Write Performance and Leader Regions   In a multiregion Spanner configuration, writes are handled by a designated **leader region**. While reads can be served from any replica, all write transactions must be routed to this leader to be committed.

Latency   Impact: Read-write transactions issued from a non-leader region require multiple round-trips to the leader replica to commit successfully. This introduces unavoidable cross-region latency.

Strategic Routing   Applications should, when possible, route write traffic directly to the leader region to minimize these round-trips.

Architectural Decisions   Selecting the leader region based on where the highest volume of write traffic originates is a critical design step to optimize global performance.

Query Execution and Parameterization   A critical best practice for Spanner is the use of **query parameters** rather than embedding literal values directly into SQL strings.

The Compilation Process   When Spanner receives a query, it compiles the string into an executable query plan, which is then cached.

Cache Misses   Building queries via string concatenation makes each query unique. This prevents Spanner from reusing cached plans, forcing a costly recompilation for every execution.

Efficiency   Parameterization (e.g., WHERE CustomerId = @customerId) separates the query structure from the values, allowing Spanner to reuse the cached plan across different inputs, saving significant CPU and reducing latency.

Advanced Schema and Tuning Techniques   Beyond basic SQL, Spanner offers specialized mechanisms to co-locate data and guide the optimizer:

Interleaved Tables   This technique allows you to physically store child table rows (e.g., Order_Items) alongside their parent row (e.g., Orders) on the same server. This dramatically improves join performance by reducing I/O and increasing data locality.

Secondary Indexes   Use these to speed up queries that do not filter on the primary key.

Query Hints   For complex scenarios where the optimizer may not choose the most efficient path, query hints (e.g., @{FORCE_INDEX=...}) can be used to manually guide the query engine.

Cost Optimization Levers   Unlike other services where cost is primarily usage-based, Spanner's cost is driven by provisioned resources.

Compute Capacity   This is the primary lever for managing costs and is measured in Processing Units (PUs) or Nodes (1 Node = 1,000 PUs). You are billed for the amount of compute capacity provisioned per hour, regardless of utilization.

The Goal of Provisioning   You must balance performance targets—such as CPU utilization and latency—against the cost of over-provisioning.

Google Cloud Recommender   This tool provides insights into idle or underutilized instances, helping you identify opportunities to scale down compute capacity and save money without impacting your application.

Benefits of Parameterization

Using query parameters separates the query structure from the values. Spanner compiles and caches the plan for the query structure once and reuses it for subsequent executions with different parameter values. This is significantly more efficient.

Nonperformant example (string concatenation)

```
-- A new query plan is compiled for every customerId
SELECT * FROM Customers WHERE CustomerId = 'customer-123';
SELECT * FROM Customers WHERE CustomerId = 'customer-456';
```

Performant example (query parameters)

```
-- The same query plan is cached and reused
-- The @customerId value changes, but the query structure is
identical
SELECT * FROM Customers WHERE CustomerId = @customerId;
```

Optimizing Bigtable Performance

Bigtable is a NoSQL, wide-column database where performance is inextricably linked to schema design. Unlike relational databases, Bigtable does not have a query optimizer to "fix" inefficient access patterns; the responsibility for performance lies entirely with the engineer's row key strategy.

The Centrality of Row Key Design   The row key is the only index in Bigtable. A poorly designed row key is analogous to a missing or incorrect primary key index in a relational system.

Preventing Hotspotting   Row keys must be designed to distribute reads and writes evenly across the cluster.

Redesigning for Scale   If a sequential row key (like sensor_id-timestamp) causes a single node to saturate (monitored via the "hottest node" metric), it should be redesigned with a salted prefix or hashed value to spread the load across other nodes.

Field Filtering   Because there are no secondary indexes, engineers must use targeted row and column filters to minimize the amount of data scanned from disk during a read operation.

Diagnosing Performance with Key Visualizer   Key Visualizer is the primary tool for diagnosing Bigtable latency and performance anomalies.

Visual Heatmaps   It generates a heatmap of row keys over time, allowing engineers to instantly see if activity is concentrated on a narrow key range (bright yellow/white bands).

Metric Correlation   It helps identify whether high latency is due to application access patterns (hot row keys) or underlying cluster resource contention.

Replication and Routing Policies   Bigtable replication is used not just for durability, but for global performance optimization and disaster recovery.

Multicluster Routing   By placing clusters in different regions (e.g., us-central1 and europe-west1), application requests are automatically routed to the nearest cluster, ensuring low-latency service for a global user base.

Failover and Availability   In the event of a regional outage, traffic automatically fails over to a healthy cluster, maintaining high availability without manual intervention.

Optimizing BigQuery Performance

In BigQuery's serverless architecture, optimization is primarily focused on reducing the volume of data scanned, as cost and performance are directly correlated under the on-demand pricing model.

Data Pruning: Partitioning and Clustering   These are the two most effective levers for reducing both query time and execution cost by limiting the data the BigQuery engine has to read.

Partitioned Tables   Dividing a table by a column (usually a DATE or TIMESTAMP) allows BigQuery to skip scanning entire years of data when only a single day is required. This "partition pruning" can reduce query costs by over 99 percent.

Clustered Tables   Clustering sorts data within partitions based on specific columns. This further refines the data pruning process for complex filters, allowing the engine to skip blocks of data that don't match the query criteria.

Query Efficiency and Execution Details   Optimizing the SQL syntax itself is critical for maintaining performance in multi-petabyte environments.

Column Selection   You must avoid SELECT * and explicitly name columns. Since BigQuery uses columnar storage, selecting extra columns directly increases the amount of data processed and billed.

Execution Details   The Query Execution Details provide a stage-by-stage breakdown of the query plan. Engineers use this to identify "bottlenecks," such as stages where too much data is being "shuffled" across the network or where a single slot is processing a disproportionate amount of data.

Materialized Views   For repeated, complex analytical queries, materialized views should be used to cache and accelerate common aggregations, reducing the need to re-scan raw tables.

Governance: Custom Cost Controls   Because BigQuery's on-demand model can lead to unexpected costs from inefficient queries, administrative controls are a core part of the performance and cost strategy.

Project-Level Quotas   These act as an aggregate hard cap for all users within a project to protect the total budget from runaway costs.

User-Level Quotas   These provide granular control, allowing individual users or service accounts to experiment freely within a daily limit (e.g., 1 TB/day) without risking the project's entire daily quota.

Optimizing a BigQuery Query with Partitioning

An analytics team runs a daily query to find the total sales from the previous day from a 50 TB sales table that holds three years of historical data. Initially, the query scans the entire table, processing 50 TB of data, taking over 3 minutes to run, and costing $312.50 for each execution (at $6.25/TB on-demand pricing).

An engineer modifies the table to be partitioned by the `transaction_date` column. The query is then updated with a `WHERE` clause: `WHERE transaction_date = CURRENT_DATE() - 1`.

Now, the query only scans the data in a single partition—one day's worth of data, which is approximately 50 GB. This change reduces the execution time to under 5 seconds and drops the cost to just $0.30. The optimization resulted in a reduction in query cost and execution time of over 99 percent.

BigQuery Cost Controls

Because BigQuery can process enormous amounts of data with its on-demand pricing model, additional controls can help protect against unexpected query costs. This is especially important in environments with multiple projects and users.

You can manage query costs for on-demand usage by setting custom quotas on the amount of query data processed. These quotas can be set at both the project level and the user level.

Project-Level Quotas: Apply to all users and service accounts within a project, acting as an aggregate hard cap.

User-Level Quotas: Apply to individual users or service accounts, providing more granular control.

These quotas reset daily at midnight Pacific Time. If a query would exceed the remaining quota, it will fail with an error, preventing further cost accrual.

Implementing BigQuery Cost Controls

A company gives its data science team access to a large BigQuery project for exploratory analysis. To prevent runaway costs from inefficient queries, the cloud administrator implements two custom quotas. First, a project-level quota of 10 TB per day is set as a safety net. Second, each data scientist is given a user-level quota of 1 TB per day. This allows individual users to experiment freely within a reasonable budget, while the project-level quota prevents the aggregate usage from exceeding the team's daily budget.

EXERCISE 7.4

Codelab: Setting Up Custom Cost Controls for BigQuery

```
https://codelabs.developers.google.com/bigquery-custom-quota
```

In this exercise, you will implement custom cost controls in BigQuery to manage on-demand usage and prevent unexpected expenses. Accessed via the URL provided, this walk-through offers hands-on practice deploying what you learned earlier in the chapter. You will focus on configuring project-level and user-level daily quotas, ensuring you can effectively govern data processing limits and enforce hard caps on resource consumption.

Summary

This chapter has covered the essential aspects of monitoring, troubleshooting, and optimizing databases in Google Cloud. We began by exploring the configuration of monitoring and troubleshooting options, including the assessment of slow-running queries, database locking, and missing indexes, for both managed and self-managed databases. We then detailed the monitoring of database vitals, management of quotas, investigation of resource contention, and setting up of alerts.

Next, we focused on optimizing for cost and performance. We discussed the differences between scaling up and scaling out, how to make informed scaling decisions based on workload, and how to optimize queries for both cost and performance. We also reviewed various replication strategies for achieving high availability and disaster recovery, and specific optimization techniques for Cloud Spanner, including the critical importance of query parameterization.

By applying the principles and techniques discussed in this chapter, you can ensure that your Google Cloud databases are performant, reliable, and cost-effective, allowing you to focus on building great applications.

Exam Essentials

Configure database monitoring and troubleshooting options.   Know how to use Cloud SQL Query Insights, Cloud Spanner query statistics, and BigQuery query execution details to identify and troubleshoot slow-running queries.

Understand how to enable, access, and centralize slow query logs for self-managed databases on Compute Engine using the Ops Agent.

Be able to identify performance bottlenecks in AlloyDB and Bigtable using tools like Query Insights and Key Visualizer.

Understand how to identify and resolve database locking issues in Cloud SQL, AlloyDB, and Cloud Spanner, and how contention manifests in Bigtable.

Be familiar with the tools available for identifying missing indexes, such as the Cloud SQL and AlloyDB Index Advisors, and understand the importance of row key design for Bigtable.

Know which key metrics to monitor in Cloud Monitoring to assess the health and performance of your databases, including the use of audit logs.

Understand the importance of monitoring and managing quotas to prevent service disruptions.

Be able to investigate and resolve database resource contention.

Know how to set up alerts in Cloud Monitoring to be proactively notified of potential problems.

Optimize database cost and performance in Google Cloud. Understand the difference between scaling up and scaling out and be able to choose the appropriate scaling strategy for a given workload.

Know how to use historical data to perform capacity planning and make informed scaling decisions.

Be familiar with the different replication strategies available in Google Cloud and be able to design a replication strategy that meets specific requirements for availability and disaster recovery.

Understand how to optimize queries for cost and performance using techniques like indexing, partitioning, and analyzing execution plans.

Know why query parameterization is critical for Cloud Spanner performance and how it prevents query plan cache misses.

Understand how Spanner's leader region architecture impacts write performance and how to optimize for it.

Know the primary levers for controlling Spanner costs, including compute capacity and the role of the Recommender.

Review Questions

1. A database engineer is troubleshooting an intermittent issue on a Cloud SQL instance that results in application errors. The errors are not consistent and seem to happen at random times. Which Cloud service would provide detailed diagnostic information, such as specific error messages and stack traces, that occurred on the database instance?

   A. Cloud Monitoring

   B. Cloud Logging

   C. Cloud IAM

   D. Cloud Storage

2. A professional Cloud Database engineer wants to identify opportunities to reduce the operational cost of their Cloud Spanner instance without negatively impacting performance. Which Google Cloud tool provides insights into idle or underutilized Spanner instances, suggesting ways to optimize compute capacity?

   A. Cloud Audit Logs

   B. Cloud Spanner Key Visualizer

   C. Google Cloud Recommender

   D. Cloud Billing reports

3. A database administrator wants to set up a comprehensive alerting system for their Cloud SQL instances. They need to be notified via email if storage utilization exceeds 80 percent and via PagerDuty if the instance becomes unresponsive. Which service is best suited to configure both these types of alerts?

   A. Cloud Logging

   B. Cloud Monitoring

   C. Cloud DNS

   D. Cloud Storage

4. A batch job is failing intermittently on an AlloyDB for PostgreSQL instance due to transaction timeouts. The database administrator suspects database locking is causing the issue. Which method should the administrator use to identify which transactions are holding locks and blocking others in AlloyDB?

   A. Analyze Cloud Monitoring metrics for I/O waits.

   B. Query the `pg_locks` view.

   C. Check `information_schema.innodb_locks`.

   D. Use the Key Visualizer tool.

5. During a sudden peak in traffic, a new component of an application fails to connect to a previously working Cloud SQL database, reporting a generic "resource unavailable" error. No changes were made to the database configuration. Based on the scenario, what is a likely cause of this issue, and what should be checked first?

   A. A network misconfiguration; check VPC firewall rules.

   B. The Cloud SQL instance ran out of disk space; check storage utilization.

   C. An API quota limit was reached; check the Quotas page in Google Cloud Console.

   D. The database machine type is too small; scale up the instance.

6. A Cloud SQL for PostgreSQL instance is experiencing high CPU usage and query latency during certain batch operations. The database engineer suspects inefficient queries are the primary cause. Which of the following is the most effective approach to optimize these problematic queries in Cloud SQL for PostgreSQL?

   A. Increase the Cloud SQL instance storage size.

   B. Analyze query plans using `EXPLAIN ANALYZE` and consider adding appropriate indexes.

   C. Enable SSL/TLS encryption for all connections.

   D. Migrate the database to a multiregion configuration.

7. A retail company's e-commerce application is experiencing slow page loads for product detail pages. The database engineer suspects a specific query is the bottleneck on their Cloud SQL for PostgreSQL instance. Which Google Cloud tool should the engineer use to quickly identify the most resource-intensive queries and analyze their performance?

   A. Cloud Logging

   B. Cloud Monitoring custom dashboards

   C. Cloud SQL Query Insights

   D. Cloud Trace

8. A newly deployed feature on a Cloud SQL Enterprise Plus edition for PostgreSQL instance is performing slower than expected. Initial investigation suggests a missing index might be the cause for some queries. Which Cloud SQL feature can help identify potential missing indexes by analyzing the database's query workload?

   A. Cloud SQL Query Insights Index Advisor

   B. Cloud Monitoring's CPU utilization reports

   C. `EXPLAIN ANALYZE` command for each query

   D. Cloud Logging's error logs

9. A database on Compute Engine experiences intermittent performance degradation, characterized by high I/O wait times. What does high I/O wait time typically indicate in a database context, suggesting a potential area for investigation?

    A. The database has too much available memory.

    B. The database is waiting for disk I/O operations to complete, suggesting contention for storage resources.

    C. The CPU is underutilized and needs more work.

    D. The network connection to the database is experiencing high latency.

10. A retail company is preparing for a major online sales event, anticipating a 10x increase in website traffic and database load for their AlloyDB for PostgreSQL cluster. What is the most effective approach to ensure the AlloyDB cluster can handle the expected surge in workload without performance degradation?

    A. Wait for the sales event to start, then manually scale up the cluster if performance drops.

    B. Proactively analyze historical workload data, perform capacity planning, and scale up/out the cluster before the event.

    C. Rely on AlloyDB's automatic scaling to handle the load dynamically.

    D. Implement database sharding during the sales event to distribute the load.

11. A global application uses Cloud Spanner with a multiregion configuration. Developers notice that write operations from users in Europe are experiencing higher latency compared to reads. What is the most likely reason for this increased write latency in a multiregion Spanner configuration, and how can it be optimized?

    A. Reads are routed to the nearest replica, but all writes must be routed to the designated leader region. Optimize by setting the leader region to Europe.

    B. Spanner uses asynchronous replication for writes, leading to eventual consistency. Optimize by enabling synchronous write replication.

    C. The Spanner instance is undersized. Optimize by adding more read replicas in Europe.

    D. The application is not using interleaved tables. Optimize by re-architecting the schema for interleaving.

12. A Cloud Spanner instance has been provisioned with three nodes but is consistently showing low CPU utilization, indicating it might be over-provisioned. How can the cost of this Cloud Spanner instance be optimized without impacting performance if the workload remains low?

    A. Decrease the number of processing units (PUs) or nodes provisioned.

    B. Convert the Spanner instance to a Cloud SQL instance.

    C. Implement a connection pooler to reduce idle connections.

    D. Enable interleaved tables to reduce storage consumption.

13. A real-time analytics application using Cloud Bigtable is experiencing high latency for write operations. The data model involves storing events with row keys like `user_id#timestamp`. Which Bigtable specific tool should the engineer use to diagnose if the write latency is due to hotspotting on certain nodes?

    A. Key Visualizer

    B. Query Insights

    C. `pg_locks` view

    D. Cloud Spanner Query Statistics

14. A data analyst submits a complex SQL query to BigQuery that consistently takes a long time to complete and consumes significant resources. Which BigQuery specific feature should the analyst use to understand how the query is executed and identify potential bottlenecks for optimization?

    A. BigQuery Query Execution Details

    B. Cloud SQL Query Insights

    C. `EXPLAIN ANALYZE` command in a local client

    D. Cloud Monitoring's I/O metrics

15. An application sporadically loses connectivity to its Cloud SQL database, leading to user errors. The database instance itself appears to be running according to logs. Which Cloud Monitoring metric would be most helpful to investigate if the database is experiencing intermittent connectivity issues or connection saturation?

    A. CPU Utilization

    B. Disk Write Operations

    C. Active Connections

    D. Storage Capacity

16. You've set up an alert in Cloud Monitoring for unusually high database error rates. You now want to automatically trigger a detailed diagnostic script on a VM when this alert fires. Which Google Cloud service can subscribe to the alert notification and execute the script for automated response?

    A. Cloud DNS

    B. Pub/Sub topic connected to a Cloud Function or Cloud Run service

    C. Cloud CDN

    D. Cloud Interconnect

17. A Cloud Spanner database stores customer orders, and for performance, related `order_items` are frequently queried together with their parent order. What Spanner schema design technique can improve query performance for frequently accessed parent-child relationships, such as `orders` and `order_items`, by co-locating data?

- **A.** Creating a separate read replica for order_items
- **B.** Using interleaved tables
- **C.** Implementing database sharding across multiple Spanner instances
- **D.** Disabling secondary indexes on the `order_items` table

18. A data warehouse application uses AlloyDB for PostgreSQL, and reports are running slowly. The team identifies that read queries are overwhelming the primary instance. Beyond scaling up the primary, what is the best AlloyDB-specific feature to alleviate the read workload pressure and improve reporting performance?

- **A.** Creating a standby instance in a different region
- **B.** Configuring a read pool with multiple read replicas
- **C.** Enabling `pg_stat_statements` on the primary
- **D.** Using BigQuery for all reporting

19. A database needs to scale to handle increasing demand. The engineering team is debating between scaling up and scaling out. What is a key characteristic of scaling out (horizontal scaling) that differentiates it from scaling up (vertical scaling) for a database, particularly in the context of large workloads?

- **A.** Scaling out always provides infinite capacity with no cost increase.
- **B.** Scaling out involves adding more powerful resources to a single machine, while scaling up adds more machines.
- **C.** Scaling out often involves distributing the workload across multiple nodes or instances, enabling linear performance increases for distributed databases.
- **D.** Scaling out is primarily used for improving write performance only.

20. A global gaming company uses Bigtable for storing player profiles and game state. They need to ensure high availability and low latency for players across North America and Europe, with automated failover in case of a regional outage. Which Bigtable feature should they configure to meet these requirements for global distribution, availability, and low latency?

- **A.** A single-cluster Bigtable instance in a central region
- **B.** Bigtable replication with multicluster routing
- **C.** Exporting Bigtable data to Cloud Storage daily for backup
- **D.** Using Cloud SQL read replicas for Bigtable data

Chapter

8

Managing and Automating Database Operations

✔ **2.4 Optimize database cost and performance in Google Cloud.**

- Continuously assess and optimize the cost of running a database solution.

✔ **2.5 Automate common database tasks.**

- Perform database maintenance (e.g., rebuilding indexes, data exports).

- Schedule database exports.

- Manage upgrades for Google Cloud–managed databases.

- Monitor database SLA/SLOs.

The responsibilities of a Google Cloud Professional Database Engineer extend beyond initial design and deployment to include the long-term operational health and cost-effectiveness of database systems. Effective operational management hinges on automation, which transforms routine, error-prone manual tasks into dependable, repeatable processes. For example, in a high-growth e-commerce application, tasks like data cleanup, table reorganization, and backups become increasingly frequent and critical. An engineer must build automated workflows to handle these operations without manual intervention, preventing performance degradation and ensuring data protection while controlling costs.

This chapter covers the strategies and tools available on Google Cloud for streamlining routine database tasks, managing the database software life cycle, monitoring service levels, and continuously optimizing costs.

Automating Common Database Tasks

Manual intervention for routine database operations in a dynamic cloud environment is unscalable and introduces risk. Automating these tasks is a requirement for maintaining performance, ensuring reliability, and allowing engineering teams to focus on higher-value activities. Google Cloud offers a suite of serverless tools that can be orchestrated to create automation workflows for any managed database service. By using services like Cloud Scheduler, Cloud Functions, and Cloud Run, you can build event-driven or time-based triggers to handle tasks ranging from routine maintenance to complex data extraction jobs.

Performing Database Maintenance

Consistent database maintenance is fundamental to a healthy system. These tasks are necessary to reclaim unused space, update table statistics for the query optimizer, and ensure data integrity. While Google Cloud's managed services handle underlying maintenance like OS patching, database-level tasks such as managing fragmentation and rebuilding indexes often remain a shared responsibility that requires proactive configuration.

In relational databases, frequent data modifications (INSERTs, UPDATEs, DELETEs) can lead to fragmentation, where data is no longer stored contiguously on disk.

This forces the database to perform additional I/O operations, degrading query performance. In PostgreSQL-based services like Cloud SQL and AlloyDB, this often manifests as "bloat," where outdated row versions consume disk space and slow down table scans.

Automating maintenance ensures these tasks are performed consistently. The combination of a trigger (the "when") and a compute service (the "what") is the standard pattern for this automation. The primary tools for this in Google Cloud are:

Cloud Scheduler: This is the trigger, or the "when." It is a fully managed cron job service used to initiate tasks on a recurring schedule (e.g., daily at 2 a.m., every Monday at midnight). Cloud Scheduler does not execute the maintenance logic itself; instead, it sends a request to a target that contains the logic. This target can be an HTTP endpoint on a Cloud Run service, a Pub/Sub topic, or an App Engine application. For database maintenance, a common pattern is to have Cloud Scheduler trigger a Cloud Function either directly via an HTTP request or indirectly by publishing a message to a Pub/Sub topic that the function subscribes to.

Cloud Functions: This is a lightweight compute service, or the "what." It is a serverless, event-driven platform for running short-lived, single-purpose code in response to triggers. A function can contain the specific logic to connect to a database instance and execute a maintenance command. For example, a Python function could use a database connector library to run a VACUUM command on a Cloud SQL for PostgreSQL instance. Cloud Functions are ideal for tasks that are relatively simple and can complete within the function's maximum timeout period (up to 9 minutes for HTTP-triggered functions).

Cloud Run: This is a more powerful and flexible compute service, also part of the "what." It is a managed platform that runs stateless containers. You would choose Cloud Run over Cloud Functions for maintenance tasks that have more complex requirements. For instance, if a maintenance script requires a specific third-party library that isn't available in the standard Cloud Functions runtime, you can package that library and your script into a Docker container image and deploy it as a Cloud Run service. Cloud Run is also the better choice for tasks that may take longer to complete than the Cloud Functions timeout allows

---

EXERCISE 8.1

Codelab: Triggering Cloud Run Jobs with Cloud Scheduler

```
https://codelabs.developers.google.com/cloud-run-jobs-and-cloud-
scheduler
```

In this exercise, you will configure Cloud Run jobs and Cloud Scheduler to automate the cleanup of invalid data within a sample service. Accessed via the URL provided, this walk-through offers

(Continued)

hands-on practice deploying what you learned earlier in the chapter. You will focus on executing and scheduling containerized tasks to handle operational workflows, ensuring you can effectively manage background processes and verify their successful completion through system logs.

Assessing and Managing Fragmentation

The first step is to assess the level of fragmentation. **For Cloud SQL and AlloyDB for PostgreSQL,** you can use SQL queries against system catalogs to estimate table and index bloat. A common query, like the following, joins system tables to compare the actual size of a table to its expected size.

Sample Query:

```
-- This is a simplified query for illustrative purposes.
-- More complex and accurate community scripts are widely available.
SELECT
  table_name,
  pg_size_pretty(pg_total_relation_size(table_name::regclass) -
           pg_relation_size(table_name::regclass)) AS index_size,
  pg_size_pretty(pg_relation_size(table_name::regclass)) AS table_size,
  pg_size_pretty(
    pg_total_relation_size(table_name::regclass) -
    (SELECT (reltuples/1000) * 8192 FROM pg_class WHERE relname=table_name)
  ) AS bloat
FROM information_schema.tables
WHERE table_schema = 'public' ORDER BY bloat DESC;
```

Sample Output:

```
| table_name | index_size | table_size | bloat |
| :--- | :--- | :--- | :--- |
| loan_applications | 12 GB | 25 GB | 8 GB |
| customer_events | 2 GB | 5 GB | 500 MB |
```

The bloat column gives an estimate of wasted space. A high amount of bloat, especially as a percentage of the total table size, indicates that maintenance is needed. For the `loan_applications` table, 8 GB of bloat is significant. The appropriate action would be to schedule a VACUUM operation during a maintenance window. If index bloat is the primary concern, a REINDEX CONCURRENTLY would be more targeted.

For Cloud SQL for MySQL, the Data_free column in the output of SHOW TABLE STATUS can indicate fragmentation within InnoDB tables. The following is a sample query.

Sample Query:

```
SHOW TABLE STATUS LIKE 'orders';
```

Sample Output (abbreviated):

```
| Name | Engine | Rows | Avg_row_length | Data_length | Data_free |
| :--- | :--- | :--- | :--- | :--- | :--- |
| orders | InnoDB | 10542891 | 256 | 2700000000 | 314572800 |
```

The Data_free column shows the number of bytes allocated but unused. In this example, there are 300 MB of free space. This space can be reclaimed by the operating system. If this value is significant, the recommended action is to run OPTIMIZE TABLE orders; during a low-traffic period, as this operation can lock the table while it rebuilds.

For Oracle on Bare Metal Solution, you can query Oracle's data dictionary views to identify segments with reclaimable space. See the following sample query.

Sample Query:

```
-- Requires running DBMS_SPACE.ASA_RECOMMENDATIONS first
SELECT segment_owner, segment_name, segment_type,
    allocated_space/1024/1024 AS allocated_mb,
    used_space/1024/1024 AS used_mb,
    (allocated_space - used_space)/1024/1024 AS reclaimable_mb
FROM TABLE(dbms_space.asa_recommendations('FALSE', 'FALSE', 'FALSE'));
```

Sample Output:

```
| SEGMENT_OWNER | SEGMENT_NAME | SEGMENT_TYPE | ALLOCATED_MB | USED_MB | RECLAIMABLE_MB |
| :--- | :--- | :--- | :--- | :--- | :--- |
| FIN | TRANSACTIONS | TABLE | 10240 | 6144 | 4096 |
| FIN | IDX_TRANS_DATE | INDEX | 5120 | 4096 | 1024 |
```

The `reclaimable_mb` column indicates space that can be freed. A large value suggests table bloat or fragmentation. For the `TRANSACTIONS` table, 4 GB of space can be reclaimed. The appropriate action would be to perform a full vacuum operation to reclaim space to the operating system, such as `VACUUM FULL FIN.TRANSACTIONS;`, or to rebuild the table online using an extension like `pg_repack`.

The **Cloud Spanner and Bigtable** services have different storage architectures, where fragmentation is not a user-managed concern; Google's underlying systems handle data compaction and distribution automatically.

Once identified, fragmentation can be managed using database-specific commands. For example, in PostgreSQL, `VACUUM` reclaims space from dead tuples, whereas `REINDEX CONCURRENTLY` rebuilds bloated indexes without blocking write operations.

Managing Index Bloat in AlloyDB

A fintech application is using AlloyDB for its high-throughput loan processing system. The `loan_applications` table contains several indexes to accelerate queries on different application statuses (pending, approved, rejected). Due to frequent updates as applications move through the workflow, the indexes were becoming significantly bloated, leading to slower `UPDATE` operations and increased storage costs.

The database engineering team implemented a Cloud Function that executes a specialized PostgreSQL query to identify indexes with a bloat percentage over 30 percent. They used Cloud Scheduler to run this function weekly. If the function detects a bloated index, it logs the finding and triggers a second function that executes `REINDEX CONCURRENTLY` on that specific index during a designated nightly maintenance window. This targeted, automated approach maintains the performance of heavily used indexes without requiring a disruptive `VACUUM FULL` or a full table reindex.

Scheduling Database Exports

Exporting data from production databases is a standard operational requirement for several purposes, including offline analysis, compliance archiving, and populating nonproduction environments. Google Cloud provides native, managed methods for exporting data from its database services, typically to Cloud Storage, a versatile and cost-effective staging location.

Export Mechanisms and Automation

Selecting the appropriate export method depends on the specific database engine and the required output format for downstream consumption.

Cloud SQL/AlloyDB: Exports can be initiated via the gcloud CLI or the Cloud SQL Admin API to create SQL or CSV files in Cloud Storage.

Cloud Spanner/Bigtable: These services integrate with Dataflow, using managed templates to export data in formats like Avro or CSV to Cloud Storage.

Firestore: Offers a managed export/import service to back up collections to Cloud Storage.

Operational efficiency is achieved by scheduling these exports using the standard pattern of Cloud Scheduler triggering a Cloud Function or Cloud Run job.

Scheduling a Daily Spanner Export to BigQuery

A global logistics company uses a multiregion Cloud Spanner instance to manage real-time shipment tracking data. The data science team requires a daily snapshot of this data in BigQuery to run supply chain optimization models.

The Cloud Database Engineer automates this workflow:

1. A Cloud Scheduler job is configured to run daily at 01:00 UTC.

2. The scheduler triggers a Cloud Function that initiates a Dataflow job using the Cloud Spanner To Cloud Storage Avro template, exporting the `shipments` and `locations` tables to a Cloud Storage bucket.

3. The Dataflow job is configured to publish a message to a Pub/Sub topic upon successful completion.

4. A second Cloud Function, triggered by this Pub/Sub topic, executes a BigQuery load job to import the new Avro files from Cloud Storage into a partitioned `shipments_daily` table in BigQuery.

This event-driven, serverless pipeline ensures that fresh data is reliably available for analysis each morning without manual intervention.

Managing Upgrades for Google Cloud–Managed Databases

Maintaining up-to-date database software is critical for security, performance, and feature access. Google Cloud simplifies this for its managed databases, but the database engineer is responsible for planning and managing major version upgrades.

There are two categories of upgrades:

Minor Version Upgrades   These include security patches and bug fixes (e.g., PostgreSQL 14.1 to 14.2). For services like Cloud SQL, Google handles these automatically during a predefined maintenance window. These upgrades are backward-compatible and typically involve minimal downtime (often under 60 seconds).

Major Version Upgrades   These introduce significant new features and potential backward-incompatible changes (e.g., PostgreSQL 13 to 14). These upgrades are user-initiated and require careful planning and testing.

The recommended process for a major version upgrade is as follows:

Testing in a Nonproduction Environment   Create a clone of the production database and perform the major version upgrade on the clone.

Validating Application Compatibility   Conduct thorough testing of your application against the upgraded clone. Verify SQL syntax, driver behavior, and query performance to identify any regressions or breaking changes.

Planning the Production Upgrade   After validating the new version, plan the production upgrade. For applications that can tolerate downtime, an in-place upgrade can be scheduled during a maintenance window.

Executing and Monitoring   Perform the upgrade and closely monitor application and database metrics (latency, error rates, CPU) to confirm normal operation.

Planning a Zero-Downtime Upgrade for Cloud SQL

An online retail company's inventory system runs on Cloud SQL for MySQL. An upgrade from MySQL 5.7 to 8.0 is needed to use new features like window functions. The system must be available 24/7, making the downtime from a standard in-place upgrade unacceptable.

The database engineer designs a near-zero downtime migration. Instead of an in-place upgrade, they provision a new, separate Cloud SQL instance with MySQL 8.0. They then use the Database Migration Service (DMS) to configure continuous replication from the 5.7 instance to the new 8.0 instance. Once the initial data sync is complete, DMS maintains near real-time replication. During a low-traffic period, the application is briefly put into maintenance mode, the replication lag is verified to be zero, and the application's connection string is switched to the new MySQL 8.0 instance. The total downtime is limited to a few seconds, completing the major version upgrade without impacting sales.

Monitoring Database SLA/SLOs

Ensuring your database meets its reliability targets is a core operational function. Doing so requires differentiating between the service provider's guarantee and your own internal goals. To design and manage these targets effectively, you must become familiar with the following key concepts and how they interact:

Service Level Agreement (SLA): A formal commitment from Google Cloud regarding service availability. For instance, a multiregion Cloud Spanner instance has a 99.999

percent monthly uptime SLA. A failure to meet the SLA may result in service credits for the customer.

Service Level Objective (SLO): An *internal* reliability target defined for your service, based on user expectations. An SLO should generally be stricter than the provider's SLA. For example, you might set a 99.95 percent availability SLO for an application that relies on a Cloud SQL instance with a 99.99 percent SLA.

Service Level Indicator (SLI): The specific metric measured to track performance against an SLO. Common database SLIs include availability (the percentage of successful requests) and latency (the percentage of requests completed within a time threshold).

Cloud Monitoring is the primary tool for achieving this level of operational visibility and compliance. You can define an SLO for a service, select an SLI (e.g., `serviceruntime.googleapis.com/api/request_count` for availability), and set a performance goal. Cloud Monitoring tracks performance against this goal and calculates your error budget— the amount of unreliability your service can tolerate without violating the SLO. Alerting policies can then be configured to notify you when the error budget is being consumed too quickly, enabling a response *before* users are significantly impacted.

Monitoring Latency SLO for Cloud Spanner

A global financial trading platform uses a multiregion Cloud Spanner instance. While Spanner's 99.999 percent availability SLA is essential, the platform's customers are more sensitive to latency; a slow response is nearly as detrimental as an error.

The site reliability engineering (SRE) team defines a strict latency SLO: "99 percent of read requests must complete in under 75 milliseconds." They configure this SLO in Cloud Monitoring, using the `spanner.googleapis.com/api/request_latencies` metric as their SLI. An alert fires, indicating that the error budget for this SLO is being consumed at an alarming rate. The on-call engineer investigates using Query Insights and discovers that a newly deployed analytics feature is running an inefficient query without a proper index, causing periodic latency spikes for all users. The feature is immediately disabled, latency returns to normal, and the SLO is preserved. This proactive monitoring prevented a widespread performance issue.

Optimizing Database Cost and Performance in Google Cloud

A primary benefit of the cloud is the ability to pay for consumed resources, but this model requires active management. Cost and performance are directly related; an over-provisioned database performs well but is expensive, whereas an under-provisioned one is cheap but suffers from performance issues that impact the business. A cloud database engineer must continuously assess and optimize the database solution to meet performance SLOs at the lowest possible cost.

Continuously Assessing and Optimizing Cost

Cost optimization is an iterative process of monitoring usage, analyzing spending, identifying inefficiencies, and taking corrective action.

Assessing Costs

Effective optimization begins with a thorough assessment of cost drivers. Google Cloud provides several tools for this purpose:

Cloud Billing Reports: The Google Cloud Console includes a dashboard for viewing current and forecasted costs, with filters for project, service, SKU, and labels.

Billing Data Export to BigQuery: For more granular analysis, detailed usage and cost data can be exported to a BigQuery dataset, enabling custom SQL queries and dashboards.

Recommender: This service uses machine learning to analyze resource usage and provide actionable recommendations, such as identifying idle or over-provisioned database instances.

Assessing Bigtable Storage Costs

An IoT company uses Cloud Bigtable to store high-volume time-series data. Their monthly bill for Bigtable storage was unexpectedly high. To investigate, the engineering team enabled the Billing Data Export to BigQuery.

By querying the billing data, they determined the majority of the cost came from the Bigtable SSD Storage SKU for their main `sensor_readings` table. The initial garbage collection (GC) policy retained data for 365 days. However, analysis of application query patterns showed that 99 percent of all reads were for data less than 90 days old. The older data was consuming a massive amount of expensive SSD storage but was rarely accessed. Based on this assessment, they changed the GC policy to 90 days, cutting storage costs by over 70 percent without impacting application performance.

Cost Optimization Strategies

Once costs are understood, several optimization strategies can be applied:

Right-Sizing Instances   Use metrics from Cloud Monitoring (e.g., CPU Utilization) to identify and downsize consistently underutilized database instances.

Storage Optimization   Select the appropriate storage tier (e.g., SSD vs. HDD in Cloud SQL) and manage backup retention policies to balance cost and recovery objectives.

Leverage Committed Use Discounts (CUDs)   For predictable workloads on Cloud SQL, Spanner, and other services, purchasing a 1-year or 3-year CUD provides a significant discount on vCPU and memory costs.

Automate Shutdowns for Nonproduction Environments   Use Cloud Scheduler to stop development and testing instances outside of business hours.

Optimize Network Costs   Co-locate applications and databases in the same region to minimize data transfer costs.

Optimizing Costs for Oracle on Bare Metal Solution

A large financial institution migrated its core banking system to Oracle on Bare Metal Solution to exit its on-premises data center. The production environment ran on a large, powerful server configuration. However, identical, equally expensive servers had been provisioned for development, testing, and disaster recovery, all running 24/7.

The Google Cloud database engineer identified two major cost optimization opportunities. First, for the predictable production workload, they purchased a 3-year Committed Use Discount for the Bare Metal Solution hardware, significantly reducing the hourly cost. Second, for the nonproduction environments, they implemented an automation script using Cloud Functions and Cloud Scheduler. The script shuts down the development and testing servers on evenings and weekends and restarts them on weekday mornings. This automation reduced non-production server costs by approximately 60 percent.

Summary

This chapter covered the critical operational responsibilities of a Google Cloud Professional Database Engineer, emphasizing automation and continuous optimization. We examined methods for automating essential database tasks, including maintenance, scheduled exports, software upgrades, and the monitoring of service levels against defined objectives.

The discussion then shifted to the intertwined goals of cost and performance optimization. We reviewed the tools and techniques for continuously assessing database spending, from high-level billing reports to deep analysis with BigQuery. Finally, we outlined actionable strategies for cost reduction, such as instance right-sizing, storage optimization, commitment discounts, and automated resource scheduling. Mastery of these operational practices is essential for building and maintaining database solutions that are not only powerful and scalable but also efficient and economical.

Exam Essentials

Know how to automate database maintenance tasks.   Be able to explain how to use Cloud Scheduler in combination with Cloud Functions or Cloud Run to perform tasks like VACUUM on Cloud SQL or AlloyDB instances, or gather statistics on Oracle.

Be able to design automated export workflows.   You should know the native export methods for services like Cloud SQL, Spanner, and Firestore, and be able to describe how to use Cloud Scheduler and Dataflow to create a scheduled export pipeline to Cloud Storage.

Understand how to manage database upgrades.   Differentiate between minor and major version upgrades for managed services. Be able to describe a safe process for performing a major version upgrade, including testing and strategies for minimizing downtime.

Know how to monitor SLAs and SLOs.   Be able to define SLA, SLO, and SLI. Understand how to use Cloud Monitoring to set up an SLO, track an error budget, and create alerts based on budget burn rate.

Know the tools for assessing cloud database costs.   Understand the roles of Cloud Billing reports, billing export to BigQuery, and the Recommender service in identifying and analyzing database-related costs.

Be able to identify and apply cost optimization strategies.   You must be familiar with key optimization levers, including right-sizing instances based on monitoring data, choosing appropriate storage tiers, applying Committed Use Discounts for predictable workloads, and automating shutdowns for non-production environments.

Review Questions

1. A Google Cloud database engineer wants to continuously assess if any of their Cloud SQL instances are over-provisioned (i.e., running on machine types larger than needed). Which Google Cloud service can provide actionable recommendations for right-sizing these database instances based on their actual usage?

   A. Cloud Billing Reports

   B. Cloud Trace

   C. Google Cloud Recommender

   D. Cloud Deployment Manager

2. A Google Cloud database engineer is setting up a new Cloud SQL for MySQL database. They need to configure a cost-effective storage solution for a noncritical application that can tolerate slightly higher I/O latency. Which storage type should they select for their Cloud SQL instance?

   A. SSD (solid-state drive)

   B. HDD (hard disk drive)

   C. NVMe (Nonvolatile Memory Express)

   D. Network attached storage (NAS)

3. When managing database maintenance for managed services like Cloud SQL, what is the shared responsibility model between Google Cloud and the user regarding tasks like applying OS patches and database-level maintenance?

   A. Google handles all tasks; users have no responsibility.

   B. Users handle all tasks, including OS patching.

   C. Google handles OS patches and hardware, whereas users often handle database-level maintenance like `VACUUM` or `OPTIMIZE TABLE`.

   D. Google handles database-level maintenance, whereas users handle OS patching.

4. What is the primary benefit of automating routine database tasks (like maintenance, backups, and exports) in a cloud environment compared to manual execution?

   A. It increases the need for specialized human intervention.

   B. It reduces consistency and increases the likelihood of human error.

   C. It frees up valuable engineering time and improves reliability and consistency.

   D. It always eliminates the need for any form of monitoring.

5. A rapidly growing e-commerce platform uses Cloud SQL for PostgreSQL, and its orders table experiences millions of updates and deletes daily. Over time, query performance has degraded due to "table bloat." What is the primary cause of this bloat and how is it typically managed in PostgreSQL?

    A. Data is being incorrectly indexed, requiring a `REINDEX` operation.

    B. Old row versions are not immediately reclaimed, requiring a `VACUUM` process.

    C. The table is too large for a single instance, requiring sharding.

    D. The database is consistently running out of disk space, necessitating a `STORAGE RESIZE`.

6. A gaming company stores player profiles in Cloud Bigtable. They need to ensure that data older than 90 days is automatically removed from the `session_history` column family to manage storage costs and compliance. How should this data life-cycle management be configured in Bigtable?

    A. By setting up a recurring Dataflow job to delete old data

    B. By configuring a garbage collection (GC) policy directly on the `session_history` column family

    C. By manually running `DELETE` statements on old rows every month

    D. By enabling automatic partition expiration for the Bigtable instance

7. A Cloud SQL for MySQL instance is suffering from poor query performance, and `SHOW TABLE STATUS` output indicates a high `Data_free` value for several tables. This suggests internal fragmentation. Which MySQL command should the database engineer use to reorganize table data and associated indexes to reclaim space and improve I/O efficiency?

    A. `VACUUM ANALYZE`

    B. `REINDEX TABLE`

    C. `OPTIMIZE TABLE`

    D. `ANALYZE TABLE`

8. A company's analytical queries against a large Cloud SQL for PostgreSQL database are performing poorly, even after adding appropriate indexes. Upon investigation, the engineer suspects significant internal fragmentation (bloat) in some tables. Which PostgreSQL command, while effective at reclaiming space, requires an `ACCESS EXCLUSIVE` lock and can cause significant application downtime?

    A. `VACUUM`

    B. `VACUUM ANALYZE`

    C. `VACUUM FULL`

    D. `REINDEX CONCURRENTLY`

9. A small startup is using a Cloud SQL for PostgreSQL instance. They noticed that their autovacuum settings are not keeping up with the rate of data changes, leading to performance issues and increased storage consumption. How can they determine the extent of table bloat within their PostgreSQL database on Cloud SQL?

   A. Check the `pg_stat_statements` view for query execution times.

   B. Query PostgreSQL system catalogs like `pg_class` to compare actual table size to expected size.

   C. Use the `SHOW TABLE STATUS` command.

   D. Analyze the Cloud Monitoring metric for CPU utilization.

10. A Cloud Database Engineer wants to identify tables in their Cloud SQL for MySQL instance that have a high amount of unused space allocated to them, indicating fragmentation. Which column in the `information_schema.TABLES` view would provide this information?

   A. `TABLE_ROWS`

   B. `DATA_LENGTH`

   C. `INDEX_LENGTH`

   D. `DATA_FREE`

11. A Google Cloud database engineer wants to automate the daily `VACUUM ANALYZE` command for a high-churn table in a Cloud SQL for PostgreSQL instance, ensuring it runs outside peak hours. Which combination of Google Cloud services would be most effective for scheduling and executing this maintenance task?

   A. Cloud Logging and Cloud Monitoring

   B. Cloud Scheduler and Cloud Functions

   C. Cloud Composer and Cloud Build

   D. Cloud CDN and Cloud DNS

12. Your company's development environment for a new application uses a dedicated Cloud SQL instance. This instance is only used during business hours (9 a.m.–5 p.m., weekdays). To significantly reduce costs without impacting development cycles, what automation strategy should be implemented?

   A. Scale down the instance to the smallest machine type during off-hours.

   B. Purchase a 3-year committed use discount (CUD) for the instance.

   C. Automate the shutdown of the instance outside business hours and restart it in the morning using Cloud Scheduler and Cloud Functions.

   D. Migrate the development database to a zonal deployment with no high availability.

13. A Google Cloud database engineer is migrating a legacy Oracle database to Google Cloud's Bare Metal Solution. They need to automate the process of gathering optimizer statistics (DBMS_STATS.GATHER_SCHEMA_STATS) on a nightly basis. How can this be effectively automated within the Google Cloud ecosystem?

   A. Rely on Oracle's internal self-tuning mechanisms, no automation needed.

   B. Use Cloud Scheduler to trigger a script on a management VM that connects to Oracle and executes the command.

   C. Set up a Cloud SQL Auth Proxy to connect to the Oracle database.

   D. Implement a Cloud Spanner Dataflow template for statistics collection.

14. A data analytics team requires a daily snapshot of a Cloud Spanner database for offline processing in BigQuery, without impacting the performance of the transactional Spanner instance. Which automated workflow pattern is best suited for this task on Google Cloud?

   A. Manually export data from Spanner to Cloud Storage and then manually import to BigQuery.

   B. Use a Cloud Scheduler job to trigger a Cloud Function that starts a Dataflow export job from Spanner to Cloud Storage, followed by another Cloud Function to load into BigQuery.

   C. Configure a continuous replication pipeline directly from Spanner to BigQuery.

   D. Use `pg_dump` on the Spanner instance to create daily backups.

15. A Google Cloud database engineer is reviewing the monthly Cloud Spanner bill and notices higher costs than expected for compute capacity. The Cloud Monitoring metrics show that the instance's CPU utilization rarely exceeds 15 percent. What is the most direct cost optimization strategy to address this over-provisioning?

   A. Migrate the Cloud Spanner instance to a single-region configuration.

   B. Decrease the number of provisioned processing units (PUs) or nodes for the Spanner instance.

   C. Enable interleaved tables for all relationships to reduce I/O.

   D. Purchase a 1-year CUD for the current Spanner configuration.

16. An engineering team uses a Firestore in Native Mode database. They need to create weekly backups of their users collection to Cloud Storage for long-term archiving and compliance. What is the recommended automated mechanism for performing these exports?

   A. Using Dataflow templates to stream data from Firestore to Cloud Storage

   B. Setting up a Cloud Scheduler job to trigger a Cloud Function that initiates the managed Firestore export/import service

   C. Manually exporting the collection using the `gcloud firestore export` command every week

   D. Configuring Firestore to automatically replicate to a Bigtable instance in Cloud Storage

17. A database engineer is responsible for a fleet of Cloud SQL instances and needs to get a holistic view of spending patterns across all projects and services. They want to identify which specific Cloud SQL SKUs (e.g., vCPU-hours, GB-months of SSD) contribute most to their monthly bill. Which Google Cloud tool provides this detailed financial breakdown?

    A. Cloud Monitoring dashboards filtered by service

    B. Cloud Logging exports to BigQuery

    C. Cloud Billing Report with SKU filtering

    D. Google Cloud Recommender with cost optimization recommendations

18. Your company has a large amount of historical data in Cloud Storage that needs to be regularly imported into a BigQuery table for reporting. The import needs to be scheduled daily. How can this automated import be configured using native Google Cloud tools?

    A. By manually running the bq load command from a Compute Engine VM

    B. By creating a Cloud Scheduler job to trigger a Cloud Function that executes a BigQuery load job

    C. By setting up a Dataflow streaming pipeline directly from Cloud Storage to BigQuery

    D. By configuring a Cloud SQL instance to ingest data from Cloud Storage into BigQuery

19. A startup's new application will have a small, unpredictable workload, initially, but is expected to grow. They want to minimize their initial database costs but ensure scalability for the future. What principle should guide their initial database provisioning and subsequent optimization?

    A. Always provision for peak expected future load immediately to avoid reprovisioning.

    B. Choose the largest available instance types for all databases to prevent performance issues.

    C. Continuously assess and optimize the cost of running the database solution, right-sizing instances based on actual usage.

    D. Utilize only on-premises solutions to control all costs directly.

20. A Google Cloud database engineer is responsible for a mission-critical Cloud SQL instance. To maintain optimal performance, they've identified the need for periodic OPTIMIZE TABLE operations on certain tables. To prevent these operations from causing unexpected downtime, what is a crucial consideration when scheduling such maintenance for a high-availability database?

    A. These operations should only be run manually during business hours for direct supervision.

    B. They should be automated and scheduled during periods of lowest expected application traffic to minimize impact.

    C. They should be executed randomly to avoid predictable performance dips.

    D. These operations are fully managed by Cloud SQL and require no user intervention.

Implementing Backup and Recovery Strategies

GOOGLE CLOUD CERTIFIED PROFESSIONAL CLOUD DATABASE ENGINEER EXAM OBJECTIVES COVERED IN THIS CHAPTER:

✔ **2.3 Design database backup and recovery solutions.**

- Given requirements, recommend backup and recovery options (automatic scheduled backups).

- Configure export and import data for databases.

- Manage data retention.

Protecting an organization's data is a primary responsibility for a database engineer. A well-designed backup and recovery strategy is the essential safety net that ensures business continuity in the face of unforeseen events. Consider a thriving e-commerce platform during its busiest holiday sale. A software bug in a new deployment accidentally corrupts the central orders database. Without a reliable and rapid recovery plan, the business could face significant losses and reputational damage. With a well-architected backup solution, however, the Google Cloud database engineer can restore the database to a consistent state from just moments before the corruption occurred, turning a potential disaster into a manageable incident.

This chapter covers the processes for protecting data on Google Cloud and ensuring it can be restored swiftly and reliably. We will review how to design and implement backup and recovery solutions tied directly to business tolerances for downtime and data loss. We will also cover the practical steps for configuring automated backups and data exports across Google Cloud's suite of managed databases. Finally, this chapter addresses the topic of managing data retention to balance compliance requirements with cost-effective storage management.

Recommending Backup and Recovery Options

A data protection strategy begins with a clear understanding of business requirements. It is not enough to simply "back up the data"; the solution must align with specific, measurable business objectives for recovery. These objectives are formally defined by service level agreements (SLAs)—contracts with users or customers—and service level objectives (SLOs)—the internal targets set to meet those SLAs. For a database engineer, the most critical SLOs related to data recovery are the recovery time objective (RTO) and the recovery point objective (RPO).

Recovery Time Objective (RTO)   This metric defines the maximum acceptable downtime for a database after a failure or disaster. It answers the question, "How quickly must we be back online?" An RTO of 15 minutes means the database must be fully operational within 15 minutes of an incident being declared.

Recovery Point Objective (RPO)   This metric defines the maximum acceptable amount of data loss, measured in time. It answers the question, "How much data can we afford to lose?" An RPO of 5 minutes means that in a worst-case scenario, any data created or modified in the 5 minutes preceding the failure may be lost.

These two metrics are the guiding principles for designing a backup and recovery solution. A low RTO necessitates solutions with rapid, often automated, failover and restore capabilities. A low RPO requires frequent backups or continuous data protection mechanisms. The role of a Google Cloud database engineer is to evaluate the features of each Google Cloud database service and recommend a solution that meets these objectives in the most reliable and cost-effective manner.

Transforming RTO/RPO on CloudSQL

A mid-sized retail company ran its inventory management system on a standard Cloud SQL for MySQL instance. Their backup strategy was simple: the default daily automated backup, giving them an RPO of up to 24 hours. Having never experienced a major incident, they considered this sufficient. During a weekend flash sale, a deployment script with a bug was executed, incorrectly updating stock levels for their most popular products and effectively zeroing out the inventory. By the time the issue was discovered, 4 hours of critical sales data had been impacted. Restoring from the last daily backup meant losing an entire day's worth of transactions, which was unacceptable. The team had to spend the next 18 hours manually reconciling sales records and correcting the database, resulting in significant revenue loss and customer frustration.

This incident prompted an immediate review of their recovery strategy. The lead database engineer conducted a postmortem and worked with business stakeholders to define clear SLOs: an RTO of 30 minutes for any incident and an RPO of no more than 5 minutes. To meet these new SLOs, the engineer reconfigured the inventory database. They enabled the high availability (HA) configuration to provide automatic failover for zonal failures, addressing the RTO. For the RPO, they enabled point-in-time recovery (PITR). When a minor data corruption issue occurred later, they used PITR to restore the database to a state just 1 minute before the event, completing the entire operation in under 20 minutes. This transformed their recovery capability from a multi-hour, manual ordeal into a swift, predictable procedure well within their new business requirements.

Options by Database Service

Each Google Cloud database service offers a unique set of features for backup and recovery. Your recommendation must be based on a careful analysis of these features against the required RTO and RPO.

Cloud SQL

Cloud SQL provides a robust and flexible set of backup and recovery features for its MySQL, PostgreSQL, and SQL Server instances, making it suitable for a wide range of RTO and RPO requirements:

Automated Backups: Cloud SQL can be configured to take a full backup of your instance automatically once every 24 hours during a specified maintenance window. This feature is excellent for establishing a baseline RPO of 24 hours.

On-Demand Backups: You can trigger a backup at any time. This is useful before performing risky operations like a major schema change or application upgrade, allowing you to create a specific recovery point.

Point-in-Time Recovery (PITR): This is the most effective feature for achieving a low RPO. When enabled, Cloud SQL continuously archives transaction logs (binary logs for MySQL, write-ahead logging for PostgreSQL) to Cloud Storage. This allows you to restore the database to a specific second within the backup retention window.

High Availability (HA) Configuration: While primarily an availability feature, the HA configuration directly impacts your RTO. An HA instance maintains a synchronous standby replica in a different zone. In case of a primary instance failure, Cloud SQL automatically fails over to the standby, typically within minutes.

Balancing High Availability and Point-in-Time Recovery for Customer Support Applications

A customer support application uses Cloud SQL for PostgreSQL and has an SLA requiring an RTO of less than 30 minutes and an RPO of less than 15 minutes.

Recommendation: Configure the instance as a high availability (HA) instance to meet the RTO requirement for zonal failures. Enable point-in-time recovery (PITR) with a backup retention window of at least 7 days. This combination ensures that in the event of logical corruption or accidental deletion, you can restore the database to a point just before the incident, easily meeting the 15-minute RPO.

EXERCISE 9.1

Skillsboost: Configuring Replication and Enabling PITR for Cloud SQL for PostgreSQL

```
https://www.cloudskillsboost.google/catalog_lab/4202
```

In this exercise, you will configure and test point-in-time recovery for a Cloud SQL for PostgreSQL instance to protect against data loss scenarios. Accessed via the URL provided, this walk-through offers hands-on practice deploying what you learned earlier in the chapter. You will focus on the process of recovering a database to a specific moment in time, ensuring you understand how to effectively restore data to a new instance and mitigate the impact of operational errors.

AlloyDB for PostgreSQL

AlloyDB, as a high-performance, PostgreSQL-compatible database, builds upon these concepts with a more advanced, continuous backup system:

Continuous Backups: Instead of daily snapshots, AlloyDB continuously backs up your data and transaction logs. This architecture is fundamental to its ability to offer fast, granular recovery.

Fast Point-in-Time Recovery: Leveraging its cloud-native storage architecture, AlloyDB can perform PITR significantly faster than traditional PostgreSQL, helping to meet very aggressive RTOs for recovery from logical errors.

High Availability: Similar to Cloud SQL, AlloyDB's HA architecture with automatic failover provides a very low RTO for instance or zonal failures.

Leveraging AlloyDB's Continuous Backup for Near-Zero RPO Trading Platforms

A financial trading platform uses AlloyDB and requires an RPO of near-zero and an RTO of less than 5 minutes for any type of failure.

Recommendation: The inherent architecture of a highly available AlloyDB cluster already meets these stringent requirements. Its continuous backup system provides a near-zero RPO for logical recovery, and its rapid automatic failover provides a sub-minute RTO for infrastructure failures. No additional complex configuration is needed beyond enabling backups and configuring the HA cluster.

Cloud Spanner

Cloud Spanner is designed for global scale and mission-critical availability, and its backup and recovery features reflect this:

Managed Backups: You can create full backups of your Spanner databases. Restoring a Spanner database is a fast operation, which helps achieve a low RTO.

Automation for RPO: Spanner supports built-in automated backup schedules. To achieve a specific RPO, you can create a backup schedule directly in the Google Cloud console or via the API to automatically run full backups at a specified frequency.

Point-in-Time Recovery (PITR): Spanner also offers PITR, allowing you to recover data from any point in time within the last 7 days. This is a powerful tool for recovering from logical data corruption with a very low RPO.

Automating Discrete Backups for Spanner Using Serverless Orchestration

A global logistics application on Spanner needs to be protected against accidental data deletion with an RPO of 1 hour.

Recommendation: While Spanner's PITR provides a much lower RPO, if the requirement is specifically for discrete backups, the solution is to configure a native Spanner backup schedule. You can set the schedule to run every hour, ensuring regular recovery points are automatically created without needing external orchestration tools.

Bigtable, Firestore, and BigQuery

These NoSQL and analytics databases have different backup paradigms, often revolving around exports and snapshots:

Bigtable: Offers managed backups that create a consistent, read-only copy of a table's schema and data. This process must be automated with Cloud Scheduler and Cloud Functions to meet a specific RPO.

Firestore: Provides a managed export/import feature to a Cloud Storage bucket. This is not a true point-in-time backup but a snapshot at the time of the export. Automation via Cloud Scheduler is the key to creating regular recovery points.

BigQuery: Data in BigQuery is highly durable and replicated. For recovery from logical errors, BigQuery supports table snapshots. You can also use the `EXPORT DATA` statement to create logical backups in Cloud Storage. Automating these operations with scheduled queries is common practice.

Table 9.1 summarizes the native backup capabilities and how they align with RTO/RPO goals.

TABLE 9.1   RPO and RTO of backup methods for Google Cloud databases

Database service	Native backup method	How it meets RPO	How it meets RTO
Cloud SQL	Automated/ On-Demand Snapshots, PITR	RPO of minutes with PITR; 24 hours with daily snapshots	RTO of minutes with HA failover; longer for restore from backup
AlloyDB	Continuous Backup, PITR	RPO of seconds to minutes	RTO of minutes with HA failover and fast PITR
Cloud Spanner	Managed Backups, PITR	RPO depends on automation frequency (e.g., hourly). Very low RPO with PITR.	RTO of minutes to hours, depending on database size.
Bigtable	Managed Backups	RPO depends on automation frequency.	RTO depends on restore time, which varies with table size.
Firestore	Managed Export/ Import	RPO depends on export frequency (automation).	RTO depends on import time, which can be significant for large databases.
BigQuery	Table Snapshots, Data Export	RPO depends on snapshot/export frequency (automation).	RTO is very low for restoring from a snapshot; longer for importing from export.

Configuring Automatic Scheduled Backups

Automating backups is a fundamental practice that ensures consistency, reduces the risk of human error, and guarantees a recent recovery point is always available. The configuration method varies across Google Cloud's database services.

Scheduling Backups on Cloud Spanner

A fintech startup used Cloud Spanner to manage its globally distributed transaction ledger. Their compliance policy required a full, auditable backup to be created at the end of every business day. In their early stages, this process was manual: the on-call site reliability engineer (SRE) had a checklist item to trigger the backup from the console before signing off. This process worked for months. However, during a major international holiday week, a handoff between the U.S.-based SRE and their European counterpart was fumbled. The checklist item was missed for two consecutive days. On the third day, a new microservice deployment contained a subtle bug that caused logical corruption in a small but critical set of ledger accounts.

The team's first instinct was to restore from the last backup, only to discover the most recent one was from 3 days prior. While they ultimately recovered using Spanner's point-in-time recovery (PITR), the process was tense. It required a painstaking investigation to pinpoint the exact moment before the corruption began, followed by a restore operation that was far more stressful than a simple restore-from-backup would have been. The incident triggered an immediate overhaul of their backup strategy. The lead database engineer configured a native Spanner backup schedule to trigger every night at midnight UTC. This built-in scheduling feature automatically initiates the Spanner backup and assigns a mandatory expiration time, completely removing the risk of human error and ensuring their daily backup SLO was always met.

Cloud SQL

For Cloud SQL, configuring automated backups is a straightforward process handled directly through the instance settings:

1. Navigate to the Cloud SQL instance in the Google Cloud Console.
2. Edit the instance configuration.
3. Go to the Data Protection section.
4. Enable automated backups. You will be presented with several options:
    a. Time Window: Select a 4-hour window during which the backup will be performed. It is important to choose a period of low activity for your application to minimize any potential performance impact.

   b. Location: Choose where your backups are stored. A multiregion location provides higher availability for your backups, while a regional location is cheaper.

   c. Retention: Specify the number of automated backups to retain, from 1 to 365.

5. Enable point-in-time recovery (PITR) by selecting the option. This will begin archiving the transaction logs.

You can also perform these configurations using the `gcloud` command-line tool.

```
# Example: Update a Cloud SQL instance to enable automated backups
gcloud sql instances patch my-instance-name \
--backup-start-time=03:00 \
--retained-backups-count=14 \
--backup-location=us

# Example: Enable Point-in-Time Recovery (for PostgreSQL)
gcloud sql instances patch my-pg-instance \
--enable-point-in-time-recovery \
--retained-transaction-log-days=7
```

Cloud Spanner, Bigtable, and Firestore

These services do not have a built-in, one-click scheduler for backups like Cloud SQL. Automation requires orchestrating a few Google Cloud services together, with the most common pattern being Cloud Scheduler and Cloud Functions.

The workflow is as follows:

1. Create a Cloud Function (e.g., in Python, Node.js, or Go) that uses the Google Cloud client libraries to initiate a backup or export operation for the desired database.

2. Configure a new Cloud Scheduler job:

   a. Define the schedule by setting the frequency using a standard cron format (e.g., 0 2 * * * for 2:00 a.m. daily).

   b. Set the target to be the HTTP trigger URL of the Cloud Function you created.

This serverless, event-driven approach is highly reliable and cost-effective.

Configuring Export and Import of Data for Databases

Beyond disaster recovery, data exports and imports fulfill several key operational requirements. An export is a logical backup, creating a copy of the data in a portable format (like CSV or SQL), independent of the underlying database storage format. This differs from a snapshot-based backup, which is a physical backup of the database's disk blocks.

Key Use Cases for Export/Import

Use cases for export and import of data for databases include:

Data Archiving: Exporting data to Cloud Storage is a cost-effective way to archive historical data for long-term compliance or analysis.

Populating Development Environments: Export a sanitized subset of your production data to populate development and testing environments.

Data Migration and Interoperability: Create data in standard formats that can be imported into other database systems or loaded into analytical platforms like BigQuery.

Offline Analysis: Allow data scientists to take an export of production data to run heavy analytical queries without impacting the performance of the live database.

Hybrid Data Pipeline for Risk Analysis

A large financial institution runs its mission-critical, legacy trading database on Oracle on Bare Metal Solution (BMS). This high-performance system processes thousands of transactions per second. A separate risk analysis team needs a daily snapshot of all settled trades to run complex risk models in BigQuery. Running these analytical queries directly against the production Oracle database was not an option, as it would severely impact the performance of the transactional workload.

The database engineering team was tasked with creating a reliable, automated pipeline to move this data. They designed a hybrid cloud workflow. First, they configured a cron job on a management VM within the BMS environment. This job executes a script that uses Oracle's native Data Pump (`expdp`) utility to export the required trade tables into a DMP file on a local filesystem. The second part of the script uses `gsutil` to securely upload this large export file to a designated Cloud Storage bucket.

The arrival of the new file in Cloud Storage acts as a trigger. A Cloud Function, subscribed to this event, automatically initiates a BigQuery load job. This entire process runs automatically every night, providing the risk team with fresh data for their analysis each morning without ever impacting the performance of the critical production Oracle database. This export/import pattern proved to be a robust and efficient bridge between their on-premises Oracle environment and Google Cloud's powerful analytics platform.

Export/Import Procedures in Google Cloud

Export and import procedures in Google Cloud include the following:

Cloud SQL   Cloud SQL provides a managed export and import service that integrates directly with Cloud Storage. You can export to SQL format (`.sql`) for portability or CSV format for loading into other tools. A critical feature of this service is the ability to perform a serverless export.

Understanding Serverless Export

A serverless export is a feature of Cloud SQL's managed export service that offloads the export operation to a separate, temporary instance managed entirely by Google. When you initiate a serverless export, Cloud SQL automatically provisions this temporary instance, performs the export there, and then tears it down upon completion.

The primary benefit of this approach is performance isolation. Because the export does not run on your primary production instance, it does not consume any of its CPU, memory, or I/O resources. This prevents performance degradation on the production database, which is crucial for heavily used applications.

Serverless export is the recommended method for exporting data from a busy production database when performance isolation is the main concern. It is the ideal choice when you need to get a copy of your data without impacting live user traffic and prefer not to run the export from a read replica.

Cloud Spanner and Bigtable   Large-scale data movement is handled by Dataflow. Google provides prebuilt Dataflow templates to export data to formats like Avro or Parquet in Cloud Storage and to import data back.

Firestore   Firestore has a managed export/import service to move all documents or specific collections to and from a Cloud Storage bucket.

EXERCISE 9.2

Skillsboost: Cloud Spanner—Loading Data and Performing Backups

`https://www.cloudskillsboost.google/catalog_lab/5727`

In this exercise, you will utilize various methods to load data into Cloud Spanner and perform a critical database backup. Accessed via the URL provided, this walk-through offers hands-on practice deploying what you learned earlier in the chapter. You will focus on inserting batch and streaming data using DML, client libraries, and Dataflow, ensuring you understand the practical steps required to manage data ingestion and resilience in a horizontally scalable environment.

Managing Data Retention

Data retention management involves defining and enforcing how long backups and archives are kept, balancing compliance requirements against storage costs. A well-defined retention policy ensures you meet legal obligations without incurring unnecessary costs.

Backup Retention Policy

A mobile gaming company used Bigtable to store high-volume player event data. To protect against data loss, they followed best practices and set up an automated daily backup of their main table to a Cloud Storage bucket using a Cloud Function triggered by Cloud Scheduler. The system worked flawlessly, and the team, focused on launching new game features, didn't give it a second thought.

Six months later, the finance department flagged a massive and unexpected increase in their Google Cloud bill, traced back to Cloud Storage. An investigation by the database engineer revealed that the daily Bigtable backups, each several hundred gigabytes in size, had been accumulating for half a year. They had never implemented a cleanup or retention mechanism. The storage bucket contained over 180 backups, consuming terabytes of storage and costing them thousands of dollars per month for data that was well past its useful recovery window.

The immediate fix was to manually delete the old backups. The long-term solution involved implementing a retention policy. The engineer configured a Cloud Storage Lifecycle Management rule on the backup bucket. The rule was simple: automatically delete any object in the bucket after it becomes 30 days old. This single configuration ensured that their backup storage would no longer grow indefinitely, bringing costs back under control and aligning their storage footprint with their actual 30-day recovery requirement.

Retention Mechanisms in Google Cloud

Retention mechanisms include:

Cloud Spanner: When you create a managed backup in Cloud Spanner, you are required to specify an expiration date. The system automatically deletes the backup once this expiration time is reached, natively handling its retention life cycle.

Cloud SQL and AlloyDB: These services have built-in retention settings. When you configure automated backups, you specify the number of backups (for Cloud SQL) or the number of days (for AlloyDB and PITR logs) to retain. The system automatically deletes backups and logs that are older than the specified retention period.

Bigtable: The managed backups for this services does not have an automatic expiration date. You are responsible for managing their life cycle. There are two common patterns for this:

Cloud Storage Lifecycle Management: If your backups are stored in a dedicated Cloud Storage bucket, this is the simplest method. You can create a life cycle rule on the bucket to automatically delete objects after a specified number of days.

Automated Cleanup Function: For more complex logic (e.g., keeping the first backup of every month indefinitely while deleting other daily backups after 30 days), you can create a second Cloud Function. This function, triggered by Cloud Scheduler, would list all backups, apply your custom retention logic to determine which ones to delete, and then call the appropriate API to delete them.

Firestore and BigQuery Exports: Data exported to Cloud Storage is also managed via Cloud Storage Lifecycle Management. You can set rules to transition data to cheaper storage classes (like Nearline or Coldline) for long-term archiving before finally deleting it.

EXERCISE 9.3

Skillsboost: Google Cloud Storage—Add and Remove Retention Policies

```
https://www.cloudskillsboost.google/catalog_lab/1352
```

In this exercise, you will utilize Cloud Storage Bucket Lock to configure and manage robust data retention policies. Accessed via the URL provided, this walk-through offers hands-on practice deploying what you learned earlier in the chapter. You will focus on defining and locking object retention rules to support regulatory compliance, ensuring you understand the practical steps required to enforce strict data governance and object preservation.

Summary

In this chapter, we established the importance of implementing backup and recovery strategies tailored to business needs. You learned that the design of any such solution must be driven by the organization's specific recovery time objective (RTO) and recovery point objective (RPO). We explored the native backup and recovery capabilities of Google Cloud's managed database services and discussed how to recommend the right options based on different SLA requirements.

We then moved into the practical aspects of configuration, detailing how to set up automatic scheduled backups and distinguishing between logical exports and physical backups. We specifically highlighted Cloud SQL's serverless export feature as a key tool for creating exports without impacting production performance. Finally, we addressed the vital task of managing data retention. We covered the built-in retention features of services like Cloud SQL and the automation patterns required for Bigtable, where life cycle policies on Cloud Storage and cleanup functions are essential for managing costs and meeting compliance mandates.

Exam Essentials

Understand RTO and RPO.   Be able to define recovery time objective (maximum downtime) and recovery point objective (maximum data loss) and explain how they drive the design of a backup solution.

Know the backup features of each database service.   You must be familiar with the backup and recovery mechanisms for Cloud SQL (automated backups, PITR), AlloyDB (continuous backup), Spanner (managed backups, PITR), Bigtable (managed backups), and Firestore (managed export/import).

Recommend solutions based on SLOs.   Given a scenario with specific RTO and RPO requirements, you should be able to recommend the appropriate Google Cloud database and backup configuration to meet those needs.

Know how to configure automated backups.   Be able to describe the steps for setting up scheduled backups for Cloud SQL and Spanner directly, and for services like Firestore using the Cloud Scheduler/Cloud Function pattern.

Differentiate between physical and logical backups.   Understand that a snapshot-based backup is for disaster recovery, while an export creates a portable, logical copy of the data for different use cases.

Know the export/import methods.   Be familiar with the tools and formats used for exporting and importing data for each service, such as SQL/CSV for Cloud SQL (including the serverless export option) and Dataflow templates for Spanner.

Know how to manage data retention.   Be able to explain the different mechanisms for enforcing retention policies, such as the built-in settings in Cloud SQL and the use of Cloud Storage Lifecycle Management and automated cleanup scripts for services like Spanner and Bigtable.

Review Questions

1. When configuring automated backups for a Cloud SQL instance, where should the backup location be chosen to provide the highest availability and protection against a regional outage, albeit at a potentially higher cost?

   A. A custom Cloud Storage bucket

   B. A regional location within the same region as the instance

   C. A multiregion location (e.g., US or Europe)

   D. An on-premises storage array

2. A large-scale analytical platform uses Cloud Bigtable. The team needs to create daily consistent backups of their Bigtable tables to meet compliance requirements. How should this automated daily backup be configured?

   A. Cloud Bigtable automatically creates daily backups that are retained for 7 days.

   B. By scheduling a Dataflow job to export data to Cloud Storage.

   C. By enabling point-in-time recovery (PITR) directly on the Bigtable instance.

   D. By using Cloud Scheduler to trigger a Cloud Function that calls the Bigtable Admin API's `create_backup` method.

3. Your company uses Firestore in Native Mode. To ensure business continuity, they need to implement a strategy for restoring data in case of logical corruption. Which Firestore feature supports creating these restorable points, and how is its frequency typically managed?

   A. Firestore's built-in PITR, automatically configured hourly

   B. Managed export/import service, automated via Cloud Scheduler and Cloud Functions

   C. By taking snapshots of the underlying persistent disks

   D. By replicating the Firestore database to a Cloud SQL instance

4. What is the primary difference between a logical backup (e.g., a SQL dump or CSV export) and a physical backup (e.g., a database snapshot) in the context of database recovery?

   A. Logical backups are faster to create, whereas physical backups are slower.

   B. Logical backups can be imported into different database systems, whereas physical backups are specific to the source database engine and version.

   C. Logical backups capture the physical state of disk blocks, whereas physical backups capture only the database schema.

   D. Logical backups are always encrypted, whereas physical backups are not.

5. A Professional Cloud Database Engineer is tasked with setting up daily automated backups for a Cloud Spanner instance. How can this be natively accomplished within Google Cloud?

    A. By creating a custom Cloud Scheduler job to trigger the Spanner API.

    B. By configuring a Dataflow job to export data to Cloud Storage.

    C. By using the built-in backup schedules feature in the Cloud Spanner console or API.

    D. Spanner only supports Point-in-Time Recovery (PITR) and does not support discrete automated backups.

6. A software development firm needs to regularly refresh development and testing environments with recent production data from their Cloud SQL for PostgreSQL database. To avoid sensitive customer information appearing in nonproduction environments, the data must be sanitized during the copy process. Which approach should the engineer recommend?

    A. Implement Cloud SQL's point-in-time recovery (PITR) to restore production data to `dev/test`.

    B. Configure automated daily backups for the production instance and restore them to `dev/test`.

    C. Export the required production tables to Cloud Storage (e.g., CSV or SQL format), sanitize the data using a script, and then import it into the `dev/test` instances.

    D. Set up a read replica of the production database for the `dev/test` environments.

7. A financial application requires its Cloud SQL for PostgreSQL database to be recoverable to a point in time with no more than 5 minutes of data loss, even in the event of an accidental data deletion. Which Cloud SQL feature is essential to meet this strict recovery point objective (RPO)?

    A. High availability (HA) configuration

    B. Automated daily backups

    C. Point-in-time recovery (PITR)

    D. Read replicas for load balancing

8. Your company's compliance policy requires a daily backup of its Cloud Spanner database, specifically a full, auditable copy that can be restored. What is the most straightforward, fully managed way to automate this process?

    A. Orchestrate Cloud Scheduler and Cloud Functions.

    B. Create a native backup schedule directly on the Spanner database.

    C. Export the database daily to Cloud Storage using Dataflow.

    D. Rely exclusively on Spanner's 7-day Point-in-Time Recovery (PITR).

9. A database engineer needs to migrate a large relational dataset from a local PostgreSQL database to a new Cloud SQL for PostgreSQL instance. The dataset is currently stored in a pg_dump SQL file. Which Cloud SQL feature is designed to facilitate importing such a file directly into the Cloud SQL instance?

   A. Cloud SQL automated backups

   B. The Cloud SQL import service from a Cloud Storage bucket

   C. Cloud SQL's point-in-time recovery (PITR)

   D. Setting up a read replica from the local PostgreSQL database

10. A company needs to archive historical sales data from its Cloud SQL for MySQL database for compliance reasons. This data is no longer actively queried by the application but must be accessible for auditing. Which method provides a cost-effective way to store this data long-term and ensures it's in a portable format?

    A. Deleting the old data from Cloud SQL to free up space

    B. Exporting the data to a Cloud Storage bucket in CSV format

    C. Relying on automated Cloud SQL backups for long-term retention

    D. Keeping the data in Cloud SQL and simply scaling down the instance

11. A Professional Cloud Database Engineer is evaluating backup strategies for a new application on AlloyDB for PostgreSQL. The business requires an RPO of near-zero and an RTO of less than 5 minutes for any failure type. How does AlloyDB's inherent architecture address these stringent requirements?

    A. AlloyDB relies on daily full backups and manual restoration for recovery.

    B. AlloyDB requires external tools to achieve continuous backup and PITR.

    C. AlloyDB's continuous backup and rapid automatic failover provide near-zero RPO and low RTO.

    D. AlloyDB only supports snapshot-based backups, which have high RPO.

12. A Professional Cloud Database Engineer is recommending a backup and recovery solution for a new application with an RTO of 4 hours and an RPO of 24 hours. The application will use Cloud SQL for PostgreSQL. Which Cloud SQL configuration should be recommended as the primary means to meet these SLOs?

    A. Enable point-in-time recovery (PITR) with a 7-day retention period.

    B. Configure the instance for high availability (HA).

    C. Configure automated daily backups with a 7-day retention period.

    D. Implement manual exports of the database to Cloud Storage monthly.

13. A Professional Cloud Database Engineer is designing a solution for a critical database. The business has stated a service level agreement (SLA) with customers that mandates database availability of 99.99 percent. Which internal target (SLO) should the engineer prioritize to ensure this SLA is met through effective recovery?

   A. Maximize the mean time between failures (MTBF).

   B. Minimize the recovery time objective (RTO).

   C. Maximize the recovery point objective (RPO).

   D. Reduce the total cost of ownership (TCO).

14. A database engineer needs to perform a risky schema change on a production Cloud SQL instance. Before proceeding, they want to create a specific, restorable copy of the database to serve as a reliable rollback point. Which type of Cloud SQL backup should they initiate?

   A. Automated daily backup

   B. Point-in-time recovery (PITR)

   C. On-demand manual backup

   D. Cross-region read replica

15. A media company uses Cloud Spanner for its customer database. They need the ability to recover from accidental data changes within the last 7 days with minimal data loss. Which Cloud Spanner feature provides this capability?

   A. Spanner's automated daily backups

   B. Point-in-time recovery (PITR)

   C. Spanner's synchronous multiregion replication

   D. Dataflow templates for Spanner exports

16. A Professional Cloud Database Engineer has created a new Cloud SQL for PostgreSQL instance. To ensure they can recover the database to a specific point in time (e.g., just before an erroneous `UPDATE` statement), which of the following actions must be performed on the Cloud SQL instance?

   A. Enable Automated Backups and configure point-in-time recovery.

   B. Create a read replica in a different region.

   C. Set the database to read-only mode after every transaction.

   D. Manually export a SQL dump file after every significant change.

17. A company wants to regularly move data from its Cloud SQL for PostgreSQL database to BigQuery for extensive analytical processing. Which method is most effective for frequent, large-scale data transfer in a BigQuery-compatible format?

   A. Using Cloud SQL's automated daily backups

   B. Configuring Cloud SQL's point-in-time recovery (PITR)

   C. Exporting data to Cloud Storage in Avro or Parquet format and then loading it into BigQuery

   D. Setting up a read replica in a separate region

18. Your team manages a Cloud SQL for MySQL database for a noncritical internal application. The business has a requirement that no more than 24 hours of data should be lost in case of a data corruption event. From a cost-efficiency perspective, which Cloud SQL feature is most appropriate to meet this RPO, assuming minimal additional requirements?

   A. Enable high availability (HA) configuration.

   B. Configure automated daily backups with sufficient retention.

   C. Enable point-in-time recovery (PITR) with a 7-day retention.

   D. Manually export the database to Cloud Storage weekly.

19. Your data analytics team relies heavily on BigQuery for daily reporting. To protect against accidental deletions or schema changes in a critical table, they need a way to quickly revert to a previous state or recover historical data. Which BigQuery feature is most similar to a logical backup or snapshot for a specific table?

   A. Using `EXPORT DATA` to save to Cloud Storage

   B. Configuring table streaming inserts

   C. Creating a BigQuery Table Snapshot

   D. Enabling continuous replication to another BigQuery dataset

20. A new mission-critical application requires a PostgreSQL-compatible database with extremely low RPO (near-zero data loss) and RTO (recovery in minutes) for both infrastructure failures and logical data corruption. Given these stringent requirements, why is AlloyDB for PostgreSQL a strong recommendation over a standard Cloud SQL for PostgreSQL instance?

   A. AlloyDB offers a cheaper storage solution than Cloud SQL, reducing overall recovery costs.

   B. AlloyDB implements continuous backups and extremely fast point-in-time recovery (PITR), combined with rapid automatic failover.

   C. AlloyDB simplifies manual `pg_dump` operations, making it faster to create logical backups.

   D. AlloyDB provides built-in cross-region disaster recovery, which Cloud SQL lacks.

Chapter 10

Planning and Executing Database Migrations

✔ **3.1 Design and implement data migration and replication.**

- Develop and execute migration strategies and plans, including zero/near-zero downtime, extended outage, and fallback.

- Reverse replication from Google Cloud to source.

- Plan and perform database migration, including fallback plans and DDL/DML conversion.

- Determine the correct database migration tools for a given scenario (e.g., databases hosted outside of Google Cloud).

Moving an existing database into a new environment is a complex and critical task for a Cloud database engineer. This process is more than a simple "lift and shift" of data; it is an engineering effort that touches every part of an application stack. It requires careful planning, precise execution, and a deep understanding of both the source and target systems. A database migration involves preparing the application, ensuring schema compatibility, moving the data with minimal disruption, and planning for any eventuality to ensure the business-critical application remains operational.

This chapter provides a guide to the life cycle of a database migration to Google Cloud. We will cover the strategic decisions that support a successful migration, starting with migration strategies tailored to different business requirements for uptime. We will then cover the tactical elements of creating a migration plan, including critical components like schema conversion and fallback strategies. A key part of modern, low-risk migrations is the ability to replicate data in both directions; we will explore how to configure reverse replication from Google Cloud back to a source database. Finally, we will review Google Cloud's migration tooling to provide clear guidance on how to select the right tool for any given migration scenario.

Designing and Implementing Data Migration and Replication

The core of any database migration project is the design of how data will be moved and synchronized between the source and target environments. The chosen approach must be tailored to the specific characteristics of the database, the nature of the application workload, and the business's tolerance for downtime. A successful design requires an analysis of these factors to create a strategy that is technically sound and aligns with business continuity requirements.

This section covers the pillars of designing and implementing a data migration and replication strategy. We will start by evaluating different migration strategies, from planned outages to zero-downtime approaches, and understand the trade-offs of each. From there, we will break down the components of a migration plan, including schema conversion and fallback planning. We will also cover the technique of setting up reverse replication, a cornerstone of modern, phased migration approaches. Finally, we will provide an overview of the native Google Cloud tools available to help determine the best tool for a specific migration challenge.

Developing and Executing Migration Strategies

The first decision in a migration plan is choosing the overall strategy. This choice is driven by the application's service level objective (SLO) for availability. Different applications have vastly different tolerances for downtime, from internal batch processing systems that can be offline for hours to customer-facing e-commerce platforms that cannot afford a single second of disruption. Understanding this requirement dictates the complexity, cost, and risk profile of the entire migration project. The three primary strategies are an extended outage, near-zero downtime, and zero downtime.

Extended Outage (Offline Migration)

The extended outage, often called an offline migration, is the most straightforward approach. In this strategy, the application is taken offline for a scheduled period. During this maintenance window, the database is shut down, a full backup is taken, the backup is transferred to Google Cloud, it is restored to the new target database instance, and then the application is reconfigured to point to the new database before being brought back online.

The main advantage is simplicity. The process is linear, easy to understand, and carries the lowest risk of data inconsistency, as no changes are being made to the data during the move. Follow these steps:

1. Schedule a maintenance window.   Communicate with all business and technical stakeholders to agree on a time when the application can be unavailable. This is often during a period of low traffic, such as overnight or on a weekend.

2. Stop application traffic.   Halt all connections to the source database to ensure a consistent state.

3. Perform a full backup.   Use the database's native tools (e.g., `mysqldump`, `pg_dump`, Oracle Recovery Manager [RMAN]) to create a full backup of the database.

4. Transfer data.   Upload the backup file to a Cloud Storage bucket. For very large datasets, this might involve using Storage Transfer Service or a physical transfer appliance.

5. Restore to the target.   Provision the target database in Google Cloud (e.g., Cloud SQL, AlloyDB) and restore the database from the backup file in Cloud Storage.

6. Validate data.   Perform integrity checks and validation queries to ensure all data has been restored correctly.

7. Reconfigure and start the application.   Update the application's connection strings to point to the new Google Cloud database endpoint and restart the application services.

8. Perform final testing.   Conduct post-migration testing to confirm the application is fully functional.

This method's primary drawback is the significant downtime required, which can range from hours to days depending on the database size and the time needed for data transfer and restoration. Therefore, it is only suitable for noncritical applications, development/test environments, or systems where extended, planned downtime is acceptable to the business.

Extended Outage with Cloud SQL

A digital marketing agency used a small, self-managed MySQL database to power their internal blog's content management system. The system was actively used only by content creators during weekdays. To reduce operational overhead, they decided to migrate to Cloud SQL for MySQL. They chose an extended outage strategy. On a Friday evening at 7 p.m., after all content for the week was published, they stopped the web server, performed a `mysqldump` of the database, and uploaded the 50 GB SQL file to a Cloud Storage bucket. The restore process into a new Cloud SQL instance took about 2 hours. After a round of validation testing on Saturday morning, they updated the application's configuration to point to the new Cloud SQL instance IP. The entire migration was completed by Saturday afternoon, with zero impact on the business and a full day to spare before employees returned on Monday.

Near-Zero Downtime Migration

For many business-critical applications, an extended outage is not an option. A near-zero downtime strategy is designed to minimize the service interruption to a very brief window, often just a few minutes, during the final cutover. This is achieved by using continuous data replication to keep the source and target databases in sync while the application remains online.

The core technology enabling this is change data capture (CDC). CDC tools read the transaction logs of the source database to capture all changes (`INSERT`s, `UPDATE`s, `DELETE`s) in real time and replicate them to the target database. Follow these steps:

1. Perform initial data load (bulk load).   While the source database is online, perform an initial full load of the data to the target Google Cloud database. This can be done from a snapshot or a backup.

2. Configure continuous replication.   Set up a replication stream using a tool like Google's Database Migration Service (DMS) or Datastream. The tool will start capturing changes from the point the initial load was taken and apply them to the target.

3. Monitor the replication lag.   Continuously monitor the replication process to ensure the target database is keeping up with the source. The time difference between a change occurring on the source and being applied to the target is known as "replication lag." The goal is to get this lag down to a few seconds.

4. Perform pre-cutover validation.   While replication is running, thoroughly test the target environment. This includes performance testing, data validation, and testing application connectivity to the new database.

5. Schedule a cutover window.   Plan a brief maintenance window for the final switch.

6. Execute the cutover.

This step involves the following:
  Stop application traffic to the source database.
  Wait for the replication lag to drop to zero, ensuring the target is fully in sync.
  Promote the target Google Cloud database to be the new primary.
  Reconfigure the application to point to the new primary database.
  Start application traffic.

The downtime in this scenario is limited to the time it takes to stop traffic, confirm sync, and repoint the application, which is typically very short. This makes it the preferred strategy for most production systems.

Near-Zero Downtime with AlloyDB

A growing online retailer was running its e-commerce platform on a self-hosted PostgreSQL database. As they prepared for the holiday season, they needed to ensure higher availability and better performance, so they chose to migrate to AlloyDB for its scalability and PostgreSQL compatibility. An extended outage was out of the question. Using Database Migration Service (DMS), they initiated the migration. DMS performed an initial bulk copy of their terabyte-scale database to AlloyDB over a few hours, all while the live site continued to take orders. For the next week, DMS continuously replicated all new orders, customer sign-ups, and inventory changes to AlloyDB. The team monitored the replication lag, which consistently stayed under 5 seconds. During their scheduled 3 a.m. maintenance window, they put the site into maintenance mode, waited for the DMS lag to reach zero, and then promoted the AlloyDB cluster to be the new primary. The cutover, including repointing the application, took only 7 minutes. Customers who visited the site moments before and after the window noticed no disruption.

Quickstart: Migrating a Database to AlloyDB for PostgreSQL by Using Database Migration Service

```
https://cloud.google.com/database-migration/docs/postgresql-to-
alloydb/quickstart
```

In this exercise, you will use Database Migration Service to migrate data to AlloyDB for PostgreSQL. Accessed via the URL provided, this walk-through offers hands-on practice deploying what you learned earlier in the chapter. You will focus on the migration workflow, ensuring you understand the practical steps required to successfully transfer data to the destination instance.

Zero-Downtime Migration

For the most mission-critical applications, such as global financial systems or high-traffic e-commerce sites, even a few minutes of downtime is unacceptable. A zero-downtime migration aims to achieve the cutover with no user-visible service interruption. This is the most complex and expensive strategy, requiring sophisticated architecture and tooling.

Achieving zero downtime typically involves a "split read/write" or "data access microservice" pattern. The application is modified to write to both the source and target databases simultaneously for a period, while reads are gradually shifted from the source to the target.

Follow these steps:

1. Perform an initial load followed by continuous replication.   The process starts similarly to a near-zero downtime migration, with a bulk load followed by continuous replication to keep the databases in sync.

2. Implement dual-write logic.   Modify the application's data access layer to write to both the source and the target database. This is a significant engineering effort and requires careful handling of potential conflicts and failures.

3. Gradually shift reads.   Configure the application or a load balancer to gradually shift read traffic from the source to the target database. This can start with a small percentage (e.g., 1 percent of reads) and slowly increase as confidence in the new system grows (a canary release pattern).

4. Perform a full read migration.   Once 100 percent of read traffic is being served by the target database and the system is stable, the application is fully reliant on the new database for reads.

5. Execute the final cutover (write migration).   At a designated time, the application is reconfigured to stop writing to the source database.

At this point, the source database is no longer active, and the migration is complete.

6. Decommission dual-write logic. The temporary dual-write code can be removed from the application.

This strategy eliminates downtime but introduces significant application complexity and potential for data divergence if not managed perfectly. It is reserved for systems where the business cost of any downtime is extraordinarily high.

Zero Downtime with Spanner

A major international airline operated a flight booking system on a complex, sharded relational database spread across multiple data centers. To improve global consistency and simplify operations, they decided to migrate to a multiregion Cloud Spanner instance. Given the critical nature of their business, any downtime meant lost revenue and stranded customers. Their engineering team rearchitected the application's data access layer to support dual writes. After an initial bulk load and setting up continuous replication with Datastream, they enabled the dual-write feature. For 2 weeks, every new booking was written to both the old database and the new Spanner instance. They then began a canary rollout for read traffic, starting with 1 percent of queries hitting Spanner, slowly ramping up to 100 percent over several days while closely monitoring performance and consistency. Once all reads were successfully served by Spanner, they performed the final, seamless cutover by simply disabling the write path to the old database in their application configuration. There was no maintenance window and no user-visible downtime.

Creating Migration Plans, Including Fallback and Schema Conversion

A migration strategy sets the high-level approach, but a detailed migration plan provides the step-by-step playbook for execution. A migration plan is a document that accounts for every technical detail, dependency, and potential risk. Two of the most critical components of this plan are the strategy for schema conversion and the plan for a potential fallback.

The Migration Plan

A migration plan should be a living document, collaboratively developed by database engineers, application owners, network engineers, and business stakeholders. It should include:

Scope and Objectives: Clearly defined goals, including which databases and applications are in scope and the target RTO/RPO for the migration.

Team Roles and Responsibilities: A clear RACI (Responsible, Accountable, Consulted, Informed) matrix.

Source and Target Environment Details: Detailed specifications of the source and target databases, including versions, configurations, IP addresses, and security settings.

Step-by-Step Execution Plan: A detailed, timed checklist for every phase of the migration (pre-migration, migration execution, post-migration).

Communication Plan: How and when to communicate with stakeholders during the migration process.

Testing and Validation Plan: A comprehensive list of tests to be performed before, during, and after the migration to ensure data integrity and application functionality.

Schema Conversion Plan: A detailed approach for handling schema differences.

Fallback Plan: A clear, tested procedure to revert to the source system if the migration fails.

DDL/DML Conversion (Schema Conversion)

Schema conversion is often one of the most complex parts of a database migration, especially in a heterogeneous migration (moving between different database engines, e.g., Oracle to PostgreSQL). This process involves translating the source database's DDL (Data Definition Language)—the CREATE TABLE, CREATE INDEX, and other statements that define the database structure—into a format compatible with the target engine. For heterogeneous migrations, it also requires converting procedural code containing DML (Data Manipulation Language), such as the INSERT, UPDATE, and DELETE statements found within stored procedures and triggers. Even in homogeneous migrations (e.g., PostgreSQL to AlloyDB), differences in versions or supported features can require schema adjustments.

Homogeneous Migrations

In a homogeneous migration, the schema is largely compatible. However, you must still account for the following:

Version-Specific Features: A feature used in an older on-premises version might be deprecated or behave differently in the newer managed version in Google Cloud.

Unsupported Extensions: The on-premises database might use extensions that are not supported in the managed service. For example, Cloud SQL has a specific list of supported PostgreSQL extensions.

Proprietary Features: Some on-premises setups might use vendor-specific performance or management features that do not have a direct equivalent in the cloud.

Heterogeneous Migrations

This is where DDL/DML conversion becomes a major project. You must translate data types, stored procedures (which contain procedural DML), functions, triggers, and even the SQL dialect itself.

Data Type Mapping: There is no perfect one-to-one mapping for all data types between different database engines. For example, Oracle's NUMBER type does not have a direct equivalent in PostgreSQL and must be mapped to NUMERIC, INTEGER, or BIGINT depending on its precision and scale.

Stored Procedures and Functions: Procedural code (e.g., Oracle's PL/SQL, SQL Server's T-SQL) is vendor-specific and must be completely rewritten in the target database's language (e.g., PostgreSQL's PL/pgSQL). This can be a massive undertaking.

SQL Dialect Differences: Even standard SQL has vendor-specific variations in syntax and function names that must be identified and refactored in the application code.

Google Cloud offers the Database Migration Service (DMS) Schema Conversion feature to assist with this process. It can analyze the source database schema (e.g., Oracle) and automatically generate a converted schema for a target like Cloud SQL for PostgreSQL, along with an assessment of the conversion complexity. While it automates much of the tedious work, manual review and refinement are always necessary for complex conversions.

Heterogeneous Schema Conversion with Oracle

A financial institution was migrating its core loan processing system from a large on-premises Oracle database to AlloyDB for PostgreSQL to modernize and reduce licensing costs. The Oracle database was over a decade old and contained hundreds of complex PL/SQL stored procedures and triggers that encapsulated critical business logic. A manual conversion was estimated to take months. They used the schema conversion feature of Database Migration Service (DMS). DMS analyzed the Oracle schema and automatically converted the majority of the tables, data types (like mapping NUMBER to NUMERIC), and constraints. More importantly, it generated a detailed assessment report that highlighted the PL/SQL code that could not be automatically converted. This allowed the development team to focus their efforts on rewriting only the most complex procedures in PL/pgSQL, saving thousands of hours of manual work. The automated conversion handled about 80 percent of the schema objects, turning a daunting project into a manageable one.

Fallback and Rollback Plan

No migration is guaranteed to be flawless. A fallback plan is an insurance policy. It defines the precise steps to take to abort the migration and revert to the original source system if an unrecoverable issue is discovered after the cutover.

A good fallback plan is:

Tested: You must perform a dry run of the fallback procedure to ensure it works and to understand how long it will take.

Specific: It should be a detailed checklist, not a general idea.

Trigger-Based: It should clearly define the conditions that would trigger a fallback (e.g., "data corruption detected," "application performance below 70 percent of baseline for 30 minutes").

The key enabler for a rapid and safe fallback is *reverse replication.*

Configuring Reverse Replication from Google Cloud Back to the Source

Reverse replication is the process of capturing data changes from the new Google Cloud database and replicating them back to the original on-premises source database. This is the ultimate safety net.

Imagine you have cut over to your new Cloud SQL instance. You discover a critical performance issue that can't be resolved quickly. With reverse replication running, all the transactions that have occurred on the new Cloud SQL database since the cutover have been replicated back to the on-premises database. To fall back, you simply repoint your application back to the on-premises database. Because it has received all the latest changes, no data is lost.

Setting up reverse replication involves using a CDC tool like Datastream or a third-party replication tool. The configuration is the mirror image of the primary migration replication:

- Source: The Google Cloud database (e.g., Cloud SQL, AlloyDB).

- Target: The original on-premises or source database.

- CDC Setup: For Google Cloud sources, this often involves enabling logical decoding (for PostgreSQL) or binary logging (for MySQL) on the managed instance. Datastream can then be configured to read these logs and stream the changes back to the on-premises target.

Reverse replication is a critical component of a near-zero downtime strategy. It allows the business to operate on the new system with the confidence that a rapid, data-loss-free retreat is possible if necessary. It transforms a high-stakes, one-way cutover into a lower-risk, reversible transition.

Reverse Replication with Firestore

A mobile gaming company decided to migrate its user profile and game state data from another cloud's NoSQL database to Firestore to take advantage of its real-time capabilities and better integration with their Firebase-based application. The integrity of player data was paramount; any data loss would be catastrophic for user trust. As part of their near-zero downtime migration plan, not only did they use Datastream to replicate data *to* Firestore, but they also configured a second Datastream job for reverse replication *from* Firestore back to the original source database. After the cutover, they monitored the new system for 24 hours. During this period, a subtle bug related to in-app purchases was discovered in the new environment. Instead of a frantic hotfix, they executed their fallback plan. They repointed the game client back to the original database. Because the reverse replication had been running, all the player activity and purchases made during the 24-hour window on Firestore had been safely replicated back to the source. They were able to revert with zero data loss, fix the bug in a staging environment, and plan a second, successful migration attempt a week later.

Pre-Migration Requirements for DMS

Using a managed tool like Database Migration Service (DMS) simplifies the migration process, but success depends on careful preparation of the source environment to meet the technical prerequisites of the service. Before initiating a DMS job, a database engineer must perform several key preparatory steps covering the source database configuration, networking, and schema structure.

Source Database Preparation: DMS relies on change data capture (CDC) to perform continuous replication. This requires specific configurations on the source database to expose its transaction log. For a PostgreSQL source, this means the `pglogical` extension must be installed and configured. The database user that DMS will connect with must be granted the `REPLICATION` role and have appropriate permissions to use the extension. For a MySQL source, you must enable binary logging (`binlog`) and set the format to ROW.

Networking: DMS needs a secure and reliable network path from its environment in Google Cloud to your source database. If your source is on-premises or in another cloud, you will typically need to establish a connection using Cloud VPN or Cloud Interconnect. You must also configure firewall rules on your source network to allow ingress traffic from the DMS IP address range. For sources within Google Cloud, such as a self-managed database on Compute Engine, VPC Network Peering can be used to establish connectivity.

Initial Load Requirements: For the initial bulk copy of data (the snapshot phase), DMS has a critical requirement: Every table that you intend to migrate must have a primary key. Tables without a primary key cannot be included in the initial snapshot and will cause the migration to fail or skip them.

Schema Objects: It is crucial to understand what DMS does and does not migrate. DMS is designed to migrate the core schema (tables, columns, data types) and the data itself. However, it does not migrate other database objects. This includes stored procedures, functions, triggers, sequences, views, and database users with their permissions. These objects must be extracted from the source and applied to the target database manually or using other tools as a separate, parallel step in the migration plan.

Foreign Keys and Indexes: To optimize the speed of the initial data load, DMS handles constraints and indexes intelligently. During the bulk load phase, foreign key constraints are temporarily disabled on the target database to avoid validation overhead on every row insertion. They are automatically reenabled once the bulk load is complete. Similarly, while secondary indexes are created on the target, it is often more efficient to configure the migration job to create them *after* the initial data has been loaded, as this significantly speeds up the data ingestion process.

Determining the Correct Database Migration Tools for a Given Scenario

Google Cloud offers a portfolio of native tools designed to facilitate different aspects of the migration process. Choosing the right tool depends on the source and target databases, the migration strategy (offline vs. online), and whether schema conversion is required.

Table 10.1 summarizes the primary Google Cloud migration tools and their ideal use cases.

Example Scenario: Choosing the Right Tool

A retail company wants to migrate its 5 TB on-premises PostgreSQL 11 database to AlloyDB for PostgreSQL. The application is business-critical and can only tolerate a 15-minute maintenance window for the final cutover.

> **Analysis:** This is a homogeneous migration (PostgreSQL to PostgreSQL-compatible) with a near-zero downtime requirement. The goal is to move the entire database.
> **Recommended Tool: Database Migration Service (DMS)** is the perfect fit.

Follow these steps:

1. Use DMS to perform the initial bulk data load from the on-premises database to AlloyDB. DMS will then automatically start a continuous replication job to keep the two databases in sync.

2. Monitor the replication lag in the DMS console.

3. During the 15-minute cutover window, stop the application, wait for the DMS lag to hit zero, promote the AlloyDB instance, and repoint the application.

By selecting the right tool and a matching strategy, the company can meet its stringent uptime requirements and execute a low-risk migration.

TABLE 10.1 Google Cloud migration tools

Tool	Primary use case	Supported sources	Supported targets	Key features	When to use
Database Migration Service (DMS)	An opinionated, end-to-end service to move a database with minimal downtime.	On-premises/ other cloud MySQL, PostgreSQL, Oracle, SQL Server	Cloud SQL (MySQL, PostgreSQL, SQL Server), AlloyDB, Cloud Spanner (from Oracle)	An integrated, serverless service for homogeneous migrations. Manages the entire life cycle: initial snapshot, continuous replication (CDC), and cutover.	The default choice for homogeneous migrations to Google Cloud's managed relational databases (Cloud SQL, AlloyDB). Its main purpose is to replace a source database with a Google Cloud target.
Datastream	A general-purpose service to stream changes from a database.	On-premises/ other cloud Oracle, MySQL, PostgreSQL	BigQuery, Cloud Storage, Cloud SQL, Spanner	A stand-alone, serverless CDC and replication service. Highly flexible and designed to be a component in a larger data pipeline.	Use when you need a flexible CDC stream for a custom pipeline, especially when the target is not a managed relational database (e.g., streaming changes to BigQuery for real-time analytics or to Cloud Storage for archival).
Dataflow	A service to process and transform data in transit.	Pub/Sub, Cloud Storage, BigQuery, etc. (as part of a pipeline)	Pub/Sub, Cloud Storage, BigQuery, etc.	A serverless, unified stream and batch data processing service with rich SDKs for complex transformations.	Use to transform data that is being moved by another tool. It is a data processing service, not a migration service. Example pipeline: Datastream (CDC) > Pub/Sub > Dataflow (Transform) > BigQuery (Load).

(Continued)

TABLE 10.1 (Continued)

Tool	Primary use case	Supported sources	Supported targets	Key features	When to use
Storage Transfer Service	Bulk data transfer for offline migrations.	Cloud Storage, AWS S3, Azure Blob Storage, on-premises file systems	Cloud Storage	High-speed, scheduled, and managed data transfers for large datasets.	For the "data transfer" step in an extended outage (offline) migration, moving large backup files to Cloud Storage.
Transfer Appliance	Physical appliance for massive offline data transfer.	On-premises data centers with limited bandwidth	Cloud Storage	A physical hardware appliance you load with data and ship to Google for ingestion.	When your dataset is so large (petabytes) that online transfer over the network is not feasible.

Combining Tools for Bigtable

An industrial IoT company had been collecting petabytes of historical sensor data as flat files on-premises. They wanted to migrate this data to Cloud Bigtable to perform large-scale anomaly detection. Given the sheer volume of historical data, an online transfer was not practical. They chose to use the Transfer Appliance. They loaded 300 TB of historical data onto the appliance, shipped it to Google, and had it ingested directly into a Cloud Storage bucket. From there, they used a Dataflow job to load the data into Cloud Bigtable. For the ongoing, real-time sensor data, they set up a Datastream job to capture new data as it arrived on-premises and stream it directly into their Bigtable instance. By combining two different tools—the Transfer Appliance for the historical bulk load and Datastream for the continuous replication—they successfully addressed both facets of their migration challenge.

Common Migration Paths to Google Cloud Databases

While every migration is unique, certain patterns emerge based on the source technology and the desired business outcome. Understanding these common paths helps a database engineer quickly identify a viable target and strategy for a given on-premises or self-managed database.

From Self-Managed MySQL/PostgreSQL/SQL Server to Cloud SQL

Common Source: Instances of MySQL, PostgreSQL, or SQL Server running on-premises, in a colocation facility, or on IaaS virtual machines (like Compute Engine or AWS EC2).

Why This Path Is Common: This is the most direct "lift-and-optimize" path for applications using standard open source or commercial relational databases. The primary driver is to eliminate the operational burden of managing the database—including patching, backups, replication, and failover—while making minimal changes to the application code. It's a move from managing a database to using a database service.

From On-Premises Oracle to AlloyDB for PostgreSQL

Common Source: On-premises Oracle databases, often running on expensive, proprietary hardware.

Why This Path Is Common: This is a classic modernization path. Organizations choose this route to escape high Oracle licensing and support costs and to move to a powerful, open-standard database. AlloyDB is an attractive target because its enterprise-grade performance and PostgreSQL compatibility provide a robust alternative for demanding workloads. Tools like DMS Schema Conversion are specifically designed to facilitate this complex, heterogeneous migration.

From Manually Sharded Databases to Cloud Spanner

Common Source: Large-scale MySQL or PostgreSQL deployments that have been manually sharded at the application layer to achieve horizontal scale.

Why This Path Is Common: Managing sharding logic within an application is incredibly complex, brittle, and operationally intensive. It makes schema changes difficult and can lead to "hotspots." Teams migrate to Cloud Spanner to offload this complexity entirely. Spanner provides limitless horizontal scaling with transactional consistency out of the box, allowing developers to focus on application features instead of distributed database management.

From On-Premises Oracle to Oracle on Google Cloud

Common Source: Mission-critical Oracle databases running on-premises, often on specialized hardware like Oracle Exadata.

Why This Path Is Common: This is a "lift-and-shift" strategy for organizations that want to exit their data centers but are not ready or able to re-architect their applications away from Oracle. By moving to a solution like Bare Metal Solution for Oracle or the newer Oracle Database@Google Cloud, they can run their existing Oracle workloads in a cloud environment, gaining infrastructure flexibility while retaining their investment and expertise in Oracle technology.

From MongoDB to Firestore

Common Source: Self-hosted MongoDB clusters or MongoDB Atlas.

Why This Path Is Common: This path is particularly popular for developers building web and mobile applications. While MongoDB is a powerful document database, Firestore offers a fully serverless experience with deep, native integration into the Firebase and Google Cloud ecosystems. Its real-time synchronization and offline capabilities are often a better fit for modern, client-heavy applications, simplifying the development stack significantly.

Figure 10.1 provides a visual framework for selecting the optimal Google Cloud target by mapping common source technologies—such as Oracle, MySQL, or HBase—against specific business objectives like cost reduction, horizontal scaling, or serverless modernization. This decision tree simplifies the migration process by identifying established paths to managed services like Cloud SQL, AlloyDB, Spanner, and Bigtable based on the original database's architecture.

From Apache HBase or Cassandra to Bigtable

Common Source: Self-managed clusters of Apache HBase or Apache Cassandra.

Why This Path Is Common: Bigtable was designed based on the same principles as these wide-column stores, and its API maintains compatibility with the HBase API. The primary motivation for this migration is to escape the extreme operational complexity and cost of running and scaling large HBase or Cassandra clusters. Teams move to Bigtable to get a fully managed, highly scalable, and performant equivalent without the overhead of managing Zookeeper, JVM tuning, compaction strategies, and cluster repairs.

FIGURE 10.1   Common migration paths to Google Cloud databases

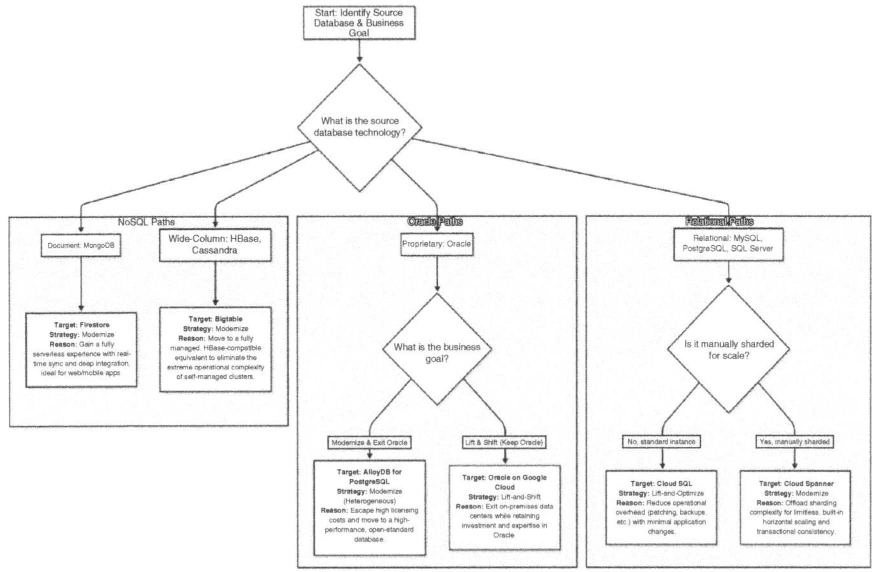

EXERCISE 10.2

Skillsboost: Migrate MySQL Data to Cloud SQL Using Database Migration Service

```
https://www.cloudskillsboost.google/paths/22/course_templates/629
```

In this exercise, you will migrate MySQL data to Cloud SQL using the Database Migration Service. Accessed via the URL provided, this walk-through offers hands-on practice deploying what you learned earlier in the chapter. You will focus on utilizing different job types and connectivity options to move both database and user data, ensuring you understand the practical steps required to execute a successful migration strategy.

Summary

In this chapter, we navigated the complex but manageable world of planning and executing database migrations to Google Cloud. We began by establishing that the choice of migration strategy—extended outage, near-zero downtime, or zero downtime—is fundamentally dictated by the business's tolerance for application unavailability. You saw that while an extended outage offers simplicity, most business-critical systems require a near-zero downtime approach powered by continuous data replication.

We then detailed the essential components of a robust migration plan, emphasizing the critical need for thorough schema conversion planning, especially in heterogeneous migrations, and the non-negotiable requirement for a well-defined and tested fallback plan. We highlighted how configuring reverse replication from Google Cloud back to the source system provides the ultimate safety net, enabling a rapid and data-loss-free rollback if necessary.

Finally, we surveyed the native Google Cloud toolset for migrations and identified common migration paths for popular databases. You learned that Database Migration Service (DMS) is the go-to solution for streamlined, near-zero downtime homogeneous migrations, while Datastream offers powerful real-time CDC capabilities for heterogeneous replication to services like BigQuery and Cloud Storage. By understanding these strategies, planning components, and tools, you are now equipped to design and execute database migrations that are efficient, low-risk, and aligned with critical business objectives.

Exam Essentials

Differentiate between migration strategies.   You must understand the trade-offs between extended outage, near-zero downtime, and zero-downtime migrations and be able to select the appropriate strategy based on a given application's availability requirements.

Know the components of a migration plan.   Be prepared to identify the key elements of a comprehensive migration plan, with a particular focus on the importance of schema conversion and fallback planning.

Understand DDL/DML conversion challenges.   You should be able to describe the differences in complexity between homogeneous and heterogeneous schema conversions and identify common issues like data type mapping and stored procedure translation. Know that DMS offers schema conversion capabilities.

Explain the purpose of reverse replication.   You must be able to articulate why reverse replication is a critical component of a low-risk migration strategy and how it facilitates a rapid, data-safe fallback.

Select the correct Google Cloud migration tool.   Be able to analyze a migration scenario (source/target databases, downtime requirements) and choose the most appropriate Google Cloud tool, primarily differentiating between Database Migration Service (DMS), Datastream, and Dataflow.

Understand the role of CDC.   Know that change data capture (CDC) is the underlying technology that enables near-zero and zero-downtime migrations by replicating changes in real time.

Identify common migration paths.   Be able to recognize typical source databases for Google Cloud targets, such as migrating from self-managed MySQL to Cloud SQL, Oracle to AlloyDB, or Apache HBase to Bigtable, and understand the primary business and technical drivers for these paths.

Review Questions

1. A company runs a legacy financial application on a large on-premises Oracle database. They want to migrate to Google Cloud to reduce their data center footprint but cannot rearchitect the application away from Oracle due to its complexity and vendor-specific features. Which Google Cloud solution is best suited for this "lift-and-shift" scenario for Oracle databases?

   A. Migrating to Cloud SQL for PostgreSQL

   B. Migrating to Cloud Spanner

   C. Deploying Oracle on Google Cloud's Bare Metal Solution

   D. Converting the Oracle database to Firestore

2. A highly critical application requires a database migration with absolutely no user-visible downtime. The application architecture allows for modifications to its data access layer. Which advanced migration strategy should be employed?

   A. Extended outage

   B. Near-zero downtime with DMS

   C. Zero-downtime migration with dual-writes

   D. Simple export/import

3. A Professional Cloud Database Engineer is planning to migrate a self-managed MySQL database from a Compute Engine instance to a managed Cloud SQL for MySQL instance, with minimal downtime. Which Google Cloud service is the most appropriate and opinionated choice for this type of homogeneous, near-zero downtime migration?

   A. Datastream

   B. Database Migration Service (DMS)

   C. Storage Transfer Service

   D. Transfer Appliance

4. A company currently runs a complex, manually sharded PostgreSQL database on-premises. They want to migrate to a database service on Google Cloud that offers limitless horizontal scaling and strong transactional consistency, without managing the sharding logic themselves. Which Google Cloud database service is the best target for this migration?

   A. Cloud SQL for PostgreSQL

   B. AlloyDB for PostgreSQL

   C. Cloud Spanner

   D. BigQuery

5. Your client is migrating a self-managed Oracle database to AlloyDB for PostgreSQL. The primary business objective for this heterogeneous migration is to reduce high licensing costs and to move to an open source compatible solution while maintaining high performance. Which aspect of AlloyDB best supports this objective?

    A. Its global distribution and strong consistency

    B. Its full PostgreSQL compatibility and enterprise-grade performance

    C. Its NoSQL document model and flexible schema

    D. Its ability to run on Bare Metal Solution

6. What is the primary purpose of using Datastream in a database migration context on Google Cloud, as opposed to Database Migration Service (DMS)?

    A. Datastream is primarily used for offline (extended outage) migrations.

    B. Datastream is specifically designed for homogeneous migrations to Cloud SQL.

    C. Datastream is a general-purpose CDC service for streaming changes to various targets, often for analytics or custom pipelines.

    D. Datastream supports physical data transfers of petabytes using appliances.

7. A software development company is migrating its existing MongoDB database to Firestore. What is a key motivation for this specific migration path, particularly for applications leveraging the Firebase ecosystem?

    A. To achieve better SQL compatibility

    B. To leverage Firestore's fully serverless nature and real-time synchronization capabilities for web/mobile applications

    C. To enable complex analytical queries using OLAP

    D. To reduce the cost of proprietary database licenses

8. When planning a database migration, what is the primary reason it is recommended to disable foreign key constraints and secondary indexes on the target database during the initial bulk data load phase?

    A. To prevent the target database from becoming read-only

    B. To speed up the data ingestion process and reduce overhead

    C. To ensure data is normalized correctly during the transfer

    D. To allow for application-level data validation before committing

9. A database engineer is planning a migration from a self-managed Oracle database to Cloud SQL for PostgreSQL. They anticipate significant challenges with data type mapping and stored procedure conversion. Which specific feature of Google Cloud's Database Migration Service (DMS) is designed to assist with this aspect of heterogeneous migrations?

    A. Automated high availability setup

    B. Continuous replication (CDC)

    C. Schema Conversion feature

    D. Cost optimization recommendations

10. For a zero-downtime database migration, the application's data access layer needs modification. What is the primary reason for this architectural change?

    A. To simplify database connection strings

    B. To enable dual-write functionality and gradual read shifting

    C. To allow for offline data processing

    D. To introduce caching mechanisms for improved performance

11. A company has petabytes of historical IoT sensor data stored in CSV files on-premises. They want to load this data into BigQuery for analytics and simultaneously set up a real-time ingestion path for new sensor data. Which combination of Google Cloud services would be most appropriate for this scenario?

    A. Dataflow for both historical load and real-time ingestion

    B. Storage Transfer Service for historical, and Datastream for real-time CDC

    C. Transfer Appliance for historical, and Pub/Sub for real-time ingestion

    D. BigQuery Data Transfer Service for historical, and Filestore for real-time streaming

12. A company is migrating its on-premises Oracle database to AlloyDB for PostgreSQL on Google Cloud. This migration involves converting data types, stored procedures, and SQL syntax. Which type of migration is this, and what is its primary challenge?

    A. Homogeneous migration; primary challenge is data transfer volume.

    B. Heterogeneous migration; primary challenge is schema and code conversion.

    C. Lift-and-shift migration; primary challenge is network latency.

    D. Zero-downtime migration; primary challenge is ensuring application compatibility.

13. Your team has successfully migrated an application to a new Cloud SQL database. However, during post-migration testing, a critical data integrity issue is discovered that cannot be quickly resolved in the new environment. To prevent data loss and ensure business continuity, you need to revert to the original on-premises database with all changes made since the cutover. Which migration technique is crucial to enable this rapid and data-safe fallback?

    A. Initial data load using Storage Transfer Service

    B. One-way continuous replication from source to target

    C. Configuring reverse replication from Google Cloud back to the source

    D. Performing a full backup of the new Cloud SQL instance immediately after cutover

14. A small internal application can tolerate a few hours of downtime for its database migration. The team wants a straightforward process with minimal complexity. Which migration strategy would be most suitable for this scenario?

    A. Zero-downtime migration

    B. Near-zero downtime migration

    C. Extended outage (offline migration)

    D. Dual-write migration

15. Your company is moving its customer analytics platform from a self-managed Apache HBase cluster to a fully managed Google Cloud service. The application benefits from HBase's wide-column, NoSQL data model. Which Google Cloud database service is the most appropriate target for this migration?

    A. Cloud SQL for PostgreSQL

    B. Cloud Spanner

    C. Cloud Bigtable

    D. Firestore

16. A database engineer is planning a migration of a MySQL database from an on-premises server to Cloud SQL for MySQL. They intend to use Database Migration Service (DMS) for a near-zero downtime migration. What is a critical prerequisite that must be configured on the on-premises source MySQL database for DMS's continuous replication to function?

    A. The `pglogical` extension must be installed.

    B. The MySQL `binlog` (binary logging) must be enabled with the ROW format.

    C. The database must be in read-only mode for the entire migration.

    D. A Cloud Interconnect connection must be established to Azure.

17. A company wants to move its data from a large on-premises database to Google Cloud. They are evaluating two strategies: an extended outage and a near-zero downtime migration. What is the main trade-off when choosing a near-zero downtime migration over an extended outage?

    A. Near-zero downtime is simpler to implement but riskier.

    B. Near-zero downtime results in longer overall migration time but lower complexity.

    C. Near-zero downtime is more complex and costly but results in minimal business disruption.

    D. Near-zero downtime requires manual data reconciliation after cutover.

18. When migrating a PostgreSQL database to Cloud SQL for PostgreSQL using DMS, a critical prerequisite for the initial data load phase is that every table in the source database must have:

A. An associated foreign key constraint

B. A primary key

C. A `created_at` timestamp column

D. No specific requirements; DMS handles all table types

19. Your company is migrating its existing on-premises production SQL Server database to Cloud SQL for SQL Server. To establish a secure and performant connection between your on-premises environment and Google Cloud for DMS replication, which Google Cloud networking service would be most appropriate?

A. Cloud CDN (Content Delivery Network)

B. Cloud Interconnect or Cloud VPN

C. Google Kubernetes Engine (GKE) Gateway

D. Cloud Load Balancing

20. The Database Migration Service (DMS) can migrate schema and data, but it explicitly does not migrate certain database objects. A Google Cloud database engineer must account for these objects separately in the migration plan. Which of the following is a type of object that DMS does not typically migrate and requires manual or alternative tool handling?

A. Tables and columns

B. Primary keys

C. Stored procedures and triggers

D. Indexes

Deploying and Validating Database Solutions

GOOGLE CLOUD CERTIFIED PROFESSIONAL CLOUD DATABASE ENGINEER EXAM OBJECTIVES COVERED IN THIS CHAPTER:

✔ **4.1 Apply concepts to implement scalable and highly available databases in Google Cloud.**

- Provision highly available database solutions in Google Cloud.
- Test high availability and disaster recovery strategies.
- Set up multiregional replication for databases.
- Deploy and scale read replicas.
- Automate database instance provisioning.
- Configure monitoring for highly available databases.

The transition from an architectural design to an operational, resilient database solution requires translating theoretical plans into tangible infrastructure. An architectural blueprint, no matter how precise, must be validated by its real-world implementation and its ability to withstand operational stress. This chapter covers the practical steps of constructing the database infrastructure and, critically, verifying that it meets the design requirements for scale and availability.

This chapter shifts from design to execution. We will cover the provisioning of highly available database solutions using the features built into Google Cloud's managed services. We will use infrastructure as code (IaC) to automate provisioning for consistency and speed. We will then configure replication to achieve both read scalability and disaster recovery. Finally, this chapter will cover the discipline of testing and monitoring to validate that HA and DR strategies function as designed.

Applying Concepts to Implement Highly Scalable and Available Databases

The successful implementation of a database solution is measured by its ability to perform reliably under load and recover from failure. This requires a practical understanding of how to translate architectural concepts into specific configurations within the Google Cloud ecosystem. A database engineer must be proficient with the services, commands, and orchestration required to build a system that is both scalable and resilient.

This section covers the hands-on application of these concepts. We will walk through provisioning database solutions that are highly available by default. We will then explore the automation of this provisioning process to reduce manual effort and the risk of human error. From there, we will discuss the implementation of replication for scaling and disaster recovery. Finally, we will address the necessary practice of periodically testing and monitoring these systems to ensure they will perform as expected during a failure event.

Provisioning High Availability Database Solutions in Google Cloud

High availability (HA) is a foundational characteristic of any production-grade database. It refers to the system's ability to remain operational despite the failure of one or more of its components. In Google Cloud, HA is achieved through redundancy, where critical components are duplicated across different failure domains, such as zones. If one component fails, traffic is automatically redirected to a redundant, healthy component, ensuring minimal service disruption. Provisioning for HA from the outset is a core responsibility of a Google Cloud database engineer.

Storage Configuration

It's important to understand that storage type (SSD vs. HDD) is a core configuration of a database instance, separate from its high availability or replication topology. To improve I/O performance, you would change the storage type from HDD to SSD by editing the primary instance's configuration. This change will then be automatically propagated to its HA standby. Creating a read replica or enabling HA does not, by itself, change the underlying storage type from HDD to SSD.

Cloud SQL

For relational databases like MySQL, PostgreSQL, and SQL Server, Cloud SQL provides a direct HA configuration. When you provision a Cloud SQL instance with the HA option enabled, Google Cloud automatically creates a primary instance and a standby instance in two different zones within the same region. This regional configuration relies on several key architectural components to ensure continuous service and data integrity:

Architecture   The primary instance handles all read and write traffic. The standby instance is an exact, up-to-date replica of the primary.

Replication   Data is replicated synchronously from the primary to the standby instance's persistent disk. This means a transaction is committed only after it has been written to both the primary and standby disks, guaranteeing zero data loss (an RPO of 0) in the event of a failover.

Automatic Failover   Cloud SQL continuously monitors the health of the primary instance. If the primary instance becomes unresponsive for any reason (e.g., a zonal failure, a hardware issue), Cloud SQL automatically initiates a failover. The standby instance is promoted to become the new primary, and all application traffic is redirected to it. This process typically completes within minutes, providing a very low RTO for zonal failures.

Provisioning this involves selecting the High Availability (Regional) option during instance creation in the Google Cloud Console or using a flag in the `gcloud` command.

```
gcloud sql instances create my-ha-instance \
   --database-version=POSTGRES_14 \
   --tier=db-n1-standard-4 \
   --region=us-central1 \
   --availability-type=REGIONAL
```

AlloyDB for PostgreSQL

AlloyDB, Google Cloud's PostgreSQL-compatible database, uses an architecture designed for HA that decouples compute from storage, allowing for more efficient and faster HA operations. This design relies on a distributed storage system and rapid instance failover to maintain availability without the performance penalties of traditional synchronous replication.

Architecture   An AlloyDB cluster consists of a primary instance for reads and writes, and a highly available, distributed storage layer that is replicated across multiple zones within a region. You can also add one or more read pool instances for scaling reads.

HA Mechanism   In the event of a primary instance failure, AlloyDB can promote a standby replica (if configured) or create a new primary instance very quickly—often in under 60 seconds. Because the storage layer is independent and already zonally redundant, there is no need to copy data during a failover, which significantly reduces the RTO.

Provisioning a highly available AlloyDB cluster involves creating the cluster and then adding a primary instance to it.

```
# Create the regional AlloyDB cluster
gcloud alloydb clusters create my-alloydb-cluster \
   --database-version=POSTGRES_14 \
   --password="YOUR_PASSWORD" \
   --network=default \
   --region=us-central1

# Create the primary instance within the cluster
gcloud alloydb instances create my-primary-instance \
   --instance-type=PRIMARY \
   --cpu-count=4 \
```

```
--cluster=my-alloydb-cluster \
--region=us-central1
```

Cloud Spanner

Cloud Spanner is designed for global scale and mission-critical availability, offering an industry-leading 99.999 percent availability SLA. This extreme resilience is achieved through a combination of distributed architecture and a robust consensus-based replication protocol:

Architecture   Spanner distributes data across multiple zones (in a regional configuration) or multiple regions (in a multiregion configuration). It uses a synchronous, Paxos-based replication protocol (a distributed consensus algorithm that ensures multiple nodes agree on a single data value even if some nodes fail) to maintain multiple, consistent copies of the data.

HA Mechanism   A regional Spanner instance maintains at least three read-write replicas, each in a different zone within the region. If a single zone fails, the instance remains fully available for reads and writes with zero downtime, as the remaining replicas can continue to serve traffic and elect a new leader via a majority vote. A multiregion instance extends this protection across entire regions, providing both extreme high availability and built-in disaster recovery.

Provisioning a regional Spanner instance automatically configures it for multizone high availability.

```
# Create a regional Spanner instance with 1 node (1000 processing units)
gcloud spanner instances create my-spanner-instance \
  --config=regional-us-central1 \
  --description="My HA Spanner Instance" \
  --nodes=1
```

Bigtable

For NoSQL workloads, Bigtable achieves HA through multicluster routing. The following components define how Bigtable maintains continuous operation during infrastructure outages:

Architecture   You can create a Bigtable instance with two or more clusters in different zones or regions. An application profile is then configured to route traffic to these clusters.

HA Mechanism   With a multicluster routing policy, Bigtable can automatically fail over traffic from an unavailable cluster to the nearest healthy cluster. This provides high availability for both reads and writes, protecting against zonal or even regional failures.

To provision a highly available Bigtable instance, you create it with at least two clusters in different failure domains (e.g., different zones).

```
# Create a Bigtable instance with two clusters in different zones for HA
gcloud bigtable instances create my-bigtable-instance \
    --display-name="My HA Bigtable Instance" \
    --cluster-config=id=cluster-a,zone=us-central1-a \
    --cluster-config=id=cluster-b,zone=us-central1-b
```

Table 11.1 summarizes the HA provisioning options for key Google Cloud databases.

TABLE 11.1   HA provisioning options for key Google Cloud databases

Database service	HA mechanism	Replication type	Typical failover time	Primary use case
Cloud SQL	Primary/standby instances in different zones	Synchronous	Minutes	Regional HA for traditional RDBMS workloads
AlloyDB	Primary/standby instances with distributed storage	Synchronous	Under 60 seconds	High-performance, regional HA for PostgreSQL workloads
Cloud Spanner	Multizone or multiregion read-write replicas	Synchronous (Paxos)	Zero downtime for zonal failure	Mission-critical, global applications needing extreme HA
Bigtable	Multicluster routing	Asynchronous	Seconds to minutes	Globally distributed, HA NoSQL workloads

---

Averting a Holiday Sales Disaster with Cloud SQL HA

An online gift basket company was running its entire e-commerce platform on a single Cloud SQL for MySQL instance. Ahead of the busy holiday season, their Cloud database engineer convinced leadership to invest in upgrading the instance to a high availability configuration. The change was simple: a few clicks in the console and a brief maintenance window.

Two weeks later, during the peak of Black Friday sales, Google Cloud experienced an unexpected, full-zone outage in the region where their primary instance was located. The engineer received an automated alert from Cloud Monitoring. By the time they logged in to investigate, the failover had already happened. Cloud SQL had automatically detected the unresponsive primary, promoted the standby instance in the unaffected zone, and redirected all traffic. The website experienced a brief blip in connectivity lasting less than 3 minutes, after which orders continued to flow seamlessly. A postmortem revealed that without the HA configuration, they would have faced hours of downtime and tens of thousands of dollars in lost revenue on their busiest day of the year.

EXERCISE 11.1

Skillsboost: Creating Spanner Instances and Databases (CLI and Terraform)

`www.cloudskillsboost.google/catalog_lab/6636`

In this exercise, you will automate the deployment of Google Cloud Spanner resources using both the `gcloud` CLI and Terraform. Accessed via the URL provided, this walk-through offers hands-on practice deploying what you learned earlier in the chapter. You will focus on programmatically provisioning instances and databases to streamline infrastructure management, ensuring you understand how to implement reproducible and scalable database environments without relying on the Cloud Console.

Automating Database Instance Provisioning

In a modern cloud environment, manual provisioning is a liability. It is slow, prone to human error, and leads to configuration drift, where environments that are supposed to be identical slowly diverge over time. Automating the provisioning of database instances using infrastructure as code (IaC) is a fundamental MLOps and DevOps practice that solves these problems. IaC allows you to define and manage your infrastructure using code and declarative configuration files, making the process repeatable, consistent, and version-controlled.

Terraform

Terraform is the most widely used open source IaC tool and is fully supported by Google Cloud. You define the desired state of your infrastructure—including database instances, networks, and firewall rules—in a human-readable configuration language called HCL (HashiCorp Configuration Language). By using Terraform, database engineers can manage infrastructure through a consistent workflow characterized by three core pillars:

Declarative Syntax   You describe *what* you want (e.g., "a Cloud SQL PostgreSQL instance with 4 vCPUs, 16 GB of RAM, and HA enabled"), and Terraform figures out *how* to create, update, or delete resources to match that state.

Execution Plan   Before making any changes, Terraform generates an execution plan that shows you exactly what it will do. This allows for a safe review process before applying any changes.

State Management   Terraform maintains a state file that maps your configuration to the real-world resources it manages, allowing it to track changes over time.

Here is a simplified example of a Terraform configuration to provision a Cloud SQL for PostgreSQL instance:

```
# main.tf

provider "google" {
  project = "your-gcp-project-id"
  region  = "us-central1"
}

resource "google_sql_database_instance" "main" {
  name             = "my-automated-instance"
  database_version = "POSTGRES_14"
  region           = "us-central1"

  settings {
    tier             = "db-n1-standard-4"
    availability_type = "REGIONAL" # This enables High Availability

    backup_configuration {
      enabled          = true
      point_in_time_recovery_enabled = true
    }
  }
}
```

By storing this code in a version control system like Git, you can track every change to your infrastructure, collaborate with teammates, and integrate it into a CI/CD pipeline for fully automated deployments.

gcloud Command-Line Interface (CLI)

For simpler automation tasks or for use within shell scripts, the `gcloud` CLI is an excellent tool. Every action you can perform in the Google Cloud Console can also be done using the `gcloud` command. You can write scripts that chain together `gcloud` commands to provision a database, configure its settings, and set up networking.

```bash
#!/bin/bash
# A simple script to create a database and a user

INSTANCE_NAME="scripted-instance"
REGION="us-east1"
DB_NAME="app_db"
USER_NAME="app_user"
PASSWORD="a-very-secure-password"

# Create the HA Cloud SQL instance
gcloud sql instances create $INSTANCE_NAME \
   --database-version=MYSQL_8_0 \
   --region=$REGION \
   --availability-type=REGIONAL \
   --tier=db-n1-standard-2 \
   --root-password=$PASSWORD

# Create a database within the instance
gcloud sql databases create $DB_NAME --instance=$INSTANCE_NAME

# Create a user
gcloud sql users create $USER_NAME --instance=$INSTANCE_NAME --password=$PASSWORD
```

While scripting is powerful, Terraform is generally preferred for managing complex environments because its declarative nature and state management capabilities make it more robust and easier to maintain over time.

Standardizing Global Deployments with Spanner and Terraform

A global fintech company was building a new payment processing platform on Cloud Spanner. Their architecture required identical Spanner instances to be deployed across three regions (Americas, EMEA, Asia) for development, staging, and production environments—a total of nine instances. The initial manual provisioning process was slow and error-prone. One engineer forgot to enable specific audit logging on a staging instance, which caused a compliance check to fail for days before the issue was discovered.

The lead Cloud database engineer mandated a move to IaC. They developed a single, reusable Terraform module for provisioning a Spanner instance. The module was parameterized, allowing them to specify the region, node count, and environment (e.g., `dev`, `stg`, `prod`) as variables. They integrated this module into a Cloud Build CI/CD pipeline. Now, provisioning a new, perfectly configured Spanner instance in any region is a matter of running the pipeline with the correct parameters. This has eliminated configuration drift, reduced provisioning time from hours to minutes, and ensured that every environment, from development to production, is a perfect, auditable replica of the defined configuration.

EXERCISE 11.2

Skillsboost: Cloud SQL with Terraform

```
https://www.cloudskillsboost.google/focuses/1215
```

In this exercise, you will create Cloud SQL instances using Terraform and configure the Cloud SQL Proxy to establish secure connections. Accessed via the URL provided, this lab offers hands-on practice deploying what you learned earlier in the chapter. You will focus on automating database provisioning and verifying connectivity with a MySQL client, ensuring you possess the practical skills to manage infrastructure as code and securely access your managed database instances.

Deploying and Scaling Read Replicas

Many applications have a workload pattern where reads are far more frequent than writes (e.g., blogs, product catalogs, social media feeds). In these scenarios, the primary database instance can become a bottleneck handling all the read requests. Read replicas are designed to solve this problem by offloading read traffic, thereby improving overall application performance and scalability.

A read replica is a copy of the primary instance that serves only read traffic. They use *asynchronous replication*, meaning there is a small delay (replication lag) between when data is written to the primary and when it becomes available to read on the replica. Keep the following in mind:

Use Case   Offloading read queries from the primary instance to one or more read replicas. This frees up the primary to handle writes and improves overall application performance and scalability.

Implementation   In Cloud SQL, you can easily create one or more read replicas for a primary instance. Your application can then be configured to direct write operations to the primary and read operations to the replicas. For AlloyDB, this is accomplished via a "read pool," which is a group of read-only instances that can be scaled independently and sit behind a single endpoint for easy load balancing.

Consideration   Because replication is asynchronous, read replicas are not suitable for reading data that must be perfectly up-to-date (read-after-write consistency). The application must be able to tolerate a small replication lag.

Cloud SQL Parallel Replication

For Cloud SQL for MySQL 8, you can enable parallel replication on a read replica. This feature allows the replica to use multiple threads to apply transactions from the primary's binary log simultaneously. For workloads where the primary instance has a very high write throughput, parallel replication can significantly reduce replication lag, ensuring the data on read replicas is more up-to-date and improving the performance of read-heavy applications that rely on them.

Connecting Applications to Replicas for Global Scale

While cross-region read replicas can dramatically reduce latency for global users, a critical implementation detail is how to direct application traffic to the geographically closest replica.

The Challenge of Global Endpoints

Cloud SQL read replicas each have their own unique IP address. Google Cloud does not provide a single, global endpoint that automatically routes application connections to the nearest replica. This means the responsibility for intelligent routing falls to the application architecture. Without a routing strategy, an application in Europe might unnecessarily connect to a replica in Asia, negating the latency benefits.

Application-Side Routing Strategies

There are two primary strategies for solving this routing challenge:

DNS-Based Routing: This approach uses a managed DNS service to handle the routing logic.

How It Works: Services like Cloud DNS can be configured with latency-based routing policies. You create a DNS record set (e.g., `reads.my-app.com`) with multiple records, each pointing to the unique IP address of a different read replica.

Implementation: When an application server or end-user client makes a DNS query for `reads.my-app.com`, Cloud DNS intelligently responds with the IP address of the replica located in the region that provides the lowest latency to the source of the DNS query (the user's DNS resolver). The application simply connects to the generic hostname, and the routing happens transparently at the DNS level.

Application Logic: This approach embeds the routing intelligence directly into the application code or a proxy layer.

How It Works: The application itself determines the user's location or its own serving region (e.g., by inspecting request headers or using metadata services).

Implementation: Based on this location, the application logic selects the appropriate replica's connection string from its configuration files or a secure store like Secret Manager. For example, if the application detects it's serving a request from europe-west1, it retrieves and uses the connection string for the europe-west1 read replica. This method provides granular control but increases application complexity.

Choosing between these strategies depends on the desired level of control and complexity. DNS-based routing is simpler to manage for the application, while application-side logic offers more fine-grained control over connection decisions.

Case Surviving a Viral Marketing Campaign with Read Replicas

A fashion startup launched a new line of sneakers with a clever social media campaign. The campaign went viral overnight, driving 100 times their normal traffic to their e-commerce site, which was built on Cloud SQL for PostgreSQL. The site quickly slowed to a crawl as the single primary database struggled to handle the flood of users browsing the product catalog.

The on-call engineer, seeing the CPU on the primary instance pegged at 100 percent, quickly provisioned two read replicas. They updated the application's connection manager to route all product catalog queries to the replicas while sending Add To Cart and checkout operations to the primary. Within minutes, the load on the primary instance dropped dramatically and the website's performance returned to normal. The read replicas absorbed the massive influx of read traffic, allowing the primary to focus on the critical job of processing orders, turning a potential site crash into a huge sales success.

Skillsboost: Creating and Managing AlloyDB Instances

```
www.cloudskillsboost.google/paths/22/course_templates/642/
labs/557016
```

In this exercise, you will perform core AlloyDB operations, migrate from PostgreSQL, and accelerate analytical queries using the Columnar Engine. Accessed via the URL provided, this walk-through offers hands-on practice deploying what you learned earlier in the chapter. You will focus on administering the database and optimizing performance, ensuring you understand the practical steps required to manage hybrid transactional and analytical workloads effectively.

Setting Up Multiregional Replication for Disaster Recovery

While HA configurations protect against failures within a region, a true disaster recovery (DR) strategy must account for the possibility of an entire region becoming unavailable. Multiregional replication is the key to building this level of resilience.

A cross-region replica is a specific type of read replica where the replica is provisioned in a different geographical region from the primary instance. While it can also be used to serve read traffic to users in that region (reducing latency), its primary purpose is disaster recovery. Here are the details:

Use Case   To provide a recovery option in the event of a full regional outage. If the primary region becomes unavailable, you can manually promote the cross-region replica to become a new, stand-alone primary instance.

Implementation   The setup is similar to a standard read replica. You create a replica of your primary Cloud SQL instance but specify a different region for its location.

RTO/RPO   Because replication is asynchronous, there is a potential for data loss (RPO > 0) if the primary region fails before all transactions have been replicated. The RTO will be longer than an automatic HA failover, as it involves a manual promotion process, DNS changes, and application reconfiguration. This process can take minutes to hours, depending on the preparedness of the team.

It is crucial to differentiate this from a multiregion Spanner instance, which provides synchronous replication across regions for an RPO of zero and can handle a regional failure with a very low RTO automatically.

Creating a Cross-Region Replica

Setting up a cross-region replica for Cloud SQL is a straightforward process. The following steps walk you through creating a DR replica using the `gcloud` CLI.

1. Before creating any replica, the primary instance must have automatic backups enabled. This is a mandatory prerequisite for the replication process. You can verify this using the `describe` command.

```
# Verify backups are enabled on the primary instance
gcloud sql instances describe my-primary-instance
```

In the output, confirm that `settings.backupConfiguration.enabled` is set to `true`.

2. Use the `gcloud sql replicas create` command. The key is to specify a `--region` flag that is different from the primary instance's region.

```
# Create a read replica named 'my-dr-replica' in the us-east1 region
# for the primary instance 'my-primary-instance'
gcloud sql replicas create my-dr-replica \
    --instance=my-primary-instance \
    --region=us-east1 \
    --async
```

3. After the operation begins, you can check the status of the new replica:

```
# Describe the new replica to check its status
gcloud sql instances describe my-dr-replica
```

4. Look for `state: RUNNABLE` to confirm the replica is operational. You should also verify that its `region` is `us-east1` and its `instanceType` is `READ_REPLICA_INSTANCE`.

Table 11.2 provides a concise comparison of three different database replication and high-availability strategies available in Google Cloud. It highlights the trade-offs between them, focusing on their primary use case, recovery objectives, and data consistency models.

TABLE 11.2   Replication options in Google Cloud databases

Feature	Read replica (in-region)	Cross-region replica	Multiregion Spanner
Primary purpose	Read scaling	Disaster recovery	HA and DR
Replication	Asynchronous	Asynchronous	Synchronous
RPO on failure	N/A (not for failover)	Seconds to minutes	Zero
RTO on failure	N/A (not for failover)	Minutes to hours (manual)	Seconds to minutes (automatic)
Consistency	Eventual	Eventual	Strong

Delivering Low-Latency Personalization with Bigtable Replication

A major media streaming service used Cloud Bigtable to store user profiles and watch history, which powered their content personalization engine. As their service expanded from North America to Europe and Asia, users in the new regions complained of slow recommendations. The root cause was network latency; their application servers in Europe were making cross-continent requests to the single Bigtable cluster in us-central1.

To solve this, the engineering team configured Bigtable replication. They added new Bigtable clusters in europe-west1 and asia-east1 to their instance and created an application profile with a multicluster routing policy. This policy automatically routes application requests to the nearest cluster. With the change deployed, European user requests were served from the europe-west1 cluster and Asian requests from asia-east1, while the data was asynchronously replicated between all three clusters. This change dramatically reduced read latency for their international users, leading to a measurable increase in user engagement and watch time. The replication provided both a better user experience and a robust, multiregion HA/DR posture.

Testing High Availability and Disaster Recovery Strategies Periodically

A disaster recovery plan that has never been tested is not a plan; it's a theory. Periodically and rigorously testing your HA and DR strategies is the only way to ensure they will work when you need them most. These tests, often called "game days" or "disaster recovery drills," are essential for building confidence in your system's resilience, identifying hidden flaws, and training your team to respond effectively under pressure.

Testing High Availability (HA)

Testing your HA setup involves validating the automatic failover process. For services like Cloud SQL and AlloyDB, you can manually initiate a failover by following these steps:

1. Schedule the test.   Announce the test to all stakeholders.

2. Establish baselines.   Monitor key application metrics (e.g., error rates, latency) before the test.

3. Initiate failover.   Use the Google Cloud Console or the `gcloud` command to trigger a manual failover of your HA instance. This simulates a primary instance failure and forces the system to promote the standby.

4. Monitor and measure.   Observe the application's behavior during the failover. Measure the exact time it takes for the database to become available again (the actual RTO). Check for any errors or unexpected behavior.

5. Validate.   Once the failover is complete, run a suite of tests to confirm the application is fully functional.

6. Fail back (optional).   You can perform the process in reverse to return to the original primary instance.

This test validates that the automatic failover mechanism works and gives you a real-world measurement of your RTO, which is often more accurate than the documented estimates.

Testing Disaster Recovery

Testing a DR plan is more involved, as it simulates a complete regional outage and requires manual intervention:

1. Perform a tabletop exercise.   Before a live drill, walk through the entire DR plan with the team. Discuss each step, role, and responsibility. This step often uncovers logical flaws or outdated information in the documentation.

2. Isolate the primary.   In a controlled manner, make the primary database inaccessible to the application (e.g., by changing firewall rules), simulating a regional outage.

3. Execute the plan.   The response team follows the documented DR plan. This includes:

Promoting the Replica   The cross-region read replica is promoted to a stand-alone, writable instance.
Reconfiguring the Application   Application connection strings and DNS records are updated to point to the new primary in the DR region.
Validating Data   The team must verify the state of the data on the new primary, measuring the actual data loss (RPO) by comparing it with the last known state of the old primary.

4. Perform a full system validation.   Once the application is connected, run a full suite of functional and performance tests to ensure the system is operating correctly in the DR region.

5. Perform postmortem and cleanup steps.   After the test, have the team conduct a postmortem to discuss what went well, what went wrong, and how to improve the plan. Then carefully reset the environment to its original state.

A DR Drill Uncovers a Critical Storage Misconfiguration for Oracle on BMS

A large insurance company migrated its core claims processing system, running on a massive Oracle database, to Oracle on Bare Metal Solution (BMS) in us-central1. Their DR strategy involved using Oracle Data Guard to asynchronously replicate data to a standby Oracle instance on BMS in us-east4. They had a detailed, 200-step runbook for failing over.

During their first annual DR drill, the team began the failover process. The database promotion itself went smoothly. However, when the application was pointed to the DR instance, performance was abysmal—queries that took seconds in the primary region were taking over 15 minutes. The application was unusable. After hours of investigation, the root cause was found: The storage LUNs provisioned for the DR Oracle instance in us-east4 were configured with a lower performance tier than the primary to save costs. While the storage had enough capacity, it lacked the IOPS to handle the production workload.

The DR test was a failure from a business RTO perspective, but a massive success in identifying a critical flaw. The company immediately reprovisioned the DR storage to match the primary's performance specifications. The test proved that a DR plan must validate not just data availability, but also performance under load, ensuring the recovery environment is truly capable of running the business.

Executing and Verifying Failover and Promotion

Understanding the practical commands and procedures for executing a failover or promotion is critical during a testing drill or a real event. It's essential to distinguish between these two key operations:

Failover   An automatic or manual process for an HA-configured instance where the standby takes over for the primary. The connection endpoint (IP address) does not change. This provides high availability.

Promotion   A manual process where a read replica is converted into a stand-alone, writable primary instance. The original primary is unaffected. This is a key step in a disaster recovery plan and results in a new database with a new IP address.

Executing with *gcloud*

Here are the specific `gcloud` commands to initiate these operations for Cloud SQL.

HA Failover (Cloud SQL):

```
# Initiate a manual failover for an HA instance.
# This command triggers the same process as an automatic failover.
gcloud sql instances failover YOUR_INSTANCE_NAME
```

Promote Read Replica (Cloud SQL):

```
# Promote a read replica to a standalone, writable instance.
# This is an irreversible action for the replica.
gcloud sql instances promote-replica YOUR_REPLICA_NAME
```

Troubleshooting a Failed Failover

If a failover or promotion operation does not complete successfully, a systematic approach like this is needed to diagnose the issue:

1. Check the Operations log.   The first place to look is the Operations log for the Cloud SQL instance in the Google Cloud Console. This log provides detailed, human-readable status messages and specific errors for all administrative actions, including failovers.

2. Use `gcloud` to view operations.   You can retrieve the same information from the command line, which can be useful for scripting or quick checks.

```
gcloud sql operations list --instance=YOUR_INSTANCE_NAME
```

3. Review Cloud Monitoring metrics.   Check the dashboards in Cloud Monitoring for the period leading up to the failover attempt. Look for signs of instance overload (e.g., sustained 100 percent CPU utilization, low available memory) or storage issues (e.g., disk full) on either the primary or standby instance, as these can prevent a successful failover.

4. Verify IAM permissions.   Ensure the Cloud SQL service account (`service-`*<project-number>*`@gcp-sa-cloud-sql.iam.gserviceaccount.com`) has the necessary `cloudsql.admin` role and other required permissions. While rare, incorrect IAM configurations can interfere with instance management operations.

EXERCISE 11.4

Skillsboost: Configuring Replication and Enabling PITR for Cloud SQL for PostgreSQL

`www.cloudskillsboost.google/catalog_lab/4202`

In this exercise, you will configure and test point-in-time recovery (PITR) for a Cloud SQL for PostgreSQL instance. Accessed via the URL provided, this walk-through offers hands-on practice deploying what you learned earlier in the chapter. You will focus on enabling recovery features and restoring a database to a precise moment, ensuring you understand how to mitigate data loss by creating new instances based on specific historical states.

Configuring Monitoring for Highly Available Databases

Deploying a highly available database is only half the battle; you must also monitor the health of the HA system itself. Monitoring for HA goes beyond standard performance metrics like CPU and memory. It focuses on the specific signals that indicate the health of your redundancy and replication mechanisms, ensuring that your safety net is intact and ready when you need it.

The key metrics for HA monitoring are as follows:

Replication Lag   For any system using asynchronous replication (like Cloud SQL read replicas or Bigtable replication), replication lag is the most critical metric. It measures the time delay between a write occurring on the primary and that same write being applied to the replica. High replication lag jeopardizes your recovery point objective (RPO) because it represents the window of data that could be lost in a DR scenario. In Cloud SQL, this metric is available in Cloud Monitoring as `cloudsql.googleapis.com/database/replication/replica_lag`.

Instance Health   You must monitor the health of all instances in your topology—primary, standby, and replicas. An unhealthy standby or replica means your HA or DR protection is compromised. Cloud Monitoring provides simple uptime and health status checks for this purpose.

Failover Events   An automatic failover is a critical event that needs immediate attention. While the system handles the recovery, you need to investigate the root cause of the original failure to prevent it from happening again. You can create alerts based on System Event audit logs in Cloud Logging or specific log entries that indicate a failover has occurred.

Setting Up Alerts

Proactive alerting is crucial. You should configure alerts in Cloud Monitoring to notify you immediately if:

- Replication lag on a DR replica exceeds your defined RPO (e.g., >5 minutes).
- A standby or replica instance becomes unhealthy or stops replicating.
- An automatic failover is initiated.

These alerts should be routed to a system like PagerDuty or Slack to ensure the on-call team can respond quickly.

Proactive Monitoring Prevents DR Failure for AlloyDB

A logistics company used an AlloyDB cluster in us-west1 as their primary database, with a cross-region read replica in us-east1 for disaster recovery. Their business requirement was an RPO of no more than 10 minutes. The database engineering team set up a critical alert in Cloud Monitoring to trigger if the replication lag to the DR replica ever exceeded 300 seconds (5 minutes).

One afternoon, the alert fired. The team was notified that replication lag was steadily climbing and had reached 7 minutes. Investigation in Cloud Monitoring revealed a spike in network latency between the two regions, which was slowing down the replication stream. Although there was no outage, the high lag meant their DR strategy was out of compliance with their RPO. The team was able to work with Google Cloud support to diagnose the transient network issue. The lag returned to normal within an hour. Without the proactive alert on replication lag, they would have been unaware that their DR protection was compromised, and a real disaster during that window could have resulted in unacceptable data loss.

EXERCISE 11.5

Skillsboost: Monitoring and Managing Bigtable Health and Performance

```
www.cloudskillsboost.google/paths/22/course_templates/650/
labs/557005
```

In this exercise, you will monitor disk usage, configure node autoscaling, implement replication, and back up data. Accessed via the URL provided, this walk-through offers hands-on practice deploying what you learned earlier in the chapter. You will focus on managing the health and performance of your instance to improve durability and availability, ensuring you understand the practical operational controls required to maintain a scalable NoSQL database.

Summary

In this chapter, we transitioned from design and theory to the practical realities of implementation and validation. We explored the hands-on steps required to build robust, scalable, and highly available database solutions on Google Cloud. We began by provisioning HA configurations for key services like Cloud SQL, AlloyDB, and Spanner, understanding how their different architectures provide resilience against failure. We then emphasized the critical importance of automating these provisioning tasks using tools like Terraform and the `gcloud` CLI to ensure consistency and speed while reducing human error.

We dissected the dual role of replication, learning how to deploy and scale in-region read replicas for performance and how to set up cross-region replicas as the cornerstone of a sound disaster recovery strategy. Most importantly, we established that a plan for HA or DR is incomplete without rigorous, periodic testing and monitoring. We detailed the procedures for conducting HA failover tests and DR drills, including the specific commands and troubleshooting steps, and outlined how to monitor the health of the HA system itself. These exercises are the only true way to validate that your systems will behave as expected when a crisis occurs. By mastering these implementation and validation techniques, you can confidently build and manage database systems that are not just powerful, but truly resilient.

Exam Essentials

Know HA configurations for key services.   You must be able to describe the high availability mechanisms for Cloud SQL (primary/standby with synchronous replication), AlloyDB (decoupled compute/storage), and Cloud Spanner (multizone/multiregion synchronous replication).

Understand automation with IaC.   Be prepared to explain why automating database provisioning is essential and be able to identify Terraform and `gcloud` CLI as the primary tools for accomplishing this.

Differentiate between replica types and connection strategies.   You must clearly distinguish between the use case for in-region read replicas (read scaling) and cross-region replicas (disaster recovery). Understand that both typically use asynchronous replication and know the strategies (DNS-based, application-side logic) for connecting to them.

Explain the purpose of testing.   Be able to explain why periodic testing of HA and DR plans is non-negotiable. You should be able to describe the high-level process for both an HA failover test and a DR drill.

Differentiate failover vs. promotion.   Understand that a failover is an HA operation where the endpoint remains the same, whereas a promotion is a DR operation that creates a new, stand-alone database from a replica. Be familiar with the `gcloud` commands to execute these actions.

Configure monitoring for HA.   Be able to identify key metrics for monitoring an HA system, such as replication lag and instance health, and know how to use Cloud Monitoring and Logging to create alerts for them.

Connect features to RTO/RPO.   Understand how different solutions impact recovery objectives. An automatic HA failover provides a very low RTO. A manual DR promotion of a cross-region replica results in a higher RTO and a non-zero RPO due to asynchronous replication.

Recognize the role of synchronous vs. asynchronous replication.   Know that synchronous replication (used in Cloud SQL HA and Spanner) guarantees zero data loss on failover (RPO = 0), while asynchronous replication (used for read replicas) implies a potential for data loss.

Review Questions

1. What is the primary reason why it is crucial to perform periodic testing of high availability (HA) and disaster recovery (DR) strategies, often through "game days" or DR drills?

   A. To validate theoretical RTO/RPO values and train response teams

   B. To reduce the ongoing operational costs of the database

   C. To confirm that all database instances are running the latest software versions

   D. To provide real-time performance metrics to application teams

2. What is the main use case for an in-region read replica in Cloud SQL?

   A. To serve as a direct failover target for the primary in case of an outage

   B. To enable point-in-time recovery (PITR) for the primary instance

   C. To offload read queries from the primary instance, improving read scalability

   D. To provide a disaster recovery option in a different Google Cloud region

3. A small startup is provisioning its first Cloud SQL for PostgreSQL instance. They prioritize minimal initial cost and are comfortable with manual intervention for database recovery. Which provisioning choice would align with their current priorities?

   A. A regional instance with high availability (HA) enabled

   B. A zonal instance without a standby replica

   C. A multiregion instance for global resilience

   D. A zonal instance with point-in-time recovery (PITR) enabled

4. Your team is conducting a "game day" exercise to validate the DR plan for a critical Cloud SQL instance. The scenario involves simulating a regional outage and performing a full failover to a cross-region replica. During the exercise, it becomes apparent that the documentation for updating DNS records and application connection strings is outdated, causing significant delays. What is the most important lesson learned from this experience regarding DR planning?

   A. Regular testing is unnecessary if the documentation is perfect.

   B. The RPO (recovery point objective) needs to be lowered.

   C. DR plans must be periodically tested and documentation kept up-to-date.

   D. Automated backups are sufficient for a DR strategy.

5. A development team wants to test their disaster recovery plan for a Cloud SQL for MySQL database. The plan involves promoting a cross-region read replica to a new stand-alone primary in a different region. What is the correct `gcloud` command to execute this critical step in the DR drill?

A. `gcloud sql instances failover MY_INSTANCE_NAME`

B. `gcloud sql instances promote-replica MY_REPLICA_NAME`

C. `gcloud sql instances patch MY_INSTANCE_NAME --availability-type=REGIONAL`

D. `gcloud sql export sql MY_INSTANCE_NAME gs://my-bucket/backup.sql`

6. A database engineer wants to ensure that all newly provisioned Cloud SQL instances always have high availability, automated backups, and point-in-time recovery enabled. Which IaC tool would allow them to define this desired state once and apply it consistently across all new deployments?

A. `gcloud sql create` commands for each instance

B. Python scripts that manually configure each setting

C. Terraform with a `google_sql_database_instance` resource

D. Cloud Monitoring custom dashboards

7. A large-scale IoT application collects massive amounts of time-series data and stores it in Cloud Bigtable. To ensure continuous data availability and low latency for users across different continents, what is the recommended Bigtable configuration for high availability and global distribution?

A. A single Bigtable cluster in a central region with a public IP

B. Multicluster routing with two or more Bigtable clusters in different regions

C. Automated daily backups of the Bigtable instance to Cloud Storage

D. Setting up a Bigtable instance on a Compute Engine VM with a custom replication solution

8. A financial services company needs to provision a new Cloud SQL for MySQL instance that must sustain operations even if an entire Google Cloud zone becomes unavailable. Their application demands a very low RTO (recovery time objective) in such a scenario. Which Cloud SQL configuration provides this high availability within a region?

A. A zonal instance with automated daily backups

B. A regional instance with a high availability (HA) configuration

C. A multiregion instance with cross-region read replicas

D. A zonal instance with point-in-time recovery (PITR) enabled

9. A social media application uses a Cloud SQL for PostgreSQL database. The primary instance is experiencing performance bottlenecks during peak hours due to a high volume of read queries. To alleviate this pressure and scale read operations, which replication strategy should be implemented?

   A. Create a cross-region read replica in a different geographic region.

   B. Provision a high availability (HA) configuration for the primary instance.

   C. Set up one or more in-region read replicas.

   D. Convert the entire database to Cloud Spanner.

10. A critical internal application's Cloud SQL HA instance failed over unexpectedly. The SRE team needs to quickly diagnose why the failover occurred and understand the sequence of events leading up to it. Which specific resource should they check first to get detailed information about the failover operation itself?

    A. The application's own error logs

    B. The Cloud SQL instance's Operations log in the Google Cloud Console

    C. Cloud Monitoring metrics for CPU utilization

    D. The billing reports for the Cloud SQL instance

11. A global gaming company uses Cloud Spanner for its leaderboard data. They need a database solution that offers extreme availability (99.999 percent SLA) and transparent protection against entire regional outages, maintaining strong global consistency. How does Cloud Spanner achieve this resilience and low RTO for regional failures?

    A. By performing daily full backups to Cloud Storage

    B. By synchronously replicating data across multiple zones and regions

    C. By relying on manual failover to a hot standby in another region

    D. By automatically sharding data across different project IDs

12. A Google Cloud database engineer provisions a new Cloud SQL for MySQL instance. The business requires high write performance, so the engineer selects SSD storage. They also provision it for high availability (HA). If the primary instance's SSD disk were to fail, how does Cloud SQL's HA configuration help maintain service?

    A. It automatically switches to a cheaper HDD disk for the standby.

    B. It creates a new, larger SSD disk and migrates the data there.

    C. It leverages the synchronously replicated data on the standby instance's SSD disk for failover.

    D. It falls back to read-only mode until a new disk can be attached.

13. An engineering team wants to automate the provisioning of their AlloyDB for PostgreSQL clusters. They are comfortable with shell scripting and `gcloud` commands. Which automation approach would be most suitable for creating, configuring, and managing these clusters in a programmatic way?

   A. Manual provisioning through the Google Cloud Console

   B. Writing custom Python scripts using the AlloyDB client library

   C. Utilizing `gcloud` CLI commands within shell scripts

   D. Deploying Cloud Composer workflows for each cluster

14. A company needs to ensure its critical Cloud SQL for PostgreSQL database can recover from a widespread regional outage. They decide to set up a cross-region read replica. What is the primary characteristic of the replication between the primary and this cross-region read replica in Cloud SQL, and what does it imply for RPO?

   A. It is synchronous, guaranteeing zero data loss (RPO = 0).

   B. It is synchronous, meaning higher latency but faster RTO.

   C. It is asynchronous, implying potential data loss (RPO > 0).

   D. It is asynchronous, but only for writes; reads are synchronous.

15. A Google Cloud Professional Database Engineer is building a new application on AlloyDB for PostgreSQL that requires extremely low RTO (under 60 seconds) for primary instance failures. How does AlloyDB's architecture specifically achieve this rapid failover capability?

   A. By relying on manual intervention to promote a standby

   B. By using a physical standby that requires data copying during failover

   C. By decoupling compute from storage, allowing for rapid promotion of a new primary instance leveraging shared, zonally redundant storage

   D. By automatically sharding the database across multiple projects

16. A company is planning its annual disaster recovery (DR) drill. The DR plan involves manually promoting a Cloud SQL cross-region read replica to a new primary. After the promotion, the application connection strings need to be updated. What is the key difference between this "promotion" operation and an automatic "failover" in a Cloud SQL HA configuration?

   A. Promotion is automated and restores data from a backup, whereas failover is manual and involves data loss.

   B. Promotion is for read scaling, whereas failover is for write scaling.

   C. Promotion converts a replica to a new primary with a new endpoint, whereas failover switches to a standby keeping the same endpoint.

   D. Promotion is only for PostgreSQL, whereas failover is for MySQL.

17. A Google Cloud database engineer has used Terraform to provision a Cloud SQL instance. Later, they update the Terraform configuration to change the database version and enable a new extension. After running terraform apply, the changes are successfully deployed. What is the key benefit of using Terraform for making such changes, rather than manual CLI commands?

    A. Terraform provides a graphical user interface for easy management.

    B. Terraform automatically backs up the database before every change.

    C. Terraform tracks the state of the infrastructure, allowing for consistent and auditable changes.

    D. Terraform only supports immutable infrastructure, preventing any changes.

18. When performing a manual failover test for a Cloud SQL HA instance, the `gcloud sql instances failover` command is used. What does this command simulate, and what is its expected outcome regarding the instance's connection endpoint?

    A. It simulates a full regional disaster and changes the instance's IP address.

    B. It simulates a zonal failure and keeps the instance's IP address the same.

    C. It exports the database to a new instance in a different project.

    D. It promotes a read replica to a stand-alone primary.

19. A critical application database on Google Cloud uses asynchronous replication for its read replicas. What is the implication of this asynchronous nature regarding the recovery point objective (RPO) in the event of the primary database failing?

    A. The RPO will be zero, as no data is lost.

    B. The RPO will be very high, as data needs to be manually restored.

    C. The RPO will be greater than zero, implying potential data loss.

    D. Asynchronous replication only impacts RTO, not RPO.

20. A database engineer has deployed an AlloyDB for PostgreSQL cluster. To periodically test the cluster's high availability, they plan to manually trigger a failover. After initiating the failover, what is the most critical metric they should monitor to determine the actual RTO (recovery time objective) achieved?

    A. Total storage used by the cluster

    B. Number of read replicas connected to the primary

    C. Time until new connections are successfully made to the new primary

    D. CPU utilization of the compute nodes

Appendix

Answers to the Review Questions

Chapter 1: Data Storage Technologies

1. **B.** Google Cloud Storage is designed for storing and retrieving large amounts of unstructured data. It offers high scalability, durability, and availability, making it suitable for storing images, videos, and audio files.

   Persistent Disk, Cloud Filestore, and Hyperdisk are not designed for storing large volumes of unstructured data. They are better suited for structured data or specific use cases.

2. **C.** High-frequency trading requires extremely low latency and high throughput to execute orders rapidly. Therefore, performance and scalability are the most critical considerations for this scenario.

   While cost, durability, security, and compliance are important, they are secondary to the speed and capacity required for high-frequency trading.

3. **C.** Local SSDs are directly attached to the virtual machine and offer the highest performance for I/O-intensive workloads. They are ideal for caching, scratch processing, and temporary data storage.

   Persistent Disk, Hyperdisk, and Google Cloud Storage are network-attached storage solutions and may introduce latency compared to a locally attached SSD.

4. **D.** Hyperdisk offers the highest performance and lowest latency among the listed options. It is designed for demanding workloads that require exceptional performance, such as high-end databases and real-time analytics.

   Standard, Balanced, and Extreme Persistent Disks offer good performance, but Hyperdisk is optimized for the highest performance and lowest latency.

5. **C.** Coldline is designed for data accessed a few times per year and offers a lower cost than Nearline. It is suitable for long-term data archiving, such as historical sales data that is accessed infrequently.

   Standard is for frequently accessed data, Nearline is for data accessed more frequently than Coldline, and Archive is for data accessed very rarely and has high retrieval costs.

6. **C.** Object storage is the most suitable option for storing large amounts of unstructured data, like images, videos, and text posts, due to its scalability and cost-effectiveness for handling rapid data growth.

   Block, file, and in-memory storage are not as scalable or cost-effective for managing massive amounts of unstructured data.

7. **B.** Persistent Disk offers durable block storage for virtual machines, providing the required persistence and performance characteristics for a high-performance database.

   Object storage, local SSDs, and cloud storage in general do not provide the same level of performance and persistence required for a high-performance database.

8. **C.** Local SSD provides the highest performance among the options due to its direct attachment to the virtual machine, but data is lost if the instance terminates.

   Persistent Disk, Hyperdisk, and object storage all offer data durability features to protect against data loss.

9. A. The primary distinction is that Filestore is fully managed by Google Cloud, while NetApp Volumes is a partner-managed service offered in collaboration with NetApp, providing a different level of integration and support.

While there may be some differences in protocols, scale, or performance, the key difference is the management responsibility.

10. B. Object storage like Google Cloud Storage is ideal for storing and analyzing large datasets. Key-value stores are optimized for handling large amounts of data with simple key-value pairs, making them suitable for storing and retrieving DNA sequences efficiently.

Block storage is designed for operating systems and virtual machines, not for directly storing and analyzing large datasets of genomic data. While file storage can store large files, it's less efficient and scalable than object storage for handling massive datasets and complex analysis requirements. In-memory databases are fast but don't offer persistent storage needed for long-term genomic data retention. Relational databases are less suitable for the unstructured nature and massive scale of genomic data; they can struggle with performance and scalability at this scale.

11. B. Google Cloud Filestore is a fully managed network file storage service that provides a scalable, high-performance, and reliable platform for storing and accessing data.

Cloud storage, Hyperdisk, and NetApp Volumes offer different storage functionalities and are not fully managed NFS file storage services.

12. A. Cloud Filestore is a managed file storage service that supports concurrent access from multiple virtual machines, making it ideal for shared filesystems.

Cloud storage, Persistent Disk, and Local SSD are not designed for concurrent access from multiple virtual machines in the same way as a shared filesystem.

13. C. Persistent Disk (pd-extreme) offers the highest performance and is specifically designed for demanding workloads like Oracle databases requiring high IOPS and throughput.

Cloud storage, pd-standard, and Local SSD do not provide the same level of IOPS and throughput as pd-extreme.

14. A. This combination balances performance and cost. Persistent Disk (pd-standard) provides durable storage for large video files, while Local SSD offers high-performance temporary storage for editing tasks.

Other options may be overly expensive or not provide the necessary balance of performance and cost-effectiveness.

15. C. Multiregion storage replicates data across multiple geographic regions, providing the highest level of durability and availability in case of regional outages.

Region and Dual-Region storage offer less geographic redundancy than Multiregion.

16. B. Cloud Filestore is a fully managed NFS file storage service that offers high performance and low latency, and that is accessible from multiple compute engine instances.

Cloud storage, Persistent Disk, and Local SSD are not designed as shared filesystems with NFS support.

17. A. Standard storage offers the highest throughput and lowest latency, making it ideal for data-intensive workloads like machine learning model training where data access speed is critical.

Nearline, Coldline, and Archive storage are designed for less frequently accessed data and would have higher latency and lower throughput, negatively impacting training time.

18. D. Archive storage is the most cost-effective option for long-term data archival and disaster recovery. It offers the lowest storage costs but has the highest retrieval fees and latency, making it suitable for data accessed very infrequently.

Standard, Nearline, and Coldline storage are more expensive and have higher access times than Archive storage, making them less suitable for infrequently accessed data.

19. A. Region storage allows you to store data within a specific geographic region, giving you control over data placement and helping you comply with data residency regulations.

Dual-Region, Multiregion, and Global storage options do not offer the same level of control over data placement within a specific region.

20. C. Multiregion storage provides the highest level of availability and low latency for data accessed globally. Data is replicated across multiple geographic regions, ensuring low latency and high availability for users worldwide.

Region and Dual-Region storage do not offer the same level of global availability and low latency as Multi-Region.

Chapter 2: Database Storage Models and Data Types

1. C. Structured data follows a predefined format, organized into rows and columns with a defined schema. Unstructured data, conversely, has a variable format.

A, B, and D are all characteristics of structured data. A defined schema, rows and columns, and a quantitative nature are key features.

2. C. In-memory databases store data in RAM, enabling extremely fast access and significantly lower latency compared to disk-based databases.

While in-memory databases can offer improved security and durability through specific configurations and implementations, their primary advantage lies in performance. Cost-efficiency is not inherently guaranteed.

3. C. Relational OLAP (online analytical processing) databases are designed for analytical workloads, handling complex queries and large datasets efficiently.

In-memory databases excel at speed, NoSQL databases prioritize scalability and flexibility, and OLTP databases focus on transactional processing.

4. B. Document databases are designed to store data in flexible, schema-less documents, often represented in JSON or similar formats.

Key-value stores are simple key-value pairs; graph databases model relationships; columnar databases organize data by columns.

5. C. Key-value stores are efficient for storing and retrieving time-stamped data points, making them ideal for sensor data analysis.

Relational databases are less efficient for time-series data; in-memory databases are best for speed, not massive datasets; and document databases are more suitable for complex, unstructured data.

6. B. In-memory databases provide extremely low latency, crucial for real-time leaderboards and responsive gameplay.

Relational databases can be slower; key-value stores lack the structure for complex game data; and document databases offer flexibility but may lack the speed.

7. A. The defining difference is the schema: structured data conforms to a predefined schema, whereas unstructured data does not.

While the other options might often be true, they are not the defining characteristic.

8. C. Relational OLTP (online transaction processing) databases are designed for transactional workloads, ensuring ACID properties (Atomicity, Consistency, Isolation, Durability).

NoSQL, key-value, and document databases generally don't guarantee ACID properties to the same extent.

9. D. Vector data, or embeddings, represents complex data like text or images as numerical arrays that capture semantic meaning. This allows for searches based on contextual similarity (what something means) rather than lexical matching (exact keywords), which is ideal for the described use case.

10. A. This data is typically structured, and the sensitive nature necessitates prioritizing security and compliance with regulations like GDPR or CCPA.

Scalability, flexibility, and performance are important, but security and compliance are paramount for sensitive data.

11. A, B, D. Key-value stores, in-memory databases, and OLTP relational databases are all optimized for high-throughput, short transactions.

Document databases are more flexible but not typically as optimized for speed and concurrency as the other three. BLOB and file storage are more suited for large files and not designed for low-latency access.

12. A, E. In-memory databases and key-value stores offer the low latency needed for real-time updates in gaming applications.

Relational databases can be slower; object storage is not designed for low-latency access.

13. A. Managed services abstract away operational tasks, leaving users to focus on application development. Unmanaged services require manual configuration and administration.

While managed services often offer better performance and reduced costs, the key differentiator is the level of management provided.

14. B. Document databases handle semi-structured data with flexible schemas, making them ideal for diverse data structures.

In-memory databases are for speed; key-value databases lack structural flexibility; and relational databases are less flexible.

15. C. In-memory databases provide extremely low latency, essential for real-time analytics processing of high-volume events.

Relational, key-value, and document databases would be slower for this use case.

16. B. The core principle of Approximate Nearest Neighbor (ANN) algorithms is to trade a small, often imperceptible, amount of accuracy for a significant gain in search performance. This trade-off is crucial for making similarity searches feasible and fast across massive, high-dimensional datasets.

17. B. Vertex AI Vector Search is Google Cloud's premier, fully managed, and scalable service designed specifically for high-performance, low-latency similarity searches on billions of vectors. While other options like AlloyDB AI and BigQuery offer integrated vector capabilities, Vertex AI Vector Search is the optimal choice for a dedicated, large-scale vector search workload as required by the RAG application.

18. C. Relational databases are defined by their tabular structure and support ACID properties, crucial for transaction processing.

In-memory, NoSQL, and key-value stores are different database paradigms with different strengths and weaknesses.

19. C. Unmanaged services provide maximum control over the database environment, allowing customization and fine-grained optimization.

Managed services offer simplified management, automatic backups, and reduced operational overhead, but at the cost of less direct control.

20. B. Semi-structured data, like JSON or XML, has some inherent organization but doesn't adhere to a strict schema like relational databases.

A describes structured data; C describes unstructured data; D describes in-memory data.

Chapter 3: Databases in Google Cloud

1. C. Cloud Storage is a highly scalable and durable object storage service, ideal for storing and managing large amounts of unstructured data like images, videos, and backups.

Cloud SQL is a relational database service; Cloud Spanner is a globally distributed, scalable database; and Cloud Filestore is a managed network file storage service.

2. D. The `pgvector` extension, supported by AlloyDB, allows for the storage and efficient searching of vector embeddings. This is the core technology behind RAG for finding semantically similar documents to provide as context to an LLM. While Cloud SQL's high availability is important for reliability, it doesn't directly address the needs of RAG. Cloud Firestore's real-time synchronization is not the primary requirement for this use case. BigQuery's federated query capabilities are useful for querying across different data sources, but not specifically for the efficient vector search needed for RAG.

3. A. BigQuery is a serverless, highly scalable, and cost-effective data warehouse designed for processing massive datasets and complex analytical queries with SQL.

Cloud SQL, Cloud Spanner, and Cloud Datastore are not primarily designed for petabyte-scale analytical queries.

4. B. Regional instance deployment ensures that data is stored in a specific geographical location, meeting data residency requirements. Customer-managed encryption keys (CMEKs) provide an extra layer of security, allowing the organization to control their encryption keys, which is crucial for sensitive data under HIPAA. While VPC Service Controls and Cloud Audit Logs are important for security and compliance, they don't directly address the data residency requirement. Firebase and Cloud Functions are not the primary solutions for managing large, regulated datasets.

5. D. BigQuery Federated Queries allows you to query data directly from external data sources like Cloud SQL, Cloud Storage, and even other clouds, without the need for data movement. This enables unified analysis across different systems. BigQuery Omni is for multicloud analytics, not for federating queries to on-premises databases. Database Migration Service is for migrating databases, not for querying data in place. Cloud Dataflow is a data processing service for building data pipelines, not a tool for directly querying multiple sources.

6. C. Cloud Firestore's flexible schema and offline capabilities, combined with real-time synchronization, make it ideal for mobile applications needing dynamic data models.

Cloud SQL, Cloud Spanner, and BigQuery are not designed for offline capabilities and flexible, mobile-friendly data modeling.

7. B. Bare Metal Solution provides dedicated physical servers, granting complete control over the hardware and software stack to meet stringent security and compliance needs.

Cloud SQL, Compute Engine, and GKE offer less direct control over the underlying hardware.

8. B. BigQuery is a serverless, highly scalable, and cost-effective data warehouse optimized for large-scale data analysis, offering SQL support and integration with BigQuery ML.

Cloud Bigtable is a NoSQL database; Cloud Spanner is a globally distributed database; and AlloyDB is a high-performance PostgreSQL-compatible database.

9. C. Cloud Firestore's flexible schema and scalability make it well suited for handling the diverse and evolving data structures of a social media application.

Cloud SQL and Cloud Spanner are relational databases, less flexible for evolving data structures. BigQuery is a data warehouse, not ideal for real-time updates.

10. B. MongoDB Atlas on Google Cloud offers a fully managed MongoDB service with simplified setup, automatic scaling, and high availability.

Cloud SQL, BMS, and Compute Engine do not offer managed MongoDB services.

11. D. Cloud SQL provides strong ACID properties and data integrity, crucial for transactional workloads like e-commerce, along with the scalability needed for peak traffic.

Cloud Bigtable, BigQuery, and Cloud Firestore are not designed to provide the strong consistency and ACID properties required for e-commerce transactions.

12. A. Memorystore, a fully managed in-memory datastore, provides extremely low latency and high throughput, making it ideal for caching and real-time applications.

Cloud SQL, Cloud Spanner, and BigQuery are not optimized for low-latency, in-memory data storage.

13. A. AlloyDB is a fully managed, PostgreSQL-compatible database service designed to handle both transactional and analytical workloads efficiently.

Cloud Spanner is globally distributed, but not primarily designed for analytical queries; Cloud Bigtable and BigQuery are not PostgreSQL-compatible.

14. B. Cloud Spanner is a globally distributed, strongly consistent database service that maintains low latency across multiple regions.

Cloud SQL, Cloud Firestore, and BigQuery are not designed for global distribution with strong consistency and low latency across regions.

15. B. Cloud Bigtable's wide-column store design excels at handling high-throughput, low-latency time-series data common in IoT applications.

Cloud SQL, Cloud Spanner, and BigQuery are not optimized for the high-volume, low-latency demands of time-series data from IoT devices.

16. B. Compute Engine allows users complete control over the operating system and software, including installing any supported database version.

BMS provides dedicated physical servers but still restricts to supported OS configurations. GKE and Cloud SQL limit database choices to supported managed instances.

17. D. Deploying a database directly on GKE allows for seamless integration with existing Kubernetes infrastructure and offers the maximum level of customization.

Cloud SQL and MongoDB Atlas are managed services providing less customization, while BMS is less integrated with the GKE environment.

18. C. For simple, flat data structures with a primary focus on real-time updates, Firebase Realtime Database remains a suitable option.

Cloud Firestore, in both Native and Datastore modes, offers more scalability and features but might be overkill for extremely simple applications. Cloud Datastore is an older, less flexible NoSQL service.

19. C. Oracle Databases@Google Cloud provides a simplified migration path leveraging Google Cloud commitments, unified support, and standard Oracle tools.

Oracle on Compute Engine and BMS require more manual configuration; cross-cloud interconnect is for connecting to Oracle Cloud Infrastructure, not deploying on GCP.

20. A. Managed databases handle infrastructure management (backups, patching, scaling) while unmanaged databases give users full control but require more operational effort.

While true that managed databases are on Google's infrastructure, that's not the primary distinguishing feature. Both managed and unmanaged databases can support various engine types. Licensing fees vary based on the database type, not solely on management level.

Chapter 4: Database Capacity and Usage Planning

1. B. Continuous replication is the best choice because it is the foundational strategy that directly addresses the core requirement of minimizing downtime.

Scheduled maintenance is an offline or "big bang" migration. It involves taking the application down for an extended period to export, transfer, and import the data. It's simple but fails the "minimize downtime" requirement completely, making it unsuitable for a critical e-commerce platform. These are advanced application-level architectural patterns, not just data migration strategies. While powerful, these patterns introduce immense complexity to maintain data consistency across two different database systems (e.g., handling dual writes). They are chosen to de-risk a large-scale application refactoring project, not simply to migrate data.

2. D. Understanding your current environment is fundamental to planning a successful migration. Inventorying applications and dependencies reveals the system's complexity and interrelationships.

The other options are part of the Plan or later phases.

3. C. The Google Cloud Pricing Calculator provides detailed cost projections for various resources.

Cloud Monitoring tracks performance, Cloud Billing shows past usage, and Cloud Resource Manager manages resources, not costs.

4. C. Scheduled maintenance allows for offline migration during a planned downtime window.

The other options prioritize minimal downtime, making them unsuitable for applications that can tolerate extended downtime.

5. C. Cloud Storage offers scalable storage for flat files, and BigQuery provides efficient analysis capabilities.

Cloud SQL, Cloud Spanner, and Cloud Datastore are database services not ideal for this type of data.

6. D. This phase involves designing the future state architecture and outlining the migration strategy.

The other choices belong to the Assess, Deploy, and Optimize phases, respectively.

7. D. DMS automates many database migration tasks, minimizing downtime and errors.

Cloud SQL, Cloud Spanner are databases. Cloud Resource Manager isn't a migration service.

8. B. Automation minimizes human errors and ensures consistent configurations across environments, improving repeatability.

The other options are not the primary reason for automating deployments.

9. A. It acts as an intermediary, handling complexities and enabling a phased migration with minimal client-side disruption.

The other options are not the primary benefit of a data access microservice.

10. C. Continuous improvement of performance, cost efficiency and business value are the goals.

The other options belong to different phases of the methodology.

11. A. A PoC allows for early identification and resolution of issues before full-scale migration.

It does not definitively determine the final cost, the team's skill, or application scalability.

12. D. BigQuery is a highly scalable, cost-effective data warehouse designed for large-scale data analysis.

Cloud Storage is for storage; Cloud SQL and Cloud Spanner are databases.

13. B. Caching reduces the need to access the database frequently for frequently used data.

The other options might increase costs or not improve performance.

14. C. IaC enables automated and consistent deployments, reducing errors and increasing reliability.

Manual configuration is not the goal of IaC. It doesn't directly improve monitoring, nor increase security vulnerabilities.

15. C. Ensuring the migrated database operates correctly and meets all requirements is essential before declaring a successful migration.

Optimization should start, but thorough testing is necessary first. Monitoring should continue, and the disaster recovery plan should be integrated.

16. B. A PoC allows for testing and validation of the migration strategy in a controlled environment, identifying and addressing potential issues before full-scale migration.

The other approaches are not effective or thorough.

17. C. Cloud Scheduler is specifically designed to automate tasks based on schedules.

Cloud Monitoring, Cloud Logging, and Cloud Composer are not primarily for scheduling database maintenance. While Cloud Composer can orchestrate complex workflows, Cloud Scheduler is the simpler, more direct service for basic scheduled database maintenance tasks

18. C. These factors ensure the chosen solution aligns with the application's needs and the organization's policies and regulations.

Cost alone is not sufficient for decision-making.

19. B. Automated replication and failover is the core strategy for achieving high availability (HA), which is essential for business continuity. This entire process happens within seconds or minutes without human intervention, ensuring the lowest possible recovery time objective (RTO) and recovery point objective (RPO).

While regular backups (A) and point-in-time recovery (D) are crucial for disaster recovery (e.g., recovering from data corruption or a regional outage), they are not HA solutions. Restoring a database from a backup is a much slower process that leads to significant downtime. Manual failover (C) introduces delay and a high risk of human error during a critical incident, making it less reliable than an automated system.

20. B. Understanding the interdependencies helps in planning a successful migration and identifying potential impact points.

The other options are not a comprehensive definition of dependency mapping.

Chapter 5: Designing for High Availability and Disaster Recovery

1. B. Cloud Monitoring allows you to create custom alerts based on metrics or logs, while Cloud Logging captures detailed operational logs, including those related to maintenance events. Together, they enable comprehensive monitoring and alerting for database health and maintenance.

A is incorrect because Cloud DNS is for domain name resolution and Cloud CDN is for content delivery, neither of which are primary tools for monitoring database maintenance. C is incorrect because while Cloud Storage can store logs and Cloud Functions can process them, Cloud Monitoring and Cloud Logging are the foundational services for active monitoring and alerting on events. D is incorrect as BigQuery is a data warehouse and Dataflow is a data processing service, not directly used for real-time operational monitoring of database maintenance.

2. B. Regular and rigorous testing of recovery procedures through disaster recovery drills is the most critical activity. It validates that the entire recovery process, including automation, documentation, and team coordination, functions as expected in a simulated real-world scenario, identifying any gaps before a real disaster strikes.

A is incorrect because reviewing logs only confirms backup completion, not the ability to actually restore and recover data successfully. C is incorrect as increasing backup frequency impacts RPO but doesn't validate the entire recovery process or its RTO. D is also incorrect; although monitoring is important for operational health, it doesn't replace the active validation of recovery capabilities that testing provides.

3. B. Configuring a Cloud SQL instance for high availability (HA) ensures that a standby instance in a different zone within the same region is kept in sync. In the event of a primary zonal failure, Cloud SQL automatically fails over to this standby, providing robust protection against zonal outages and minimizing downtime.

A is incorrect because multiregional deployment protects against regional outages, which is overkill and more costly for mitigating a single zonal failure. C is incorrect as migrating to a custom Compute Engine setup requires significant management overhead and does not inherently provide automated HA without complex configuration. D is incorrect because increasing storage size does not improve the instance's resilience against zonal failures; it only provides more disk space.

4. B. Automation is paramount in disaster recovery because it significantly reduces the potential for human error during stressful recovery operations and dramatically accelerates recovery times. Automated scripts and orchestration ensure consistent and rapid restoration processes.

A is incorrect because manual intervention slows down recovery and introduces a higher risk of errors, which is contrary to the goal of speed and consistency. C is incorrect as reducing backup frequency would worsen RPO (more data loss) and potentially increase recovery time by having fewer recovery points. D is incorrect because relying on a single backup mechanism (e.g., only snapshots) limits flexibility and might not cover all RTO/RPO needs or data integrity scenarios.

5. B. To guarantee a consistent and usable database from a persistent disk snapshot, the database must be "quiesced" (e.g., by flushing buffers, pausing writes, or using database-specific tools like `pg_start_backup`) to ensure all pending transactions are written to disk before the snapshot is taken. This prevents data corruption upon restoration.

A is incorrect because stopping the instance is a valid way to ensure consistency but often results in higher RTO; quiescing allows the instance to remain running. C is incorrect as disk size is unrelated to snapshot consistency; snapshots capture the state, not require more space for the original disk. D is incorrect as disabling network connectivity does not guarantee data consistency at the disk level.

6. B. A Cloud SQL cross-region read replica allows replication of data to a different geographical region. While it typically uses asynchronous replication, which means a small RPO window (potential data loss) in case of a primary region failure, it enables recovery from a regional outage by promoting the replica. It should also be noted that a cross-region replica is read-only until promoted.

A is incorrect because Cloud SQL HA protects against zonal failures within a single region, not against a complete regional outage. C is incorrect because while Cloud Spanner multi-region provides synchronous replication and zero data loss, the question specifies Cloud SQL and accepts a small RPO. D is incorrect because managed backups are for point-in-time recovery, but restoring from them takes significant time, leading to a higher RTO, and don't provide continuous replication for cross-region resilience.

7. B. Cloud SQL cross-region replication is typically asynchronous. This means that data is copied from the primary to the secondary with a slight delay (replication lag). If the primary region fails before all transactions have been fully replicated to the secondary, any transactions committed during that lag window could be lost, resulting in a non-zero RPO.

A is incorrect; replicas maintain data for recovery and do not automatically purge it without configuration. C is incorrect; Cloud SQL read replicas can be promoted to become primary instances in a disaster scenario. D is incorrect; the replica contains a full copy of the data, not just the schema.

8. B. Performing a data classification exercise helps identify which data is most critical to the business. This, combined with a business impact analysis (BIA), determines the true cost of downtime and data loss, allowing you to set appropriate (and often tiered) RTO and RPO targets for different datasets.

A is incorrect because automation is a means to achieve RTO/RPO, not a way to define them or prioritize data. C is incorrect because while Cloud Spanner offers high availability, it's not the universal solution for all data and might be overkill or unsuitable for some; prioritizing helps determine the right service. D is incorrect as purchasing the most expensive storage without understanding requirements is fiscally irresponsible and not a strategy for defining recovery objectives.

9. B. For an application to effectively leverage a multi-region database for failover, it must be designed with mechanisms (e.g., global load balancing, smart connection strings, service discovery) that allow it to dynamically re-point its database connection to the primary instance in the currently active, healthy region.

A is incorrect because relying solely on IP addresses makes failover more complex and less dynamic; using DNS or service discovery is generally preferred. C is incorrect as storing local copies of all database data would lead to massive data inconsistencies and is not a practical approach for multi-region resilience. D is incorrect because while some multiregion strategies involve eventual consistency, the application's ability to re-point is crucial regardless of the consistency model; also, many critical multiregion databases (like Spanner) aim for strong consistency.

10. B. Achieving very low RTO and RPO often requires extensive infrastructure duplication (e.g., warm/hot standbys, active-active setups across regions/zones), continuous data replication, and the inherent complexity of managing and testing such highly available and distributed systems, all of which contribute to significantly higher costs.

A is incorrect because manual backups are typically less efficient for very low RPO/RTO; automated solutions are preferred and often more expensive. C is incorrect because open source solutions themselves do not guarantee low RTO/RPO without significant investment in HA/DR infrastructure and expertise, potentially costing more than managed services. D is incorrect because achieving low RTO/RPO usually increases the need for specialized and often premium cloud services and configurations.

11. B. Cloud Spanner's multiregion configuration is specifically designed for global applications requiring extreme availability and strong consistency across geographically distant regions, often achieving 99.999 percent SLA. It uses synchronous replication across regions to ensure zero data loss (low RPO) and automatic failover for low RTO.

A is incorrect because Cloud SQL cross-region read replicas are typically asynchronous, meaning potential data loss (higher RPO) and requiring manual promotion for recovery. C is incorrect as Cloud Bigtable is a wide-column NoSQL database, not a relational one suited for transactional financial applications, and its multicluster routing focuses on read/write distribution, not necessarily strong global transactional consistency as Spanner. D is incorrect because managing synchronous replication for a custom PostgreSQL instance on Compute Engine across regions is complex, difficult to achieve true global strong consistency, and doesn't offer the automated, built-in resilience of Spanner.

12. B. For major version upgrades, rigorously testing your application with the new database version in a nonproduction environment is paramount to identify compatibility issues and performance regressions. A full backup is also essential for a reliable rollback point.

    A is incorrect because this is a major version upgrade, which is not automatically handled like minor versions and can be disruptive. C is incorrect as while Google Cloud manages the service, the upgrade process for major versions often requires customer-initiated action and careful scheduling outside of peak business hours. D is incorrect because while scaling up might be part of performance optimization, it's not the most critical preparatory step for a major version upgrade's success and compatibility.

13. B. Minor version upgrades (e.g., 14.1–14.2) typically involve bug fixes, small performance enhancements, and security patches; are often nondisruptive; and are automatically managed by Google Cloud. Major version upgrades (e.g., 14–15) involve significant changes, new features, and potentially breaking changes, requiring more extensive planning, testing, and potential downtime or migration.

    A is incorrect as it swaps the definitions; 14.1–14.2 is minor, and 14–15 is major. C is incorrect because minor versions are typically automated, not manual, and major versions require customer planning. D is incorrect because both types can include security patches; minor versions focus on fixes, whereas major versions introduce new features and architectural improvements.

14. C. Point-in-time recovery (PITR) in Cloud SQL, achieved by combining full backups with continuous transaction log archiving, allows restoration to any specific second within the retention period. This capability directly addresses the need for a near-zero RPO for logical corruptions or accidental deletions.

    A is incorrect because automated daily backups only allow restoration to the last full backup, meaning data created between the last backup and the incident would be lost. B is incorrect because on-demand backups provide a specific recovery point but not the fine-grained, "to the second" recovery needed to avoid losing subsequent transactions. D is incorrect as read replicas primarily serve to offload read traffic and improve performance, not to enable granular point-in-time recovery for the primary instance.

15. A. Export/import (logical backups) typically involves extracting data, which can be very time-consuming, especially for large datasets. The subsequent import process also takes significant time, making this method generally unsuitable for scenarios requiring a very low RTO (rapid recovery).

    B is incorrect as export/import provides high data portability, allowing data to be moved between different database systems or environments. C is incorrect as logical backups are excellent for auditing because they provide a human-readable format of the data and schema. D is incorrect as archiving data to cost-effective storage like Cloud Storage is a common and appropriate use case for export/import.

16. B. Recovery time objective (RTO) precisely defines the maximum acceptable duration of time an application can be unavailable following a disaster. For a real-time stock trading application, minimizing interruption means achieving an extremely low RTO.

    A is incorrect because RPO focuses on the maximum acceptable data loss, not the time to recover the service. C is incorrect as an SLA is a formal agreement about service availability, while RTO is the internal metric defining the recovery speed. D is incorrect as data consistency index is not a standard disaster recovery metric.

17. B. Recovery point objective (RPO) represents the maximum acceptable amount of data loss, measured in time, that an application can tolerate after a disaster. A tolerance of "up to 15 minutes of recent data loss" directly defines the RPO for this database.

    A is incorrect because RTO defines the maximum acceptable downtime for recovery, not the amount of data loss. C is incorrect as MTTR is the average time taken to repair a failed component, not a business tolerance for data loss. D is incorrect as uptime percentage measures service availability, not the acceptable amount of data loss in a disaster.

18. B. Cloud SQL's point-in-time recovery (PITR) works by combining a recent full database backup with continuous archiving of transaction logs (write-ahead logs for PostgreSQL, binary logs for MySQL). This allows the database to be restored to virtually any specific second within the retention period by applying the logs from the last full backup.

    A is incorrect because creating full snapshots every second would be prohibitively expensive and resource-intensive; PITR uses transaction logs for fine-grained recovery. C is incorrect as synchronous multi-region replication is more about high availability and strong consistency across regions, not the specific mechanism for PITR within a single instance. D is incorrect because while manual restoration from full backups is possible, it does not provide the "point-in-time" granularity of PITR, only restoring to specific backup points.

19. B. For mission-critical databases with very low downtime tolerance during major version upgrades, the recommended strategy is to provision a new instance with the target version. Data is then migrated/replicated, allowing for a controlled cutover with significantly reduced, or even near-zero, downtime.

    A is incorrect as in-place major version upgrades for Cloud SQL typically involve downtime, which is unacceptable for a low-downtime tolerance application. C is incorrect as scheduling during peak hours would maximize business impact due to inevitable downtime. D is incorrect as postponing upgrades indefinitely would lead to security vulnerabilities, performance issues, and lack of new features.

20. C. Maintaining clear, concise, and up-to-date documentation, including runbooks, contact lists, and escalation procedures, is critical. This ensures that recovery efforts are well coordinated, reduce reliance on individual knowledge, and can be executed consistently and efficiently even during high-stress situations.

    A is incorrect because RPO focuses on data loss, not the efficiency of the recovery process itself. B is incorrect as monitoring and alerting are for detection and readiness, not for the execution of the recovery steps themselves. D is incorrect as reducing costs is a financial goal, not a direct driver for consistent and efficient execution during a disaster.

Chapter 6: Designing Secure Database Connectivity and Access

1. B. Authentication is the process of verifying a user's or application's identity (e.g., username/password, IAM credentials). Access control (or authorization) is the process of determining what actions an authenticated user is permitted to perform once they have gained access (e.g., `SELECT` on `table X`, `CREATE USER`).

    A is incorrect because it reverses the definitions of authentication and access control. C is incorrect because both authentication (e.g., IAM database authentication) and access control (e.g., IAM roles for the database service, internal database roles/privileges) can involve Google Cloud IAM and internal database mechanisms. D is incorrect because both authentication and access control primarily apply to active access, not data at rest or in transit, although the secure transport of credentials and commands is part of the overall security.

2. C. Deploying the Cloud SQL Auth Proxy as a sidecar container in the GKE pod is the recommended best practice. It uses IAM for authentication, automatically encrypts all traffic, and eliminates the need for IP allowlists, which is crucial for dynamic GKE environments.

    A is incorrect because it exposes the database to public internet (even with allowlists) and requires manual management of dynamic GKE node IPs, which is not practical. B is incorrect because while direct SSL/TLS provides encryption, it requires manual certificate management and doesn't simplify IAM-based authentication or IP allowlisting. D is incorrect because a VPN is an overkill for secure connectivity within Google Cloud for a single Cloud SQL instance, as the Auth Proxy provides a simpler, more integrated solution.

3. B. Admin Activity Logs record administrative actions that modify the configuration or metadata of a Google Cloud resource, including schema changes for a Cloud Spanner database. These logs are always enabled by default and are crucial for auditing administrative actions.

    A is incorrect because Data Access Logs capture user-driven API calls that read or modify user-provided data, not administrative schema changes. C is incorrect because System Event Logs record actions taken by Google Cloud systems, such as automated failovers, not user-initiated administrative changes. D is incorrect as "Operational Logs" is a generic term and not one of the specific Cloud Audit Log types that captures schema modifications.

4. B. Assigning a private IP to the Cloud SQL instance within the same VPC ensures that the database is not accessible from the public internet, enhancing security through network isolation. VPC firewall rules then precisely control which internal resources can establish connections, adhering to the principle of least privilege.

    A is incorrect because it exposes the database to the public internet, which is contrary to the goal of maximizing security and minimizing exposure. C is incorrect because while the Cloud SQL Auth Proxy is recommended for secure connections, it still needs network connectivity, and disabling All Other Network Settings would make it inaccessible. D is incorrect as IAM database authentication and client certificates secure the authentication and encryption of the connection, but not the underlying network access which is controlled by private IP and firewalls.

5. B. Serverless platforms like Cloud Run can scale rapidly, and each instance creating its own database connection can quickly exhaust the database's connection limit. Implementing a session pooler (e.g., PgBouncer or a built-in pooler like AlloyDB's) decouples the number of application instances from the number of database connections, efficiently reusing a smaller pool of connections and preventing exhaustion.

A is incorrect because while undersizing is possible, "too many connections" specifically points to connection limit issues, which scaling CPU/memory alone might not fix if the limit is architectural. C is incorrect because network latency from not using private IP would affect performance, but not directly cause "too many connections" errors. D is incorrect because Cloud SQL Auth Proxy simplifies secure connections but does not inherently provide connection pooling to prevent "too many connections" if not combined with a pooler.

6. D. To establish a secure, encrypted connection (mTLS) directly with a Cloud SQL instance that enforces SSL/TLS, the client application needs the server's Certificate Authority (CA) certificate (to verify the server's identity), its own client certificate, and its corresponding client private key (for client authentication to the server).

A is incorrect because username and password are for authentication, not for encryption or secure connection establishment. B is incorrect because IP address and port are for network connectivity, not for SSL/TLS encryption. C is incorrect because client private IP and server DNS name are for network routing, not SSL/TLS certificate-based authentication and encryption.

7. B. To get a comprehensive view, both Google Cloud platform-level auditing and database-native auditing are needed. Cloud Audit Logs (Admin Activity) capture administrative changes to the instance, and Data Access Logs capture API calls related to data access. Additionally, enabling MySQL's native auditing features (like the general query log or a specific audit plug-in) captures detailed `SELECT`/`INSERT` queries within the database.

A is incorrect because slow query log captures slow queries, and general query log captures all queries, but they don't encompass administrative changes to the Cloud SQL instance itself or integrate cleanly with Cloud Audit Logs. C is incorrect as Cloud Monitoring focuses on performance metrics, not detailed security auditing. D is incorrect because VPC Flow Logs capture network flow information, not specific database queries or administrative actions.

8. B. The pgaudit extension for PostgreSQL is designed for fine-grained auditing of SQL statements, including `SELECT` queries, against specific tables or users. It provides detailed logs required for compliance and security analysis within the database.

A is incorrect because while Cloud Audit Logs (Data Access) capture API calls to read data, they generally don't log individual `SELECT` statements with the granularity required for specific table/user auditing within the database engine itself. C is incorrect because a custom metric counts queries but doesn't provide the detailed logs (who, what, when, query text) needed for auditing. D is incorrect because a load balancer logs network traffic, not specific SQL queries executed within the database.

9. C. Customer-managed encryption keys (CMEKs) allow organizations to use encryption keys managed within Cloud KMS to protect their database data. This provides an additional layer of control, including the ability to disable or destroy the key, which effectively renders the encrypted data permanently inaccessible and meets strict compliance requirements for key lifecycle management.

A is incorrect because SSL/TLS certificates encrypt data in transit, not at rest, and do not provide key management control. B is incorrect as the Cloud SQL Auth Proxy handles authentication and encryption in transit but does not give control over the encryption keys used for data at rest. D is incorrect as Private IP provides network isolation and prevents public access but does not relate to the management of encryption keys for data at rest.

10. B. Exponential backoff prevents clients from overwhelming the database or service with a "retry storm" during a transient issue or recovery. By progressively increasing the wait time, it gives the system time to recover, preventing further resource contention and allowing it to stabilize.

A is incorrect because exponential backoff introduces delays, not speeds up initial connection time. C is incorrect because it's an error handling strategy, unrelated to network encryption like SSL/TLS. D is incorrect because it's a connection retry mechanism and does not directly ensure strong data consistency, which is a property of the database system and replication model.

11. C. The `roles/spanner.databaseReader` IAM role provides read-only access to data and schema within a Spanner database. This perfectly aligns with the principle of least privilege for a security analyst needing to audit data without modification capabilities.

A is incorrect because `roles/spanner.databaseAdmin` provides full control over schema and database-level IAM policies, which violates the principle of least privilege for read-only access. B is incorrect because `roles/spanner.databaseUser` allows for data manipulation (`INSERT`, `UPDATE`, `DELETE`), which is more than read-only access. D is incorrect because `roles/owner` grants full administrative control over all resources in a project, which is a significant security risk and far exceeds the required permissions.

12. B. IAM Database Authentication for Cloud SQL allows users and service accounts to authenticate using their Google Cloud identity, completely eliminating the need to manage database passwords directly in application code. This centralizes authentication within IAM and simplifies credential management.

A is incorrect because IAM Database Authentication is for authenticating to the database, not for providing SSH access to the underlying server. C is incorrect because it's an authentication method and does not directly impact query execution times. D is incorrect because it's an authentication method and does not relate to multiregion failover, which is an HA/DR feature of the database service.

13. C. Google Cloud Secret Manager is the recommended service for securely storing sensitive data like database passwords. It provides versioning, access control via IAM, and automatic rotation, allowing applications to fetch credentials at runtime without hardcoding them.

A is incorrect because storing passwords in plaintext files is a significant security vulnerability. B is incorrect because environment variables can be easily exposed through process listings or logs, making them insecure for sensitive credentials. D is incorrect because storing credentials directly in a configuration file on the database server is not where the application should retrieve its credentials from.

14. B. For databases on Bare Metal Solution, a secure and low-latency connection from your VPC is established using Cloud Interconnect, creating a private link. VPC firewall rules are then used to strictly control which Compute Engine instances can communicate with the Oracle database servers over this private connection, ensuring security.

A is incorrect because direct public internet access is highly insecure and generally not recommended for sensitive database traffic. C is incorrect because the Cloud SQL Auth Proxy is specifically designed for Cloud SQL instances and does not support Oracle databases on Bare Metal Solution. D is incorrect because while a bastion host can provide SSH tunneling, it's typically for administrative access, not the primary high-throughput, low-latency application connectivity needed for a production database on Bare Metal Solution when Cloud Interconnect is available.

15. C. The `roles/cloudsql.admin` IAM role grants full administrative control over Cloud SQL instances, including creating and deleting instances, managing users, and configuring databases. This is appropriate for an application requiring broad administrative access.

A is incorrect because `roles/cloudsql.client` only grants permission to connect to an instance, typically used by applications for data access. B is incorrect because `roles/cloudsql.viewer` provides read-only access to Cloud SQL resources, which is insufficient for administrative tasks. D is incorrect because `roles/iam.serviceAccountUser` allows a user to impersonate a service account, but it doesn't grant specific Cloud SQL permissions on its own.

16. B. When using the Cloud SQL Auth Proxy, the application connects to localhost on a specific port (e.g., 5432 for PostgreSQL, 3306 for MySQL) on the same machine or container where the Auth Proxy is running. The proxy then handles the secure, authenticated communication to the actual Cloud SQL instance.

A is incorrect because the application connects to the proxy, not directly to the Cloud SQL instance's private IP when the proxy is in use for this connection pattern. C is incorrect because the proxy eliminates the need for public IP access for secure connections. D is incorrect because while Cloud SQL instances have DNS names, the application connects through the proxy's local endpoint.

17. C. The `roles/cloudsql.client` IAM role grants permissions to connect to a Cloud SQL instance, which is precisely what's needed for users or service accounts leveraging the Cloud SQL Auth Proxy. It adheres to the principle of least privilege for connection purposes.

A is incorrect because `roles/cloudsql.admin` grants full administrative control, which is excessive for developers who only need to connect to the database. B is incorrect because `roles/cloudsql.viewer` only allows viewing Cloud SQL resources, not connecting to them. D is incorrect because `roles/editor` grants broad editing capabilities across many Google Cloud services, far exceeding the specific permission required for database connectivity.

18. B. AlloyDB for PostgreSQL has a built-in connection pooler, which effectively manages and reuses database connections without requiring the application to implement its own pooling logic or integrate with an external pooler. This is particularly beneficial for legacy applications that are difficult to modify.

A is incorrect because AlloyDB does not have an automatic sharding feature; it's a fully managed relational database. C is incorrect because while read replicas distribute read traffic, they don't inherently provide connection pooling for the primary writer or manage the number of connections from the application itself. D is incorrect because although AlloyDB supports connections, its support for public IP is for accessibility, not connection efficiency.

19. C. System Event Logs record actions taken by Google Cloud systems rather than by users. An automatic failover of a Cloud SQL HA instance is an example of such a system-generated event, and thus would be recorded in the System Event Logs.

    A is incorrect because Admin Activity Logs capture user-initiated administrative actions, not automated system events. B is incorrect because Data Access Logs capture user interactions with data, not infrastructure events. D is incorrect as "Export Logs" refers to the process of exporting logs to another destination, not a type of audit log itself.

20. C. Using a public IP with authorized networks means the database is exposed to the public Internet, even if only from specified IP ranges. This increases the attack surface compared to a private IP connection or using the Cloud SQL Auth Proxy, which creates a secure tunnel and does not require managing public IP allowlists.

    A is incorrect; the Auth Proxy provides automatic encryption, and public IP with authorized networks usually requires manual SSL/TLS setup for encryption. B is incorrect; the Auth Proxy integrates directly with IAM for authentication, simplifying it significantly compared to authorized networks. D is incorrect because managing static IP allowlists is challenging and impractical for dynamic, autoscaling environments where IPs change frequently, making it unsuitable.

Chapter 7: Monitoring, Troubleshooting, and Optimizing Performance

1. B. Cloud Logging collects and stores all types of logs, including error logs, slow query logs, and general activity logs from Cloud SQL instances. This detailed log data is invaluable for troubleshooting intermittent issues by providing specific error messages, timestamps, and context.

   A is incorrect because Cloud Monitoring provides metrics and dashboards, not detailed error messages or stack traces. C is incorrect because Cloud IAM manages access control. D is incorrect because Cloud Storage is for object storage.

2. C. The Google Cloud Recommender service provides proactive recommendations for optimizing resource usage across various Google Cloud services, including identifying underutilized Cloud Spanner instances and suggesting adjustments to compute capacity (PUs/nodes) to save costs.

   A is incorrect because Cloud Audit Logs record activities for security and compliance, not cost optimization recommendations. B is incorrect because Cloud Spanner Key Visualizer is for identifying hotspotting and schema design issues. D is incorrect because Cloud Billing reports show current and past costs, but they don't provide actionable recommendations for optimization.

3. B. Cloud Monitoring is the central Google Cloud service for setting up alerts based on various metrics, including storage utilization and instance availability/responsiveness. It supports different notification channels like email and PagerDuty, making it ideal for comprehensive alerting.

A is incorrect because Cloud Logging collects logs, but Cloud Monitoring is specifically designed for metric-based alerting. C is incorrect because Cloud DNS manages domain name resolution. D is incorrect because Cloud Storage is for object storage.

4. B. For PostgreSQL-compatible databases like AlloyDB, the `pg_locks` view provides detailed information on current locks held by transactions, including the type of lock and the process holding it. This view is essential for diagnosing and understanding database locking issues.

A is incorrect because while I/O waits can be a symptom, they don't directly identify specific transactions holding locks. C is incorrect because `information_schema.innodb_locks` is specific to MySQL/InnoDB, not PostgreSQL. D is incorrect because Key Visualizer is used for hotspotting analysis in Bigtable and Spanner, not for relational database locking.

5. C. A sudden "resource unavailable" error during a traffic peak, especially without database configuration changes, strongly suggests that an API quota limit for Cloud SQL operations (like creating new connections) has been reached. Checking the Quotas page is the immediate action to verify this.

A is incorrect because a network misconfiguration would likely prevent any connections, not just during a peak. B is incorrect because running out of disk space would typically result in different, more specific errors related to storage. D is incorrect because while an undersized machine type can cause performance issues, "resource unavailable" often points to a hard limit like a quota, not just performance degradation.

6. B. Analyzing query plans using `EXPLAIN ANALYZE` helps illustrate how the database executes a query, revealing inefficiencies like full table scans or suboptimal join orders. Based on this analysis, adding appropriate indexes can significantly speed up query execution and reduce CPU usage.

A is incorrect because increasing storage size affects disk capacity, not query performance or CPU usage directly. C is incorrect because SSL/TLS encryption secures data in transit but doesn't optimize query performance. D is incorrect because migrating to a multiregion configuration improves disaster recovery and global availability, not specific query performance within an instance.

7. C. Cloud SQL Query Insights provides a visual dashboard specifically designed to help identify and analyze resource-intensive queries in Cloud SQL instances, showing CPU consumption and allowing drill-down into query plans. It helps pinpoint bottlenecks for optimization by revealing query-level performance metrics.

A is incorrect because Cloud Logging collects general logs but doesn't provide the specialized query performance analysis of Query Insights. B is incorrect because Cloud Monitoring dashboards show system-level metrics (CPU, RAM) but not detailed query-level performance. D is incorrect because Cloud Trace is primarily for distributed tracing across microservices, not direct database query performance analysis.

8. A. For Cloud SQL for PostgreSQL, the Index Advisor component of Query Insights analyzes your query workload and provides specific recommendations for new indexes that could significantly improve query performance by reducing full table scans. This proactive tool helps identify indexes that would benefit your overall workload.

   B is incorrect because CPU utilization reports show overall resource consumption, not specific missing indexes. C is incorrect because while `EXPLAIN ANALYZE` helps you understand an individual query plan, the Index Advisor proactively recommends indexes based on a broader workload analysis. D is incorrect because error logs capture database errors, not insights into missing indexes.

9. B. High I/O wait times in a database context signify that the CPU is idle, waiting for disk operations (reads or writes) to finish. This often points to a bottleneck or contention related to the underlying storage performance or the I/O subsystem's ability to keep up with demand.

   A is incorrect because too much memory would generally lead to less disk I/O, not more wait time. C is incorrect because high I/O wait means the CPU is waiting, implying it's not underutilized but blocked. D is incorrect because while network latency is a factor in overall performance, high I/O wait specifically refers to the database's interaction with its storage.

10. B. Proactive capacity planning involves analyzing historical data (e.g., from Cloud Monitoring) and anticipating future workload increases. This allows for pre-scaling (scaling up the primary, scaling out read pools) of the AlloyDB cluster before the event, ensuring it can handle the surge without reactive performance degradation.

    A is incorrect because reactive scaling during a peak event can lead to significant performance issues and potential downtime, negatively impacting the user experience. C is incorrect because while AlloyDB is highly scalable, it currently requires manual scaling of nodes/PUs based on expected workload, unlike services like Spanner or BigQuery, which have more automatic scaling of resources. D is incorrect because implementing database sharding is a complex architectural change, not something done dynamically during a peak event, and AlloyDB handles horizontal scaling within its managed architecture.

11. A. In a multiregion Spanner configuration, all write operations are handled by a single designated leader region to ensure strong global consistency. This means writes originating from other regions will incur cross-regional latency to reach the leader. Optimizing involves routing writes to the application's leader region or strategically placing the leader region closer to the highest volume of write traffic.

    B is incorrect because Spanner uses synchronous replication for writes across regions to guarantee strong consistency, not asynchronous. C is incorrect because read replicas are for read scaling, and adding more wouldn't directly reduce cross-region write latency to the leader. D is incorrect because interleaved tables optimize join performance and I/O for specific query patterns, not general cross-region write latency due to the leader region architecture.

12. A. The primary way to control Cloud Spanner costs is by adjusting the provisioned compute capacity, which is measured in processing units (PUs) or nodes. If current utilization is low, reducing the number of PUs/nodes will directly decrease the cost without affecting performance for the current workload.

B is incorrect because converting to Cloud SQL is a major architectural change that impacts functionality and availability, not a direct cost optimization for an existing Spanner instance. C is incorrect because a connection pooler optimizes application-to-database connections, not the inherent cost of provisioned Spanner compute capacity. D is incorrect because interleaved tables are a performance optimization for specific query patterns, not a direct cost reduction mechanism, and they don't reduce the base cost of provisioned nodes.

13. A. Key Visualizer is a specific Google Cloud Bigtable tool that provides a visual heatmap of your table's row key ranges. It allows you to quickly identify if reads or writes are disproportionately concentrated on a small set of keys or nodes, which is known as hotspotting and is a common cause of write latency in Bigtable.

    B is incorrect because Query Insights is for Cloud SQL and AlloyDB. C is incorrect because `pg_locks` is for PostgreSQL-compatible databases. D is incorrect because Cloud Spanner Query Statistics are for Cloud Spanner.

14. A. BigQuery Query Execution Details provide a comprehensive breakdown of the query plan, including the stages, time spent in each stage, and data shuffled and processed. This detailed information is crucial for pinpointing bottlenecks and optimizing complex BigQuery query performance.

    B is incorrect because Cloud SQL Query Insights is for Cloud SQL, not BigQuery. C is incorrect because `EXPLAIN ANALYZE` is a command used in traditional relational databases, whereas BigQuery has its own web-based execution details. D is incorrect because while I/O metrics are important for underlying infrastructure, BigQuery's execution details provide much more specific insight into the query's internal operations and efficiency.

15. C. Monitoring the Active Connections metric provides insight into the number of concurrent connections to the database. Spikes or sustained high values nearing the database's connection limit could indicate connection saturation, leading to connection refusals and application errors.

    A is incorrect because CPU utilization indicates processing load, not direct connectivity issues. B is incorrect because Disk Write Operations relate to I/O performance, not connection availability. D is incorrect because Storage Capacity indicates disk space usage, not connection health.

16. B. Cloud Monitoring alerts can publish messages to a Pub/Sub topic. A Cloud Function or Cloud Run service can then be configured to subscribe to this Pub/Sub topic and execute custom code, such as a diagnostic script or an automated remediation action, enabling automated responses to alerts.

    A is incorrect because Cloud DNS manages domain name resolution. C is incorrect because Cloud CDN is for content delivery. D is incorrect because Cloud Interconnect provides private network connectivity to Google Cloud, none of which are used for automated script execution based on alerts.

17. B. Interleaved tables in Cloud Spanner allow you to physically store child table rows alongside their parent row on the same server. This design improves query performance for joins between parent and child tables by reducing I/O and improving data locality, as related data is retrieved more efficiently.

A is incorrect because read replicas scale read operations but don't optimize the physical storage or join performance of parent-child relationships on the primary instance. C is incorrect because Spanner already handles distributed storage internally, and manual sharding across instances is generally not recommended unless for very specific advanced use cases. D is incorrect because disabling secondary indexes would likely harm, not improve, query performance for specific access patterns.

18. B. AlloyDB supports read pools, which consist of one or more read replicas. By configuring a read pool, read queries can be offloaded from the primary instance and distributed across these replicas, significantly improving performance for read-heavy workloads like reporting without impacting the primary's write capabilities.

    A is incorrect because a standby instance in a different region is for disaster recovery, not specifically for read scaling. C is incorrect because `pg_stat_statements` is for performance analysis, not a scaling mechanism. D is incorrect because using BigQuery is a data warehouse migration, not an AlloyDB-specific scaling strategy.

19. C. Scaling out (horizontal scaling) involves adding more nodes or instances to a database cluster, distributing the workload across them. For distributed databases like Spanner or Bigtable, this allows for linear performance increases by adding more capacity units and is essential for handling massive, growing workloads.

    A is incorrect because scaling out still incurs cost, and although it provides greater capacity than scaling up, it's not infinite or free. B is incorrect because it swaps the definitions; scaling up adds more resources to a single machine, whereas scaling out adds more machines/nodes. D is incorrect because scaling out can improve both read and write performance, depending on the database architecture (e.g., read replicas for reads, sharded distributed databases for both).

20. B. Bigtable replication allows you to replicate data across multiple clusters in different regions. With multicluster routing, applications can connect to the nearest cluster for low latency, and traffic automatically fails over to a healthy cluster in another region in case of an outage, ensuring high availability and disaster recovery.

    A is incorrect because a single cluster provides no protection against regional outages and will have high latency for distant users. C is incorrect because daily backups are for recovery, not for real-time high availability or low latency across regions. D is incorrect because Cloud SQL is a relational database and cannot serve as a read replica for Bigtable data.

Chapter 8: Managing and Automating Database Operations

1. C. The Google Cloud Recommender service uses machine learning to analyze your resource usage patterns and proactively provides actionable recommendations, including identifying over-provisioned Cloud SQL instances that can be right-sized (scaled down) to save costs without compromising performance.

A is incorrect because Cloud Billing Reports show historical costs but don't provide recommendations for optimization. B is incorrect because Cloud Trace is for analyzing application latency and distributed requests. D is incorrect because Cloud Deployment Manager is for provisioning infrastructure, not for providing optimization recommendations.

2. B. For noncritical applications that can tolerate higher I/O latency, HDD storage is the most cost-effective option for Cloud SQL instances. SSDs offer higher performance but come at a higher cost.

A is incorrect because SSDs are more expensive and are for performance-critical workloads. C is incorrect because NVMe is typically a local storage technology and not a configurable option for Cloud SQL managed storage. D is incorrect because NAS is a general storage type and not a specific, configurable storage option within Cloud SQL.

3. C. In the shared responsibility model for managed database services, Google Cloud is responsible for the underlying infrastructure, OS patching, and hardware management. However, users are typically responsible for database-level maintenance tasks like `VACUUM` (for PostgreSQL), `OPTIMIZE TABLE` (for MySQL), and managing statistics, or configuring service-specific settings for these.

A is incorrect as users do have responsibilities for database-level maintenance. B is incorrect as Google manages the underlying OS. D is incorrect as Google handles OS patching.

4. C. Automating routine database tasks frees up valuable engineering time, allowing teams to focus on more complex, higher-value activities. It also significantly improves reliability and consistency by eliminating the potential for human error inherent in manual processes.

A is incorrect because automation reduces the need for constant human intervention, not increases it. B is incorrect because automation improves consistency and reduces human error. D is incorrect because monitoring remains crucial to ensure automated processes are running as expected and to detect any issues.

5. B. In PostgreSQL, `UPDATE` and `DELETE` operations mark old row versions ("dead tuples") as invisible rather than immediately removing them. This accumulated dead space, or "bloat," requires a `VACUUM` process to reclaim it and make the space reusable, which in turn helps maintain query performance.

A is incorrect because while reindexing addresses index bloat, table bloat is primarily managed by `VACUUM`. C is incorrect because sharding addresses horizontal scalability, not internal table bloat. D is incorrect because storage resize is for increasing disk capacity, not for reclaiming fragmented space within tables.

6. B. Cloud Bigtable manages data retention through garbage collection (GC) policies, which are configured directly on column families. Setting a GC policy for `max age` (e.g., 90 days) or `max versions` allows Bigtable to automatically delete old or stale data, optimizing storage and compliance.

A is incorrect because while Dataflow can manipulate data, a GC policy is the native and more efficient way to manage data retention in Bigtable. C is incorrect because manual deletions are not scalable or reliable for continuous data life-cycle management in a high-volume system. D is incorrect because automatic partition expiration is a BigQuery feature, not Bigtable.

7. C. The OPTIMIZE TABLE command in MySQL (for InnoDB tables, it's equivalent to ALTER TABLE ... FORCE) reorganizes the physical storage of table data and its associated indexes. This process reclaims fragmented space, improves I/O efficiency, and ultimately enhances query performance.

A is incorrect because VACUUM ANALYZE is a PostgreSQL command, not applicable to MySQL. B is incorrect because REINDEX TABLE is a PostgreSQL command, and while MySQL rebuilds indexes as part of OPTIMIZE TABLE, it's not a stand-alone command for this purpose. D is incorrect because ANALYZE TABLE only updates statistics used by the optimizer; it does not reclaim space or defragment the table.

8. C. The VACUUM FULL command in PostgreSQL aggressively reclaims all dead space by rewriting the entire table to a new disk file. However, it requires an ACCESS EXCLUSIVE lock on the table, blocking all other operations (reads and writes) until it completes, making it highly disruptive for production systems.

A is incorrect because VACUUM (without FULL) reclaims space without typically blocking reads or writes. B is incorrect because VACUUM ANALYZE also typically doesn't block operations. D is incorrect because REINDEX CONCURRENTLY is specifically designed to rebuild indexes without blocking writes, minimizing disruption.

9. B. In PostgreSQL (used by Cloud SQL and AlloyDB), you can query system catalogs like pg_class, pg_catalog.pg_database, and pg_statistic to get information about table and index sizes. By comparing the actual size to the logical size based on row count, you can estimate the amount of bloat.

A is incorrect because pg_stat_statements provides query statistics, not information about table bloat. C is incorrect because SHOW TABLE STATUS is a MySQL command, not PostgreSQL. D is incorrect because CPU utilization is a performance metric, not directly indicative of table bloat.

10. D. The DATA_FREE column in the information_schema.TABLES view for MySQL indicates the amount of allocated but currently unused space within the table's data file. A high value in this column suggests internal fragmentation or bloat.

A is incorrect because TABLE_ROWS indicates the number of rows in the table. B is incorrect because DATA_LENGTH indicates the actual length of the data file, including used and unused space. C is incorrect because INDEX_LENGTH indicates the length of the index file.

11. B. Cloud Scheduler is ideal for defining recurring schedules (like daily at 3 a.m.), and Cloud Functions can execute a serverless script that connects to the database and runs the VACUUM ANALYZE command, providing a fully managed and automated solution.

A is incorrect because Cloud Logging collects logs and Cloud Monitoring provides metrics; neither can execute scheduled commands. C is incorrect because Cloud Composer is for complex workflow orchestration, which is overkill for a single command, and Cloud Build is for CI/CD. D is incorrect because Cloud CDN is for content delivery and Cloud DNS for domain resolution, unrelated to database automation.

12. C. Automating the shutdown of nonproduction instances outside business hours is a highly effective cost optimization strategy. By stopping the instance when it's not needed, you eliminate compute charges for those periods, significantly reducing the overall cost. Cloud Scheduler and Cloud Functions can orchestrate this.

A is incorrect because scaling down still incurs compute costs, albeit at a lower rate, and might not be sufficient. B is incorrect because CUDs are for predictable, continuous workloads, not for intermittent usage, and won't save as much as shutting down. D is incorrect because although zonal deployment is cheaper, it still runs 24/7 and doesn't address the intermittent usage pattern for maximum savings.

13. B. For Oracle on Bare Metal Solution, automation can be achieved by using Cloud Scheduler to trigger a script (e.g., on a Compute Engine management VM) that contains the necessary SQL*Plus or SQL commands to connect to the Oracle database and execute the `DBMS_STATS.GATHER_SCHEMA_STATS` procedure.

    A is incorrect because while Oracle has auto-stats, explicit scheduling is often preferred for critical production systems to ensure timely updates. C is incorrect because the Cloud SQL Auth Proxy is specific to Cloud SQL, not Oracle on Bare Metal. D is incorrect because Cloud Spanner Dataflow templates are for data processing/migration for Spanner, not for managing Oracle database statistics.

14. B. This pattern leverages serverless components for a robust, automated ETL pipeline. Cloud Scheduler provides the daily trigger, the first Cloud Function orchestrates the Dataflow job for efficient, large-scale export from Spanner to Cloud Storage, and the second Cloud Function loads the exported data into BigQuery.

    A is incorrect because manual processes are not scalable, reliable, or efficient for daily tasks. C is incorrect because there is no native continuous replication pipeline directly from Spanner to BigQuery that is managed in this manner. D is incorrect because `pg_dump` is a PostgreSQL tool and not applicable to Cloud Spanner.

15. B. Cloud Spanner's primary cost driver for compute capacity is the number of provisioned processing units (PUs) or nodes. If the instance is consistently underutilized (low CPU), reducing the number of PUs/nodes is the most direct and effective way to reduce costs without impacting performance for the current workload.

    A is incorrect because migrating to a single-region configuration impacts availability and global consistency, not directly addressing over-provisioned compute for the current region. C is incorrect because interleaved tables are a performance optimization for specific query patterns and do not directly reduce the cost of over-provisioned compute. D is incorrect because purchasing a CUD would reduce the rate, but it locks in the cost for the current (over-provisioned) configuration for a long term.

16. B. Firestore offers a managed export/import service. Automating this can be done by using Cloud Scheduler to trigger a Cloud Function, which then calls the Firestore export API to send the specified collection data to a Cloud Storage bucket.

    A is incorrect because while Dataflow can be used for custom ETL, Firestore provides a native managed export service that is simpler for regular backups. C is incorrect because manual exports are not scalable or reliable for weekly tasks. D is incorrect because Firestore does not automatically replicate to Bigtable or store its data directly in Cloud Storage in that manner.

17. C. The Cloud Billing Report in the Google Cloud Console allows users to filter costs by various dimensions, including specific Google Cloud services (like Cloud SQL) and down to individual SKUs (stock keeping units). This provides a detailed financial breakdown of where costs are incurred, which is essential for understanding spending patterns.

A is incorrect because Cloud Monitoring dashboards show resource utilization, not detailed cost breakdowns by SKU. B is incorrect because Cloud Logging exports capture log data, not billing data. D is incorrect because the Google Cloud Recommender provides optimization recommendations, not a detailed historical cost breakdown by SKU.

18. B. This is a common pattern for automating BigQuery loads. Cloud Scheduler can define the daily schedule, and a Cloud Function can then execute the bq load command or use the BigQuery client library to import the data from Cloud Storage into the BigQuery table.

    A is incorrect because manual execution is not automation. C is incorrect because a streaming pipeline is for continuous, real-time data, not typically for daily batch imports of historical data from Cloud Storage. D is incorrect because Cloud SQL is a relational database and does not directly ingest data from Cloud Storage into BigQuery.

19. C. Cost optimization is a continuous process in the cloud. It involves starting with appropriate sizing, continuously monitoring actual usage with tools like Cloud Monitoring and Recommender, and then right-sizing instances (scaling up/down) based on current workload to ensure optimal performance at the lowest possible cost.

    A is incorrect because provisioning for future peak load immediately leads to significant over-provisioning and unnecessary costs in the present. B is incorrect because choosing the largest instance types is expensive and inefficient for small or unpredictable initial workloads. D is incorrect because although on-premises solutions offer direct control, they come with high up-front capital expenditures and ongoing operational overhead, often making them less cost-effective than cloud solutions in the long run.

20. B. OPTIMIZE TABLE (for MySQL) or similar operations for other databases can involve table locking and resource consumption. Therefore, they should be automated and scheduled during periods of lowest expected application traffic to minimize any potential impact on application performance or user experience.

    A is incorrect because manual execution during business hours is risky and inefficient; automation is key. C is incorrect because random execution can lead to unpredictable performance dips when traffic is high. D is incorrect because while Cloud SQL manages the underlying infrastructure, database-level maintenance like OPTIMIZE TABLE often requires user configuration or scheduling.

Chapter 9: Implementing Backup and Recovery Strategies

1. C. Choosing a multiregion location (e.g., US, Europe, Asia) for Cloud SQL automated backups provides the highest availability and protection against a single regional outage. Backups stored in a multiregion location are replicated across multiple geographic regions, ensuring resilience even if an entire Google Cloud region becomes unavailable.

   A is incorrect because while you can export to a custom bucket, automated backups are managed differently and location choice is within Cloud SQL settings. B is incorrect because a regional location protects against zonal failures but not against a complete regional outage.

D is incorrect because on-premises storage is outside Google Cloud and would not benefit from its built-in availability features.

2. D. Bigtable provides a managed backup feature, but it needs to be triggered. Automating this typically involves using Cloud Scheduler for the daily schedule and a Cloud Function to programmatically call the Bigtable Admin API's `create_backup` method to initiate the backup.

   A is incorrect because Bigtable does not automatically create daily backups; it requires explicit configuration/triggering. B is incorrect because while Dataflow can export data, Bigtable has a native managed backup feature that is generally preferred for creating consistent, restorable backups. C is incorrect because Bigtable does not have a native PITR feature in the same way as Cloud SQL or Spanner.

3. B. Firestore's managed export/import service is the primary way to create restorable copies of your data. To meet specific RPO requirements, this service can be automated by using Cloud Scheduler to trigger a Cloud Function that calls the Firestore export API on a defined schedule.

   A is incorrect because Firestore does not have a built-in PITR feature like Cloud SQL or Spanner. C is incorrect because Firestore is a managed NoSQL database, and you do not manage its underlying persistent disks directly. D is incorrect because replicating Firestore to Cloud SQL is not a native backup mechanism and would involve significant custom ETL.

4. B. Logical backups (like SQL dumps or CSV exports) contain the data in a portable, human-readable format that can often be imported into different database systems or versions. Physical backups (like disk snapshots) capture the raw block-level data and are specific to the database engine, version, and often the underlying storage technology.

   A is incorrect; physical backups are often faster to create for large databases because they're block-level copies. C is incorrect because it reverses the definitions; physical captures disk blocks, logical captures schema and data. D is incorrect; encryption depends on configuration for both types, not inherent to the type itself.

5. C. Cloud Spanner's managed backup feature creates a full, consistent backup of your database. However, this operation must be explicitly initiated via its API. There is no native, recurring scheduler for these backups within the Spanner service itself, which is why external orchestration, typically using Cloud Scheduler to trigger a Cloud Function, is required for automation.

   A is incorrect because Spanner's managed backups are specifically designed to be consistent and distributed. B is incorrect; while large, the cost of storage isn't the primary reason for lacking an internal scheduler for backups. D is incorrect because Spanner PITR is for granular recovery from logical changes, whereas managed backups are for broader recovery points, compliance, and cloning, fulfilling distinct needs.

6. C. Exporting data to Cloud Storage in a portable format (like CSV or SQL) provides the flexibility needed to perform an intermediate step for data sanitization (e.g., anonymization or pseudonymization) using a script or data processing tool. After sanitization, the data can then be safely and easily imported into the development and testing environments, ensuring compliance and data privacy.

A is incorrect because PITR restores the entire database and doesn't inherently offer a mechanism for data sanitization during the restore process. B is incorrect because restoring automated backups also restores the entire dataset without an easy way to sanitize it during the restore operation. D is incorrect because a read replica would directly expose all production data, including sensitive information, to the dev/test environment without allowing for sanitization.

7. C. Point-in-time recovery (PITR) continuously archives transaction logs, enabling restoration of the database to any specific second within the retention window. This feature allows for a very low RPO, meeting the requirement of no more than 5 minutes of data loss from accidental deletion.

   A is incorrect because HA configuration primarily addresses recovery time objective (RTO) by providing automatic failover for infrastructure failures, not granular data recovery from logical corruption. B is incorrect because automated daily backups only allow recovery to the time of the last full backup, meaning up to 24 hours of data could be lost. D is incorrect because read replicas are for read scaling and disaster recovery, not for granular point-in-time recovery of the primary instance.

8. B. Cloud Scheduler can define a recurring schedule (e.g., daily at a specific time). A Cloud Function, triggered by the scheduler, would then execute code using the Spanner API to initiate the managed backup of the Spanner database. This creates a fully automated, serverless solution for regular backups.

   A is incorrect because Cloud Logging is for logs and Cloud Monitoring is for metrics; neither orchestrates backups. C is incorrect because while Dataflow is used for Spanner exports, it's not the primary service for scheduling regular Spanner backups, and Pub/Sub is for messaging. D is incorrect because Cloud Build and Cloud Source Repositories are for CI/CD, not routine database backups.

9. B. The Cloud SQL import service allows you to import data from SQL dump files (or CSV files) that are stored in a Cloud Storage bucket directly into your Cloud SQL instance. This is the standard and most efficient way to load large datasets from such files.

   A is incorrect because automated backups are for creating backups from Cloud SQL, not importing. C is incorrect because PITR is for restoring a Cloud SQL instance to a specific point in time, not for initial data import. D is incorrect because setting up a read replica is for replication and ongoing synchronization, not for a one-time import from a static file.

10. B. Exporting the data to a Cloud Storage bucket in a portable format like CSV (or SQL dump) is a cost-effective solution for archiving. Cloud Storage is cheaper than Cloud SQL storage, and CSV allows for easy access and processing by other tools or for long-term compliance without needing a running database instance.

    A is incorrect because deleting data means it's no longer accessible for auditing. C is incorrect because automated Cloud SQL backups are primarily for disaster recovery, not for long-term, accessible archiving in a portable format for compliance. D is incorrect because keeping large amounts of inactive data in Cloud SQL is more expensive than archiving to Cloud Storage.

11. C. AlloyDB's architecture includes continuous backups and transaction logging that enable fast, granular point-in-time recovery, leading to a near-zero RPO. Combined with its rapid automatic failover mechanism, it natively meets very aggressive RTO requirements for infrastructure failures.

A is incorrect because AlloyDB offers continuous backup and PITR, not just daily full backups and manual restoration. B is incorrect because it provides these capabilities inherently. D is incorrect because AlloyDB's continuous backup and PITR offer highly granular recovery, unlike typical snapshot-based systems.

12. C. For an RPO of 24 hours, Cloud SQL's automated daily backups are sufficient, as they create a full backup once every 24 hours. For an RTO of 4 hours, restoring from a standard automated backup is typically achievable within this timeframe, making this the most straightforward and cost-effective primary solution.

A is incorrect because PITR provides a much lower RPO than required (seconds to minutes) and thus incurs higher costs than necessary for a 24-hour RPO. B is incorrect because HA primarily focuses on a very low RTO for zonal failures (minutes), which is more stringent than the 4-hour RTO and higher cost than needed if standard backup/restore meets the RTO. D is incorrect because manual monthly exports would lead to an RPO of up to 30 days, far exceeding the 24-hour requirement.

13. B. To meet a stringent availability SLA (like 99.99 percent), the engineer must prioritize minimizing the recovery time objective (RTO). A low RTO means the database can be brought back online quickly after an outage, directly contributing to higher overall availability and helping meet the SLA.

A is incorrect because MTBF relates to system reliability, not directly to recovery post-failure. C is incorrect because maximizing RPO means tolerating more data loss, which is usually not a goal for critical systems, and a high RPO doesn't directly improve availability. D is incorrect because reducing TCO is a financial goal, not an operational one directly linked to meeting an availability SLA through recovery.

14. C. An on-demand manual backup allows you to trigger a full backup of your Cloud SQL instance at a specific moment. This is ideal before risky operations as it provides a known good state to which you can restore if the operation causes unforeseen issues, serving as a reliable rollback point.

A is incorrect because the automated daily backup occurs at a fixed time and might not capture the exact point before the risky operation. B is incorrect because PITR enables recovery to a specific second but doesn't create a distinct, easily referenceable "rollback point" backup that can be used directly for a restore operation as simply as a manual backup. D is incorrect because a cross-region read replica is for disaster recovery or read scaling, not for creating a one-time rollback point for the primary.

15. B. Cloud Spanner offers point-in-time recovery (PITR), which allows you to restore your database to any specific timestamp within a configurable retention period (up to 7 days by default). This is specifically designed for recovering from logical data corruption or accidental changes with minimal data loss.

A is incorrect because while Spanner has managed backups, they typically need to be scheduled, and PITR provides more granular recovery. C is incorrect because synchronous multi-region replication ensures high availability and consistency, but PITR is for logical recovery from user errors. D is incorrect because Dataflow templates are for exporting/importing data, not for direct point-in-time recovery.

16. A. To enable point-in-time recovery (PITR) in Cloud SQL for PostgreSQL, you must first select Automated Backups. Once automated backups are enabled, you can then configure PITR, which ensures continuous archiving of transaction logs, allowing restoration to any specific second within the retention window.

B is incorrect because a read replica is primarily for read scaling or disaster recovery, not for point-in-time recovery of the primary instance. C is incorrect because setting the database to read-only mode is not a practical solution for a transactional system and doesn't enable PITR. D is incorrect because manually exporting SQL dump files is not feasible for continuous point-in-time recovery and would lead to significant data loss between exports.

17. C. Exporting data from Cloud SQL to Cloud Storage in open formats like Avro or Parquet (or even CSV/JSON) is the most effective way to transfer large datasets to BigQuery. BigQuery can natively ingest data from Cloud Storage in these formats, making the process efficient for large-scale analytical workflows.

A is incorrect because automated backups are for restoring to Cloud SQL, not for direct transfer to BigQuery. B is incorrect because PITR is for point-in-time recovery of the Cloud SQL instance itself, not for exporting data to another service. D is incorrect because a read replica is for read scaling and disaster recovery within Cloud SQL, not for large-scale data transfer to BigQuery for analytical purposes.

18. B. Automated daily backups create a full backup once every 24 hours. This directly meets an RPO of 24 hours by allowing restoration to the last full backup and is generally the most cost-effective solution for this specific recovery point objective, as it fulfills the requirement without unnecessary complexity or resource overhead.

A is incorrect because HA configuration primarily addresses RTO (downtime) and zonal failures, not RPO for data corruption, and incurs higher costs than necessary for a 24-hour RPO. C is incorrect because PITR provides a significantly lower RPO (seconds to minutes) than required, making it more expensive than necessary. D is incorrect because manual weekly exports would result in an RPO of up to 7 days, which does not meet the 24-hour requirement.

19. C. BigQuery Table Snapshots allow you to create a lightweight, point-in-time copy of a table. This feature is primarily useful for quickly reverting to a previous state or recovering data due to accidental deletions or schema changes, acting as a logical backup for resilience against user errors within BigQuery.

A is incorrect because `EXPORT DATA` creates a copy of the data in Cloud Storage, which is more for external use or full archival, not for quick internal recovery within BigQuery. B is incorrect because streaming inserts are for real-time data ingestion, not backup or recovery. D is incorrect because continuous replication is for high availability and redundancy, not specifically for point-in-time recovery from logical human errors or specific table history.

20. B. AlloyDB is designed with a continuous backup system that constantly streams transaction logs, enabling highly granular, near-zero RPO with very fast point-in-time recovery. Its rapid automatic failover mechanism also ensures minimal RTO for infrastructure-related issues, making it ideal for the most stringent availability and data loss requirements.

A is incorrect because AlloyDB is a premium, high-performance offering, generally not chosen primarily for cost savings. C is incorrect because AlloyDB is a managed service that aims to automate and enhance backup capabilities beyond traditional manual `pg_dump` methods. D is incorrect because Cloud SQL offers cross-region read replicas and backups, supporting cross-region DR strategies, and AlloyDB's high-availability features are typically within a region or multiregion cluster setup.

Chapter 10: Planning and Executing Database Migrations

1. C. For organizations needing to "lift-and-shift" their existing Oracle workloads to Google Cloud without extensive re-architecture, Google Cloud's Bare Metal Solution (BMS) allows running Oracle databases on dedicated hardware within Google Cloud's data centers, providing the infrastructure and licensing flexibility while retaining the native Oracle environment.

A is incorrect because migrating to Cloud SQL for PostgreSQL is a heterogeneous migration requiring significant schema and code changes. B is incorrect because migrating to Cloud Spanner requires a complete rearchitecture of the database and application data model. D is incorrect because converting to Firestore (a NoSQL document database) is a major rearchitecture, not a lift-and-shift.

2. C. A zero-downtime migration, often involving techniques like dual writes (where the application writes to both source and target databases simultaneously) and gradual read shifting, is the most advanced strategy designed to achieve a cutover with no user-visible service interruption.

A is incorrect because an extended outage involves significant downtime. B is incorrect because while DMS provides near-zero downtime, it still has a brief cutover window, which is not "absolutely no user-visible downtime." D is incorrect because a simple export/import is an offline migration technique with downtime.

3. B. Database Migration Service (DMS) is specifically designed as an opinionated, end-to-end service for homogeneous database migrations (e.g., MySQL to Cloud SQL for MySQL) with minimal downtime. It handles the initial load and continuous replication seamlessly.

A is incorrect because Datastream is a more general-purpose CDC service, often used when the target is not a managed relational database or for custom pipelines. C is incorrect because Storage Transfer Service is for bulk data transfer to Cloud Storage, typically for offline migrations. D is incorrect because the Transfer Appliance is for physical transfer of petabytes of data, not online database migration.

4. C. Cloud Spanner is Google Cloud's globally distributed, strongly consistent, and infinitely scalable relational database. It is specifically designed to handle massive workloads without requiring application-level sharding, making it ideal for migrating from complex manually sharded systems.

   A is incorrect because Cloud SQL offers vertical scaling and read replicas but doesn't handle application-level sharding. B is incorrect because AlloyDB is a high-performance, PostgreSQL-compatible relational database, but it also doesn't handle application-level sharding or provide global, unlimited horizontal scaling like Spanner. D is incorrect because BigQuery is a data warehouse for analytics, not a transactional OLTP database for live application data.

5. B. AlloyDB for PostgreSQL is specifically designed to be fully compatible with PostgreSQL, an open source database, thus eliminating Oracle licensing costs. Its enterprise-grade performance often matches or exceeds commercial databases for many demanding workloads, making it a robust alternative.

   A is incorrect because global distribution and strong consistency are features of Cloud Spanner, not AlloyDB (though AlloyDB is highly available). C is incorrect as AlloyDB is a relational database with strict schema, not a NoSQL document database. D is incorrect because AlloyDB is a fully managed service, not designed to run on Bare Metal Solution, which is used for lift-and-shift of native Oracle.

6. C. Datastream is a highly flexible, serverless change data capture (CDC) and replication service that can stream data changes from various sources to a wide array of targets, including BigQuery, Cloud Storage, or other databases. It is designed to be a component in broader data pipelines, not just a full end-to-end migration tool like DMS.

   A is incorrect because Datastream is for online, real-time data streaming, not offline migrations. B is incorrect because while DMS is for homogeneous migrations to Cloud SQL, Datastream is more general-purpose and supports many targets beyond Cloud SQL. D is incorrect because physical appliance transfers are handled by the Transfer Appliance.

7. B. Firestore offers a fully serverless experience with deep integration into the Firebase ecosystem, providing real-time data synchronization and offline capabilities that are highly beneficial for modern web and mobile applications, simplifying development significantly compared to managing a MongoDB cluster.

   A is incorrect because Firestore is a NoSQL document database, not designed for SQL compatibility. C is incorrect because Firestore is an OLTP database, not primarily for complex OLAP. D is incorrect because MongoDB is open source, so licensing cost reduction isn't the primary driver for a migration to Firestore, though operational cost might be.

8. B. Disabling foreign key constraints and secondary indexes during the initial bulk data load significantly speeds up the data ingestion process. Each insertion doesn't require immediate validation of foreign key relationships or updates to multiple index structures, reducing overhead and improving load performance. They are typically re-enabled after the load.

   A is incorrect; foreign keys and indexes do not make a database read-only. C is incorrect; data normalization is a design concern, not a loading optimization. D is incorrect; although validation is important, it's a separate step, and disabling constraints/indexes doesn't directly enable application-level validation before commit.

9. C. DMS provides a Schema Conversion feature that can analyze the source database schema (e.g., Oracle) and automatically generate a converted schema for a target like Cloud SQL for PostgreSQL, assessing the complexity and facilitating the translation of data types, functions, and stored procedures.

A is incorrect because automated HA setup is for the target database, not for schema conversion. B is incorrect because continuous replication is for data movement, not schema translation. D is incorrect because cost optimization recommendations are provided by the Recommender service, not a direct feature of DMS for migration execution.

10. B. In zero-downtime migrations, the application's data access layer is modified to implement dual writes (writing to both source and target databases simultaneously). This also allows for gradually shifting read traffic from the source to the target, ensuring continuous availability during the transition.

A is incorrect as simplifying connection strings is a minor benefit and not the primary driver for such complex modifications. C is incorrect as offline data processing is unrelated to the real-time requirements of zero-downtime migrations. D is incorrect as caching is a performance optimization, not a core requirement for a zero-downtime database cutover itself.

11. C. For petabyte-scale historical data where network bandwidth is a bottleneck, Transfer Appliance is the most efficient way to physically ship data to Google Cloud (loading into Cloud Storage and then BigQuery). For new, incoming IoT data, Pub/Sub is the managed service designed to ingest high-frequency, real-time event streams from distributed sensors.

A is incorrect because while Dataflow can process data, it is not a physical transfer mechanism for petabytes of on-premises files, nor is it the entry point for raw IoT streams.

B is incorrect because Datastream is a Change Data Capture (CDC) service for relational databases (like MySQL or Oracle); it cannot ingest raw IoT sensor events or flat CSV files. Additionally, Storage Transfer Service is typically for online transfers, which may be too slow for petabyte-scale on-premises data.

D is incorrect because BigQuery Data Transfer Service is primarily for scheduling transfers from SaaS apps (like Google Ads) or other cloud providers, not for massive on-premises hardware moves. Filestore is a managed NAS (Network Attached Storage) and is not used for real-time stream ingestion.

12. B. This is a heterogeneous migration because it involves moving between different database engines (Oracle to PostgreSQL). The primary challenge in such migrations is the conversion of incompatible schema elements (data types, functions, stored procedures written in different SQL dialects like PL/SQL to PL/pgSQL).

A is incorrect because homogeneous implies the same database engine, and data transfer volume is a common challenge for both types. C is incorrect because lift-and-shift usually implies minimal changes to the application or database, which is not the case here. D is incorrect because while application compatibility is an issue, the core database conversion itself is the first hurdle in heterogeneous migrations.

13. C. Configuring reverse replication means that changes made on the new Google Cloud database are continuously streamed back to the original source database. If a critical issue arises after cutover, the application can be quickly repointed back to the source database without data loss, as the source has been kept up-to-date.

A is incorrect because initial data load is part of the forward migration, not for fallback. B is incorrect because one-way replication only keeps the target in sync, not the source. D is incorrect because while a backup is important, restoring from it takes time and doesn't update the old source system with new changes.

14. C. An extended outage (offline) migration is the simplest approach where the application is taken completely offline for a scheduled period while the database is moved. Given the tolerance for a few hours of downtime, this strategy minimizes complexity and is often sufficient for non-critical applications.

A is incorrect because zero-downtime is the most complex and expensive, unnecessary for this scenario. B is incorrect because near-zero downtime is also more complex than needed for a multi-hour tolerance. D is incorrect because dual write is a technique used within a zero-downtime migration, implying higher complexity.

15. C. Cloud Bigtable is Google Cloud's fully managed, highly scalable wide-column NoSQL database, designed to be API-compatible with Apache HBase. It is the natural choice for migrating existing HBase workloads to a fully managed environment while retaining the data model benefits.

A is incorrect because Cloud SQL is a relational database. B is incorrect because Cloud Spanner is a globally distributed relational database. D is incorrect because Firestore is a document-oriented NoSQL database.

16. B. For MySQL sources, DMS relies on binary logging (`binlog`) to capture changes for continuous replication. Specifically, the `binlog_format` must be set to ROW to ensure all changes are captured accurately.

A is incorrect because pglogical is a PostgreSQL extension, not applicable to MySQL. C is incorrect because DMS supports online migrations, so the source database does not need to be in read-only mode for the entire process. D is incorrect because Cloud Interconnect would connect to Google Cloud, and the destination is Cloud SQL, not Azure.

17. C. A near-zero downtime migration strategy is significantly more complex to plan and implement (due to continuous replication, cutover orchestration, and potential application changes) and typically more costly. However, its primary advantage is that it results in minimal to no business disruption, which is crucial for critical applications.

A is incorrect because near-zero downtime is more complex and generally less risky when properly executed. B is incorrect because it can involve a longer planning/replication phase but aims for minimal cutover time. D is incorrect because if implemented correctly, continuous replication should eliminate the need for manual data reconciliation after cutover.

18. B. For the initial bulk copy of data, DMS requires that every table intended for migration must have a primary key. Tables without a primary key cannot be included in the initial snapshot, which would cause the migration to fail or skip them.

A is incorrect because not all tables necessarily need foreign keys. C is incorrect as `created_at` timestamps are common but not a strict DMS requirement for migration. D is incorrect because DMS does have an important prerequisite regarding primary keys for tables.

19. B. For establishing secure and performant connectivity between an on-premises environment and Google Cloud services like DMS, Cloud Interconnect or Cloud VPN are the most appropriate networking services. They provide either dedicated network connections or encrypted tunnels, respectively.

A is incorrect because Cloud CDN is for content delivery, not private network connectivity for database migration. C is incorrect because GKE Gateway is for managing traffic to services within GKE, not for connecting on-premises databases. D is incorrect because Cloud Load Balancing distributes traffic within Google Cloud or from the Internet; it does not establish private connectivity from on-premises.

20. C. DMS is designed to migrate the core schema (tables, columns, data types) and the data itself. However, it does not typically migrate other database objects such as stored procedures, functions, triggers, sequences, and users with their permissions, which must be handled as separate steps in the migration plan.

A is incorrect because tables and columns are core schema components that DMS does migrate. B is incorrect because primary keys are also migrated and are a requirement for DMS initial load. D is incorrect because DMS provisions indexes on the target; while it optimizes how they are created, it does not mean it fails to migrate their definition.

Chapter 11: Deploying and Validating Database Solutions

1. A. Periodic testing of HA and DR strategies through drills is essential to validate that the theoretical RTO (time to recover) and RPO (data loss) objectives can actually be met in a real-world scenario. It also helps train the response teams, identify gaps in documentation, and uncover hidden flaws in the recovery plan.

B is incorrect; testing is an operational cost, not a cost reduction method. C is incorrect; software versions are managed through maintenance windows, not DR drills. D is incorrect; performance metrics are for monitoring, not the primary purpose of DR testing.

2. C. An in-region read replica is primarily used to offload read traffic from the primary Cloud SQL instance. By directing read queries to the replica, the primary instance can focus on write operations, thereby improving the overall read scalability and performance of the application.

A is incorrect because although it's a replica, Cloud SQL's HA configuration provides automated failover, not typically an in-region read replica. B is incorrect because PITR relies on automated backups and transaction logs on the primary, not on read replicas. D is incorrect because cross-region read replicas are used for disaster recovery in different regions.

3. B. A zonal instance without a standby replica is the lowest cost configuration for Cloud SQL. It provides a single point of failure in case of a zonal outage but aligns with the priority of minimal initial cost and comfort with manual recovery, as it would require restoring from a backup in such an event.

A is incorrect because HA adds cost and automates recovery, which contradicts "minimal initial cost" and "manual intervention." C is incorrect because multiregion is the highest cost for global resilience, far beyond initial cost minimization. D is incorrect because PITR adds cost for low RPO and implies automated recovery, not manual intervention.

4. C. The most important lesson is that DR plans, including all associated documentation (like updating DNS records and connection strings), must be periodically tested and continuously updated. Testing reveals gaps and outdated information, ensuring the plan is viable when a real disaster occurs.

A is incorrect because even perfect documentation needs to be validated through testing, and real-world scenarios always reveal unforeseen challenges. B is incorrect because RPO relates to data loss, not the efficiency of the recovery process itself. D is incorrect because while automated backups are a component of DR, they are not a substitute for a comprehensive plan that includes testing and updated procedures.

5. B. The `gcloud sql instances promote-replica MY_REPLICA_NAME` command is used to convert a read replica into a stand-alone, writable primary instance. This is a key step in a disaster recovery scenario where the original primary is unavailable and the replica needs to take over as the new primary.

A is incorrect because failover is used for HA-configured instances to switch between a primary and its standby within the same region, not to promote a separate read replica. C is incorrect because `patch --availability-type=REGIONAL` is used to configure an instance for HA, not to promote a replica. D is incorrect because `export sql` is for creating a logical backup, not for failover or promotion.

6. C. Terraform allows the declarative definition of the desired state of resources, including Cloud SQL instances. By defining the `availability_type`, `backup_configuration`, and `point_in_time_recovery_enabled` within a `google_sql_database_instance` resource, Terraform ensures all new deployments adhere to these settings consistently.

A is incorrect because while gcloud create can include these flags, it's a procedural approach; Terraform ensures the desired state and manages changes over time. B is incorrect because manual scripting is less robust and harder to maintain for complex environments than IaC. D is incorrect because Cloud Monitoring is for monitoring, not for provisioning.

7. B. Bigtable achieves high availability and global distribution through multicluster routing. By creating two or more clusters in different regions and configuring an application profile, Bigtable can automatically route traffic to the nearest healthy cluster, ensuring low latency and continuous availability even if an entire region fails.

A is incorrect because a single cluster is a single point of failure and will have high latency for distant users. C is incorrect because daily backups are for recovery, not for real-time high availability or low latency. D is incorrect because Bigtable is a fully managed service, and running it on a Compute Engine VM would reintroduce operational overhead and complexity.

8. B. A regional Cloud SQL instance configured for high availability (HA) automatically provisions a primary and a synchronized standby in different zones within the same region. This setup ensures automatic failover to the standby in case of a zonal outage, providing a very low RTO for such failures.

A is incorrect because a zonal instance is a single point of failure against a zonal outage. C is incorrect because a multiregion setup primarily protects against regional outages, not just zonal ones, and is typically for disaster recovery rather than regional HA. D is incorrect because PITR is for RPO (data loss) and logical recovery, not for high availability against zonal infrastructure failures.

9. C. Setting up one or more in-region read replicas for Cloud SQL allows you to offload read queries from the primary instance. This distributes the read workload and significantly improves performance and scalability for read-heavy applications, freeing the primary to focus on writes.

A is incorrect because a cross-region read replica is primarily for disaster recovery against regional outages or to serve users in other regions, not the most direct solution for scaling reads in the primary region. B is incorrect because HA configuration provides resilience against zonal failures and improves RTO, but it doesn't inherently scale read capacity beyond the primary. D is incorrect because converting to Cloud Spanner is a major architectural change, not a simple replication strategy.

10. B. The Cloud SQL instance's Operations log in the Google Cloud Console (or via `gcloud sql operations list`) provides detailed, human-readable status messages and specific error codes for all administrative actions, including both automatic and manual failovers. This is the primary place to diagnose failover events.

A is incorrect because application logs show the symptom (connection failure), but not the cause of the database failover itself. C is incorrect because although Cloud Monitoring can show performance metrics that might indicate a problem leading to failover, it doesn't detail the failover operation's sequence or cause. D is incorrect because billing reports are for cost analysis, not operational troubleshooting.

11. B. Cloud Spanner achieves its industry-leading availability and strong global consistency by synchronously replicating data across multiple zones (in a regional configuration) or multiple regions (in a multiregion configuration) using a Paxos-based protocol. This allows it to automatically handle failures with zero downtime for zonal failures and very low RTO for regional failures.

A is incorrect because daily backups are for RPO and disaster recovery, not real-time extreme availability. C is incorrect because Spanner's failover is automated, not manual, for regional outages when configured multiregion. D is incorrect because sharding across project IDs is not a built-in Spanner HA mechanism; Spanner manages its distribution automatically within an instance.

12. C. When a Cloud SQL instance is provisioned with HA, its data, including the selected storage type (SSD in this case), is synchronously replicated to the standby instance's disk in a different zone. If the primary's disk fails, Cloud SQL automatically promotes the standby, which already has an up-to-date, consistent copy of the data on its own SSD disk.

A is incorrect; the standby uses the same configured storage type as the primary. B is incorrect; HA is about immediate failover to an existing standby, not creating a new disk. D is incorrect; HA aims for full read/write functionality immediately upon failover, not read-only mode.

13. C. Using `gcloud` CLI commands within shell scripts is a powerful and flexible way to automate the provisioning and management of AlloyDB clusters. `gcloud` provides commands for virtually every action available in the console, making it suitable for programmatic control and integration into CI/CD pipelines.

A is incorrect because manual provisioning is slow and error-prone. B is incorrect because while Python scripts with client libraries are powerful, `gcloud` scripts are often simpler for direct provisioning tasks. D is incorrect because Cloud Composer is primarily for orchestrating complex data pipelines, which would be overkill for simple cluster provisioning.

14. C. Cross-region replication in Cloud SQL is typically asynchronous. This means data is copied with a slight delay. Therefore, in the event of a regional failure before all transactions are replicated, there is a potential for some data loss, leading to an RPO greater than zero.

A is incorrect because Cloud SQL cross-region replication is asynchronous, not synchronous, which allows for lower latency between regions but implies potential data loss. B is incorrect because asynchronous replication does not guarantee faster RTO. D is incorrect because asynchronous replication applies to all data changes replicated, not just writes.

15. C. AlloyDB's architecture decouples compute from storage. Its distributed, zonally redundant storage allows for rapid promotion of a new primary instance (often under 60 seconds) without needing to copy large amounts of data, as the storage is already available and consistent across zones.

A is incorrect because AlloyDB's failover is automated and extremely fast. B is incorrect because its compute/storage decoupling means data doesn't need to be copied during failover, which is critical for its speed. D is incorrect because sharding across projects is not an inherent HA mechanism of AlloyDB.

16. C. Promotion is a manual operation typically used in DR to convert a read replica into a stand-alone, writable primary instance, often resulting in a new connection endpoint for the application. Failover, in an HA setup, is usually an automatic process that switches traffic to a standby instance, but crucially, the connection endpoint remains the same, providing transparent high availability.

A is incorrect; failover is automated and aims for zero data loss (RPO = 0) in HA. Promotion of a replica is manual and might have some data loss (RPO > 0). B is incorrect; both relate to availability and recovery, not just read/write scaling. D is incorrect; both operations are available across Cloud SQL's supported database engines.

17. C. Terraform maintains a state file that maps the defined configuration to the real-world resources it manages. This state tracking allows Terraform to understand the current infrastructure, plan changes, and apply them consistently. It also makes changes auditable by tracking them in version control alongside the code.

A is incorrect; Terraform is primarily a CLI tool, though it can integrate with UIs. B is incorrect; Terraform does not automatically back up databases; that's a separate configuration. D is incorrect; Terraform manages mutable infrastructure by default, allowing changes.

18. B. The `gcloud sql instances failover` command simulates a zonal failure for a Cloud SQL HA instance. The expected outcome is that the service automatically switches the active primary to the standby instance in the unaffected zone, and crucially, the instance's connection endpoint (IP address) remains the same, ensuring transparent high availability.

A is incorrect; it simulates a zonal failure, and the IP address does not change. C is incorrect; it's a failover command, not an export. D is incorrect; promoting a read replica is a different command and operation.

19. C. Asynchronous replication means that data is copied from the primary to the replica with a slight delay. If the primary fails before all transactions are replicated, any data committed during that lag period will be lost on the replica. Therefore, the RPO (maximum acceptable data loss) will be greater than zero.

A is incorrect; synchronous replication guarantees RPO = 0. B is incorrect; while recovery time can vary, the RPO (data loss) is directly tied to the replication lag, not necessarily "very high" or manual restoration. D is incorrect; asynchronous replication directly impacts RPO, as it determines the window of potential data loss.

20. C. The RTO is precisely defined as the maximum acceptable downtime. Therefore, the most critical metric to measure the actual RTO achieved during a failover test is the time it takes for the database to become fully available again, specifically when new application connections can successfully establish and perform operations on the newly promoted primary instance.

A is incorrect because total storage usage is for capacity planning, not RTO. B is incorrect because the number of read replicas is for scalability, not RTO. D is incorrect because while CPU utilization is a performance metric, it doesn't directly measure the time to recover service availability during a failover.

Index

Note: Page numbers in *italics* and **bold** refers to figures and tables respectively.

A

admin activity logs, 167
AlloyDB, 76–80, **78**, 191, 209, 210
   near-zero downtime, 249
   for PostgreSQL, 272–273
application logic, 280
application-side routing strategies, 279–280
assess phase
   application catalog, 120, **121**
   application inventory, 119, **119**
   assess data, 121
   business requirements, 122
   dependency map, 119, **120**
   future requirements, 122–123
   workload metrics, 122
automated backups, 5, 228
automated cleanup function, 237
automate shutdowns, 217
automatic failover, 271
automatic scheduled backups
   Bigtable, 233
   Cloud Spanner, 233
   Cloud SQL, 232–233
   Firestore, 233
automating common database tasks
   assessing and managing fragmentation,
      210–212
   database maintenance, 208–210
   Google Cloud–managed databases
      upgrades, 213–214
   monitoring database SLA/SLOs, 214–215
   scheduling database exports, 212–213

B

backup and recovery strategies
   AlloyDB for PostgreSQL, 229
   automatic scheduled backups,
      231–233
   BigQuery, 230
   Bigtable, 230
   Cloud Spanner, 229–230
   Cloud SQL, 228–229
   data retention, 236–237
   export/import procedures in Google Cloud,
      235–236
   Firestore, 230
   key use cases for export/import,
      234–235
   options by database service, 227
backup retention policy, 236
Bare Metal Solution (BMS),
     211, 234
BigQuery, 89–93, **92**, 230
   dataset, 216
   load job, 235
Bigtable, 230, 273–274
   replication, 283
   services, 212
   storage costs, 216
billing data export, 216
block storage
   in Google Cloud, 12, **13**
   hyperdisk, 9–11, **11**
   Local SSDs, 11–12
   persistent disk, 6–8, *8*

C

change data capture (CDC), 248
Cloud Audit Logs, 167–168
Cloud Bigtable, 83–86, **85**
Cloud billing reports, 216
Cloud Database Engineer, 213
Cloud Firestore, 86–89, **87**
Cloud Functions runtime, 209
Cloud Monitoring, 275
Cloud Run service, 209
Cloud Scheduler, 209, 212, 213
Cloud Spanner, 80–83, **81**, 212, 215,
    229–230, 273
Cloud SQL, 74–76, **75**, 209, 210, 214
    parallel replication, 279
    transforming RTO/RPO on, 227
Cloud SQL Auth Proxy
    auditing policies, 167–168
    automatic encryption, 164
    connection methods, 165
    connection pooling, 167
    customer-managed encryption keys
      (CMEKs), 166
    recommended pattern, 164–165
    secure authorization, 164
    simplified network configuration, 164
    SSL/TLS configuration, 166
Cloud SQL connection methods
    private IP address, 163–164
    public IP address, 163
Cloud storage, 3
    lifecycle management, 237
communication plan, 252
connection pooler, 161
continuous backups, 229
cost and performance, Google Cloud
    AlloyDB performance, 193–194
    BigQuery performance, 196–198
    Bigtable performance, 196
    Cloud Spanner performance, 194–195
    Cloud SQL performance, 193
    optimizing queries, 192
    replication strategies, 191–192
    scaling out (horizontal scaling), 189
    scaling strategies, 190–191, **190**
    scaling up (vertical scaling), 189
critical storages misconfiguration, 284–285
cross-region replica creation, 281–283, **282**

D

data access logs, 167
data archiving, 234
database cost
    assessing costs, 216
    cost optimization strategies, 216–217
Database Migration Service (DMS), 214, 248,
    249, 253, 255
database solutions
    AlloyDB for PostgreSQL, 272–273
    application-side routing strategies, 279–280
    automating database instance provisioning,
      275
    Bigtable, 273–274
    Cloud Spanner, 273
    Cloud SQL, 271–272
    connecting applications to replicas, 279
    failed failover troubleshooting, 286
    gcloud Command-Line Interface (CLI),
      277–278
    gcloud execution, 285
    high availability (HA), 271
    monitoring for highly available databases,
      286–287
    multiregional replication for disaster recov-
      ery, 281–283
    read replicas, deploying and scaling,
      278–280
    setting up alerts, 287–288
    Terraform, 276–277
    testing disaster recovery, 284–285
    testing high availability (HA), 283–284

database storage technologies
    in-memory databases, 44–47
    NoSQL databases, 45, 50–52
    OLTP databases, 47–50
    relational databases, 44, 47
    semi-structured data, 40–41
    structured data, 37–38
    types of data, **44**
    unstructured data, 38–40
    vector data, 41–43
    vector databases, 45, 52–53, **53**
data encryption, 5
Data_free column, 211
data migration
    common migration paths, 259–261, *260*
    configuring reverse replication, 254–255
    correct database migration tools, 256–259,
      257–258
    DDL/DML conversion (schema conversion),
      252
    developing and executing, 247
    extended outage (offline migration),
      247–248
    fallback and rollback plan, 253–254
    heterogeneous migration, 252–253
    homogeneous migration, 252
    interoperability and, 234
    migration plan, 251–252
    near-zero downtime migration, 248–249
    pre-migration requirements, 255–256
    zero-downtime migration, 250–251
data storage design
    block storage, 6–12
    cost optimization, 4
    data protection and recovery, 5
    decision tree, 27, *28*
    file storage, 19–27
    object storage, 12–19
    performance and scalability, 4
    security and compliance, 5
    workload's characteristics, 3–4
Datastream, 248
data type mapping, 253

DDL/DML conversion (schema conversion),
    252
deploy phase
    configure security, 128
    data migration, 128
    deployment process, 128
    resource setup, 127
    testing, 129
DNS-based routing, 279–280

F

fallback plan, 252–254
fast point-in-time recovery, 229
file storage
    Google Cloud Filestore, 20–23
    Google Cloud NetApp Volumes, 23–26, **27**
    visual representation of, *19*
firebase-based application, 254
Firestore, 230
foreign keys and indexes, 256

G

gcloud Command-Line Interface (CLI),
    277–278
gcloud execution, 285
Generative AI and LLMs
    Google Cloud database, 107–108
    retrieval-augmented generation (RAG), 107
GlobalConnect, 146–147
global endpoints, 279
Google Cloud, 208
    AlloyDB, 76–80, **78**
    BigQuery, 89–93, **92**
    Cloud Bigtable, 83–86, **85**
    Cloud Firestore, 86–89, **87**
    Cloud Spanner, 80–83, **81**
    Cloud SQL, 74–76, **75**
    configuring reverse replication, 254–255
    Console, 216

Google Cloud (*Cont.*)
databases, **274**
export/import procedures in, 235–236
high availability (HA), 271
managed services, 270
Memorystore, 71–72, **73**
migration tools, **257–258**
MongoDB, 93–95
Oracle databases, 95–100, 97–99
organizational policies, 109
performance, 215–217
regulatory and compliance support, 108–109
retention mechanisms in, 237
Google Cloud database, **231**
endpoint, 247
managed databases, 66–68
managed database services, 62, **63**
partner-managed databases, 68–70
unmanaged database services, 62–66, **63**
Google Cloud Implementation Methodology
assess phase, 118–123
deploy phase, 127–129
optimization phase, 129–130
plan phase, 123–127
Google Cloud NetApp Volumes
additional factors, 25
configuration options, 24–25
key features, 24
options, **27**
use cases, 25–26
Google Cloud Professional Database Engineer, 3, 208
Google Compute Engine (GCE), 63
Google Kubernetes Engine (GKE), 63
Google-managed databases
advantages, 67
challenges, 67
in Google Cloud, 71–93
key characteristics, 66–67
use cases, 68
Google's Bare Metal Solution (BMS), 63

H

heterogeneous migration, 252–253
heterogeneous schema conversion, 253
high availability (HA) and disaster recovery (DR)
backup and recovery strategy, 149, **150**, 151
characteristics of, 139, **139**
deployment strategies, **143**
GlobalConnect, 146–147
maintenance windows, 144
major version upgrades, 145–146
minor version upgrades, 145
multiregional deployment, 141–143
notifications, 144–145
point-in-time recovery (PITR), 148–149
recovery point objective (RPO), 148
recovery time objective (RTO), 148
regional deployment, 140–141
upgrading database versions, 145
zonal deployment, 140
high availability (HA) configuration, 228
homogeneous migration, 252
hybrid data pipeline, 234–235

I

infrastructure as code (IaC), 270
initial load requirements, 255
in-memory databases, 44–47
integrating multiple database technologies
data integration and movement, 106
Federated Queries, 106
hybrid and multicloud deployments, 106–107

L

large language model (LLM) applications, 62
Leverage Committed Use Discounts (CUDs), 217

load balancer, 161
low-traffic period, 214

M

major version upgrades, 214
Master Google Cloud storage options, 29
Memorystore, 71–72, **73**
migration plan, 251–252
minor version upgrades, 213
MongoDB, 93–95
monitoring and troubleshooting
    alerts for errors and performance metrics,
        188–189
    cloud logging, 186
    cloud monitoring, 185
    database locking, 182
    identifying missing indexes, 182–183
    performance issues in Google Cloud, 183,
        184
    quotas, 186–187
    resource contention, 187–188
    self-managed databases, 180–181
    slow-running queries, 178–180
multiregional replication, 281–283

N

near-zero downtime migration, 248–249, 254
networking, 255
NoSQL databases, 45, 50–52

O

object storage
    additional factors, 17
    autoclass, 16
    comparison of, **16**
    Google Cloud Storage (GCS), 13–14
    key features, 14–15
    location types, 16–17
    storage classes, 15
    traditional filesystems, 12
    use cases, 18–19
offline analysis, 234
OLTP databases, 47–50
on-demand backups, 228
optimization phase
    automation, 130
    cloud-native features, 130
    fine-tune configurations, 129
    performance and costs, 129
Oracle, 217
    databases, 95–100, 97–99
    heterogeneous schema conversion, 253

P

partner-managed databases
    advantages, 69
    challenges, 70
    in Google Cloud, 93–100
    key characteristics, 68–69
    MongoDB database, 69
    Oracle databases, 69
    use cases, 70
Payment Card Industry Data Security
        Standards (PCI DSS), 4
persistent disk snapshots, 5
plan phase
    communication plan, 127
    cost analysis, 125–126
    rollback plan, 126
    sizing database, 123–124
point-in-time recovery (PITR), 130,
        228–229, 230
populating development environments, 234
PostgreSQL-based services, 209, 210
PostgreSQL-compatible database, 229
PostgreSQL instance, 209
PostgreSQL query, 212
post-migration testing, 248
pre-cutover validation, 249

R

recommender, 216
recovery point objective (RPO), 226, 227
recovery time objective (RTO), 5, 226
relational databases, 44, 47
robust access controls, 5
rollback plan, 253–254

S

schema conversion plan, 252
schema objects, 255
secure database connection
    access control, 170
    authentication, 169–170
    client-side resiliency, 162
    configuring networking and security,
        163–168
    high availability, 161–162
    IAM policies, 168, **169**
    scalability, 161
    security, 162
self-hosted PostgreSQL database, 249
self-managed database options
    Bare Metal Solution (BMS), 100–102
    Google Cloud Compute Engine (GCE),
        102–103
    Google Kubernetes Engine (GKE), 104–105
semi-structured data, 40–41
service level agreements (SLAs), 214–215, 226
Service Level Indicator (SLI), 215
Service Level Objective (SLO), 215
site reliability engineering (SRE), 215
source database preparation, 255
SQL dialect differences, 253
step-by-step execution plan, 252
storage technologies

block storage, 6–12
file storage, 19–27
object storage, 12–19
stored procedures and functions, 253
structured data, 37–38
system event logs, 167

T

Terraform, 276–277

U

unmanaged databases
    advantages, 65
    challenges, 65
    on Google Cloud, 65
    key characteristics, 64
    use cases, 66
unstructured data, 38–40
unsupported extensions, 252

V

VACUUM command, 209
validating application compatibility, 214
vector data, 41–43
vector databases, 45, 52–53, 53
version-specific features, 252

Z

zero-downtime
    migration, 250–251
    upgrade, 214